D0805857

# BORROWED TIME

*Also by Roy Hattersley*

NON-FICTION

Nelson
Goodbye to Yorkshire
Politics Apart
Endpiece Revisited
Press Gang
A Yorkshire Boyhood
Choose Freedom
Between Ourselves
Who Goes Home?
Fifty Years On
Buster's Diaries
Blood and Fire
A Brand from the Burning
The Edwardians
Campbell–Bannerman
Buster's Secret Diaries

FICTION

The Maker's Mark
In That Quiet Earth
Skylark Song

# BORROWED TIME

The Story of Britain Between the Wars

## ROY HATTERSLEY

Little, Brown

LITTLE, BROWN

First published in Great Britain in 2007
by Little, Brown

Copyright © Roy Hattersley 2007

The moral right of the author has been asserted.

All rights reserved.
No part of this publication may be reproduced,
stored in a retrieval system, or transmitted,
in any form or by any means, without the prior
permission in writing of the publisher, nor be
otherwise circulated in any form of binding or cover
other than that in which it is published and without
a similar condition including this condition being
imposed on the subsequent purchaser.

A CIP catalogue record for this book
is available from the British Library.

ISBN 978-0-316-73032-7

Typeset in Bembo by M Rules
Printed and bound in Great Britain by
Clays Ltd, St Ives plc

Little, Brown
An imprint of
Little, Brown Book Group
100 Victoria Embankment
London EC4Y 0DY

An Hachette Livre UK Company

www.littlebrown.co.uk

# CONTENTS

# Contents

## PART IV: Today the Struggle

# PREFACE

Many of the families who, during the 1920s and 1930s, were buffeted about by the winds of fate had no idea that the uncertainty of their times was in any way unusual. Cynicism became fashionable and disenchantment was 'smart'. T. E. Lawrence (serving at the time as a private in the Royal Tank Corps) climbed on a ladder outside the front door of his cottage at Cloud's Hill and carved '*Ou phrontis*' (who cares?) into the lintel. It was the gesture of a generation – the claim not to care, made with such determination that it was clear that those who made it cared very much indeed. Between the wars, Britain was uncertain about most aspects of life other than the need to put on a brave face.

Some of the feelings of an anxious nation – hopes which were realised, ambitions which were unfulfilled and pleasures in the simple things of life which made it easier to bear the tribulations of those turbulent years – were recorded in diaries and letters. For permission to quote the emotion of the time I am grateful to Caroline Cudmore (Ethel Wood), His Grace the Duke of Devonshire (the Ninth Duke of Devonshire), Dr Richard Rowlatt (Mr Justice Rowlatt), Barbara Crowther (Anne Worth), Gillian Hall (Captain W. H. S. Hall), Sarah Gooderson (Doris Gooderson), Kathryn Hartley (William Hartley), Robin Constable (Daphne Thompson), Trevor Hopper (May Hopper), Judy Symonds (Rosamund Lehmann), Hannah Smith (Canon Spencer Elliott), Peter Anderson (Anne Goodison) and Chris Furniss (Harry Furniss).

Anthony Howard read the manuscript and made both corrections and improvements – a generous use of his time and invaluable assistance for which I have been indebted to him during the preparation of my last five books. Cynthia Shepherd corrected, improved – and typed. Richard Beswick (my publisher and editor) and Joe Merton (who read the manuscript on his behalf) suggested changes from which the final text greatly benefited. My sincere thanks to them all.

Of course, the errors and omissions are my sole responsibility.

# The Hush Before the Dawn

Oh what a day. Never to be forgotten. With what great enthusiasm we waited for the morning papers, but without the satisfaction of seeing that the Armistice had been signed. It was not until 11 o'clock that we knew. Then the guns boomed forth, the bells rang and the people cheered and cheered through the streets.

Ethel Wood – fashion illustrator, London

Age 26

Diary for 11 November 1918

Ethel Wood's diary reflected the feelings of the whole nation. For almost a week, it had been clear that the Germans were on the point of capitulation. David Lloyd George, speaking at his first Guildhall Banquet as Prime Minister, had made a joke to explain the delay. The Allied Forces were, he said, advancing so quickly that the Kaiser's emissaries – bound for the railway carriage in the Forest of Compiègne where Marshall Foch waited to receive the Central Powers' surrender – had lost their way. Heartened by the thought that the Berlin High Command could not even sue for peace with the much-vaunted Prussian efficiency, the bankers and brokers stood and cheered. Ten years earlier the People's Budget had made Lloyd George a figure of hate and loathing in the City. Victory, like time, is a great healer.

By Sunday 10 November, the Archbishop of Canterbury was so
confident that victory was near that he told the congregation in
Westminster Abbey that they were 'waiting . . . in the hush before the
dawn'. Next morning, according to *The Times*, 'London went to work
early and settled down with what concentration it could muster'.[1] But
several hundred impatient citizens made their way to Downing Street
rather than to their offices and shops. They were rewarded first with
the sight of the War Cabinet arriving at Number Ten one by one –
General Smuts, Lord Milner, A. J. Balfour. Then the Prime Minister
appeared. 'At eleven o'clock this morning,' he told the crowd, 'the war
will be over. We have won a great victory and we are entitled to a bit
of shouting.'

At eleven o'clock the capital erupted into a cacophony of rejoicing.
The guns and bells which Ethel Wood heard were only the beginning.
Soon the official signs that the war was over were joined by the
people's contribution to the noises of victory. Policemen blew their
whistles. Cabs hooted their klaxon-horns. Tram-cars clanged and buses
hooted. In the East End, Boy Scouts who had been trained to cycle
the streets, blowing warnings of air raids on their bugles, sounded what
they knew to be the last 'All Clear'.

*The Times* reported 'Cheering Crowds . . . Rejoicing in the
Streets . . . A Great Display of Flags'. Ethel Wood recorded the scene
with a hand which trembled with emotion. 'The excitement was
infectious . . . Everybody left their work and got on buses, taxis,
wagons, sidecars of motor cycles – in fact any vehicle . . . Officers and
nurses dashed through the streets of London, sitting on top of taxis . . .
Flags were hung in all the windows . . . People draped themselves
with them . . . Everybody was greeting one another like old friends.'

Parliament, as was only to be expected, received the news with
more decorum. But even there the House of Commons defied convention with signs of celebration which were out of order by the rules
of debate but were in keeping with the jubilant feelings of the time.
When the Prime Minister entered the chamber, the whole House –
including Mr Asquith, deposed by Lloyd George two years earlier –
rose to its feet and cheered. From then on cheers punctuated almost
every sentence as he read out the armistice terms one by one. The
assurance that 'repatriation and restitution' were to be 'secured in

full' – the policy which led to the collapse of the European currencies and sowed the seeds of the Second World War – was received with particular ecstasy.

The Prime Minister's statement ended with an explanation of its brevity. 'This is no time for words. Our hearts are too full of gratitude to which no tongue can give adequate expression.' The Commons, followed by the Lords, then marched in solemn procession to St Margaret's, the parish church of Parliament. Lloyd George and Asquith (who had led the nation during the first two years of the war) walked, side by side, at the head of the column. The service began with 'O God our Help in Ages Past' and included a reading from Isaiah: 'He hath sent me to bind up the broken hearted, to proclaim liberty to the captives and the opening of the prison to them that are bound . . . They shall raise up the former desolations and they shall repair the waste cities.'

In the West End the rejoicing went on throughout the afternoon and into the night – despite the steady rain. Street lamps, once blacked out as protection against enemy Zeppelins, had their covers torn away. Theatres and shops blazed with light. In places of entertainment the national anthem was sung with gusto. In the streets and squares it was augmented with choruses of 'Land of Hope and Glory' and 'Rule Britannia'. One bookmaker pinned up a notice declaring Foch and Haig joint winners, with Allenby in third place and Hindenburg nowhere. Then, a little before midnight, the searchlights – stationed in London parks to help the artillery train its guns on German aircraft – were turned on and great beams of light illuminated the sky above the capital.

At two minutes after eleven, a copy of the Prime Minister's announcement had been hung on the gates of Buckingham Palace. By quarter-past an estimated crowd of five thousand cheering subjects had assembled to demand a sight of the King. Their wish was granted. The King – wearing the uniform of an Admiral of the Fleet and accompanied by the Queen, the Duke of Connaught and Princess Mary – appeared on the Palace balcony. In the courtyard the band of the Irish Guards struck up the national anthem and, to the relief of the *Times* reporter on the spot, almost everybody behaved with complete decorum. 'Officers stood to attention, civilians removed their hats.

Men and women took up the refrain joyously.' But two men climbed the Victoria Monument. They were later identified as Australians.

When the band played 'Rule Britannia' an extraordinary thing happened. The King removed his naval cap and waved it to the crowd. Thus encouraged, the bolder spirits outside the Palace gates began to cry 'Speech!' The cries continued as the band – having brought tears to eyes with 'La Marseillaise' and a selection of Belgian airs – moved on to 'Tipperary' and 'Keep the Home Fires Burning'. Then, to delighted astonishment, the King spoke. The crowd had grown to ten thousand strong, so few of them heard what he had to say. But his words were printed in the following day's Court Circular. 'With you, I rejoice and thank God for the victories which the Allied Armies have won, bringing hostilities to an end and peace within sight.'

It was a day for the defiance of protocol. When the King visited the City to receive the salutations of the Mayor and Corporation he passed through Temple Bar without, as tradition required, receiving the permission of the City Fathers. At about the same time soldiers returning from the front arrived at Victoria Station. They seized bells, usually employed by porters to attract attention and clear their passage, and rang a joyous peal of victory. It was a day for breaking rules and defying conventions.

In the rest of the country local dignitaries led the rejoicing. In Bristol the Lord Mayor and the Bishop both read addresses from the steps of the Council House. The Lord Provost of Aberdeen spoke to a gathering of several thousand citizens and took the salute from a march past of Gordon Highlanders. The Mayor of Scarborough announced the news from a tram-car which, as part of a national savings campaign, had been converted to look like a howitzer. The Lord Provost of Edinburgh sent a telegram of congratulations to the Welsh Prime Minister and similar messages to two Scottish heroes – Field Marshal Sir Douglas Haig and Admiral Beatty. The Lord Mayor of Manchester declared (without any authority) that the rest of the day was a holiday. In Belfast and Birmingham work stopped even in the absence of a municipal announcement and in Plymouth the breweries – fearful that the navy would celebrate too enthusiastically – ordered the closure of their public houses.

There were some exceptions to the rejoicing. Duff Cooper – then a young diplomat, who had served in France with the Grenadier Guards – 'could not resist a feeling of profound melancholy, looking at the crowds of cheering people and thinking of the dead'.[2] At the time, no one knew how great the casualties had been. More than three quarters of a million British servicemen had died in France and Belgium. Twenty thousand of them had died in the Battle of the Somme – a pointless slaughter retained in the national memory as a major indictment of the generals who planned the 'war of attrition'.

Field Marshal Haig, Commander-in-Chief of the British Army in France, seemed, on the day the war ended, to feel no emotion at all. He told his subordinate generals to continue their advance and noted that 'the state of the German Army is said to be very bad'. Then he lived up to his reputation as 'the educated soldier' by philosophising. 'We hear this morning that the Kaiser is in Holland. If the war had gone against us no doubt the King would have had to go, and probably our army would have become insubordinate like the German Army. He was reminded of John Bunyan's remark on seeing a man on his way to be hanged. "But for the Grace of God John Bunyan would have been in that man's place".'[3]

Back in London the jubilant people had no time for philosophical speculation. The King, accompanied by members of the royal family, attended an official service of thanksgiving at St Paul's Cathedral. Once again the crowds were outside Buckingham Palace to see them come and go. Ethel Wood was just in time to glimpse the rear of the procession disappearing through the Palace gates. 'Saw the Queen, Princess Mary, General French, the Duke of Connaught and other nobility return from a service.' On the following day the excitement was 'still going strong'. Indeed it was too strong to gain her approval. 'Revelling in Trafalgar Square last night. The crowd lit a huge bonfire, burnt German guns (part of a display in the Mall), the watchman's hut, wooden blocks out of the road and a side car. When the fire brigade came to put it out, two Australians cut the hose.'

Field Marshal Haig, writing on the same day, described the penalty of defeat. 'Reports from Foch's HQ state that . . . Germans pointed out that if the rolling stock and supplies of the Army . . . are given up, then Germans east of the Rhine will starve . . . Foch was rather brutal . . . and replied that was their affair.'[4] It was not the first time that what was left of the German High Command had raised the like-lihood of mass starvation sweeping their country. In a message to Woodrow Wilson, President of the United States – thought to be the least vengeful of the Allied leaders – the Secretary of State for Foreign Affairs in Berlin had warned both of certain deaths and of their equally certain consequences. 'After a blockade of fifty months, those conditions, especially the surrender of the means of transport and the sustenance of the troops of occupation, would make it impossible to provide Germany with food and would cause the starvation of mil-lions of men, women and children. All the more if the blockade is to continue. We had to accept the conditions. But we feel it our duty to draw President Wilson's attention most solemnly and with all earnest-ness to the fact that the enforcement of these conditions must produce among the German people feelings contrary to those upon which alone the reconstruction of the community of nations can rest, guar-anteeing a just and desirable peace.'[5]

Ethel Wood grasped the point. 'The German people.' she wrote, 'are taking the terms of the Armistice very badly.' The generals and the politicians knew it too but did not care. So for almost twenty-one years Europe lived on borrowed time. Then the war between France and Britain, Germany and Austria broke out again.

# PART I

# Years for the Locusts to Eat

It was Stanley Baldwin — the avuncular pragmatist — who came to represent all the political failures of Britain between the wars. He failed to re-arm either because he did not recognise or feared to challenge Germany's aggressive intentions. Until then he had enjoyed a reputation for imposing his will — almost imperceptibly — on colleagues who were thought to possess both more courage and greater intellect. Perversely Lloyd George — Prime Minister when the First World War was won — has escaped almost all blame for the catastrophes which followed. At Versailles he supported whatever terms were necessary for his survival as leader of the coalition government — irrespective of the consequences for world peace and economic stability.

Four years later his lies to the leaders of the Irish national parties precipitated a bloody civil war. But the creation of the 'Free State' was the first tumultuous step towards independence. India made almost imperceptible progress along the same road. But most of the protests against the continuing Raj were peaceful — or at least began that way. Gandhi emerged from exile in South Africa as a leader whose almost mystical hold over his followers was matched by his unpredictable changes in the strategy he wished them to follow.

Winston Churchill — egocentric and irresponsible — contributed to most of the errors which he later condemned. His attitude towards Indian nationalism was as extreme as his language on the subject was intemperate and cost him a place in the Tory Party leadership. Indeed, until rejuvenated and rehabilitated by war, he assumed that he would never hold high office again.

The nadir of his fortunes came when, despite popular opinion and common logic, he continued to support the vain attempts of Edward VIII to defy Parliament and public opinion and to retain both the crown and Mrs Simpson. But he ended a speech which condemned Baldwin's failure to improve air defences with a phrase which characterised two decades of disillusion and disappointment. 'These,' he said, 'were the years for the locusts to eat.'

CHAPTER ONE

# A Child Weeping

Try to keep cheerful, dear lad, and think of the good times we all will have when this war is over and you are home.

Augusta 'Gus' Hattersley to her brother Bert,
private 2042 1$^{st}$/7$^{th}$ Sherwood Foresters
Killed in Action 1 July 1916

Among all the leaders of the victorious Allies who assembled in Paris on 18 January 1919, only President Woodrow Wilson of the United States thought of the Conference as the chance to build a lasting peace. And, according to John Maynard Keynes, the Treasury's representative in the British delegation, Wilson was a 'blind and deaf Don Quixote' who came to Europe with 'no plan, no scheme, no constructive ideas whatsoever for clothing with the flesh of life the commandments which he had thundered down from the White House' in the form of a fourteen-point plan.[1] But his aspirations were undoubtedly noble. The same could not be said of Georges Clemenceau, Prime Minister of France, whose country's size and sacrifice allowed him to talk on equal terms to the leader of the most powerful nation in the world. Between them they represented the politics of the two decades which followed. Good intentions were confounded by timidity and incompetence. Cynicism and self-interest triumphed as the allies of ruthless determination.

Reasonably enough, Clemenceau wanted a settlement which guaranteed that Germany would never again march west across the Rhine. But he also wanted revenge and the major share of the booty he regarded as the victors' due. To him, 'the idea that France, bled white in the fields of Flanders, should emerge from the Great War without her share of conquered territory was insupportable'.[2] When President Wilson urged moderation the French Prime Minister replied

If I accept what you propose as ample for the security of France, after the millions who have died and the mothers who have suffered, I believe – indeed I hope – that my successor in office would take me by the nape of the neck and have me shot.[3]

It was the French determination to exact recompense and revenge which inspired Will Dyson's 1919 cartoon. As Clemenceau leaves Versailles, he tells his colleagues, 'Curious, I seem to hear a child weeping.' The weeping child, hidden behind one of the pillars of the palace, is peace. Prophetically, the child is labelled 1940.

Even if a real weeping child had confronted Clemenceau it is unlikely that it would have caused him much anguish. He had made slow but decisive progress from the far left to the far right of the political spectrum – radical deputy in the National Assembly and supporter of the Paris Commune of 1870 to nationalistic Prime Minister in 1917. Along the way he acquired the nickname 'Tiger' – initially a tribute to his debating style. He had confirmed his reputation by prosecuting critics of the war for treason. David Lloyd George – who led the British coalition which, in his own estimation, had changed the course of the war – was of a less punitive disposition. But he was not a politician of high principle. And all the pressures upon him – some of them created by his own reckless populism – pushed him in the direction of imposing penalties on Germany which were both salutary and severe. Occasionally his radical conscience stirred and he argued for moderation. But he was determined that the country he led should obtain the lion's share of the spoils. So he hovered – often cynically – between the poles of reconciliation and retribution.

Emotionally he was in favour of the nationalities of Europe determining their own destiny. A nineteenth-century Welsh Liberal could not believe anything else. And he understood the dangers of humiliating Germany to the point at which resentment turned into revolt. But the self-interest with which he approached the Peace Conference was illustrated by his own account of a conversation which took place when Clemenceau visited London. 'He asked me what I particularly wanted from the French. I instantly replied that I wanted Mosul attached to the new state of Iraq and Palestine from Dan to Beersheba under British control. Without hesitation, he agreed.'[4]

Wilson would have reacted differently. He believed that 'people and provinces are not to be bartered about from sovereignty to sovereignty as if they were mere chattels and pawns in a game' and he was irrevocably opposed to 'special, selfish economic combinations'. His ambitious rules for managing the dissolution of the Ottoman, Austro-Hungarian, German and Russian empires were set out in a speech to both Houses of Congress on 8 January 1918.

According to Woodrow Wilson's detractors, he had been persuaded to stand – first for the Governorship of New Jersey and then for the Presidency of the United States – by colleagues at Princeton who could no longer tolerate the pedantic and self-righteous certainty with which he led the university. His speech to Congress on 8 January 1918 portrayed all the qualities to which his critics objected. It came to be called 'The Fourteen Points' and was, in consequence, an easy target for derision. Clemenceau observed that 'the good Lord himself required only ten'.[5] But, with all their faults, the Fourteen Points were a brave and honest attempt to find a better way than war for determining the future of the world.

Open treaties should be 'openly arrived at'. Freedom of the seas must be guaranteed. Trade barriers were to be eliminated. Rearmament was to be 'reduced to the lowest level consistent with domestic safety'. Russia, still convulsed with revolution and civil war, must enjoy 'an unhampered development . . . under institutions of her own choosing'. Claims to the possession of colonies should be 'adjusted' with due regard to the interests of the indigenous people. The occupation of Belgium was to end and its sovereignty to be restored. The wrong done to France over Alsace-Lorraine (by German annexation after the Franco-Prussian war) 'should be righted'. Italy's frontiers were to be adjusted 'along clearly recognisable lines of nationality . . .' The people of Austria-Hungary should 'be accorded opportunity for autonomous development . . . Balkan relationships should be determined by friendly counsel along historically established lines.' Nations under Turkish rule were to be afforded 'unmolested opportunity for autonomous development . . . An independent Polish state must be erected which should include territories inhabited by indispensably Polish populations and should be afforded secure access to the sea.' The fourteenth point was meant to secure a permanent peace after the new world, created by the other thirteen imperatives, had been put in place. It proposed 'a general association of nations under specific covenants for affording mutual guarantees of political independence'. The association came to be called the League of Nations.

The precision of the Fourteen Points was matched by the piety of a series of subsequent speeches which Wilson called, with a magnificent disregard for ridicule, the Four Principles, the Four Ends and the Five Particulars. Each one emphasised a precept which, the President reminded America, was confirmed by the history of their own republic. 'Self determination is no mere phrase, it is a principle of action which statesmen ignore at their peril.'[6] It was a moral imperative to which the delegates to the Peace Conference responded – whenever it was not in conflict with their national interests.

Three months after Woodrow Wilson set out his plan for lasting peace Haig told the Allied troops, 'With our backs to the wall and believing in the justice of our cause, each one of us must fight to the end.' So it seemed that the President had spoken of peace too soon. But in one sense he was almost too late. David Lloyd George had anticipated many of the Fourteen Points in an address to British trade unionists and the President feared that, if he repeated them, he would seem to be limping along behind the British Prime Minister. But Lloyd George's speech received little publicity and Wilson judged that peace proposals, backed by the authority of the President of the United States, would catch and hold the world's attention. His judgement was vindicated. But the Fourteen Points received no more than a cautious welcome from European politicians. Only the European people showed real enthusiasm for Wilson's hope that 'war shall be no more'.

It was not the dangerous nobility of Woodrow Wilson's proposals –
or the President's transparent sincerity – which worried Europe's
leaders. The Fourteen Points, by their nature, were an assertion of
America's right to intervene in parts of the world well outside its
traditional spheres of influence. Wilson had given notice that the
United States proposed to play a dominant world role. The assumption
that the President could draw lines on a blank map threatened the
territorial ambitions of the European Allies.

During the war the European Allies had negotiated several of the
secret treaties which the Fourteen Points specifically condemned. In
London in 1915 Italy had been promised the Dalmatian Coast and
Trentino as an inducement to declare war on Germany. In May 1916
the Sykes–Picot Agreement had arranged for the division of the
Ottoman Empire between Russia, France and Britain with France
controlling Syria and Britain dominating Mesopotamia. Then Italy,
dissatisfied with the spoils of war she had been promised, demanded
that Fiume (Hungary's outlet to the sea) should be added to her
bounty. A binding commitment to self-determination would prejudice
the prospect of expansion – even for the countries which won the
war.

Great Britain was in specific disagreement with the second of
Woodrow Wilson's Fourteen Points – the freedom of the seas. For
more than a hundred years the Royal Navy had exercised the dubious
right to stop, search and, if necessary, sink any ship it regarded as either
a threat to British interest or in contravention of various maritime
laws which, from time to time, it unilaterally announced. Lloyd
George was adamant. The Royal Navy's 'rights' must be preserved.

Woodrow Wilson had doubts about the constitutional propriety of
leaving the United States to attend the peace conference. But Lloyd
George sent a theatrical message to the White House. 'The President's
presence is necessary for the proper organisation of the world which
must follow the peace . . . If he sits in the conference . . . he will exert
the greatest influence that any man has ever exerted in expressing the
moral value of free government.'[7] That did not mean that he endorsed
the details of Wilson's plan. When Clemenceau, in a mood of
European resentment, asked him, 'Have you ever been asked by
President Wilson whether you accept The Fourteen Points?', adding,

'For I have not', Lloyd George replied, 'I have not been asked either.'[8] Nor had either of them been asked to support the President's judgement on the treatment of defeated Germany. Wisely, Wilson had avoided discussing the subject, knowing that his formula would be regarded as unacceptably lenient.

European concerns about the American position were increased by the discovery that on 4 October 1918 – a month before the Armistice – the German High Command had asked President Wilson to negotiate a peace settlement based on the Fourteen Points. Wilson did not tell his allies of the approach until four days later. But the French had intercepted the German telegram. The discovery hardened Clemenceau's resolve to demand that Germany pay a harsh penalty for its aggression. When the Allied leaders met at the Supreme War Council in Paris on 5 October, Marshal Foch – Commander-in-Chief of the Anglo–French army which had won the war – proposed final terms which amounted to unconditional surrender. The apparent conflict between American and French aims strengthened Lloyd George's conviction that Woodrow Wilson must be persuaded to travel to Europe and lead the Allies' peace treaty negotiations. Without Wilson to assist in restraining Clemenceau the French would almost certainly insist on such a punitive settlement that Germany, even though humiliated and emasculated, would rise up in revolt against the injustice it had suffered.

Woodrow Wilson, realising that he was wanted, perhaps even needed, by the Allies, extracted a price for his participation. Lloyd George feared that, if the Peace Conference was held in Paris, the bitterness of a nation which had suffered so much – and the desire for revenge of a Prime Minister who had been the Mayor of Montmartre during the Prussian occupation of 1870 and 1871 – would prejudice its proceedings. So he proposed Geneva. But Wilson – for some reason fearful of a Bolshevik revolution in Switzerland – wanted Paris. So Paris it was. But when the work was finished the statesmen of Europe wanted a grander setting for their moment of history. They moved on to Louis XIV's palace at Versailles and signed the treaty in the shadow of the Sun King.

President Wilson could not leave the United States until the end of the year. Congressional elections were to be held in November 1918 and Wilson was determined to play a major part in a contest which he said would enable the American people to give him 'a strong hand' to play in Europe. Wilson's Democrats lost control of both the Senate and the House of Representatives – leaving the President to travel to Paris in the knowledge that he needed Republican support to obtain the necessary ratification of the treaty he hoped to negotiate. A shrewder or more emollient man would have invited sympathetic Republicans to join him as senior members of his delegation. Woodrow Wilson took only friends and known supporters.

During the time which was wasted in waiting for the President, elections were also held in Britain. They could not have been postponed for long. The Representation of the People Act of 1918 had trebled the electorate by giving a vote to every man over twenty-one and every woman over thirty. There had been no general election since 1910. Lloyd George led a coalition which governed without an explicit mandate of the people and many, perhaps most, of the men who won the war had been either too young or unqualified to vote in the last peacetime election. Nor did Lloyd George wish to delay the poll. It was certain, in the glow of triumph, that the Prime Minister who had led the country to victory would win a 'khaki election'. So it turned out, but the campaign had disastrous consequences for the Peace Conference. Its proceedings were prejudiced as much by Lloyd George's victory in Britain as by the defeat of Woodrow Wilson's Democrats in America.

Inevitably the British general election campaign of 1918 was fought on the parties' rival ideas of post-war reconstruction. The Labour Party (with the exception of George Barnes, one of its nominees in the War Cabinet) withdrew from the coalition after the Armistice and was happily reunited with the pacifists who had refused to support Lloyd George's government. 'Our battle cry, above all else,' said Jimmy Thomas, the railwaymen's leader, 'is "No More War".'[9] That battle cry became the most popular slogan of the whole campaign. But other, less idealistic, demands were also included in the coalition's speeches. 'Make the Germans Pay' and 'Hang the Kaiser' were two of the most frequent. The politicians, as politicians often do, chose to identify with the lowest common denominator. F. E. Smith, the Attorney General, told the Cabinet that unless the Kaiser was put on trial it would be impossible to indict anyone who was under his command and Eric Geddes, then Secretary of State for War, promised 'to squeeze the German lemon until the pips squeak'.[10] Lloyd George could argue that his election pledge was – as befitted a Prime Minister – more measured. But it encouraged the vengeful hope that the reparations made by the vanquished to the victors would be punishment as well as compensation. The Germans, he said, would be required to pay 'to the limit of their capacity and we shall scratch their pockets for it'.[11] Thus began the process which amounted to competitive bids to determine how great a penalty could be exacted from Germany. The coalition won by a landslide.* Lloyd George was committed to imposing severe penalties on Germany. And another step had been taken towards the pauperisation of a nation and the creation of a country so resentful about its treatment that it was prepared to rally behind any rabble-rousing politician who promised to restore national self-respect. Lloyd George also became party to the imposition of economic sanctions which were so severe that they precipitated the greatest economic crisis of the twentieth century.

The two months between the Armistice and the opening of the Peace Conference should have been used to plan the way in which the formal proceedings would be organised. Sadly the Supreme War Council, which might have performed that task, was too preoccupied with managing Germany's capitulation to think about much else. The Allied leaders assembled in Paris with conflicting ideas about what they had to do but united by the lack of any notion about how anything might be done.

The European heads of government were continually irritated by Woodrow Wilson's unremittingly high-minded tone which, they feared, confirmed his commitment to a high-minded policy. France, as represented by its Prime Minister, wanted the emasculation and humiliation of Germany. That, in Clemenceau's judgement, required – in addition to the return of the territories annexed by Prussia in 1870 – the creation of either an independent or French state west of

---

*The coalition won 484 seats, the Labour Party 59, Asquith Liberals 26, Irish Nationalists 6 and Sinn Fein 73.

the Rhine, the expansion of Poland and Czechoslovakia at the expense of Germany and reparations so severe that the German economy would remain, for the foreseeable future, too weak to sustain any resurgence of its military aspirations.

The 'peace aims' of America and France were clearly at variance with each other. And Lloyd George – occasionally a statesman but always a politician – vacillated between the two positions but eventually, with his election promises in mind, moved closer to Clemenceau. The three leaders had no clear plan of how their differences were to be resolved. But some decisions were urgently needed. The desire to bring the troops back home – prompted more by cost than by compassion – meant that the naval blockade must be maintained as the only way of ensuring that Germany observed the terms of the Armistice which its leaders had signed on 11 November. But until the blockade was lifted Germany – women and children no less than soldiers – starved. Woodrow Wilson was reluctant to make progress towards a treaty which did not include the creation of the League of Nations. It seemed to him – wrongly, as it turned out – that the inclusion of his plans for world peace was the one way to ensure Congress ratified the eventual treaty.

The Armistice terms – as far as they went – had amounted to German surrender. All artillery, machine guns and aircraft were to be immediately handed over to the Allies. Submarines and ships were to be put under Allied control pending decisions about their eventual destiny. German troops were to withdraw from the right bank of the Rhine within thirty-one days. The Allies would occupy (without hindrance) the left bank of the Rhine and establish bridge-heads on the right. All German troops occupying or garrisoned in territory outside Germany – from Alsace-Lorraine in the west to Turkey, Romania and the Austro-Hungarian Empire in the east – were to be evacuated, with the exception of forces stationed in Russia.

Russia, an ally in the war against the Central Powers, posed a particular problem. In recompense for his support Tsar Nicholas II had been promised Constantinople and the Straits. But the Tsar had been deposed in 1917 and executed a year later. The Communists, who had become the government in Moscow, had made peace with Germany and renounced, as a matter of principle, the annexation of territory.

Decisions about what to do with Constantinople were, however, dwarfed by the need to decide what to do about Russia itself. Tsarist forces fought on against the revolutionary government. In London influential voices – chief among them Winston Churchill, the Secretary of State for War – were demanding that Britain intervened in the dying days of the civil war to secure the return of the *ancien régime*.

The Allies had a principled – that is to say ideological – antipathy to the new regime in Russia. But the antagonism was fuelled by fear. There had been abortive Communist uprisings in Munich and in Budapest and, even in Britain, Bob Williams (the secretary of the Transport and General Workers' Union) had expressed the hope that he would soon 'see the Red Flag flying over Buckingham Palace'.[12] King George urged his ministers to do all they could to destroy the Bolsheviks who had murdered his cousin, the Tsar. Dealing with the Communists was complicated by the part their country had played in the war.

Tsarist Russia had held back half the forces of the Central Powers. Indeed, had Lenin not signed the Treaty of Brest–Litovsk in March 1918, the war might well have ended earlier. The peace treaty, if it was to conform to the Fourteen Points, would require independence for the Ukraine. The west had long-term worries about the security of Caspian and Ukrainian oil and the Allies were uncertain about how to respond to the determination of three Tsarist generals – Kornilov, Alexeev and Denikin – to ignore the Armistice and fight on against Germany, as they saw it, for Holy Russia.

The Allies were committed to the Tsarist 'White Russians' both materially and emotionally. Millions of tons of stores had been landed at Murmansk and at Archangel. Bases had been established at Vladivostok and in distant Siberia. British troops, no longer needed in Mesopotamia, had occupied Batum on the Black Sea and Baku on the shores of the Caspian. Allied expeditionary forces were sent to Vladivostok, Murmansk and Archangel with the theoretical task of protecting the armaments and supplies which had been stored there. The real purpose was the encouragement of the faint hope that the Tsarist cause might prevail.

In the month before the Armistice was signed, Clemenceau had set out to his general staff his policy towards Communist Russia.

The main line of the plan of action (which should be adopted)
is not only to continue to struggle against the Central Powers but
to encircle Bolshevism and bring about its downfall.[13]

The French had a vested interest in saving the *ancien régime*. Tsarist
Russia's pre-war debt to France was 25,000 million francs (£1,000
million), to which had been added half as much again in Allied war
loans. None of that would be repaid by the Bolsheviks. And France's
substantial investment in Russian banking, oil, coal and railways would
all be expropriated if Lenin remained head of state and government.

Winston Churchill – the chief British advocate of military intervention – was motivated by aristocratic, rather than economic, fears
about the Soviet regime. According to Lord Curzon, 'his ducal blood
revolted against the wholesale slaughter of Grand Dukes' and he was
a major factor in his hope that the government in which he was
Secretary of State for War would consider 'whether we should . . . bol-
ster up the Central Powers (that is to say defeated Austria and
Germany) if necessary to stem the tide of Bolshevism'.[14] The failure
of Tsarist Admiral Kolchak – who had assumed command of the
White Russian forces in Siberia – to link up with General Denikin in
the south cooled the ardour of some anti-Bolshevik crusaders. But the
more militant Tsarist sympathisers, led by Churchill himself, continued
to campaign for intervention in a way which complicated an already
confused attempt to re-draw the map of the world and guarantee lasting peace.

When the formal conference got under way it followed a plan of
procedure which the French had drafted two months earlier.[15] The
'Big Four' – Britain, America, France and Italy – would dictate the
preliminary terms to Germany without any discussion with the Berlin
government. The smaller Allies would be consulted when decisions
affecting their frontiers were taken. At a second stage all the Allies
would join with both neutrals and enemies to discuss the new world
order. The early exclusion of some affected powers was not to Wilson's
liking. When he landed in Europe, from the USS *Washington*, he determined that the French scheme should be 'quietly disregarded' while
Clemenceau was making clear (equally quietly) that the Fourteen
Points 'were not sufficiently defined in their character to be taken as

a concrete basis for a concrete settlement of the war'.[16] The result of the different views on procedure combined with the absence of any effective machinery for discussion resulted in the official meetings being downgraded, leaving the real decisions to cabals of the most powerful ministers. Paul Gambon, a veteran professional French diplomat, complained, 'Nobody knows anything because everything happens behind the scenes.'[17]

International conferences make politicians believe they have become statesmen – a transformation which they attempt to make public by surrounding themselves with clear evidence of their world status. The size and composition of the Paris delegations did nothing to help the expeditious conclusion of business. Wellington and Castlereagh took a staff of seventeen to the Congress of Vienna. Lloyd George and A. J. Balfour, his Foreign Secretary, took 750 civil servants and expert advisers to Paris. The American party was just as large, and every delegation included men and women of personal brilliance but unpredictable temperament. Keynes represented the British Treasury. Colonel T. E. Lawrence, technically advising Lloyd George on the Middle East, became the confidant and spokesman for Prince Faisal, son of Emir Hussain, the 'Guardian of the Sacred Cities of Arabia'. Both men predicted that disaster would follow the implementation of those parts of the Treaty on which their advice was offered but not taken. Both men were proved right.

Harold Nicolson recorded in his diary the account of the proceedings which he had given to Marcel Proust (who 'lunched in white gloves') over dinner at the Paris Ritz. 'So I tell him everything. The sham-cordiality of it all; the handshakes, the maps; the rustle of papers; the tea in the next room; the macaroons.'[18]

When the Peace Conference began its work its effective executive was the 'Council of Ten', to which Great Britain, the United States, France, Italy and Japan each contributed two ministers. Clemenceau's original intention was that its decisions would be at least ratified by plenary sessions of the Conference which all participating states would attend. But the plenary sessions were only convened on eight occasions, while the Council of Ten met seventy-two times and much of the work, after the first week, was done in 'special commissions'.

Clemenceau grew tired of even pretending that every nation represented in Paris influenced events with equal weight. 'I make no secret
of it,' he told one meeting of the plenary session. 'There is a conference of the great powers going on in the next room.'[19]

Although all the heads of government participated throughout the
days of early meetings, the major players were distracted by events at
home. In Britain a nation tired by war witnessed, with some sympathy, a series of minor mutinies in the armed forces. In early January
1919 troops at Folkestone and Dover refused to embark for France.
Royal Army Service Corps drivers took a 'protest convoy' from
Osterley to Whitehall. At Grove Park and Kempton 'soldiers' councils'
demanded the right to be consulted about accommodation, pay and
rations. And at Rosyth the crew of a minesweeper refused to obey
orders. Weeks of industrial unrest followed, with some trade unions
threatening a general strike if Britain attempted to restore the House
of Romanov to the throne of Holy Mother Russia.

During the third week in February an attempt was made on
Clemenceau's life. He survived but his wounds kept him out of action
for several weeks. President Wilson returned home to begin his campaign to convince the United States Senate and the American people
that his plans for 'a general association of nations . . . formed under
specific covenants for the purpose of affording guarantees of political
independence and territorial integrity to great and small nations alike'
were worthy of their support.[20] When he returned to Paris he was
adamant that there could be no preliminary treaty that redrew the
map of Europe unless it also created an international agency which
secured a permanent peace. America would only sign an agreement
which included the creation of the League of Nations.

Faced with the need to deal with both the complicated long-term
question of a League and the immediate problems of borders and
repatriation, Clemenceau, Lloyd George and Colonel Edward House
(representing the absent Woodrow Wilson) began to meet informally
to chart the route along which the Council of Ten should be steered.
Gradually the meetings evolved into a Council of Four – or sometimes Five – representing Great Britain, America, France, Italy (except
when Vittorio Emanuele Orlando withdrew in protest against the
rejection of his claim to Fiume) and occasionally Japan. The leaders of

government met in private with, at first, only an interpreter present. Then Sir Maurice Hankey, from the British Cabinet Office, was appointed official secretary of the group. Woodrow Wilson's hopes of open treaties were not realised. But at least the Peace Conference had evolved a mechanism which allowed it to make progress. Lloyd George began to wonder if the progress would be in the right direction. Perhaps it had been a mistake to persuade Wilson that Clemenceau must be accommodated.

During the third week of March 1919 the British Prime Minister retired to Fontainebleau where – with Sir Henry Wilson (the Chief of the Imperial General Staff), Jan Christiaan Smuts (South African defence minister and member of the Imperial Cabinet), Maurice Hankey, John Maynard Keynes and Philip Kerr (his private secretary) – he drafted a memorandum setting out 'the kind of Treaty of Peace to which alone we [are] prepared to append our signature'.[21] France must be prevented from insisting on a settlement so brutal that Germany would 'throw in her lot with Bolshevism and place her resources, her brains and her vast organising power at the disposal of the revolutionaries whose dream is to conquer the world for Bolshevism'.[22] Perhaps Germany could be persuaded to see the justice of a settlement which was punitive but not vindictive. 'Our terms may be severe. They may be stern and even ruthless. But at the same time, they can be so just that the country on which they are imposed will feel in its heart that it has no right to complain.'[23] Germany's obligation to pay reparations should end with the passing from power of the generations which had been responsible for the war. It would obviously be unreasonable 'to cripple [Germany] and still expect her to pay'.[24] So the defeated enemy must, out of necessity, be allowed access both to world markets and raw materials. Britain would not agree to 'transferring more Germans from German rule to some other nation' than was necessary to draw new boundaries which, by and large, represented the ethnic composition of the majority within them. Lloyd George concluded, 'If we are wise, we shall offer Germany a peace which, while just, will be preferable to all sensible men to Bolshevism.'[25]

Had Lloyd George's revised position been accepted the Peace Treaty would have been quite different from what was eventually

agreed. The new state of Czechoslovakia would not have included the
Sudetenland and France would not have been given a ten-year
suzerainty over the Saar. The boundary between Poland and Germany
was modified at Lloyd George's insistence. But Germany's loss of part
of East Prussia – the heartland of the federation and the home of the
Junkers who dominated the Berlin government – was remembered
long after the concessions which Lloyd George had negotiated had
been forgotten. And reparations were set at a level which was far too
high for Germany to pay. It was not to Bolshevism that Germany
turned. But in 1919 that was the threat which preoccupied the leaders of the western democracies.

President Wilson – true to character – hoped that the 'Bolshevik
threat' could be eliminated by convening a conference at which the
still-warring factions within Russia would meet to resolve their differences. He invited 'every organised group that is now exercising, or
attempting to exercise, political authority or military control anywhere in Siberia or within the boundaries of European Russia, as they
were before the war just concluded (except Siberia), to send representatives to the Princes' Islands in the Sea of Marmara'.[26] Lenin
agreed. The Tsarist White Russians did not.

Although Lenin's willingness to discuss the future might have been
taken as evidence of the Bolshevik wish to work with the Allied
Powers, the opponents of Soviet Communism insisted that the collapse of the Conference was conclusive proof of the need for military
action. Chief among the British advocates of intervention was again
the Secretary of State for War, Winston Churchill.

Lloyd George complained that, while he was away in Paris,
Churchill had exercised a powerful and 'exceedingly pernicious influence in Cabinet'.[27] When the Prime Minister returned to London
Churchill 'very adroitly seized the opportunity . . . to go over to Paris
and urge his plans, with regard to Russia, upon the consideration of
the French, American and British delegations'.[28] The freedom with
which Churchill pursued his anti-Bolshevik obsession illustrates more
than his cavalier approach to the collective responsibility which usually constrains a Cabinet. It confirms that Lloyd George – feeling
insecure in the leadership of a coalition which was dominated by his
historic opponents – was reluctant to impose his will on a minister

who, although technically still a Liberal, remained close to the Tory Party, which he had deserted, and to which nobody doubted he would return. The messages with which he responded to news of Churchill's free enterprise were more entreaties than instructions. 'I am very alarmed at your . . . telegram about planning a war against the Bolsheviks. The Cabinet has never authorised such a proposition.' He went on to 'beg' his Secretary of State for War 'not to commit the country to what would be a mad enterprise, out of hatred of the Bolsheviks'.[29]

Lloyd George was not, by nature, the man to steer a steady course. Distracted by London intrigues when he was in Paris and by Paris machinations when he was in London, his capacity for consistency was further limited by the rival pressures of domestic politics and what he knew to be right for the future peace of Europe. Georges Clemenceau was ruthless in his determination to secure a single objective. France must be strengthened and Germany weakened to the point at which the territorial ambitions of Berlin could never be realised. When Lloyd George recognised the folly of humiliating Germany it was too late. He had supported Clemenceau's punitive approach and persuaded Woodrow Wilson to at least not veto the French Prime Minister's proposals.

> To his horror, Mr Lloyd George, desiring at the last moment all the moderation he knew to be right, discovered that he could not in five days persuade the President of error in what it had taken him five months to prove to him to be just and right. After all, it was harder to de-bamboozle this naïve Presbyterian than to bamboozle him.[30]

There was no difficulty in the Allies agreeing to what Lloyd George and Woodrow Wilson called righting 'of the great wrong of 1871'. So Alsace and Lorraine were, after some minor dispute about where the frontier lay, returned to France. But Clemenceau regarded that as only the beginning. Initially he hoped to annex the whole left bank of the Rhine – thus reversing the decision taken by the Congress of Vienna in 1815 when the object was to protect Germany against France, not France against Germany. Lloyd George was dubious about the proposition and Woodrow Wilson was categorically opposed. Colonel House, Wilson's alter ego, told A. J. Balfour, the British Foreign Secretary, 'The French have but one idea and that is military protection. They do not seem to know that to establish a Rhenish republic against the will of the people would be contrary to the principle of self determination.'[31] The result was the sort of compromise which satisfies no one. The Allies would be in technical occupation for fifteen years though – if Germany fulfilled its other treaty obligations – troops would be withdrawn after five or ten. In the meantime French security would be guaranteed by an Anglo-American non-aggression pact.

The French approach to the future of the Saar was wholly materialistic. Whatever the inclinations of its population, France was entitled to its coal in compensation for the destruction of the mines in its north-western *départements*. Wilson rejected the notion outright. There followed an episode in the continuing pantomime in which, at various intervals, each man threatened to abandon negotiations and bring the Peace Conference to a crashing end. Clemenceau walked out. Wilson told the USS *Washington* to prepare for the voyage home. The inevitable result was a compromise. The Saar would be under French control for fifteen years, during which it would be obliged to supply France with thirty million tons of coal. A referendum would then decide whether or not the people of the Saar were French or German.

Belgium failed in its attempt to annex Luxembourg – part of Bismarck's empire and clearly sympathetic to the Central Powers during the war. The French wanted to give Denmark more of Schleswig-Holstein than the Danes felt able to accept. A plebiscite – a concession to Wilson's demand for self-determination – solved the dilemma by confirming that half of Schleswig wanted to remain German. Poland acquired 260 square miles of what had been German territory. Hungary – being in partnership with Austria, a defeated power – was emasculated by the creation of new nations. Yugoslavia was made up of 7 per cent of the old empire. Czechoslovakia encompassed 22 per cent – including the Sudetenland in which the population was almost entirely German. Romania, although not a new creation, was rewarded for its support of the Allies with 39 per cent of old Austria-Hungary. All the new nations were required to sign 'minority treaties' promising the full rights of citizenship and freedom of language and religion to their whole populations. Only Woodrow Wilson had much confidence in them being observed.

Poland, oppressed by Russia and Germany for two hundred years, demanded recognition as a great power and borders which confirmed that status. Dissatisfied with their proposed frontier in the east, it invaded the Ukraine. The Red Army drove the Ukrainian army back almost to Warsaw. But a counter-attack succeeded in saving the city. The result – a combination of Polish courage and Russian moderation – was the expansion of Poland a hundred miles to the east. Originally Woodrow Wilson – in fine disregard of his Fourteen Points – agreed to a settlement in east Germany which Lloyd George claimed would 'hand over millions of people to a distasteful allegiance'.[32] The initial plan was modified to make Danzig a free port under League of Nations protection rather than part of Poland. But the 'Polish Corridor', by which it was connected to the sea, split East Prussia from the rest of Germany. Upper Silesia was to determine its future by plebiscite and was eventually divided between Poland and Germany. Lloyd George accepted that 'it was hardly possible to draw any line which would not have Germans on both sides of it'.[33] When the Allies knew that frontiers could not be drawn along ethnic boundaries, they always made sure that Germany and the Germans came off worst.

The emasculation of Germany and its allies was intended to be the long-term protection against a resurgence of Prussian militarism. Short-term security was to be guaranteed by limitation of the German military capability. The army was to be limited to 100,000 volunteers – all of whom, to prevent the recruitment of a large reserve, were to serve for at least twelve years. The navy was to consist of no more than six battleships, six cruisers and twelve destroyers. Germany was to possess no military aircraft or submarines. President Wilson insisted that Part V of the eventual treaty which imposed the limitation should begin with a statement which asserted that the intention was pacific rather than vindictive. 'In order to render possible the initiation of a general limitation on the armaments of all nations . . .' Nobody was deceived.

It would have been impossible to justify the Middle East settlement with any such principled declaration. The future of Syria and Mesopotamia was determined by the crudest sort of power politics. The Balfour Declaration of 1917 which had made clear that the British government 'viewed with favour the establishment, in Palestine, of a Jewish national home for the Jewish people' had little influence on the proceedings. Prince Faisal, the son of Emir Hussein, who had led the 'revolt in the desert' against the Turks, had written (with the assistance of T. E. Lawrence) to the *New York Times* to welcome the idea of 'Jews and Arabs working together for a reformed and revived Middle East'. The letter ended with the assurance 'the Jews are most welcome here. There is room in Syria for both of us.' The question which hung over the Peace Conference was could Syria accommodate both British and French aspirations?

In May 1916, conscious that the Turks were being driven out of Arabia with the assistance of British army officers, Clemenceau had begun to fear that Lloyd George planned to dominate the whole region. It was not a moment for disagreement between the Allies. So an accommodation was necessary. The Sykes–Picot Agreement decided, bilaterally, that France would control Syria, Britain Mesopotamia. Tsarist Russia would be given Armenia. The Arabs would be allowed to maintain control over those parts of Arabia which the Great Powers did not claim as their own.

The Arabs complained but were ignored. However, with British encouragement, Faisal and Lawrence captured Damascus from the Turks and made clear that they regarded it as the Hashemite capital. More important, Lloyd George could not see why the French, who had made no contribution to the Turks' expulsion, should be handed land that had been won by the leadership (and the gold) which Britain had supplied to Emir Hussein and the thousand horsemen who followed his warlike sons.

In Paris Faisal argued the case for Arab autonomy – though it was later suggested that he did no more than read passages from the Koran while Lawrence, officially providing the translation, offered his improvised view on the proper disposition of power in the Middle East. It did not matter. The speeches on behalf of the Hashemites counted for nothing. Lloyd George was always determined to keep Iraq under

British 'protection'. The Royal Navy needed the oil. If that required him to agree to France gaining effective control of Syria it was a price he was prepared to pay.

Lawrence, believing that the Arabs had been betrayed, sent his medals back to the War Office. Hussein and his sons accepted – with undisguised bitterness – the kingdom which the Treaty offered them. Other Arabs were less willing to allow their fate to be decided in Paris. Ibin Saud invaded the Hejaz and was almost annihilated by the force which was sent by Hussein to repel him. The British intervened to protect their nominee – by threatening to send Whippet armoured cars from Palestine. But the price which Lloyd George, and Hussein, had to pay was the creation of a new Arab state to satisfy Ibn Saud's claims. Saudi Arabia became one of the countries of the Middle East which, directly or indirectly, owe their existence to the Paris Peace Conference.

The division of Asia Minor between the Great Powers was only one of the problems created by the dissolution of the Ottoman Empire. Constantinople had been promised to the Tsar. As a result it could not be offered to Lenin who, in any event, had forsworn the acquisition of territory outside Russian borders. It was eventually agreed that America would take responsibility for free passage through the Straits. But Woodrow Wilson could not accept 'the mandate' without the approval of Congress. While the world waited, Greece agreed to act as 'bailiff' in return for the acquisition of Smyrna, a town on the Turkish mainland with a substantial population which was ethnically, if not legally, Greek. The Sultan capitulated. But the Turkish people did not. The Sultan was repudiated and Mustafa Kemal – leader of the Turkish National Movement and Commander-in-Chief of the forces which had driven the Allies out of Gallipoli – seized power with popular sup-port if not a democratic mandate. In September 1922 he reoccupied Smyrna. The invasion was followed by a massacre of (it was claimed) 100,000 Greek and Armenian settlers. The international community watched from afar.

Now it seems incredible that politicians as sophisticated as Lloyd George, high-minded as Woodrow Wilson and experienced as Georges Clemenceau could have believed that a series of meetings in

Paris hotel rooms – often without the help of expert advisers or a sec-
retariat – could have redrawn the map of the world in a way which
would result in anything but upheaval. Almost all their work resulted
in war or revolution and the best Paris hopes were dashed by the
League of Nations' inability to protect the smaller nations against the
aggression of great powers. But, even if there had been the will and the
courage to defend the 1919 settlement, some of their decisions would
have been unsustainable in the long term. The peace imposed on
Germany made a second world war inevitable.

The seeds of hatred and bitterness were sown in Germany even before
the terms of the eventual settlement were known. While the pro-
tracted discussions went on in Paris, Germany – under an Allied
blockade – starved. General Plumer, Officer Commanding the British
Forces of Occupation, telegraphed the War Office.

> The mortality among women, children and the sick is most
> grave and sickness due to hunger is spreading. The attitude of the
> population is becoming one of despair and the people feel that
> an end by bullets is preferable to death by starvation.

The general's compassion was compounded by concern for military
discipline. In defiance of orders, British troops were giving starving
civilians food from army stores.[34]

The Armistice Agreement had contained the ambiguous assurance
that 'the Allies contemplated the provisioning of Germany to the
extent that shall be deemed necessary'. The intention was to lift the
blockade and allow the importation of food and raw materials for
which Germany would pay. The only possible source of payment was
Berlin's gold reserves, which France forbade the German government
to touch. They were, in Clemenceau's opinion, earmarked for the
payment of reparations. After two months of delay and death Lloyd
George insisted that the gold be released. It was his one success in a
campaign to conclude quickly the debate on reparations. Clemenceau
claimed that 'countries which have not known invasion' could not
understand the importance of obtaining 'total and definite guarantees'.
By that he meant the need for reparations of a size and type which

could be guaranteed to incapacitate Germany for the rest of the century.

The French proposed an initial payment of two billion pounds sterling and subsequent annual payments of six million pounds a year for an indefinite (or at least undetermined) period. Lloyd George's conclusions on the proper level of reparations owed less to careful calculation of what Germany could pay than to a crude guess as to what the British Parliament and public expected. The War Cabinet had set up a reparations sub-committee which had come to the farcical conclusion that the total sum should be twenty-four billion pounds, to be paid (allowing for interest) at £1,200,000,000 a year. In his *Life of Keynes*, Roy Harrod compares that figure with the thirty-five million pounds annual loan repayment to the United States which Ramsay MacDonald argued (successfully) was beyond Britain's means in 1931. The Treasury had been calculating Germany's ability to pay some sort of indemnity since 1916. 'Keynes estimated that under the terms of the Armistice Agreement the Allies were legally entitled to claim between £160,000,000 and £3,000,000,000 which it would have been "wise and just" to compound to £2,000,000,000.'[35] But wisdom and justice were not Lloyd George's chief preoccupations. He had published the War Cabinet's estimate of just reparations during the 'Hang the Kaiser' election campaign and it was, in consequence, difficult to argue for less. What inclination he had towards moderation was undermined by the publication of a letter signed by 380 Tory (that is to say, government) backbenchers demanding that Germany pay the full cost of the war. Naturally enough, Lord Northcliffe's *Daily Mail* entered the argument on the MPs' side and added that it possessed information to suggest that the French wanted to strike a harder bargain than the British would contemplate. Lloyd George refuted the suggestion by relying on the technicality that no figures had been officially tabled.

You are quite wrong about France STOP No allie has named figure STOP Allies in complete agreement as to demand for indemnity STOP Inter-allied commission will investigate on behalf of all on identical principles STOP Don't be always making mischief [36]

In the House of Commons his rejection of Northcliffe's criticism was even more robust. The *Daily Mail* had published what it described as appropriate peace terms. They were not as exacting as those which it had only recently demanded Lloyd George must obtain. He ended his speech with an interpretation of Northcliffe's motives. 'The war was won without him. There must be something wrong.'[37] But, despite his spirited defence of moderation, he knew that he had to give the appearance of keeping Geddes' promise to 'squeeze Germany until the pips squeak'. The idea that ruining Germany's economy might have adverse effects on Britain seems never to have entered his head. Yet Keynes, a member of his delegation, knew that if reparations were set at a crippling level the banking system, certainly of Europe and probably of the world, would be in danger of collapse. The crisis was longer delayed than Keynes anticipated. The shockwaves hit the already unsteady pound in the summer of 1931.

The dispute about how much Germany should pay turned into an argument which, although superficially semantic, was really about how to share the spoils. Did reparation mean payment sufficient to restore damage done and, if so, should it be limited to the cost of material damage? Should damage done to countries which neither fought nor were occupied be included in the calculation? General Smuts and 'Billie' Hughes, the Prime Minister of Australia, wanted the cost of widows' and disability pensions, and compensation for family separations, to be added to the total. Keynes argued that 'if words have any meaning or engagements any force we have no more right to claim for those war expenses which arose out of Pensions and Separation Allowances than for any other costs of war'.[38] Lloyd George was not disposed to exclude anything and Woodrow Wilson found an ingenious justification for what he knew to be wrong. His economic adviser explained that he 'conceded on pensions on the theory that it would not materially increase the actual amount that Germany would have to pay, but would rather affect the method of distribution because we regard Germany's capacity as being agreed to within a thirty year limit'.

President Wilson knew, or should have known, that there was no agreement on a total amount or a time limit on payments. Lloyd George, fearful that whatever sum was decided would not sound

enough, had persuaded the Allies to delegate both decisions to a
Reparations Committee that would review the position from time to
time. Keynes warned that, by leaving the size of Germany's national
debt undetermined, the Allies made it impossible for the Berlin
government to negotiate international credit. But not even Woodrow
Wilson was in a mood to be moved by such considerations. In the eyes
of the general public – in Britain and America no less than in France –
reparations had become an indemnity exacted less as compensation
than for punishment. The final settlement – motivated as much by
pride, greed, vengeance and the fear of public dissatisfaction as by the
desire for self-protection – was justified by Article 231 of the Treaty
which ended the war with Germany.*

> The Allied and the Associate Powers attest and Germany accepts
> the responsibility of Germany and its allies for causing all the loss
> and damage to which they and their nationals have been sub-
> jected as a consequence of war imposed on them by the
> aggression of Germany and its allies.

It was not a view which Count Brockdorff-Rantzau – the professional diplomat who led the German delegation – was willing to
endorse. His reluctance to accept the outright condemnation of his
country had been increased by the treatment he had received on
arrival in Paris. The Allies were not ready to sign. But the Kiaochow
Peninsula, part of the Chinese mainland which had been occupied by
Germany, was to be returned to Japan and the Japanese insisted that
the Germans apologised for their conduct and renounced all future
claim to the colony at a face-to-face meeting with the Emperor's
representative. While the wrangle over protocol went on, Brockdorff-
Rantzau and his colleagues were kept under guard and behind barbed
wire in what they regarded as a prison.

---

*Separate treaties were signed with each of the other major Central Powers:
    Saint Germain with Austria on 10 September 1919
    Neuilly with Bulgaria on 27 November 1919
    Trianon with Hungary on 4 June 1920
    Sèvres with the Ottoman Empire on 10 August 1920

On 7 May 1919, after a week of waiting, victors and vanquished met in the Hotel Trianon. Count Brockdorff-Rantzau spoke without rising from his seat. Whether or not that was an intentional discourtesy remains unclear. But his words were unambiguous.

> We cherish no illusions as to the extent of our defeat, or the degree of our impotence. We know the forces of hatred which confront us here . . . We are far from seeking to exonerate Germany from all responsibility . . . but we emphatically combat the idea that Germany, whose people were convinced that they were waging a defensive war, should alone be laden with guilt.
>
> Crimes in war may not be excusable, but they are committed in the struggle for victory in the heat of passion which blunts the conscience of nations. The hundreds of thousands of non-combatants who have perished since November 11 through the blockade were killed with cold deliberation after victory had been won and assured to our adversaries.[39]

No debate was permitted. But, for almost a month, notes passed between Germany and the Allies. The Germans sought amendments to language and substance. The Allies rejected both. Lloyd George, fearing that the Germans would refuse to sign, called the whole British Cabinet to Paris and obtained permission to propose a series of concessions. All of them — with the exception of Silesia's right to determine its future by plebiscite and a half-promise that Germany would be allowed future membership of the League of Nations — were rejected by Clemenceau. Then Woodrow Wilson, at last realising the folly of the earlier decision, tried to persuade his colleagues to determine the full extent of the expected reparations. Lloyd George and Clemenceau combined to make sure that the subject was not reopened.

Count Brockdorff-Rantzau advised the German government not to sign. It fell, in the chaos which followed, and was replaced by a social democratic administration which accepted the Treaty but asked for changes in the clauses which attributed sole guilt to Germany. The proposal was dismissed out of hand. On 22 June 1919 the new Chancellor was solemnly warned that, unless an unqualified

agreement to sign the Treaty was made within twenty-four hours, hostilities would be renewed and the whole of Germany occupied. On
Saturday 28 June 1919 the Treaty was signed in the Hall of Mirrors in
the Palace of Versailles.

Harold Nicolson wrote in his diary, 'Celebrations in the hotel afterwards. We are given free champagne at the expense of the
tax-payer . . . To bed, sick of life.'[40] But the most eloquent epitaph on
the six-month negotiation was written by John Maynard Keynes.
Before the draft treaty was shown to the Germans he warned Austen
Chamberlain, the Chancellor of the Exchequer, that it contained
'much that is unjustified and much more that is inexpedient'.[41] When
it was accepted, he told his wife 'the peace is outrageous and impossible and can bring nothing but misfortune behind it'.[42]

One misfortune followed more quickly than he anticipated.
Woodrow Wilson, unable to sign the Treaty until he had been
endorsed by Congress, began the long and wearisome campaign to
convince both the Senate and the House of Representatives that
America should lead the way to a lasting peace. Both Houses voted in
favour of the Treaty and membership of the League of Nations. But
the Senate majority was seven votes short of the two-thirds majority
which the Constitution required for the ratification of a treaty. The
United States signed a separate peace with Germany in August 1921.
Its provisions did not include the lasting commitment to membership
of 'a general association of nations under specific covenants for affording mutual guarantees of political independence'. The high hopes of
the most idealistic of the peace-makers were confounded. The fears of
the men who realised the folly of imposing a punitive settlement
were gradually justified. No wonder the child wept.

# CHAPTER TWO

# Inherit the Wilderness

Irish loyalists are really the most hopeless collection of people I ever came across. Afraid I rather jumped on them.

Went to (Colonial) Office but no news from Dublin. The evening papers tell of terror. But we hear nothing.

Diaries of 9<sup>th</sup> Duke of Devonshire
22 and 25 November 1922

When, in December 1916, David Lloyd George became Prime Minister of the United Kingdom he took with him to Downing Street the promise of Irish Home Rule which he had inherited from his predecessors. The Bill had been passed in 1914, under the provision of the Parliament Act after its rejection by the House of Lords. But Asquith – who had a long and ignoble history of repudiating Gladstone's crusade – agreed to an amending bill which promised partition to the Protestant counties of the north. With war imminent and the principle of Home Rule established John Redmond – the leader of the Irish National Party – had agreed that the boundaries could be drawn when the war was over. Everybody knew that Germany would be defeated by Christmas.

By the autumn of 1915 over 130,000 Irishmen – most of them Catholics – were serving in the British army.[1] But a militant minority

regarded England's peril as Ireland's opportunity. The Easter Rising of
1916 was the most obvious manifestation of impatience with Redmond's 'Parliamentary solution'. Dublin's apparent contempt for the
men who had captured and held the General Post Office convinced
the British government that there was little or no support for armed
revolt. But the execution of the Rising's leaders awoke dormant
desires for more than Home Rule. Nationalists (who wanted devolved
government within the United Kingdom) became republicans (who
demanded complete independence). In 1917 (Papal) Count Plunkett –
father of an executed Easter rebel – stood as a candidate in the
Roscommon by-election and, in what was thought to be a Home
Rule constituency, beat the Redmondite nominee by a majority of
two to one. It was the first in a series of parliamentary triumphs
which, paradoxically, confirmed that Ireland was rejecting the parliamentary route to self-government.

Count Plunkett convened what he chose to call the Irish Assembly.
In Dublin 1,200 delegates met in the Mansion House – many of
them representing Sinn Fein, an organisation built around Arthur
Griffith's magazine of that name. Redmond, fearing the extinction of
his party, proposed an all-party convention to determine the future
shape of Ireland and Lloyd George promised to endorse a proposal
which attracted 'substantial support'. But another by-election – this
time in East Clare – intervened. The candidate, Éamon de Valéra, had
been sentenced to death for his part in the Easter Rising but reprieved
because, as the son of an Irish emigrant, he was technically a citizen of
the United States. He had been released from prison under the provisions of an amnesty which was designed to solidify Irish-American
support for the war against Germany. De Valéra contested the seat on
a single-issue manifesto – no partition of Ireland. He won with a
majority of three thousand votes in an electorate of eight thousand.
Redmond's convention was killed stone dead. De Valéra was to
become the dominant force in Irish politics for the next thirty years –
part sea-green incorruptible who would sacrifice anyone and anything
for Ireland free and united, part scheming politician.

In the by-election in Kilkenny William Cosgrave – another 1916
rebel – stood with the formal support of Sinn Fein. He won by a two
to one majority. Both his election meeting and those which Éamon de

Valéra had held in East Clare ended with an innovation alien to British politics. Supporters – most of them members of the soon-to-be-amalgamated Irish Volunteers and Irish National Volunteers – formed up in column of route and marched off like a military unit. The Volunteers' conduct – according to de Valéra, 'the best protection that England will not rob or cheat us'[2] – led to arbitrary arrest and imprisonment without trial, though identical behaviour by the Ulster Volunteers in the north escaped even censure. The detainees insisted that they were political prisoners, refused to wear prison uniform and began a hunger strike. Thomas Ashe – President of the Supreme Court of the Irish Republican Brotherhood – died after being force-fed. Forty thousand mourners followed his hearse to the cemetery. The oration was to be spoken by Michael Collins, a member of the Irish Republican Brotherhood who had left his job as a London bank clerk in anticipation of the 1916 Rising. He had stayed in the burning Post Office to the end, been captured, convicted and imprisoned but was released alongside de Valéra under the provisions of the amnesty. He was to become the most successful, and most ruthless, of Republican organisers. His few words in the churchyard anticipated his policy. A volley fired over the coffin was, he said, the only speech which 'it is proper to make at the grave of a dead Fenian'.[3]

The *Daily Express* feared that 'the circumstances of [Ashe's] death and funeral made 100,000 Sinn Feiners out of 100,000 constitutional nationalists' and the *Daily Mail* judged that 'Sinn Fein today is pretty nearly another name for the vast bulk of the youth of Erin'.[4]

At the Sinn Fein Convention in October 1917, de Valéra was elected President. An amendment, moved and seconded by Catholic priests, limited the campaign for a free and independent Ireland 'to means which are deemed legitimate and effective'.[5] The amalgamated Volunteers, meeting at the same time, scorned convenient ambiguities. Their duty was 'to complete by force of arms the work begun by the men of Easter week'.[6] That view of their role was enthusiastically endorsed by Michael Collins, at twenty-four their appointed director of operations. The era of violence had begun.

Lloyd George had more than Ireland on his mind. In the spring of 1918, the Ludendorff Offensive drove the Allied armies back almost to the gates of Paris. The general staff decided that a war of attrition could only be won if there were more men at their disposal. On 19 April conscription was extended to Ireland. As a *quid pro quo* the Prime Minister offered immediate Home Rule with partition providing a special constitutional status for the northern counties – an offer which Redmond had rejected in 1914. This offence was compounded by the Prime Minister's assertion that 'when young men of Ireland are brought into the firing line, it is imperative that they should not be fighting to establish a principle abroad which they are denied at home'.[7] Redmond had said much the same four years earlier on behalf of the eighty thousand Irishmen who had responded to Kitchener's call and he had been ignored.

A meeting, called by the Lord Mayor of Dublin, unanimously passed a resolution (drafted by Éamon de Valéra) which denied 'the right of the British government to enforce compulsory service of this country'.[8] The Catholic hierarchy echoed that judgement. The old Nationalist Party MPs walked out of the House of Commons in protest – imitating the tactics of Sinn Fein which they had previously deplored. In Ireland the Republicans regrouped.

The unity of the movement was confirmed and illustrated by de Valéra becoming president of the Volunteers as well as Sinn Fein. Cathal Brugha (christened Charles Burgess) became the Sinn Fein chief-of-staff. The theft of weapons (sporting rifles from private individuals and Lee Enfields from the army) continued. Dynamite was stolen from quarries and British apprehensions were increased by the capture, on the west coast of Ireland, of a man who had been put ashore by a German submarine.* His mission was to discover the likelihood of open rebellion – proof that neither Sinn Fein nor the Volunteers were in close communication with Germany. But the new Viceroy, Lord French, had been appointed to crush the republican movement and he announced the discovery of a 'German plot' which confirmed that Sinn Fein was in 'treasonable association' with the enemy. Seventy-three Sinn Feiners – including de Valéra and Arthur Griffith – were

---

*Roger Casement, a more famous emissary, had arrived in the same way two years earlier.

arrested. Collins began his habit of evading capture. So did Cathal Brugha. Both men saw themselves as soldiers rather than politicians and, as they waged war during the months that lay ahead, they developed a mutual animosity which was to end in both their deaths.

Yet another by-election tested the mood of the Irish people. Arthur Griffith, imprisoned without trial, was nominated the Sinn Fein candidate in East Cavan. He fought the campaign as 'The Man in Jail for Ireland' with the slogan 'Put Him In To Get Him Out'. Support for Sinn Fein was confirmed in the 'khaki election' which followed the war. In mainland Britain, Lloyd George's coalition triumphed but in Ireland Sinn Fein swept all before it. The party won seventy-three seats. The Home Rule Party had lost all but six of the sixty-eight seats it had won in the last pre-war election. Republicans polled more than twice as many votes as Nationalists – even though in twenty-five constituencies Sinn Fein candidates were returned unopposed.

Initially Sinn Fein hoped that the Peace Conference, opening in Versailles, would discuss Ireland's claim to independence and that Woodrow Wilson would support self-determination for the subject people of the United Kingdom as he had supported it for the previously enslaved nationalities within the Austro-Hungarian empire.

While they waited for the Peace Conference to assert Irish nationhood republicans attempted to prove it a reality by convening their own parliament. Every MP who had been returned for an Irish constituency in the 1918 general election was summoned to the First Meeting of Dáil Éireann. It was held in the Dublin Mansion House on 21 January 1919 – the day after the Peace Conference opened in Paris. All but one of the Members who heeded the call had fought and won the election as Sinn Fein candidates. They issued a Declaration of Independence – legitimised, Members claimed, by both the Easter Rising of 1916 and the election results of 1918. The constitution drafted by the Sinn Fein leadership was debated and, not surprisingly, adopted. It gave Dáil Éireann full legislative and executive powers and the right to appoint a President or Prime Minister who would nominate other members of a provisional government. Éamon de Valéra was appointed Prime Minister in his absence. He was in Lincoln Gaol – though he was not destined to remain there for long.

The story of de Valéra's escape reads like an episode from the *Boy's*

*Own Paper*. It was organised by Michael Collins but the plan was laid by de Valéra himself. In part it was the reward of piety. While acting as a server at prison Mass he noticed that the priest always left his keys in the vestry. Impressions were made in the wax remnants of altar candles which had been laboriously collected in a tobacco tin. A drawing of the keys – in their exact dimensions – was incorporated into the decoration of a home-made Christmas card. Duplicate keys and a file were smuggled into the prison. One of the first set did not turn the crucial lock. So a second set was made and smuggled into the gaol. Then, on the moonless night of 13 February 1919, Éamon de Valéra opened the gate of Lincoln prison and walked out through a hole in the barbed wire fence that had been cut by a band of Volunteers. Collins was waiting to meet him. They walked together, as nonchalantly as they could, across the open land between gaol and town. Soldiers and their girlfriends clung together at intervals along their path and they called out cheery greetings as they passed. A succession of cars took de Valéra first to Worksop, then on to Sheffield, Manchester and Liverpool. He was back in Dublin – hiding in the gate house of Archbishop's House – on 20 February 1919.

Four months later – initially against the wishes of other Sinn Fein leaders, but eventually with their agreement if not their blessing – de Valéra, titular head of the recently proclaimed republic, set sail for America to argue Ireland's cause with the President and people of the United States. Forty years later, when both his reputation and the constitution of Ireland had changed, President de Valéra – head of state but not of government – addressed a joint meeting of the American Congress. He described the purpose of what he called his 'three fold mission'. His task was

> first to ask for official recognition of independence and the Republic . . . second to try to float an external loan . . . and thirdly . . . to plead with the American people that the United States . . . was not pledging itself to maintain Ireland as an integral part of British territory.[9]

Although de Valéra stayed in America from June 1919 to December 1920, far longer than he originally intended, only one of his objectives was achieved. Both the Republican and Democratic Conventions expressed sympathy, but neither offered help. Sean O'Kelly (a long-standing member of the Irish Republican Brotherhood) supported de Valéra's efforts by lobbying President Wilson in Paris, but Ireland's claim to nationhood was not discussed at the Peace Conference. However de Valéra did raise over five million dollars in 'bond certificates' – according to the *Wall Street Journal*, largely subscribed by 'Irish domestic servants and persons of a like lower standard of intelligence'.[10] During de Valéra's absence Cathal Brugha fulfilled the duties of 'Prime Minister'. A month before the Lincoln Gaol break he had sanctioned the publication of a 'directive to Volunteers' which listed those agents of the occupying power whom it was 'morally and legally [justified] to slay . . . if it is necessary to overcome their resistance'.[11] It included the Armed Forces of the Crown, police officers and every sort of public servant not excluding postmen. Despite what amounted to a declaration of war, on 31 January 1919 the British government announced that there would be no further restrictions on the movement of Sinn Fein MPs who – unlike de Valéra – were not explicitly suspected of treasonable acts. Dáil Éireann could sit in public.

The faint hope of constitutional progress towards some sort of independence did not satisfy the more extreme republicans. Indeed it frightened them, with the thought that Ireland might, after all, be persuaded to settle for Home Rule. So, to guarantee there would be no negotiated peace, what Sinn Fein's enemies called 'a reign of terror' began. In the week which followed the first meeting of Dáil Éireann, Constables McDonnell and O'Connell (both Catholics and one a widower with children) were stopped by Volunteers while escorting a cargo of gelignite to the quarry at Soloheadbeg. The officers put up no resistance but were shot dead at point-blank range. Two months later R. M. Millings, a former police inspector who had become a resident magistrate, was murdered in his drawing room. Both killings were condemned by the Catholic hierarchy. In St Michael's Church, Tipperary, the local priest, Monsignor Ryan, ended his sermon with a prayer which represented most Catholics' fear of continued violence, 'God help Ireland if she follows this deed of blood'.[12] A year of systematic killing had begun.

Inevitably the full rigour of martial law was reinstated. When, on 12

May 1919, the American Commission for Irish Freedom arrived in
Dublin to meet Dáil Éireann and discuss another appeal to the Great
Powers at Versailles it found the Mansion House surrounded. British
troops were searching for Michael Collins. The *Irish Times* regarded the
incident as a significant milestone along the road to independence.

> Three weeks ago only fools and fanatics believed in the possibil-
> ity of an Irish Republic. Today a large number of Irish
> Nationalists hope, and a large number of Unionists fear, that an
> Irish Republic may come to be through the grotesque union of
> British folly and American sentiment.[13]

The killing continued, much of it under the supervision of Michael
Collins who, as both 'finance minister' and the Volunteers' Chief of
Staff, divided his time between raising funds in Ireland (to match de
Valéra's American loan) and managing the campaign of intimidation
against the police. Irish republicans have a long history of ignoring
reality and the nomination of 'ministers' was part of the fantasy with
which the hopes of 1919 were sustained. But such was the mood of
the Irish people that the creation of a phantom government was
accepted as practical progress. Collins enthusiastically promoted investment in agriculture and fisheries, and created an independent
Consular Service (the dream of Roger Casement) to represent the
nascent Republic. But he also devoted much attention to creating
'The Squad' – assassins dedicated to murdering policemen. In late
1919 the Royal Irish Constabulary set up G-Division to combat this
new threat. It was infiltrated and its members identified. They were
then shot, one by one. The members of G-Division numbered among
the thirteen policemen who were murdered in that year. In 1920 the
number of assassinated officers rose to 182.

Amongst them was Aston Bell. Before retirement from the RIC he
had investigated the finances of the Irish Land League, an organisation
set up to resist increases in farm rents. He was brought back into service to locate the funds which were being accumulated by Sinn Fein.
One day, travelling to his Dublin office by tram-car, he was
approached by two young men who suggested that he got off at the
next stop. When he did not move another 'respectably dressed' man

descended from the upper deck and told him, 'Come on, Mr Bell. Your time has come.' They all left the tram-car and Bell was shot dead on the pavement.

In December 1919 Cardinal Logue, Primate of All Ireland, spoke out against the escalating violence.

> Holy Ireland, the land of Saint Patrick, shall never be regenerated by deeds of blood or raised up by the hand of the midnight assassin . . . Among the body of the people those crimes inspire horror, contempt and reprobation.[14]

Hope that the Irish people were opposed to the maiming and murder was provided by the municipal elections of January 1920. Sinn Fein, the only small party to defend violence, won 550 seats. Other parties – all of whom explicitly condemned the killings – won 1,256. But persons of authority were, at best, ambivalent – condemning murder but adding that they understood what provoked it. The *Chronicle*, a prominent supporter of the Liberals in the Westminster Parliament, even managed – after a constable was shot in broad daylight and a village sacked in retaliation – to denounce violence and defend its extension in one paragraph.

> Nobody can fail to deplore such occurrences but, equally nobody can wonder at them. Indeed it is obvious that if those murderers pursue their course much longer, we may see counter clubs spring up and the life of prominent Sinn Feiners becoming as unsafe as prominent officers.[15]

Even the hierarchy – as represented by Maynooth Seminary, the heart of intellectual Irish Catholicism – equivocated. It 'deplored' the killings but insisted that they had 'one cause alone . . . We have the evils of military rule exhibited at our doors. In this ancient civilisation, the people are not permitted to rule themselves through men of their choice.'[16]

The predicted counter-attacks on republicans began in the spring of 1920. On 16 March, Tomás Mac Curtain, the moderate Lord Mayor of Cork, received death threats written on Dáil Éireann writing paper – a large quantity of which had been seized by the police some days before. Four days later, Constable Mortagh was murdered by a Volunteer assassination squad. Later that night a party of men with blackened faces broke into Mac Curtain's house and shot him dead. Lord French, the Viceroy, and Lloyd George both announced – with incriminating speed – that he had not been the victim of Royal Irish Constabulary violence. A coroner's jury – containing a number of Unionists – thought differently. It judged that his 'murder was organised and carried out by the RIC officially directed by the British government'. It returned a verdict of 'wilful murder' and named, amongst others, Lloyd George and Lord French as culpable.

The courage of the RIC was rarely questioned, even by those who had least cause to love them. So it was generally assumed that it was not Sinn Fein death threats which caused a sudden increase in the number of resignations. No doubt some officers left because they were either sympathetic to the republican cause or deplored the methods which were used to suppress it. The morally fastidious must have been influenced by the growing chorus of condemnation of police conduct. Herbert Samuel, ex-Home Secretary, told the St Albans Liberal Association, 'If what is going on in Ireland had been going on in the Austrian Empire, England would be ringing with the tyranny of the Hapsburgs'.*[17] Whatever the reason, between August 1918 and August 1920 almost 10 per cent of the RIC had resigned.

It was because of the loss of manpower that the RIC began to recruit in Britain. In all, 4,400 English, Scottish and Welsh ex-servicemen joined the force. They were enlisted at such a speed that there were not enough traditional black police uniforms for every new officer to be issued with both regulation tunic and trousers. So the Chief Constable bought army surplus. At an inquest on a young man shot dead by the police on 20 April a witness reported that the officers were wearing khaki trousers. The new recruits became the 'Black

---

*It was one example of the attitude which made the notably anti-Semitic Lloyd George suggest that 'when Samuel was circumcised they threw away the wrong bit'.

and Tans' – a pejorative nickname borrowed from a pack of Tipperary hounds.

The brutality of some Black and Tans is beyond doubt. But most of them did not behave as badly as the Auxiliaries (officially called Cadets) who were engaged on the unusual terms – for police officers – of a pound a day. Nor was their record of sacking and burning whole villages any worse than that of the RIC. The invariable excuse – repeated throughout all time by 'The Forces of Law and Order' – was that the conduct of the Republican Volunteers left them with no choice but to exact exemplary punishment as a deterrent. Whatever the justification of that claim, the brutality of the police and its irregular allies alienated moderate opinion to the point at which large parts of the country accepted the legitimacy of self-proclaimed republican government. By the summer of 1920 Sinn Fein Courts had been established in twenty-one of the thirty-two Irish counties and during the first two weeks of June Sinn Fein Police made eighty arrests. A Sinn Fein Land Commission was examining 'land hunger' – the chronic sickness of rural Ireland – and Sinn Fein civil servants were collecting income tax. The *Irish Times* only just overstated the extent of the organisation's dominance when it wrote that 'the King's government has virtually ceased to exist south of the Boyne and west of the Shannon'.[18]

Lloyd George reacted by introducing the Government of Ireland Act, which offered a constitutional framework for a new settlement, and the Restoration of Order in Ireland Act, which increased the power of the police and army to suppress subversive republicans. Two parliaments were to be established – one for the six Protestant counties of the north, and the other for the rest of Ireland. Both north and south were to be represented in the 'Imperial Parliament', but the number of Irish MPs at Westminster was to be reduced. A Council of Ireland was to promote cooperation between the two parts of the partitioned nation. It was another revival of the package which Asquith had offered John Redmond before the war.

Although republicans dismissed the constitutional proposals as irrelevant to the mounting crisis, the Restoration of Order Act was implemented with increasing severity. The hopes of its title were not realised. In Thurles, after a policeman was murdered, six of his colleagues entered the house of known republican sympathisers (none of whom was connected with the assassination) and shot two young men dead. After two constables were murdered in an ambush at Tuam the whole village was ransacked and the Town Hall burned down. The villagers were told to say their rosaries and prepare for death. In Limerick, following the assassination of a police inspector, a young Sinn Fein supporter was pulled out of bed, dragged into the street and shot. Twenty people were killed in Belfast in one week. The pattern was repeated all over Ireland. It was Cork which felt the worst of the loyalist wrath.

In August the army – mistakenly believing that the town council was a Sinn Fein Court – raided the Cork City Hall and arrested Terry MacSwiney, the Lord Mayor, and held him in custody. He immediately went on hunger strike. When transferred to Mountjoy Prison he recklessly announced that his death in custody would bring a republican Ireland closer. The Viceroy responded with the announcement that MacSwiney would not be released, however long he rejected food. MacSwiney stubbornly refused either to eat or die.

The King sensibly suggested to his ministers that 'the probable result arising from MacSwiney's death will be far more serious and far more far-reaching than if he were taken out of prison and moved to a private house, where his wife could look after him, but kept under strict surveillance so that he could not return to Ireland'.[19] After six weeks the British government began to defend its position by telling friendly journalists that MacSwiney was receiving secret sustenance from his family. The washbasin, into which he spat his teeth-cleaning water, was examined for signs of food and rumours that a priest smuggled bread into gaol in his beard were encouraged. MacSwiney was later transferred to Wormwood Scrubs, where he died on 25 October 1920.

Cork struck back. On the early morning of 11 December a government convoy, making its way to the town, was attacked by republican gunmen. The Black and Tans decided to take punitive action against the whole Cork population. Later that night they appeared on the streets and imposed curfew an hour before the legally appointed time. City Hall was set alight. The shops in St Peter's Street were first looted and then burned down. Then the rest of the city was gutted. The brothers Delaney – with no known association with the earlier ambush – were shot in their beds. The results of an official inquiry were never published but, two days after telling the House of Commons that he had seen 'no evidence that the fires had been started by forces of the Crown', Hamar Greenwood, the Chief Secretary for Ireland, got very near to admitting that police or soldiers might have been involved. He could hardly have done much else. On the day after Cork was sacked both soldiers and Black and Tans appeared in the city with burned corks in their hatbands.

The Prime Minister, speaking to his Caernarfon constituency in early October, admitted that the army and the police had sometimes taken the law into their own hands. 'There is no doubt that at last their patience has given way and there has been some severe hitting back.' But they had been 'unendurably provoked. Take the conditions . . .'[20] He left his audience to imagine the rest.* A month later he was less apologetic. In his speech to the Lord Mayor's Banquet he denounced 'organised assassination of the most cowardly kind' and then concluded a passage on the success of his policy with the claim, 'We have murder by the throat.'[21]

The government had certainly intensified its campaign. Colonel Ormonde de l'Epée Winter (codename W) had been sent to Dublin to set up a network of agents who would locate and kill Michael Collins. Winter's 'Cairo Gang' – given that name because of the café in which they regularly met, as well as their service with General Allenby in Palestine – made little attempt to hide their identity. So it was easy for Collins supporters – janitors, maids and porters – to provide duplicate keys to the houses in which they lodged and lived. On the evening of Saturday 20 November 1920 Collins was enjoying the music hall in the Gaiety Theatre when one of his companions pointed out the Cairo Gang in the next box. Despite what he knew was planned to happen the next day, Collins watched the rest of the performance unperturbed.

---

*Lloyd George was less willing to condone violence than his speech suggested – 208 Black and Tans and 59 Auxiliaries were dismissed for misconduct, and 28 RIC officers prosecuted before dismissal.

On the morning of 21 November, Volunteers – among them Seán Lemass who, forty years later, was to become Taoiseach – broke into eight Dublin houses and shot dead eighteen English soldiers. Most were members of the Cairo Gang, but some were officers serving with the regular garrison. *The Times* reported that a Captain Crawford asked to be shot outside the house so as not to disturb his sick wife. The gunmen relented and reprieved him to supervise her convalescence. Captain Newbury was less fortunate. His wife attempted to close the door on the gunmen but failed and she watched as her husband was first wounded and then killed by seven shots from close range. All but one of the Volunteers escaped and it was assumed throughout the city that the army's one hostage – whatever his fate – would not satisfy the lust for revenge. Priests told their congregations to go home and lock their doors. Collins recommended that the afternoon's Gaelic Athletic Association football match at Croke Park be cancelled. It was too late. The teams had arrived and the crowd was gathering.

Auxiliaries and Black and Tans surrounded the ground – ostensibly with the intention of searching the suspects. According to the official report, the first shot came from the crowd and the security forces did no more than return fire. Twelve spectators were killed by the fusillade which left a human thigh and various gobbets of human flesh on the Croke Park terrace. One woman was crushed to death as the crowd panicked and rushed from the ground, and several hundred others were injured. They were not the last casualties of the day. At Dublin Castle two republican detainees and one man, who had been arrested in error, were shot 'while trying to escape'. The bodies were returned to their families for Christian burial. All three men had been beaten and bayoneted before they were shot.

Retaliation provoked retaliation. A week later a convoy of Auxiliaries was ambushed by one of the 'flying columns' in which the Volunteers – who had begun to call themselves the Irish Republican Army – were increasingly organised. Three IRA men were killed and all but one Auxiliary died in the fighting. According to John Barry, the leader of the column, the Auxiliaries pretended to surrender and then opened fire. The government's counter-claim was that the Volunteers bayoneted the wounded and mutilated the corpses. The terror grew daily more terrible. In the last nine months of 1920 there were 125 killings and 235 woundings.

It may well be that the horrors of the dying months of 1920 and the warning, issued by the *Irish Times* – 'the whole country runs with blood. Unless it is stopped and stopped soon, early prospects of political settlement and material prosperity will perish and our children will inherit a wilderness' – convinced both politicians and people of the need for strong action.[22] On 8 October 1920 a letter from retired Brigadier Cockerill MP had appeared in *The Times*.[23] It urged the opening of early negotiations 'unhampered by previous conditions' – between Lloyd George and 'representative Irish leaders'. Arthur Griffith had already held private and tentative talks with the Foreign Office. They were interrupted when the RIC arrested him. But Griffith spoke for only a faction of Sinn Fein. Brugha and Collins wanted to fight on for as long as fighting was possible. The Volunteers 'were ready to face the military and were not to be deterred by weaklings and cowards'.[24] Intransigence was not the exclusive preserve of the republicans. Winston Churchill, Secretary of State for War, told his constituents that he would 'never surrender to a miserable gang of cowardly assassins like the human leopards of South Africa'.[25]

Belatedly, Lloyd George realised that the slaughter must be stopped. He was prepared to consider a new settlement but he insisted on the precondition which was to prejudice peace in Ireland for the next eighty years. The IRA must completely and visibly disarm before the talks could begin.

On 10 December 1920 Lloyd George made an offer which at first seemed to echo traditional Liberal policy towards Ireland – hope for those who obeyed the law matched with unremitting pursuit and punishment for those who do not. The Prime Minister was happy to talk to anyone who sought a settlement 'consistent with the unbroken unity of the United Kingdom'. But there could be no negotiations with any group which 'controls the organisation of murder and outrage'. The terms under which the proposed talks would take place were, he knew, unacceptable to Sinn Fein. Ireland could not secede from the United Kingdom. The Protestant counties must be given the right to make independent arrangements for their future. The security of Great Britain had to be guaranteed by an agreement which allowed

the Armed Forces of the Crown to use Irish ports and Irish bases in
perpetuity. In short, Lloyd George had returned again to the formula
of 1914.

To confirm the government's determination to suppress those who
would not negotiate, Lord French – the Viceroy – declared martial law
in Cork, Tipperary, Kerry and Limerick. That meant that the death
penalty could be imposed on persons convicted of treason, arson or
sedition. The reaction from the IRA Volunteers was immediate and
violent. Far from leading to a negotiated settlement, the 'dual
approach' produced an immediate increase in murder and mayhem.
During the first three months of 1921 174 soldiers and police officers
were killed. George V repeated his doubts about the wisdom of continuing the policy of oppression. In May, Lord Stamfordham, the
King's private secretary, wrote to the Chief Secretary for Ireland to tell
him.

> The King does ask himself and he asks you if the policy of
> reprisals is to be continued and, if so, where will it lead Ireland
> and us all? It seems to His Majesty that, in punishing the guilty,
> we are inflicting punishment, no less severe, upon the innocent.[26]

Desperate remedies were considered. Field Marshal Sir Henry
Wilson, Chief of the Imperial General Staff, suggested the confiscation
of every motor car, motorcycle, bicycle and horse, and the compulsory
closure of every bank and post office, to be followed by a 'sweep' to
flush out every IRA Volunteer. He calculated that it would require the
disposition of one hundred thousand troops and result in the permanent alienation of most of the Irish population. Winston Churchill
was the only member of the Cabinet to find the idea attractive.

Ministers were then presented with another military memorandum.
General Sir Neville Macready – GOC Ireland – warned that guerrilla
warfare was beginning to take its toll on morale and stamina. 'Unless
I am entirely mistaken, the present state of affairs in Ireland must be
brought to a conclusion . . . or steps must be taken to relieve practic-
ally the whole of the troops together with commanders and staff.'[27]
The thought of replacing eighty thousand troops added to Lloyd
George's determination that, one way or another, the 'Irish question'

must be answered. While he considered how to fulfil that aim, the slaughter intensified. During the nine months to June 1921 there were four hundred killings and seven hundred woundings.

The Volunteers – thinking of themselves as no longer guerrillas but rather the army of the new republic – changed tack. Instead of hit-and-run raids on country police stations and convoys they decided to meet the enemy in battle. Two weeks after General Macready's warning reached London the Second Battalion of the Irish Republican Army – protected by covering fire from a recently formed elite Active Service Unit – occupied the Dublin Customs House and set it alight. They were instructed not to open fire unless fired on themselves, but there was never the slightest chance that they would be allowed to occupy one of Ireland's most distinguished buildings and then retire in good order. Joe MacGuiness of the ASU described the debacle.

> An armoured car crossed O'Connell Bridge . . . It was followed by three or four armoured Lancia cars . . . this party opened machine-gun fire on the windows of Liberty Hall (the trade union headquarters to which some Volunteers had retired) . . . another party of Black and Tans . . . came towards the Customs House at the double. We opened fire on them . . . other lorries arrived almost immediately. When our ammunition was used up we withdrew.[28]

Six Volunteers were killed, twelve wounded and seventy captured. It was a severe blow to the Volunteers' self-confidence and further reduced the IRA's dwindling manpower. When Collins was told by his commanders in the field that arms and ammunition were in short supply, and that there was no certainty of the armouries being replenished, the provincial government in Dublin began to consider alternatives to continual war.

The Westminster Parliament, unintentionally, offered excuse for a respite. Elections for the two parliaments, set up by the Government of Ireland Act, were held in May 1921. Sinn Fein accepted the electoral machinery as legitimate, but not the pattern of divided parliaments which was its constitutional objective. So, when it won 124 of the 128 southern seats (in all of which its candidates were unopposed) only the

four Unionist Members for Trinity College agreed to serve in the
Southern Parliament. In the north Unionists won forty of the fifty-
two seats and a more representative parliament was convened. But the
newly-elected Sinn Fein Members came together in a 'parliament' of
dubious constitutional standing, which they again called the Dáil. It
had an acknowledged leader of status and ability. Éamon de Valéra was
back in Ireland.

He had returned on 23 December 1920. Initially the British
government, anticipating his arrival, had decided that he was an 'undesirable alien' and would be deported to America, the country of his
birth. It was then thought wiser to wait until he was party to some
illegal act and could be treated as a common criminal. Sinn Fein's
intelligence system discovered the original plan but not the subsequent decision not to implement it. So de Valéra stayed, unnecessarily,
in hiding and, from his secret address, won election for the South
Down constituency.

The Government of Ireland Act had been accompanied by what
Lloyd George believed to be two conciliatory gestures – one public
and one private. Lord French was replaced as Viceroy by Lord Fitzalan,
a Catholic, and he asked Lord Derby to make a semi-official, and
absolutely secret, approach to the Sinn Fein leadership. The public gesture was publicly rejected. Cardinal Logue, not the most militant of
nationalists, welcomed Fitzalan's arrival in Dublin as confirmation
that Ireland 'would soon have a Catholic hangman'. The private gesture bore no more fruit. Derby, with dubious authority, suggested that
'something more generous' than the Government of Ireland Act was
on offer and asked if the principle of independence had to be conceded before formal talks could begin. Typically, de Valéra responded
with a question of his own. Would the British government refuse to
meet 'representatives of the Government of Ireland unless the principle of independence is conceded?'[29]

Unionists – no doubt influenced by the outcome of the Northern
Ireland elections – were more accommodating and Sir Edward Carson
(once the implacable opponent of Home Rule who had been
forced by ill health to retire from the leadership of the Ulster Unionist
Party) made a speech which was as emollient as it was unexpected.
'Look here, we have to run our own country and we have to run it

together.'[30] He was beginning to come round to the idea of 'dominion status' – a notion that was acceptable to some nationalists, if not republicans, and which, to de Valéra's fury, the Catholic hierarchy had discussed with Lord Derby. In the interests of peace and unity Carson agreed 'to accept the handshake' and, after the election, his successor, James Craig, made the metaphor reality by holding a secret meeting with de Valéra. Craig listened to a three-hour discourse on Irish history and then left without speaking more than half a dozen sentences.

On 22 June 1921 King George V opened the Northern Ireland Parliament. The first draft of his speech, a bellicose restatement of the determination to crush terror, was rejected. The second version was placatory. It was written under the guidance of General Smuts who – having fought for the Boers in 1900 and served on the Committee of Imperial Defence fifteen years later – was regarded as an expert in the process of converting rebels into patriots. The King's speech was accepted with astonished delight in most of Ireland.

> I appeal to all Irishmen to pause, to stretch out the hand of forbearance and conciliation, to forgive and forget and to join in making for the land they love a new era of peace, contentment and goodwill . . . May this gathering be the prelude of the day in which the Irish people, North and South, under one Parliament or two . . . Still work together in common love for Ireland.[31]

The speech – which reflected the King's own view – was a publicly acknowledged triumph. It was only one of the interventions into Irish politics with which George V demonstrated more wisdom than was shown by the ministers who advised him. Two days after his homecoming – which included Lloyd George leaping on the royal bandwagon by waiting to welcome him at Euston Station – the King sent the Prime Minister two messages which complemented his publicly expressed view. One was a suggestion, the other a complaint. The government, he wrote, should take advantage of the mood that the speech had stimulated and attempt another peace initiative. There was no time to be lost. 'When dealing with a quick-witted, volatile and sentimental people' it was necessary to seize the moment.[32] How unfortunate, the second memorandum said, that Winston Churchill in the House of Commons and his friend, Lord Birkenhead,* in the Lords had chosen so inappropriate a time to make aggressive speeches.

Later that week Lord Stamfordham, anxious that Irish Americans should know that the Crown did not want to retain the throne of Ireland at the expense of years more suffering and slaughter, spoke to a reporter from the *New York Times*. The story was published in the paper in more lurid terms than Stamfordham intended.

> At the last meeting he had with Lloyd George before leaving for Ireland, the King asked him, 'Are you going to shoot all the people in Northern Ireland?' 'No, your Majesty', the Premier replied. 'Well then,' said the King, 'you must come to some agreement with them. This thing cannot go on. I cannot have my people killed in this manner.'[33]

Unlikely though it is that such a conversation ever took place, there is no doubt that Lloyd George – ever the opportunist – realised that the King's real wish to see peace in Ireland was recognised throughout the country and that, by changing the climate from fear to hope, he had created the possibility that negotiations might at last succeed. The Prime Minister responded to the King's suggestion by inviting de Valéra to meet him in London. The wording of both the invitation and the subsequent reply were carefully chosen. Lloyd George wanted to imply – without being explicit – that, although de Valéra had triumphed in the election, he had no constitutional status. So he called him 'the chosen leader of a great majority of southern Ireland'. De Valéra wanted to make clear that he would attend the proposed conference without either appearing too eager or letting there be any doubt about his right to speak for Ireland. He therefore agreed to 'consult such principal representatives of our nation as are available' – a reference to the continual imprisonment of Arthur

---

*Lady Soames (née Churchill) told me that her mother heartily disliked 'the three Bs', Birkenhead, Beaverbrook and Bracken. But Clementine Churchill regretted her husband's friendship with Birkenhead most of all. When 'they spent a night gambling and lost, Birkenhead could make up his losses in the court. Papa could not'.

Griffith – and 'certain representatives of the minority community' – a reminder that he claimed suzerainty over the counties of the Unionist (and Protestant) north. General Smuts was employed to persuade de Valéra to accept an invitation which, in truth, he never intended to refuse. Smuts also used his influence to secure a ceasefire which, once negotiated, held – although both sides went out of their way to perform acts of exemplary brutality in the last minutes before it came into effect. On Monday 11 July 1921 the British troops in Ireland returned to their barracks. The scene was set for negotiations about negotiations.

A Sinn Fein delegation, headed by de Valéra, met the Prime Minister on 14 July. Their only point of agreement was the name they should employ to describe the new Ireland which they had met to consider. De Valéra's letter, accepting the Downing Street invitation, had been headed Saorstát Éireann – Irish Free State. Lloyd George, to de Valéra's surprise, was happy with that description. He was content with very little else. Nor was de Valéra. The anticipated offer of dominion status was made and rejected. Ireland demanded 'amicable but absolute' separation.[34] The discussions degenerated into angry correspondence. The Prime Minister wrote, 'We are reluctant to precipitate the issue but must point out that a prolongation of the present state of affairs is dangerous . . .' De Valéra replied, 'Threats of force must be set aside . . .'

Towards the end of Parliament's summer recess Lloyd George – judged to be exhausted by his doctors – went to Scotland for rest and recuperation. Warned that the ceasefire would not hold much longer, he called the Cabinet to Inverness. It met on 7 September in the town hall and agreed, without much dissent, to invite de Valéra (once again) to discuss Ireland's future. The terms of reference were subtly, though substantially, changed. The conference, if held, would 'ascertain how the association of Ireland with the community of nations known as the British Empire can best be reconciled with Irish national aspirations'.[35] De Valéra accepted the invitation but thought it necessary to point out that he would attend as the representative of a sovereign state – a status which he knew would not be recognised by the British government. The idea of a meeting in Scotland was abandoned. But Lloyd George had become convinced that a settlement of some sort must be secured. So he suggested an October meeting with terms of reference identical to those which had been proposed for September. No doubt de Valéra thought that the government's persistence was proof that it was ready to shift its position. He accepted and an Irish delegation led by Arthur Griffith – released from prison so that he could take part in the 'truce conference' – landed in Britain on 8 October 1921. The stage was set for the last act of the tragedy.

De Valéra had refused to take Michael Collins with him to London for Sinn Fein's first meeting with Lloyd George. When the second negotiations were arranged – and de Valéra chose to stay in Dublin – he insisted that Collins, against his will, join the delegation. The reasons why de Valéra chose to remain in Ireland are, like his motives for virtually ordering Collins to act as Griffith's deputy, hotly disputed. Frank Longford, in his sympathetic biography, claimed that the President/Prime Minister of the republic could not be party to negotiations which ended in concessions which some of the citizens he represented did not support. Longford also argued – undermining his first justification – that, by staying in Ireland, de Valéra would be able, day by day, to justify any retreat which the delegation was forced to make. He did, however, concede that de Valéra was worried about Collins' dominant position in the Irish Republican Brotherhood – which certainly regarded him as Ireland's true leader. Collins was also thought to have developed ideas above his subordinate station. Long after he was dead, de Valéra complained, 'He did not always accept my view of things . . . and was inclined to give public expression to his own opinions . . .'[36] Tim Pat Coogan, whose biography of Michael Collins is unashamedly biased in its subject's favour, quotes him as telling friends, 'It was an unheard of thing that a soldier who had fought in the field should be elected to carry on negotiations.'[37] Collins himself put more or less the same point directly to de Valéra – unfortunately in terms which were less likely to persuade than to infuriate. 'Bring me into a spotlight at a London Conference and quickly will be discovered the common clay of which I am made. The glamour of the legendary figure will be gone.'[38] Collins made an even more gloomy judgement of his own prospects on 11 October 1921, the opening day of the conference. 'You know the way it is. Either way it will be wrong. You might say the trap is sprung.'[39] For reasons which might have been noble or squalid, political or personal, de Valéra had decided that when Sinn Fein failed to achieve its objective – as fail it must – Michael Collins must be associated with the failure.

The delegation, operating under the authority set out in a memorandum of the Sinn Fein Cabinet dated 7 October 1921, believed that the opening assertion overruled all others. 'The plenipotentiaries have full powers as defined in their credentials.' However, that sweeping statement was qualified by the clauses which followed. Despite the authority – and the elevated name they had acquired – Griffith and his colleagues had to 'notify' the final decision to Dublin and it was 'further understood that the full text of the draft treaty about to be signed will be similarly submitted and a reply awaited'. The ambiguity of those instructions was the result of Sinn Fein's inexperience of anything other than armed rebellion. It was also the cause, at least in part, of the tragedy which followed. The confusion was compounded by the complication of the negotiating position. The realistic aim was 'external association', a concept which de Valéra (once a mathematics teacher) had worked out as a geometric formula which, if Euclid could be relied upon, would both satisfy Lloyd George and allow republicans to claim that Irishmen were no longer subjects of the Crown. But first of all they must demand an independent and unified Irish republic. Partition was unthinkable.

The discussions got off to a bad start. The Pope sent a message to the King wishing the conference Godspeed. The King, replying in language which, no doubt, the Court and the Foreign Office thought unexceptional, hoped that the Downing Street discussions would initiate 'a new era of peace and happiness for my people'. Of course, de Valéra took exception to the personal pronoun and wrote to Rome on behalf of the Irish nation which he described as 'confident that the ambiguities' in the King's letter would not 'mislead' His Holiness into the mistaken belief that 'the people of Ireland owe allegiance to the British King'.[40] The jingoistic London press were outraged. But the frisson caused by what the *Express* called de Valéra's 'irresponsible mischief' quickly passed. A more permanent problem for the delegation was the disagreement in tactics and objective among its members.

The nominal leader was Arthur Griffith but, although only in his

forties, he was wearied by years of battle. He had fought with the Irish
Republic Battalion for the Boers, against Britain, in South Africa and
supported – sometimes against his better judgement – every Home
Rule initiative for twenty years. He was an honest Irish patriot.
Michael Collins, despite being a reluctant member of the delegation,
was temperamentally incapable of playing a supplementary part in the
negotiations. Formally the discussion revolved around four issues but,
in reality, the negotiators only disagreed about two of them. Both
parties knew that, eventually, the Irish would agree to a free trade
agreement and guarantee the Royal Navy bases in the Free State. The
sticking points were partition and the status of the twenty-six counties – part of, or separate from, the Empire and Commonwealth.

Lloyd George, the master of manipulation, realised from the start
that the Irish delegation could be split. But he mistakenly believed that
Collins – who was, according to Winston Churchill, negotiating with
a gun in his pocket [41] – was leading the extremists. In fact, Erskine
Childers, the secretary to the Irish delegation, was far more of an
obstacle to compromise. Despite his establishment credentials –
Haileybury and Cambridge, Clerk to the House of Commons
wartime infantry officer and successful novelist* – he both argued for
the extreme course and ensured that de Valéra was notified of any
deviation from what he regarded as the mandate to insist on a united
Ireland wholly free of allegiance to the British Crown.

Although Lloyd George misunderstood the make-up of the delegation, he realised the importance of dividing the moderates from the
ultras. He therefore suggested to Griffith that they 'clear some of the
ground' in private meetings. The first took place at Winston
Churchill's house in Sussex Gardens on 30 October, the day before the
Prime Minister faced a vote of censure in Parliament from the
Unionist rump which opposed even emasculated Home Rule. Lloyd
George made an offer. If Griffith would recommend 'Irish recognition
of the crown . . . and a free partnership with the United Kingdom' he
would 'go to the House and smite the diehards'. Better still, he would
fight to secure the 'essential unity' of Ireland, Sinn Fein's first and

---

*He wrote *The Riddle of the Sands*.

greatest objective.[42] Griffith, convinced of the Prime Minister's sincerity, agreed.

The House of Commons debate was won and the hardline Unionists defeated, but it is not clear how hard Lloyd George fought thereafter for a united Ireland. However bitter the battle, it was Sir James Craig, the new Ulster Unionist leader, who won. Unable to keep his promise to defeat proposals for partition, the Prime Minister decided to proceed with a warning and an offer. If he was defeated in Parliament on the Irish issue he would be forced to resign. Bonar Law, a hardline Unionist, would then succeed him and the whole idea of Home Rule would be abandoned. However, there was a possible solution to the 'Ulster Question' which, if Sinn Fein would accept it, would safeguard Irish unity and Lloyd George's position.

Initially, the Six Counties should be allowed to remain separate from the Free State, and enjoy a special relationship to Great Britain. The boundary between north and south would be determined by a Boundary Commission, which would base its proposals on the wishes of the local population. Lloyd George implied, and Griffith assumed, that so many northern Catholics would choose to be part of the Free State an autonomous Ulster would be impossible. At a second 'informal' meeting, held on 12 November, the Prime Minister first convinced Griffith that he felt more sympathy for the nationalists than the Unionists and then persuaded him to sign a document which endorsed partition along a line to be determined by a Boundary Commission and accepted formal association of Britain and the Free State.

It is impossible to understand why Griffith put his faith in Lloyd George's integrity, the inclinations of the Northern Irish people and the objectivity of the Boundary Commission. But he put his signature to a document which offered far less than full and formal independence. Then, having personally accepted what he must have known would outrage republican opinion, he was reluctant to recommend, or even submit, the agreed formula to the Irish delegation. But the British Cabinet grew impatient. On 21 December 1922 the Prime Minister sent Arthur Griffith what he described as 'a draft of the Treaty which we are prepared to submit for the approval of Parliament'.[43] It was based on what had been 'agreed' at the private meetings. Griffith was obliged to put it to his colleagues. The hardline members of the delegation were outraged. 'If you sign this thing you will split Ireland from top to bottom.'[44] It was agreed that they should return to Dublin to consult the Irish Cabinet – where they were told that there could be no question of accepting Lloyd George's plan.

The sticking point was the oath of allegiance. Pragmatists might regard it as no more than an inconvenient formality. But the sea-green incorruptibles of Sinn Fein saw it as an admission of British sovereignty. De Valéra, displaying his usual ingenuity, drafted an oath which it would be acceptable for Irishmen to take if his idea of external association was adopted. 'I do solemnly swear true faith and allegiance to the Constitution of the Irish Free State, to the Treaty of Association and to recognise the King of Britain as head of the Association.'[45] The delegation returned to London where they found British ministers in general (and Winston Churchill when dealing with matters of defence in particular) responsive to all issues except the vital questions of partition and sovereignty.

The issue came to a head on the evening of Sunday 5 December when Lloyd George accused the Irish of going back on previous undertakings and, in a typically theatrical gesture, suddenly brandished the note of Griffith's agreement.* Griffith, his honour questioned, reacted as Lloyd George hoped. 'I have never let a man down in my whole life and never will.' He would sign the treaty. The rest of the delegation would decide for themselves. Desperately anxious to avoid communication between the delegates and the Sinn Fein Cabinet, the Prime Minister then performed his final trick. He had, he said, made a promise to the Northern Ireland Prime Minister.

> I have to communicate with Sir James Craig tonight. Here are the alternative letters which I have prepared, one enclosing Articles of Agreement reached by His Majesty's Government and yourselves and the other saying that Sinn Fein representatives refuse to come within the terms. If I send this letter, it is war and

---

*Biographers have claimed that he forgot the note's existence but subsequently found it in a suit pocket. The story is implausible.

war within three days. Which am I to send? Whichever you choose travels by special train to Holyhead tonight and by destroyer to Belfast. The train is waiting, steam up, at Euston . . . We must know your answer by 10pm tonight. You have till then, but no longer, to decide whether you give peace or war to your country.[46]

No one in the Irish delegation questioned any of the imperatives in Lloyd George's statement. Nobody asked why, if the decision was between peace or war, Craig must have had his doubts about the future resolved next day. And no one even expressed surprise that – with all the methods of communication, civil and military, open to the government – the letter to Belfast must be sent by train and a specially chartered destroyer. The Irishmen, initially ignoring the deadline, agonised until eleven o'clock. Then Collins supported Griffith on the merits of the agreement. Brugha, convinced that the republic was being betrayed, opposed the agreement root and branch. Just before midnight, the train still in Euston Station, Arthur Griffith returned to Downing Street. 'Mr Prime Minister, the Delegation is willing to sign the agreement.'[47] Michael Collins went back to his hotel and wrote,

Think – what have I got for Ireland? Something she has wanted these past 700 years. Think – will anyone be satisfied with the bargain? I tell you this, early this morning I signed my death warrant – a bullet might as well have done the job five years ago.[48]

Dáil Éireann met on 14 December to consider the Treaty. The Cabinet, which might well have endorsed Griffith's agreement, was persuaded by de Valéra to make no recommendation. Instead, at the last minute, he drafted an alternative statement, described in the discussion which followed as 'Document Two'. He introduced it with the dubious assertion that the London delegates had ignored both its mandate and its instructions to consult the Dublin Cabinet at every stage of the negotiation. The Treaty was approved (and Document Two defeated) by sixty-four votes to fifty-seven.

What de Valéra had called a sovereign parliament had spoken. But de Valéra and the anti-Treaty faction did not listen. And they were not content to fight against the agreement in the Dáil. They chose open rebellion. The result was a civil war in which the Free State army borrowed artillery from the hated English to bombard Volunteers who, only a year before, had been their allies. Cork, always a republican stronghold, was first besieged, then stormed and captured by the Free State army in August 1922. The following day Arthur Griffith, who had become the first president of the new Ireland, died of a brain haemorrhage.

Michael Collins, Commander-in-Chief of the republic's new army and part of the establishment for the first time in his life, was killed in an ambush at Bealnamblath in his home county of Cork. Éamon de Valéra – devious or worse, according to taste – having led the insurrection against the government he had helped to create, eventually accepted the need to make gradual progress. He became the grand old man of Irish independence.

Irishmen still argue about whether the Treaty delegation betrayed their country or they were betrayed by their countrymen. But one thing is clear. Collins was right to argue that the Treaty gave Ireland the freedom to fight to be free. After de Valéra became Prime Minister of an Ireland which was accepted within the community of independent nations, dominion status was repudiated and any question of allegiance to the English King forgotten. Two years later Ireland and Great Britain signed a commercial treaty dealing with coal and cattle. They were prosaic subjects but the treaty signified the realisation of the Irish dream. Ireland was accepted by the Imperial Parliament as a sovereign state.

# CHAPTER THREE

# A Wind of Freedom

The natives (in Calcutta) are much more manly than the Bengalis and play tennis quietly and naturally, like Englishmen.

Mr Justice Rowlatt
Writing home while leading the committee of inquiry
into changes in the law necessary to suppress terrorism

It is Mohandas Gandhi's fate to be remembered on the one hand as the saint and martyr of Indian independence and, on the other, as the 'naked fakir' whose acceptance as a man fit to negotiate with ministers of the Crown was, according to Winston Churchill, an affront to Parliament and an insult to the King-Emperor. In fact the Mahatma, as he came to be called, possessed so complex a character – and behaved with such a bewildering inconsistency – that he could be legitimately described as both a visionary who devoted his life to righting every sort of wrong and an opportunist who exploited every chance to enhance his righteous reputation. Only one thing about him can be said with certainty. At some time, in early middle age, he heard the voice of destiny. From then on he never doubted that he had been called to change as well as liberate India.

He had made a long, and often painful, journey to his rendezvous with fate. His ambition to become a lawyer was gratified by an elder brother who paid for him to read for the Bar in London. For a time he tried, without much success, to become an English gentleman. Little work came his way. So he returned home only to find that he had neither the character nor the courage to argue a case in court. He moved on to South Africa – without knowing that Indian immigrants in the newly established Dominion were patronised by the British settlers, despised by the Afrikaner and hated by indigenous Africans. During a railway journey to Durban, he was put off the train for the crime of refusing to leave a first-class carriage. It was a moment of Pentecost. For his remaining years in South Africa he represented Indians in their battle for better wages and civil rights – both in court and on the streets. He was a highly unsuccessful advocate and often lost his nerve when about to address judge and jury. His strength was his conviction. It remained the source of his strength and power for the rest of his life.

Gandhi returned to India in January 1915 to represent the Indian poor – a vocation which he believed required him to live like the Indian poor. It was the beginning of his transformation from man to saint. The aura of sanctity with which he was surrounded meant that his followers forgave him the human weaknesses he retained – including the attributes which held back the campaign he came to lead.

The independence movement, which he joined, generated all the noble passions which are aroused by talk of freedom. The determination to protect and preserve the British Raj had more complicated causes. Lord Curzon – sometime Viceroy – claimed, 'With India we are everything. Without it we are nothing.' That view owed something to a mystical belief in imperial greatness. But it also reflected hard economic reality. Britain's balance of trade was in permanent deficit. The balance of payments was kept in surplus by invisible earnings from India.

Until the turn of the century no British politician of substance deviated from the simple proposition that India must remain British. On the other hand Gandhi, certain that he had been called to great work, was able to follow, with a clear conscience, an unpredictable course through Indian politics. When the All India Home Rule League was formed in December 1916, he refused to join on the surprising grounds that it was wrong to embarrass the British government while it was at war with Germany. He told Annie Besant – who had abandoned her campaigns against sweated labour in London in favour of leading the theosophist movement in India – 'You are distrustful of the British. I am not and will not help in any agitation against them during the war.'[1] He had come to the firm conclusion that, when the war was over, steps towards independence would inevitably follow as the product of British gratitude.

India had itself been at war with Germany. The Viceroy and the Governor General of each province had issued declarations on behalf of the King-Emperor. It was all part of the Byzantine process by which 250 million Indians – of many different religions, races and cultures – were governed from London by a Secretary of State for India who rarely, if ever, visited the subcontinent but issued decrees from an office designed in the Mogul tradition as a gesture of respect towards the subject people.

The Secretary of State's direct responsibilities were confined to the states which, until 1859, were effectively governed by the East India Company. Some states were still theoretically ruled by 'native princes'. In fact, they almost always accepted advice from Whitehall and appointed retired British civil servants as their 'Prime Ministers'. If they deviated from Whitehall policy it was usually to oppose steps towards independence more vehemently than they were opposed by the India Office.

Gandhi's optimism that everything would change seemed to be justified when, in August 1917, Edwin Montagu, the Secretary of State, announced that the object of government policy was 'responsible government [for India] as an integral part of the British Empire'. In the following year Montagu, together with Lord Chelmsford, the Viceroy, produced a 'Joint Report on Indian Constitutional Reforms'.[2] Its proposals – for what it called a 'dyarchy' – were as arcane as the scheme's name. In the provinces, ministers were to be responsible to an elected legislative council, but the power to administer justice, raise taxes and control the police remained with the provincial governor. Central government was to take the form of an executive council, in which Indians would be in a minority. The council would be answerable to a bicameral legislature which would be largely, but not entirely, elected. The Viceroy would nominate both the executive council and some members of the two houses. He would also retain power over external affairs, defence, justice and finance. The Report was incorporated into the Government of India Act (1919), with the undertaking that its operation would be reviewed in ten years' time. Only fantasists believed that India would wait in peace so long.

In fact, even as the Montagu-Chelmsford Report was being published, the campaign for independence – divided by religion like everything else in imperial India – was attempting to pool its strength. The All-India Muslim League and the predominantly Hindu National Congress signed the Lucknow Pact which joined (although it did not unify) the two great forces of Indian nationalism. Gandhi was temporarily out of the mainstream of Indian politics. But he had no doubt that his judgement about Britain's good intentions was vindicated by the statement which accompanied the proposals for constitutional reform. The government 'intended to increase the association of India in every branch of the administration and the gradual development of self governing institutions'.[3]

The declaration was proof that the home rule movement should have seized the moment to negotiate rather than offer its grateful thanks. The war in Europe was going badly for the Allies. Men were needed for the Western Front. During the early months of 1918 the Viceroy assembled a meeting of 'patriotic' Indian leaders and asked them to support his call for volunteers. Gandhi answered, 'With a full sense of my responsibility, I beg to support the resolution.'[4] He then toured the state of Gujarat, speaking at recruitment meetings. He justified his sudden abandonment of pacifism with the explanation, 'Loyalty is not merit. It is a necessity of citizenship.'[5]

Gandhi – like all men on whom the hand of fate has rested – made all his pronouncements with total certainty. Even the admission that he had erred allowed no room for doubt or contradiction. He lived the life of a mendicant and presented himself with constant temptations for the character-improving exercise of resisting them. He was, in consequence, an irresistible moral force in the battle for self-government. He was also often impossible to work for or with. Fortunately the cause of Indian nationalism was to find another leader of more conventional talents, Jawaharlal Nehru.

★

Unrest in India was not solely the result of the desire for home rule. The normal disputes between workers and employers were exacerbated by differences of caste and religion. During his temporary reconciliation with the British, Gandhi led local fights against exploitation. He travelled to Champaran in Bihar to support the Indian peasants against the European indigo merchants, to Ahmedabad to lead the textile workers in their strike against the mill owners and to Kheda to argue that taxes should not be levied from tenant farmers whose crops had failed. He always urged that the battles should be fought by the use of satyagraha – the 'soul force' of passive resistance. There were more sinister forces at work, exploiting with violence both the grievances, which Gandhi believed could and must be ended by brotherly love, and the demand for independence which Gandhi had, temporarily, declined to support. The India Office in London determined to suppress the violence, reject the call for independence and ignore the essentially un-British talk of brotherly love.

The Defence of India Act allowed arbitrary detention. But a nervous government in Whitehall regarded the existing powers as inadequate. So, side by side with the hint of home rule, the Secretary of State had initiated an inquiry into the best way of suppressing the incipient rebellion and ending the campaign of terror which seemed like a prelude to open revolution. As what the India Office called 'responsible leaders' awaited the reward of their patriotism Mr Justice Rowlatt chaired a committee of inquiry into the need for more repressive laws. The spirit in which he approached his tasks was made transparent by his letters home – written in pencil on pages torn from legal notebooks. From Lahore on 2 February 1918, he wrote

> We have had some Sikh notables to give evidence – splendid big chaps with their beards and all their hair turned up under their turbans. One fellow, a Deputy Inspector of Police . . . sent us a statement of what his evidence was to be. Among other things, he said 'I am against judicial proceedings. The noble offices of the judicial department have to go by evidence. No one is willing to tell the truth and there is no way of persuading them.'

Mr Justice Rowlatt added, 'in which there is a good deal of truth'. Two weeks later in Calcutta he

> went to the gaol to see some of our detainees under the defence of India Act. Of course, they all come into the story our Committee is investigating, I never spoke to so many murderers in my life. Most of them have several assassinations to their credit, though one can't legally prove it to the satisfaction of the idiotic courts here.

It was only to be expected that a judge – educated at Eton and Oxford in Victorian England – would propose that the arbitrary powers of arrest and detention be extended and that the right of free association should be severely limited. The recommendations of the Rowlatt Committee were unanimously rejected by the Indian members of the Imperial Legislative Council. Nevertheless, thanks to the Viceroy's residual powers, they passed into law.

The 'Rowlatt Laws' provided a perfect example of what Ramsay MacDonald – in a moment of frustration – was to call the India Office's habit of 'working blindly, putting up backs, miscalculating the value of this section and that'.[6] What little benefit might have been gained from the publication of the Montagu–Chelmsford Report – never, in the opinion of out-and-out nationalists, more than a palliative – was dissipated. And Gandhi, recently recovered from a severe attack of dysentery, decided that it was time for him to mobilise opposition to what he, at last, accepted was a repressive government. Satyagraha would persuade the Viceroy and Secretary of State to change their minds.

Gandhi planned to begin the protest with a hartal, a day of protest and rededication on which all businesses would be closed and the righteous would fast and pray. The idea had come to Gandhi 'in the twilight condition between sleep and consciousness'.[7] The revelation did not include the obvious risk that, in some parts of the country, what was meant to be a peaceful protest would turn into mob violence.

The nationwide hartal was to be held on 7 April. Delhi, which always wanted to be at the forefront of news, would not or could not wait. It held its solemn protest on 30 March. By midday there was rioting in the city. In the evening it spread north into the Punjab. Believing that his presence might restore calm, Gandhi set off to preach the gospel of satyagraha. The police, fearing that his arrival would increase rather than reduce tension, removed him from the train and sent him back to Bombay – to which the riots had spread during his journey.

The troubles intensified in the Punjab – always the centre of Indian political discontent. At Amritsar on 10 April, two local nationalist leaders were arrested on suspicion of subversion. A mob swept through the town, burnt down the town hall and the post office, cut the telephone wires (thus preventing all communication with the outside world) and murdered four Europeans. Martial law was declared and troops, under the command of Brigadier-General R. E. H. Dyer, occupied the streets. For three days order was restored. Then, on the day of the Baisakhi Festival, a crowd assembled in the Jallianwala Bagh walled garden.

The purpose of the assembly was not clear. Whatever the original intentions, when ordered to disperse the crowd refused. Dyer ordered his troops to open fire. The soldiers fired 1,650 rounds in ten minutes. According to the official statement, issued by the military authorities, 379 people were killed and 1,208 injured. Gandhi – more as result of the rioting than of the massacre – came to the conclusion that he had made a 'Himalayan miscalculation'[8] in attempting to launch a mass movement without preparing a basically naive people for the obligations of the discipline it required. He observed a three-day fast of atonement then, on 18 April, called for an end to civil disobedience.

The sudden changing of tactics became the pattern of Gandhi's informal leadership – much to the bewildered anger of the nationalist movement's formal leaders. But none of his sudden volte-faces – made all the more incomprehensible by the fact that he must have known that riots followed each of his calls for satyagraha – was quite as dramatic as his change of heart in 1919. On 24 December, when George V gave royal assent to the Government of India Bill and announced an amnesty for political prisoners, Gandhi's response bordered on the obsequious.

This is a document of which the British people have every
reason to be proud and with which every Indian ought to be satisfied. The proclamation has replaced mistrust with trust . . .[9]

By the end of the year Gandhi had changed his mind again. The
Viceroy's policy, which he had endorsed so emphatically, was, he
decided, 'a subtle method of emasculation'.[10] The national campaign
of disobedience was renewed and augmented with a call for swadeshi,
the boycott of foreign goods. Domestic cotton spinning and home
weaving took on a mystic significance. Gandhi himself regarded his
spinning hour as an obligation second only to prayer. Incapable of
understating the force of Indian feeling, the imperial government had
initially dismissed the campaign as 'so intrinsically foolish . . . that the
common sense of India will reject it'.[11] But when, in April 1921, Lord
Reading replaced Lord Chelmsford, the new Viceroy admitted that,
although he had not before his appointment 'been unduly depressed',
he was 'compelled after investigation . . . to take a more serious view'
of the situation.

A visit to India by the Prince of Wales had long been planned and
recently announced. Despite anxiety about the Prince's safety the
Viceroy was determined that it should go ahead. Postponement
would, he argued, have created 'both in England and the Dominions,
and throughout the world, the impression that India was so disloyal
that it was not safe for the Prince to visit'.[12] On the morning of the
Prince's arrival in Bombay, Gandhi visited the city to speak at a meeting called to celebrate the ritual burning of foreign cloth. As always, he
urged his supporters to abjure violence. As always, violence followed.
In Bombay on 17 November 1921 it took the ugly form of inter-
communal riots. Parsis were gratuitously attacked on the pretext that
they had taken part in the official reception for the Prince. Although
His Royal Highness passed through Bombay unharmed, he noted
that he was greeted with 'empty streets, shuttered windows and brood-
ing silence'.[13]

Because of the Bombay riots, Gandhi once again put a temporary
halt to his civil disobedience campaign. But, during the month of
December, almost thirty thousand alleged subversives were imprisoned throughout India and, at a meeting of the Indian National

Congress in Allahabad, Gandhi was granted 'full executive authority' to launch a mass satyagraha – which he described as a 'sort of general upheaval on the political plane . . . government ceases to function . . . courts, offices etc all cease to be government property and shall be taken charge of by the people'.[14] Self-imposed rules required Gandhi to notify the Viceroy of what he proposed. Lord Reading's reply was made public.

> The issue facing the country is no longer between this or that programme of political advance but between lawlessness, with all its consequence, on one hand and the maintenance of those principles which lie at the root of civilised government.[15]

On 1 February 1922 the Viceroy's judgement of the consequence of the new policy was vindicated. In the Gorakhpur district of the United Provinces a demonstration – initially peaceful – ended with the police station set on fire. Some accounts suggest that a policeman was provoked by the marchers' jeers and retaliated by opening fire. Others insist that the police did not start firing until attacked. Whatever the cause, the result was not in doubt. Twenty-two people – including the young son of a sub-inspector – were burned to death. Despite the displeasure of other Congress leaders, Gandhi again abandoned his campaign of civil disobedience. But he was not in a mood to abandon his role as India's conscience.

Naïveté – combined with his unshakable conviction that he was destined by providence to speak for all of India – made Gandhi the champion of highly unlikely causes. They included the campaign by pious Indian Muslims to save the Turkish Caliphate – the moral suzerainty of the Sublime Port over all the people of Asia Minor – and to restore the Sultan's authority over the Holy Places in Jerusalem which are sacred to Muslims as well as to Christians and Jews. In February 1920, a meeting of the Khilafat Conference accepted Gandhi's proposal for 'non-cooperation with the British government'. The consequent two years of unrest so disturbed the colonial administration that Lord Reading felt it necessary to make a gesture which, he hoped, would placate Muslim opinion.

On the morning of 1 March 1922 Edwin Montagu, still Secretary of State for India, received a telegram from the Viceroy. It recommended, even though Reading had no *locus* in the matter, that the Allies should withdraw their troops from Constantinople and reinstate the Sultan. The Viceroy's request was published in India – the result of a combination of incompetence and misunderstanding – before the proposal it contained was agreed by the Cabinet and, on the same evening, news of an apparent change of policy reached London. It was greeted with outrage by the yellow press.

The next day Austen Chamberlain (deputising for the Prime Minister) made a statement to the House of Commons.

> His Majesty's Government are unable to reconcile the publication of the telegram of the Government of India on the sole responsibility of the Secretary of State with the collective responsibility of the Cabinet . . . the Secretary of State has tendered his resignation to the Prime Minister and His Majesty has been pleased to approve its acceptance.[17]

When the subject was debated in the House of Lords, Lord Curzon explained – characteristically but not altogether accurately – that 'a subordinate branch of government, six thousand miles away, [had] dictated to the British government' and the British government had resisted a challenge to its authority. The government benches cheered. Montagu, an instinctive reformer, had been removed from office. The diehards had tasted blood.

The hardliners were already in the ascendant. Despite the suspension of the satyagraha, Gandhi had been arrested. At his trial on 10 March, three articles published in *Young India* were offered in evidence of his subversion. He pleaded guilty. Most of the hundred minutes which the hearing lasted were taken up by the defendant's statement from the dock.

> The only course open to you Mr Judge is . . . either to resign your post or inflict on me the severest penalty, if you believe that the system and the law you are assisting to administer are good for the people.[18]

His Honour C. N. Broomfield, the district judge, chose neither alternative. Instead he sentenced Gandhi to six years' imprisonment – 'as light as any judge could inflict' according to the recipient, who set off for prison in good heart. 'Freedom,' he said, 'is to be wooed only inside prison and sometimes on the gallows'.[19] He took with him an eclectic collection of books, including Shaw's *Man and Superman*, Goethe's *Faust* and Kipling's *Barrack Room Ballads*.

Gandhi was released from prison on 11 January 1924, after an operation for acute appendicitis. Briefly it seemed that the world was beginning to change. In Britain a Labour government took minority office and Labour was traditionally in favour of Indian independence. But its tenure was brief and, by its nature, indecisive. For three years India remained discontented but not in open revolt. Perhaps the most important development of the entire period was the appointment in 1926 of Edward Wood (subsequently Lord Irwin and eventually Lord Halifax) as Viceroy. Wood was an upright Christian gentleman and a close friend of Stanley Baldwin, two attributes which were to prove invaluable during his turbulent years in India.

The Government of India Act of 1919 required that, after the new constitution had been in operation for ten years, the government set up a Royal Commission to 'consider the desirability of establishing, extending or restricting the degree of responsible government existing there.' Baldwin set up the Commission two years before the appointed date. One explanation was that Lord Birkenhead (Secretary of State for India) feared the election of a Labour government and wanted India's future settled before Ramsay MacDonald was in a position to promote independence. Birkenhead had made his position clear after the riots of 1922. 'It is frankly inconceivable that India will ever be fit for Dominion self-government.'[20] But Baldwin took a different view. He may have hoped that the Royal Commission would help in the fulfilment of his ambition. Early in the year he had insisted that, 'In the fullness of time we look forward to seeing [India] in equal partnership with the Dominions.'[21]

The Chairman of the Commission was Sir John Simon, Attorney General and Home Secretary in Asquith's government, and a man whose temperament guaranteed a sober report. Its membership included Major C. R. Attlee, sometime Mayor of Stepney and MP for Limehouse. Attlee very nearly refused to serve. He was sure that the Commission would produce unpopular recommendations which reason would oblige him to endorse, and he was fearful that association with its findings, combined with a long absence from the country, would prejudice his prospects of political office. And, as a good family man, he was reluctant to spend long weeks away from his two young children and pregnant wife. In the end he yielded to the demands of duty. But at least one of his fears proved justified. When Labour was re-elected in 1929, he was not included in the government.*

The composition of the Commission was most notable for the names which were missing from the list of members. No Indian was asked to serve on a body which was charged to make recommendations about the future of India. Even moderate Indian opinion was outraged.

As both inter-communal violence and the agitation for self-government increased, both Baldwin (very much influenced by Edward Wood) and MacDonald (back in Downing Street) were convinced of the need for an urgent initiative. The Simon Commission worked on, but India would not wait. Both party leaders were equally sure that they must act in something like unison, though Lloyd George, 'the Goat, [was] in his naughtiest mood and evidently looking forward to trying to make trouble and to attract [Tory] diehards to his imperial flag'.[22]

It was agreed that the Viceroy should issue a statement promising eventual self-government, accompanied by background notes which demonstrated that the idea was not new. However, although the party leaders saw and approved drafts of the proposed statement, Sir John Simon knew nothing of the plan to seize the initiative until he read about it in the *Sunday Times* of 13 October.

Simon was understandably outraged. By authorising a statement of policy, in advance of his report and without his knowledge, the government had humiliated him. And it had created a practical problem

---

*When Oswald Mosley resigned from the government in 1930 (see Chapter 6) Atlee was appointed Chancellor of the Duchy of Lancaster.

which had swiftly to be solved. Edward Wood's proposal that 'India's future should be discussed at a Round Table Conference' cut across Simon's assurance that Indian leaders – both rulers of the princely states and Congress – would be given a chance to talk over his recommendations 'before the government formulated any draft proposals of their own'.[23]

Baldwin, despite his friendship with Wood, withdrew the Opposition's support from the idea of the Viceroy making the statement which everyone knew was already prepared and agreed. Philip Snowden, leading the Labour government during MacDonald's absence in America, was told that Wood had already hinted to Indian leaders that a statement was likely and, in consequence, felt unable to change course. So he authorised its publication. A copy was made available to Parliament on 31 October. Baldwin did his best to minimise the uproar. He accepted that Wood did no more than emphasise the declaration 'implicit in the Declaration of 1917 that the natural issue of India's constitutional progress is the attainment of Dominion status'.[24] But he feared that the very act of emphasising that intention prejudiced the status, and therefore the work, of the Simon Commission.

Tory imperialists – and the newspapers which supported them – accused Baldwin of betraying the Tory Party's principles. During Prime Minister's Question Time, one Tory backbencher repeated the *Daily Mail*'s allegation that only the anger of the Conservative rank and file had prevented Baldwin from giving unequivocal support to the Viceroy's declaration. Baldwin then made the first of the assaults on Lord Rothermere* and all his works which were to enliven his premiership. 'It is sufficient for me at the moment to say that every statement of fact and every implication of fact contained in that article is untrue and, in my opinion, gravely injurious to the public interest, not only in this country but throughout the Empire.'[25] Lloyd George, urged on by Churchill, made a gratuitous attack on William Wedgwood Benn, the Secretary of State for India, whom he accused of being 'a pocket edition of Moses smashing the tablets of the Indian

---

*For a full account of the long battle between Baldwin and the press, see Chapter 16.

Covenant'. Benn destroyed his speech with a brief intervention. 'But I never worshipped the golden calf.'[26]

The Simon Commission published its recommendations on 24 June 1930. It proposed cautious advance towards self-governing provinces and eventual central self-government. Even those limited proposals were hedged about with warnings. The rights of the princes should be respected. Whenever independence came there would be the risk of inter-communal violence. An army entirely composed of Indians would be short of officers. Its timidity was in stark contrast to MacDonald's wildly optimistic forecast of the prospect for self-government, made while the Commission was still at work. 'Within a period of months, rather than years, there will be a new Dominion added to the Commonwealth . . . I refer to India.'[27]

Gandhi had played virtually no part in Indian politics or protest during 1926 or 1927. The leadership of Congress was firmly in the hands of Jawaharlal Nehru – a far more sophisticated figure than the Mahatma. He was also, in his way, more extreme. But his extremism had a rational basis and the consistency of purpose which Gandhi's often instinctive reaction lacked. But Gandhi had a mystical hold over millions of Indians. So when Nehru decided to move policy forward he wisely determined to include the Mahatma in the consensus. When he invited Gandhi to the Calcutta Congress (held in December 1928) his letter was a clever combination of affectionate humour and moral blackmail. 'You have made me sit in the Presidential chair and put upon my head the crown of thorns; but at least do not look at my difficulties from a distance.'[28] Gandhi accepted, explaining that the full period of his remitted prison sentence had passed and that, in consequence, he felt morally entitled to return to the battle. Undoubtedly from time to time Nehru was infuriated by Gandhi's saintly egoism. But he did more than recognise the moral force which the Mahatma added to the independence campaign. He regarded it as essential to the triumph of his hopes of a new India. Gandhi, he wrote,

> was like a powerful current of fresh air that made us stretch our-
> selves and take deep breaths; like a beam of light that pierced the
> darkness and removed the scales from our eyes; like a whirlwind

that upset many things but most of all working people's minds. He did not descend from the top; he seemed to emerge from the millions of India, speaking their language and increasingly drawing attention to them and their appalling condition.[29]

Congress accepted Nehru's proposal that the British government should be given a year to make proposals on India's progress to dominion status. If there was no response by 31 December 1929 Congress would demand full independence and fight for it with civil disobedience. 'The name of independence,' said Nehru, 'must be on your lips as the Muslims utter the name of Allah or the pious Hindus utter the name of Krishna and Rama.'[30] Gandhi would have preferred to give the British two years' grace, but accepted the will of Congress.

Jawaharlal Nehru could not have possibly believed that a British government would respond to a colonial ultimatum. Nor did it. So when Congress met at Amritsar in December 1929 the campaign for Swaraj – complete independence – was launched. The time for constitutional action had passed. Congress members were now instructed to resign their seats on the central and provincial legislature. A national campaign of civil disobedience was planned. Wood telegraphed home to the India Office that 'revolutionaries' and 'irreconcilables' were on the march.

The campaign began with a gesture 26 January 1930 was to be 'Independence Day' on which the whole nation would be asked to pledge its belief that it was 'a crime against God and man to submit to British rule'. At Gandhi's suggestion, the programme of civil disobedience began with an attack on the Salt Law. Wisely he chose to attack one of the most preposterous, as well as the most repressive, items of imperial legislation. Salt is essential in hot climates. The law stipulated that it could only be produced in government-approved factories and all salt sales were to be taxed. Gandhi proposed that all production would be halted in the licensed establishments and 'contraband' salt, made from sea water, would be sold at minimum prices or given away free. Not surprisingly, the government ridiculed the idea. Gandhi himself led the first band of protesters. The spirit – if not the size – of the demonstration earned its place in history as the 'March to the Sea'. Initially the Indian government chose virtually to ignore the march and instructed the police to avoid confrontation and make no arrests. Jokes were made in high places about the chances of achieving independence by boiling water in a kettle. But the symbol inspired more robust action throughout India. Foreign cloth was again boycotted and shops selling imported goods were picketed. The government changed course and the arrests started again – first Nehru, who was accused of making seditious speeches, and then, on 5 May 1930, Gandhi.

The Round Table Conference opened in London on 12 November while Gandhi, Nehru and almost all of the Congress leadership were still in prison. So, at the moment when it could have rightly laid claim to the leadership of the independence movement, Congress was not represented at the talks which, at least in the view of the British Prime Minister, prepared the way for ultimate independence.

Ramsay MacDonald chaired the plenary session of the Conference himself and, bravely if not wisely, also presided over the sub-committee which dealt with the traditionally intractable issue of minority rights and representation. He found both tasks highly uncongenial.

> Yesterday, a Muslim–Hindu gathering at Chequers showed the worst side of Indian politics . . . India was not considered. It was communalism and proportions of reserved seats. Hindu–Muslim not working together . . . They have no mutual confidence and Hindu too nimble for Muslim brethren.[31]

Some progress was made. MacDonald announced that the British proposed to create a federation of all India – subject to safeguards being put in place to protect the interests of the Muslim minority and acceptance by the rulers of the princely states. Responsibility for Indian affairs would be transferred to provincial 'governments', answerable to provincial legislatives, and a central 'executive', which reported to a central legislature. The difference in terminology went to the heart of the problems that had yet to be solved. Would the executive be appointed by the elected legislature or nominated by the India Office? Clarification of that crucial issue was to be left to a second Round Table Conference that MacDonald announced he would convene after consultations to test Indian opinion.

In January 1931 Gandhi was released from prison and the ban on meetings of Congress was lifted. On 17 February, Gandhi and the Viceroy held the first of a series of meetings which, after eight days, produced the 'Delhi Pact'. Civil disobedience was abandoned. All prisoners detained because of real or imagined threats of subversion were released. Martial law was suspended, but the request for an inquiry into police violence against Gandhi's followers was rejected out of hand. However the only discussion on the subject of dominion status ended in a concession to British prejudice. Whenever colony turned into dominion, special safeguards would be needed to ensure that, 'in the interests of India', defence and external affairs, finance and the protection of minorities were all administered with the efficiency that only the India Office in Whitehall could guarantee. Gandhi, typically, justified his capitulation with a mystical aphorism. 'Having clipped our wings, it is their duty to give us wings wherewith we can fly.'[32]

Back in the House of Commons, Members of Parliament debated the conclusion of the first Round Table discussions in more prosaic terms. Ramsay MacDonald described the alternative to the progress he proposed as 'repression, nothing but repression. The repression of masses of the people.'[33] Baldwin insisted on giving guarded support to the government but Winston Churchill opposed the proposition root and branch. It was the beginning of his increasingly bitter dispute with the Conservative leadership which led to his alienation from the party for most of the decade. Even those Tories who sympathised with his views found the language in which he described his policy intolerable. On 23 February 1931 he gave the West Essex Conservative Association his view on the Delhi Pact. It was, he said,

alarming and also nauseating to see Mr Gandhi, a seditious Middle Temple lawyer, now posing as a fakir of a type well known in the East, striding half naked up the steps of the Vice-Regal Palace while still organising and conducting a defunct campaign of civil disobedience, to parley on equal terms with the representative of the King-Emperor.[34]

Gandhi travelled to London to take part in the second Round Table
Conference. By the time it met, the Labour government had fallen and
Ramsay MacDonald led a 'national coalition'. Congress, despairing of
progress, called Gandhi home. But he had decided that the hour had
come. He ignored the instruction and remained in London, living not
in the West End hotel which the government had booked for him but
with a 'quietist' community in Kingsley Hall, Bow. His refusal to accept
imperial hospitality mirrored his general attitude towards the discussions. He was politely and often piously unreasonable. Although
accompanied by Sikhs, Muslims and Hindus whose views on independence were radically different from his own, he insisted that only
Congress represented India and only he represented Congress.

Ramsay MacDonald had both time and inclination to return to a
subject which revealed, in part, the survival of his radical instinct. He
began to draft a federal constitution in May 1932. His plan was
approved by the government's India Committee. But the Cabinet, as
a whole, rejected it. Tory ministers had capitulated to a secret delegation of angry MPs and peers which had demanded that progress
towards self-government be slowed almost to a halt.

The government's behaviour united a previously divided Indian
delegation. The plan which the Tory Imperialists rejected as too radical was rejected by Congress as too cautious. On 25 November *The
Times* published a letter which expressed their collective resentment at

> repeated attempts by the members of the dominant political
> party in Parliament . . . to bring proceedings of the Conference
> to an immediate end . . . No political party of standing in India
> will, in the slightest degree, favour the introduction of provincial
> autonomy as the first instalment with a mere promise of estab-
> lishing responsibility on a formal basis in the future.[35]

Gandhi's name did not appear at the bottom of the letter. He did not
sign other people's statements. But he did make a comment of his own.
He saw 'no tangible results coming out of the conference'.[36] A third
session of the Round Table Conference was convened. It ended on 1
December with a long speech by the Prime Minister. He promised
parallel progress towards regional and all-India autonomy after a joint

committee of both Houses examined the idea in detail. An intemperate speech by Winston Churchill in the House of Commons helped to secure a victory for the government by 369 votes to forty-three.

> There are mobs of neighbours . . . who when held and dominated by these passions will tear each other to pieces, men, women and children, with their fingers. Not for a hundred years have the relations between Moslems and Hindus been so poisoned as they have been since England was deemed to be losing her grip and was believed to be ready to quit the scene and told to go.[37]

Churchill then turned his attention to the composition of the select committee which, he argued, must contain Members who were critical of government policy. Hoare, the Secretary of State for India, responded by offering the chairmanship to the Marquess of Salisbury, Churchill's chief ally in the House of Lords. Salisbury declined with only perfunctory thanks. Churchill himself, offered committee membership, reacted with even less grace.

> I see no advantage in joining your committee merely to be voted down by an overwhelming majority of the distinguished persons you have selected. I will have neither part nor lot in the deed you seek to do.[38]

After an acrimonious exchange with the Marquess of Linlithgow – who had been made chairman after Salisbury's refusal – Churchill began a guerrilla campaign against both the bill and the joint select committee which examined it. On 16 April 1934 he fired off what he believed to be a broadside. There had, he claimed, been a major breach of parliamentary privilege. The Manchester Chamber of Commerce had been expected to oppose the bill root and branch. Lancashire milled Indian cotton and exported the finished cloth back to India. An independent India would make its own shirts and saris. But the Manchester businessmen had been, at most, neutral in their attitude. Churchill claimed that they had been subject to improper pressure from Lord Derby – 'the uncrowned king of Lancashire' – and the Secretary of State for India himself.

The Committee of Privileges was unanimous in its conclusion that nothing improper had occurred, but Churchill – who had been rebuked by both the Attorney General and Austen Chamberlain for the offensive manner in which his evidence was presented – refused to accept its findings. Nothing could have been more calculated to offend the House of Commons. Churchill's personal conduct – and the disapproval it attracted – played a major part in securing the passage of the Government of India Bill. Attlee, writing to his brother, described one of Churchill's faux pas in typical language.

> Winston made an awful bloomer in the House last week and was severely castigated by Lloyd George. He takes things very badly. I thought one moment that he was going to burst into tears. His stock is much down just now.[39]

The Select Committee report proposed an All–India Federation, if at least half of the princely states agreed to join. There would be elections to the central assembly on a limited franchise, but the Viceroy would retain reserve powers. Clement Attlee, who wanted more, set out his fears in a radio broadcast. 'Will these reforms be accepted and worked by Indian politicians? Can we be sure that "self-government" will not be handing over the poor to be exploited by the rich? Will they so satisfy Indians that, eventually, India will have an equal status with other Dominions within the Commonwealth?'[39]

Baldwin broadcast too. The style he adopted was typical of his hugely successful method of treating great issues. His homely language and 'plain man's' reasoning were employed in support of the principle in which he believed.

> I sometimes think that if I were not leader of the Conservative Party, I should like to be the leader of people who do not belong to any party. At any rate, I should like to think that I have got them behind me as I have already got the great bulk of the Conservative Party . . . We have learned from experience that we shall preserve our Empire if we succeed in giving the units of it the right amount of liberty at the right time. We are pledged to

self-government in India since 1919. We should have failed in one of our main imperial undertakings if we were not able to extend the field of self-government to India.[40]

That endorsement of the Select Committee's proposals was made in the face of a Conservative campaign by Tory diehards to prevent any progress on the new proposals. But Baldwin would not be shifted from the position which he had taken up at the Central Council of the Conservative Party in the Queen's Hall on 4 December 1932. His reference on that day to 'a wind of freedom blowing round the world' was adopted by Harold Macmillan forty years later. 'The time has now come . . .' Baldwin insisted. 'You have a good chance of keeping India in the Empire for ever. If you refuse it you will infallibly lose India before two generations have passed.'[41]

The Queen's Hall meeting had taken the form of a debate, with Churchill, amongst others, supporting a motion to reject the Select Committee's reports. It was the climax of a campaign which he had conducted with gusto (but not enough commitment to attend the annual Conservative Party Conference when the offer of a holiday on Walter Guinness's yacht provided an alternative attraction). His speech antagonised more Tories than it enthused. The government proposals were endorsed by a majority of 1,102 to 390 votes. When the Select Committee Report was debated in the House of Commons the motion for approval was carried by an equally convincing majority. The time had come for the Government of India Bill to be tabled.

The bill contained 473 clauses and was dismissed by Winston Churchill as a 'gigantic quilt of jumbled crochet work' and 'a monstrous monument to shame, built by pygmies'.[42] It was considered by a Committee of the Whole House but passed through all its stages without amendment. All that changed was Winston Churchill's oratorical style.

At sixty I am altering my method of speaking . . . and now talk to the House of Commons with garrulous unpremeditated flow. They seem delighted. But what a mystery the art of public speaking is! . . . There is apparently nothing to the literary effect I have sought for forty years.[43]

Churchill spoke sixty-eight times during the committee stage of the bill and lost more friends than he made. After his final speech Leo Amery (described by Churchill as an 'insect' who buzzed around his head) announced, 'Here endeth the last verse of the last chapter of the book of Jeremiah.'[44] The third reading of the bill was approved by 386 votes to 122. It was not as good a result for the Tory diehards as the majority of more than three to one suggests. Half of the Members of Parliament in the 'No' lobby believed that the bill's proposals for evolution to self-government were either too timid or too slow to take effect.

According to the *Manchester Guardian*, Britain – unable either to govern India or to get out – had 'devised a constitution that seemed like self-government in India and at Westminster like the British Raj'.[45] It took Congress some time to realise what little progress was being made towards the achievement of their aspiration. But once they had decided that their hopes had been confounded they turned on the new constitution with uninhibited ferocity. Jawaharlal Nehru described it as a 'charter for slavery'[46] which offered India responsibility without power. His proposal that the reforms should be rejected in their entirety was unanimously agreed – itself an extraordinary state of affairs for Congress.

The problem, from the point of view of Congress, was the impossibility of reconciling the two simultaneous demands – a federation of all India and immediate progress towards democratic self-government. The first aim required the princely states to be incorporated into the new nation. The Princes, who were their effective owners, had never contemplated giving the vote to people they regarded as their property. Their representatives in the legislative would instead be nominees of the ruling houses. Congress, belatedly, came to realise that – since most of those ruling houses were, in one way or another, dependent on the British government – a quarter of the legislative would be selected by 'residents' who had been chosen to administer the princely states by the India Office in Whitehall. The limitations on the powers of the national assembly were rejected by Congress as a denial of democracy. The constitution offered neither independence nor federation.

However, as in Ireland so in India. The independence movement contested the elections which were held under a constitution which it rejected. In February 1937 Congress won majorities in the United Province, Bihar, Orissa, Central Province and Madras and was the largest party in the Bombay, Assam and North West Frontier Province Parliaments. A second dilemma therefore arose. Should Congress form provincial governments and implement the decisions of the hated constitution? The eventual decision was based on an abdication and a forlorn hope. Leaders of Congress in the provinces were told to take the decisions for themselves. But governments would only be formed if the provincial governor publicly agreed not to use his reserve powers to frustrate ministers 'in regard to their constitutional activities'. Gandhi equivocated, but since his equivocation was expressed in gnomic language it was accepted as wisdom.

> The boycott of legislation . . . is not an external principle like that of truth and non-violence. My opposition has lessened but that does not mean that I am going back on my former position. The question is of strategy and I can only say what is most needed at a particular moment.[47]

The Viceroy contrived a statement both consistent with the constitution and acceptable to Congress, and the new ministers concentrated on policies which did not require the Viceroy's assurance to be tested. In particular they promoted schemes to implement Gandhi's vision of popular education – a curriculum based not on the European principle of academic learning but built around craft training which equipped pupils for the struggle to survive in impoverished India.

The arrangement – dependent as it was on the manipulation of language rather than a genuine unity of purpose – could not last. But the break, when it came, was not the result of either Congress or the Viceroy losing patience with what was never more than an accommodation. The effective end of provincial government came about because of factors so obvious that the failure to acknowledge them can only be attributed to a wilful refusal to face reality. India was not one country. A whole subcontinent – made up of states with widely different forms of government and degrees of autonomy, embracing all the world's major religions and encompassing innumerable races – had been offered a constitution more suitable to Italy at the time of the Risorgimento.

Mohammad Ali Jinnah, the leader of a group of independent Muslims in the Old Central Legislative Assembly, had attended the Round Table Conference in London but, as 'he never seemed to wish to work with anyone',[48] made almost no contribution to its final report. After it was presented to the government, he played very little part in the continuing debate. For a while he settled in England. But when the new constitution was in place he returned to India to lead the Muslim League – one of the many Islamic parties. In the subsequent election the Muslim League won 5 per cent of the vote. But, because of a level of ability which none of his rivals could match, he soon took command of the whole spectrum of Muslims who had been elected to the provincial Parliaments.

Congress had agreed to invite Muslims into the government of the provinces in which it took office, but only if they signed the 'Congress Pledge' of principle. Jinnah believed that the creation of separate electorates – the 'communal award' which MacDonald had imposed on the parties to the Round Table Conference – would guarantee a share of power to Indian Muslims. It seemed that it was only available on terms which he regarded as a humiliation. 'The fact is,' he announced, 'the Congress wants domination of India under the shelter of British bayonets.' He ridiculed the creation of a national assembly and accused Gandhi of planning 'to subjugate and vassalise the Muslims under a Hindu Raj'.[49] It was the beginning of Jinnah's determination to see free India partitioned and the virtual end of the provincial assemblies as an effective legislative force. They continued in being – uncertain and uncreative – until the war changed everything.

The slow death of the provincial parliaments did not in itself prevent the inauguration of the Federal Assembly. But the Government of India Act had been explicit. Federation, in all its forms, depended on the agreement and participation of the princely states. The Princes did not agree. So the All-India Federation was dead and independence had to wait until the reluctant member of the Simon Commission became Prime Minister in 1945.

# CHAPTER FOUR

# The King's Matter

'Mrs Simpson has figured on the front page for two or three weeks. We are led to believe that the details were more publicized here than in England the first week or so. It is for the most part written in a sticky romantic vein and the implication is that the King just "can't let her down now". I should think the British would dislike the whole set up and all the whispering behind the hand.'

Anne Worth
Born Pennsylvania 1910
Writing to her future husband from Wilmington,
Delaware, 21 October 1936

King George V died at Sandringham on Monday 20 January 1936. According to the official bulletin, his life 'drew peacefully to its close' and newspapers reported that, a few minutes before he died, he asked, 'How goes the Empire?' Fifty years later forensic historians claimed that 'the Palace', determined that the news should be announced in the august *Times* rather than in the less deferential regional evening papers, ensured that the deadline was met by injecting the old man with morphine. And it now seems that his last words were more provincial than imperial. Reassured that he would soon be well enough to visit his favourite holiday resort, he is said to have replied, 'Bugger Bognor.'

The last entry in his diary – recording the visit of Lord Dawson of Penn, the royal physician – was almost as gruff as his response to the promise of a trip to the seaside. 'I saw him and I feel rotten.' On 13 January, Queen Mary – in a note to her son, the Prince of Wales – described the King's condition in language which, although more restrained, left even less doubt about its seriousness. 'I think you ought to know that Papa is not very well.' The Prince of Wales flew at once to Sandringham and found his father sitting, comatose, in his old Tibetan dressing gown, 'a faded relic of his visit to India'.[1] The Prince then motored to London personally to warn the Prime Minister that the King would, at best, last for only a few more days.

Father and son were not close. The King regarded the Prince of Wales as sybaritic and self-indulgent. The Prince of Wales thought the King stuffy, boring and impossible to please. They had virtually no interests in common and rarely discussed anything of consequence. The Prince's louche friends seemed to the King wholly unsuitable companions for the heir apparent, but he never felt able to raise the subject directly with his son. He did, however, describe his anxieties to Cosmo Gordon Lang, the Archbishop of Canterbury – an intimacy which, when discovered by the Prince of Wales, turned him against the Primate for ever. George V – partly out of constitutional duty and partly out of a need to unburden himself – also told Stanley Baldwin of his anxieties about the future. 'After I am dead, the boy will ruin himself in twelve months.'[2]

The Prime Minister – touched that the King should confide in him – felt an increased obligation to protect 'the boy' (then forty years of age) from himself. However during the weeks of crisis, which ended in Edward VIII's abdication, Baldwin's care and concern was more apparent in what he said than in what he did. George V's hopes for the Prince of Wales were simple and straightforward. 'I pray to God that my eldest son will never marry and have children and that nothing will come between Bertie, Lilibet and the throne.'[3]

That was not, however, a universal view. 'Dickie' Mountbatten – Edward VIII's cousin and, in early 1934, so close a friend that the Prince of Wales was his best man when he married Edwina Ashley – presented him with a list of eighteen unmarried European princesses ranging from Duchess Thyra of Mecklenburg-Schwerin, who was fifteen, to Princess Alexandra of Hohenlohe-Langenburg, who was thirty-three.[4] There was, however, a let and hindrance to a formal union. The Prince of Wales was irresistibly attracted to unsuitable women.

The Prince of Wales met Freda Dudley Ward in March 1918. She had been walking in Belgrave Square when the sudden sound of maroons being fired across London warned her that an air raid was imminent. A party was in full swing in one of the houses and Mrs Dudley Ward joined the merry-makers, who were taking refuge in the basement. After the 'all clear' was sounded she was invited to join the dancing upstairs with the intriguing inducement, 'His Royal Highness is so anxious that you should do so.'[5] So she became one of the girls 'who danced with the Prince of Wales'. Better still, he escorted her home. It was, for both of them, love at first sight.

For sixteen years they met every day when the Prince was in London. He became attached to her daughters – who called him 'The Little Prince' – and they to him. During that time she was first separated, and then divorced, from her husband, William Dudley Ward, MP, the Liberal Chief Whip. Society knew of their relationship. Its attitude was summed up by the advice which Mrs Dudley Ward received from Lord Esher, a distant relative of her husband and a figure in Queen Victoria's court. He recalled how well the last love of Edward VII had behaved. And he urged similar self-restraint. 'Be discreet. Be like Mrs Keppel. Be discreet.'[6] Mrs Dudley Ward was more discreet than the Prince of Wales who, during enforced absences, wrote letters which were as revealing about his character as they were about the relationship. Royal duties were invariably described as taxing or tedious. Affection was often expressed in language which he presumably thought quaint – 'my vewy, vewy precious darling' – but is now no more than embarrassing. And he made extravagant promises. 'Now I am going to write something that I know I ought not to really . . . I swear I will never marry anyone but you.' At the time, he meant it.

The first long-term – and, as it turned out, final – separation came in May 1934 when Mrs Dudley Ward's daughter was in a nursing home, recovering from an appendicitis operation. Throughout the anxious weeks she heard nothing from the Prince of Wales. So she telephoned Fort Belvedere, the ugly house in Windsor Great Park which was his home. The telephonist, with whom continual calls had made her friendly, burst into tears. 'I have something so terrible to tell you that I don't know how to say it. I have orders not to put you through.'[7]

Despite his apparent devotion to Mrs Dudley Ward, the Prince had never felt an obligation to deny himself other female company. One of his most notorious amours was Lady Furness who, either because she possessed a title or was free of family commitments, was able to accompany him on his private excursions. The 'set' in which they both moved was enlivened by stories about their flagrant behaviour during an East African safari in 1928 – conduct so open that it was said to have precipitated the resignation of one of the Prince's private secretaries, Captain Alan Lascelles. At some time during the autumn of 1930 Lady Furness introduced the Prince to Mrs Wallis Simpson, the American wife of a London businessman who had the unusual distinction of having been both educated at Harvard and an officer in the Brigade of Guards.

Wallis Simpson was born Bessie Wallis Warfield in Baltimore, Maryland, on 19 June 1896. She always claimed – or at least Auntie Bessie, who guided her through London society, claimed on her behalf – that the Warfields were southern gentry who had fallen on hard times. When she was barely twenty she married Earl Winfield Spencer Jr, an officer in the US Navy's recently created air arm. He turned out to be an alcoholic and, possibly with good cause, violently jealous. When, as the punishment for some misdemeanour, she was locked in the bathroom all night Wallis Spencer decided to end the marriage. After a tour of the Far East with Auntie Bessie she petitioned for divorce. The decree absolute was granted in July 1928. She married Ernest Simpson a few months later.

Simpson, whose father was English, was sent to London to manage the British subsidiary of the family business. His sister, Mrs Keir Smiley, lived in the house in Belgrave Square which had been Freda Dudley Ward's refuge on the night she met the Prince of Wales. The change of ownership had not moved it from the centre of smart society. The Simpsons met Lady Furness and she introduced them to the Prince.

It would be wrong to suggest that the meeting changed the course of British history. Baldwin's biographer called the events that followed 'the great irrelevance'. And there is no doubt that most of the British people worried less about the future of King Edward VIII than about the prospect of war and the hope of economic recovery. Seventy years on most of the fuss seems absurd. But, for a couple of weeks, the government tottered and the whole nation was fascinated by what seemed like a glimpse into Ruritania. Even Bernard Shaw referred to the royal 'crisis' in his 'improved version' of Shakespeare's *Cymbeline*.

There is no reason to believe that the Prince, however susceptible, fell instantly in love with Wallis Simpson, as he had fallen in love with Freda Dudley Ward. Mrs Simpson's attractions – a sharp intelligence, an iron will, what passed in her circle for wit and, above all, the power to make a man think that her entire attention was concentrated on him – were, by their nature, slow to take hold. The friendship between the Prince and the Simpsons grew only gradually. There were six months between their first and second meeting and the Simpsons were not invited to Fort Belvedere until January 1932 – when, as usual, Lady Furness acted as hostess. By June 1933, they were sufficiently close to the Prince for him to host a birthday party for Mrs Simpson at Quaglino's restaurant. A month later the couple received the ultimate social accolade. The Prince of Wales dined with them at their flat in Bryanston Court, Marylebone.

In January 1934 Lady Furness left London for America. As she said farewell to Mrs Simpson she 'laughingly' made a suggestion which left little doubt about her low regard for Mrs Dudley Ward. 'I'm afraid the Prince is going to be very lonely. Wallis, won't you look after him?'[8]

According to her own account of what followed, Mrs Simpson was astonished when the Prince of Wales asked if he could call on her. As the year drew on, his visits grew increasingly frequent and often took place while Ernest Simpson was at work. The respectability of the still-unconsummated relationship was preserved by both Mr and Mrs Simpson being regularly invited to Fort Belvedere and accorded the unusual privilege of bringing friends. Lady Furness returned to England in June, preceded by gossip that she had enjoyed a brief liaison with Prince Aly Khan. The Prince of Wales ignored her. Unsure if she was being ostracised because of the scandal, or because a new favourite had taken her place, she asked Mrs Simpson if the Prince had become 'keen'. She received a straight answer. "'Thelma", I said, "I think he likes me. He may even be fond of me. But if you mean by keen that he is in love with me the answer is definitely no."'[9] Just two months later, telephone communication between the Prince of Wales and Mrs Dudley Ward was cut off.

By the summer of 1934 the Prince of Wales and the Simpsons were inseparable. The Simpsons were constant, rather than regular, visitors to Fort Belvedere where Wallis, no doubt responding to Lady Furness's original suggestion, increasingly took on the role of chatelaine – ordering flowers, rearranging the furniture and deciding menus. Chips Channon wrote in his diary, 'She has already the air of a personage who walks into a room as though she almost expects to be curtsied to . . .'[10] When the Prince planned a holiday in Biarritz the Simpsons were asked to join the party. Ernest Simpson had to go to America on business. His wife went without him.

The holiday included a short sea voyage aboard the *Rosaura*, a yacht belonging to Lord Moyne. Alone on the deck one evening, they became lovers – an event which, no doubt, made up in romance for what it lacked in comfort. The plan had been for the Prince and his friends to disembark at Cannes and make their separate ways home. But the Prince and Mrs Simpson could not bear to part. So together they travelled by train to Lake Como. In the following February the pattern of events was repeated. The Simpsons were invited to join the Prince of Wales on a skiing holiday in Kitzbühl. Once more Ernest Simpson, obliged to go to New York on business, urged his wife to join the party without him. Yet again the lovers could not face separation. So they went on together to Budapest and Vienna. Mrs Simpson returned home a changed woman. Whatever affection she had once felt for her husband had disappeared.

History owes its understanding of Mrs Simpson's attraction to the Prince of Wales to Mrs Simpson herself. In what might have been expected to be a romanticised, as well as romantic, autobiography, she describes – with damning frankness – why, initially, she was drawn towards the heir apparent.

Over and beyond the charm of his personality and the warmth of his manner, he was the open sesame to a new and glittering world that excited me as nothing in my life had done before . . . Trains were held; yachts materialized; the best suites in the finest hotels were flying open; aeroplanes stood waiting . . . It seemed unbelievable that I, Wallis Warfield of Baltimore, Maryland, could be part of his enchanted world.[11]

So materialistic an explanation of the early infatuation seems out of place in a memoir entitled *The Heart Has Its Reasons*. But there is no doubt that, as well as the love of the luxury and status which the Prince could provide, Mrs Simpson came to love the man who provided it. His affection for her seems to have been based on his need for a woman who would dominate him. Chips Channon wrote that she 'enormously improved the Prince'. At the opera she made him take a cigar out of his breast pocket, complaining that 'it doesn't look very nice', and she was said to regulate his conversation by 'kicking him under the table hard when to stop and gently when to go on'.[12] Harold Nicolson was 'impressed by the fact that she forbade the Prince to smoke during an entire act in the theatre'.[13] A member of Baldwin's staff, seeking amusement rather than revelation, sent a sample of Mrs Simpson's handwriting to a graphologist. The report he received was almost certainly an accurate analysis of her character. 'A woman with a strong male inclination in the sense of activity, vitality and initiative. She must dominate. She must have authority.'[14] It was strength of character, not 'the distinct charm and sharp sense of humour' which Lady Furness generously acknowledged, which made Wallis Simpson more desirable than the throne.

Nobody can be sure when the Prince of Wales decided that he and Mrs Simpson would never part. After the abdication and exile, emotion clouded memory. But in late 1936, with his fate only just decided, Prince Edward (no longer King and not yet Duke of Windsor) told his confidant and adviser Walter Monckton that he had decided they would marry back in 1934. Perhaps. But, whenever he began to take the relationship seriously, there is no doubt that the Court and the political establishment stubbornly refused to believe that the relationship would last. Indeed, after the accession, when King Edward told

his friends of his intentions, most of them believed that, if the choice
between love and duty could be postponed, Mrs Simpson would go
the way of earlier mistresses. Monckton could not have been more
frank in his admission of error. 'I thought, long before as well as after
there was talk of marriage, that, if and when the stark choice faced
them between their love and his obligations as King-Emperor, they
would in the end make the sacrifice, devastating though it would
be.'[15] Others came to the same conclusions for reasons which were
less to the King's credit. Mrs Dudley Ward, asked by a friend if the
Prince ever thought of going away with her, replied, 'I don't know. We
didn't go into it.'[16] It was assumed that the King would be saved from
destruction by his pathological inconstancy.

That did not mean that the Cabinet and Court did not worry
about the new King's association with a married – and previously
divorced – woman. But Mrs Simpson was only one of the causes of
their concern. Edward VIII was simultaneously autocratic and indo-
lent. His staff – some of whom had been routinely accused of spying
for his father – complained that he lacked all consideration. Lord
Wigram, private secretary to George V, asked permission to resign
immediately the period of official mourning was over – demoralised
as much by his new master's arrogance as his reluctance to work his
way through the state papers which were sent to him each night. The
job was offered to Godfrey Thomas, who had been the new King's
private secretary when he was Prince of Wales. Thomas declined with
thanks. Alexander Hardinge – assistant private secretary to George V
and son of Edward VII's private secretary – responded to the call of
duty and accepted the appointment. His attempts to warn the King of
the dangers which he faced resulted in his exclusion from the inner
circle of confidants. He later confessed that he had 'not realised how
overwhelming and inexorable was the influence exercised on the new
King by the lady of the moment' – his sobriquet for Mrs Simpson,
before whom 'affairs of state sank into insignificance'.[17]

From the very beginning of his reign, Edward VIII exhibited something approaching contempt for the routine of monarchy. He told
Stanley Baldwin – a man who held Old England's view of tradition –
that the Accession Council was 'just business to be got through'.

Worse still, he refused to receive the Privilege Bodies* individually when they were called to Buckingham Palace to swear their fidelity. Instead he gave a collective audience and addressed one, all-purpose reply to the assembly. Ministers were not amused to learn that he had climbed out of a Buckingham Palace window in order to avoid discussing urgent business with his private secretary. And they were horrified to discover that he used his official aeroplane (the predecessor of the 'King's Flight') to ferry friends around the country and to import continental luxuries. But their most serious fears concerned the King's attitude towards Germany and the Germans.

In March 1936 German troops reoccupied the Rhineland – simultaneously flouting the Treaty of Versailles and abrogating the Locarno Pact, which guaranteed the frontiers of France, Germany and Belgium. Yet the King and, to an even greater extent, his paramour were being assiduously cultivated by the German Embassy in London. Both of them were clearly enjoying the attention. There is, however, a fundamental distinction between irresponsibility and disloyalty. Before abdication and exile Edward VIII had no sympathy for either Adolf Hitler or his Nazi Party. But he was flattered by the Ambassador's gross overestimation of both his power and his knowledge of foreign affairs, and he welcomed opportunities (denied to him in Whitehall) to express his scepticism about the value of the League of Nations. His attitude was best illustrated by a conversation he had with the Duke of Coburg – a grandson of Queen Victoria who (although half English) had allied himself with the German Chancellor. While in London to represent Adolf Hitler at the funeral of George V, the Duke suggested to the King that there should be a high-level meeting between the Prime Minister and the German Chancellor. He must have found the response as encouraging as it was aggressive. 'Who is King here? Baldwin or I? I myself wish to talk to Hitler and will do that, here or in Germany. Tell him that please.'[18]

The King was closest to the Embassy during its occupancy by Leopold von Hoesch, predecessor of the notorious Joachim von Ribbentrop, described by the new monarch as 'an ex-champagne

---

*Twenty-six distinguished institutions, including the ancient universities and the Royal Society, which are afforded a special (if rarely used) status in law.

salesman'. Von Hoesch enjoyed (at least according to his own account) so close a relationship with the King that he was able to ask for his assistance in promoting appeasement. Anthony Eden, the Foreign Secretary, was summoned to Buckingham Palace and urged to take a sympathetic view of Germany's reoccupation of the Rhineland. A telegram sent to Berlin by von Hoesch described a conversation which is more difficult to authenticate. According to the Ambassador, the King told him, 'I sent for the PM and gave him a piece of my mind. I told the old so-and-so that I would abdicate if he made war. There was a frightful scene. But you needn't worry. There won't be a war.'[19]

Ministers, with German revanchism to worry about, saw no significance in the King's wish that the Civil List should include provision for a possible Queen Dowager's pension – a request which, they should have realised, signified Edward's intention to marry. But they always found reason not to worry. Whenever the fear of a public scandal arose they took comfort from the thought that Ernest Simpson must both know of, and accept, his wife's relationship. Some of them recalled the complaisant husbands who had been prepared (perhaps even proud) for their wives to be the mistresses of Edward VII. Newspapers, they felt sure, would never divulge to the general public stories which only the establishment would accept in the proper spirit. While Ernest and Wallis Simpson were married the King's private life was an embarrassment to the morally fastidious, but not a threat to the Crown and constitution. It was a belief in which the Prime Minister and Cabinet persisted, despite the growing body of evidence to suggest that their confidence in the King's infidelity was misplaced.

In the year before Edward's accession Ernest Simpson had applied to join the Masonic Lodge over which Sir Maurice Jenks, sometime Lord Mayor of London, presided. His application, although supported by the Prince of Wales, was rejected. It was the Prince himself who complained and was given the explanation that Masonic Law prohibited the membership of a man whose wife was the mistress of another member. The Prince gave his assurance – apparently without rancour or embarrassment – that Jenks had misinterpreted the relationship and Simpson was admitted. Some months later an embarrassed Sir Maurice reported to Stanley Baldwin that Simpson had, for no reason which he could imagine, thought it right to tell him that the King wanted to marry his wife. The suggestion that Simpson should be seen and warned about the consequences of making such allegations was rejected with the constitutionally impeccable explanation that the Prime Minister was 'the King's adviser, not the Simpsons''. But, as he was later to confess, Baldwin convinced himself that, if he ignored the impending crisis, it might go away. On the day that King George V died he made an admirably frank admission to Tom Jones – in retirement from the Cabinet Office, *éminence grise* at large. 'You know what a scrimshanker I am. I had rather hoped to have escaped the responsibility of having to take charge of the Prince as King . . .When I was a little boy in Worcester reading history books, I never thought that I should have to interfere between a King and his mistress.'[20]

There were rumours that in May 1936 Ernest Simpson had confronted the King after they had both dined with Bernard Rickson-Hatt – an old friend of the Simpsons but also London editor of Reuters' news agency. He was said to have announced that his wife must make a choice between her husband and her lover. According to the story, the King's reply was unequivocal. 'Do you really think that I would be crowned without Wallis at my side?' Then he added, 'Sooner or later the Prime Minister must meet my future wife.'[21] If Baldwin heard the gossip he ignored it. But a month later he was presented with a sequence of events which he could not ignore. Ernest Simpson, loyally emulating the King, acquired a mistress. His wife decided at once to institute divorce proceedings. She would be free to marry the King.

Divorce, in 1936, required one of the partners to be guilty of a 'matrimonial offence' – of which the most common and convenient was adultery. Gentlemen – whatever the merits of the case – always agreed to be the 'guilty party'. When the guilt was genuine the lady who had been party to the offence was often protected from publicity by the man acting out an indiscretion in a seaside hotel with a woman employed for the purpose.

Despite Simpson's willingness to follow the established path, finding a lawyer to act for Mrs Simpson was not an easy task. Toby Mathews of Charles Russell and Co., the King's first choice, declined outright. Divorces contrived to benefit both parties were illegal. The Simpsons' motives were not trusted. Other solicitors who were approached either temporised or equivocated. In the end, thanks to the intervention of Walter Monckton, King's Counsel as well as confidant, she secured the services of Theo Goddard, neither young nor fit but willing.

The King was an enthusiast for long holidays. In the summer of 1936 he proposed to travel from Vienna to the Dalmatian coast. At Sibenik the sailing yacht *Nahlin*, accompanied by two destroyers, waited to take him and his party on to the Greek Islands. A crowd gathered on the quayside. To great astonishment (at least of the accompanying Court) they appeared to recognise Mrs Simpson and applauded her up the gangway. When the yacht berthed at Dubrovnik the demonstrations of love and loyalty were even louder. The crowd shouted '*Zivila ljubav*', Serbo-Croat for 'long live love'. The King and Mrs Simpson, who attributed their recognition to the circulation, in Europe, of American magazines which (unlike British publications) reported the progress of the relationship, showed every sign of enjoying their enthusiastic welcome. During their holiday on the islands they walked hand in hand through the fishing villages and posed for local photographers. The fear that the King was actively promoting a general awareness of his situation was reinforced when, after his return home, he invited Mrs Simpson to join him for his autumn visit to Balmoral — and included her name in the list of guests published in the Court Circular. An invitation to open a hospital building in Aberdeen had been declined with the explanation that he could not perform public duties during the period of official mourning for his father. On the day of the opening ceremony — performed by the Duke of York — he was photographed at Ballater railway station meeting Mrs Simpson off the train. What came to be called the Abdication Crisis had begun.

When Stanley Baldwin returned to London after his own summer holiday he was confronted with a sheaf of press cuttings from American newspapers and magazines. Many of them — including both an account of Mrs Simpson's dinner with Queen Mary and the revelation that the King's mother was dying of a broken heart — were inventions. William Randolph Hearst's papers syndicated Mrs Simpson's profile. *Time* referred to her as 'Queen Wally'. *New York*

*World* speculated about the prospect of Ernest Simpson cross-petitioning for divorce and reassured its readers that there could be no question of the King himself being prosecuted since he was above the law. The Prime Minister was also shown a number of messages from the socially severe Commonwealth capitals. It seems that Mrs Simpson was unknown in New Zealand. But in Australia and Canada the King's infatuation was causing a concern which, as the crisis grew, was to prove a crucial influence on Baldwin's thinking.

Although British newspapers suppressed news of the King's exuberant social life, families with relations in America received, second-hand, reports of the King's situation. Some expressed their disgust in letters to the King himself. Baldwin admitted his concern to the King's private secretary but would not confront the King. Twenty years later Alexander Hardinge – the private secretary who bore the heat of the crisis – wrote to *The Times* with an admirably charitable explanation of the Prime Minister's reticence. His 'natural reluctance to interfere in the private life of the sovereign was reinforced by the fact that no constitutional issue could arise as long as Mrs Simpson remained married to Mr Simpson'.[22] One piece of evidence suggests that Baldwin was preparing to face the most difficult weeks of his life. At a time when the League of Nations was collapsing and France, Britain and the United States could not agree on how to meet the threat from Nazi Germany and Fascist Italy, he told Sir Anthony Eden, his Foreign Secretary, 'I hope you will try not to trouble me too much with foreign affairs just now.'[23]

Baldwin continued to wait and hope – even in the face of incontrovertible evidence that the drama was approaching its climax. Mrs Simpson moved out of the Bryanston Court flat and into a rented house in Cumberland Terrace, on Regent's Park. She also acquired a convenience address in Felixstowe, thus enabling the divorce petition to be heard in Ipswich. The location may have been chosen in the vain hope of avoiding publicity, although the decision to retain the services of Sir Norman Birkett, KC, to represent Mrs Simpson suggests that there was a determination not to appear furtive. Ernest Simpson provided the necessary evidence at a hotel in Bray. Although the Prime Minister continued to prevaricate and procrastinate, the Archbishop of Canterbury – as he recalled events years after – began to realise that he might be asked to crown a king who was married to a twice-divorced woman.

> As the months passed . . . the thought of my having to consecrate him as King weighed on me as a heavy burden. Indeed I considered whether I could bring myself to do so.[24]

Prelates have to consider principles. Prime Ministers can be more pragmatic. So, although he undoubtedly disapproved of the King's conduct, Baldwin remained passive while the general public remained ignorant of what Cosmo Gordon Lang called 'The King's Matter'. But in early October it became clear that the silence would soon be shattered. Lord Beaverbrook telephoned Theo Goddard (Mrs Simpson's solicitor) to warn him that the *Evening Standard*, one of the newspapers he owned, was about to publish the story of the divorce and there could be no question of it being suppressed. Walter Monckton suggested that the King, who had met Beaverbrook twice, should make a direct plea for his assistance – making 'clear that there is no desire whatsoever to stop any report of the proceedings but merely to avoid a press announcement beforehand'.[25] For two days Lord Beaverbrook was unavailable – according to his secretary, undergoing one of the longest examinations in dental history. When at last he was willing to take the royal call the King made a far more extensive plea than Monckton had suggested. Mrs Simpson was not well. The notoriety she endured was the result of the time she had spent as his guest aboard the *Nahlin*. He therefore felt responsible for the unhappy position in which she found herself. Honour obliged him to intercede on her behalf. Not only did Beaverbrook agree to act with discretion, he also promised to persuade other press barons to do the same. Only the King's arrogance prevented him from being amazed. From then on Beaverbrook hovered on the edges of the royal circle – more as an opponent to Baldwin than as a supporter of the King. He described his participation in the abdication crisis as 'fun'. He was the only participant to find it so.

Although Beaverbrook was as good as his word and formed an alliance of silence with Esmond Harmsworth, publisher of the *Daily Mail* and chairman of the Newspaper Proprietors' Association,

Alexander Hardinge had the good sense to recognise that the whole world would soon know of a relationship which, he feared, was about to be elevated from an affair into an impending marriage. He therefore urged the Prime Minister to face the issue head-on. The King must be convinced of the need to avert the anticipated crisis. Mrs Simpson must abandon the divorce proceedings. In future the relationship, if it was to persist, must be conducted with discretion. Baldwin agreed. But – as is so often the case with tasks reluctantly accepted – did the job very badly.

The Prime Minister visited the King at Fort Belvedere and found him in the garden. To calm his nerves, Baldwin asked for a drink. When whisky and soda arrived he invited his host to join him. According to the Prime Minister's own account, the King replied, 'gravely . . . even severely, "No thank you, Mr Baldwin, I never take a drink before seven o'clock in the evening."'26* It was an unfortunate beginning to an unhappy occasion. Baldwin began by wishing the King every happiness and went on to recall a conversation in which he had been granted leave to speak freely on any subject. Did the rule, he asked, still apply? On being assured that it did, he went on to express his fears that the respect in which the monarchy was held could easily be eroded. It was not an approach likely to impress the King.

> You may think me Victorian, Sir. You may think my views out of date, but I believe that I know how to interpret the minds of my own people; and I say that, although it is true that standards are lower since the war, it only leads people to expect higher standards from their King. People expect more from their King than they did a hundred years ago.27

The King responded remarkably calmly to a homily which would have been more appropriate to a school assembly and, in its reference to 'lower standards', was downright offensive. But he refused, point-blank,

---

*Forty years later, I was one of a group of Ministers who entertained another Prince of Wales when he visited the Cabinet Office. Offered a pre-lunch drink, he gave the same reply.

either to suggest that the divorce be abandoned or to 'let [Mrs Simpson] in by the back door'. He remained obdurate even after the Prime Minister had shown him a collection of highly critical letters which had been sent to Downing Street. He was equally unmoved by the prospect of the country being rent by factions – one sympathetic to the King, another deeply antagonistic. Baldwin left Fort Belvedere clinging to the hope that the King's ardour – which he told Mrs Baldwin was extensive and visible – would cool in time.

Hardinge did not pretend that he was satisfied with the Prime Minister's performance. Baldwin had failed to even mention the subject of a marriage, in the private secretary's view the vital issue. Events over the next few days proved him right. On 26 October Hearst's *New York Journal* published an article under the headline, 'King Will Wed Wally'. On the same day the Archbishop of Canterbury called on Hardinge to express his frustration that, despite his repeated suggestions, the King 'was very emphatic that on the subject of his relations with Mrs Simpson he would listen to nobody except Mr Baldwin, who had a right to speak to and advise him'.[28] It was then the turn of Geoffrey Dawson, the editor of *The Times*, to seek audience at Number 10. He had received a letter for publication from *Britannius in Partibus Infidelium*, 'a Briton who had been resident in America for many years'. It described the 'disgust' which British expatriates felt about the way in which the monarchy itself was being degraded. Dawson had no intention of publishing the letter. But he realised that '*The Times* would have to do something about the King and Mrs Simpson. The PM must tell him what to do.'[29] When the letter was shown to Baldwin, he passed it on to the King but advised Dawson, 'Do nothing.'

The award of the decree nisi was reported only formally in Britain. In America, however, speculation built up to the point at which Noel Coward felt it necessary to complain to Louis Mountbatten about the 'degrading and horrible publicity' which included the headline 'King's Moll Reno'd in Wolsey's Home Town'. At the first night of *Cavalcade* on Broadway, Coward had said that it had been 'pretty exciting to be English. [But] In the midst of all the scandal and vulgarity [he] could only feel that it is pretty uncomfortable to be English.'[30]

Although Baldwin was sure that it was best to sit tight, other ministers – Duff Cooper, who sympathised with his friend the King, and Neville Chamberlain, who was wholly censorious – demanded a meeting before the press broke its voluntary silence. It was called for 13 November – the day on which the King returned from a visit to the Fleet at Southampton during which officers and ratings had expressed their undying loyalty. On his arrival at Buckingham Palace he was handed a letter from Hardinge. It told him of the meeting, predicted that newspapers would soon begin to publish what they knew and warned that there was at least a possibility that the government would resign and that the general election which followed would be fought on rival views of the King's character and conduct. Hardinge judged that the only way to avoid the danger was for 'Mrs Simpson to go abroad without further delay'.[31]

A letter is a strange way for a principal private secretary to communicate with the King. But Hardinge found the King reluctant to talk seriously on any matter, and discussion about Mrs Simpson was absolutely forbidden. Hardinge knew that the crisis could not be long averted. The editor of the *Morning Post* had warned Baldwin that the press would not remain silent for long. The King's Proctor – who had the duty of invalidating bogus divorce proceedings – had received an official complaint, alleging that Simpson vs. Simpson was a contrivance. Worse still, the Commonwealth had begun to express its anxiety. Lord Tweedsmuir, the Governor General of Canada, only regarded the situation as 'disgusting'. The Australian High Commissioner went much further. 'If there was any question of marriage with Mrs Simpson, the King would have to go.'[32] Worst of all, a draft letter – which amounted to an ultimatum – was circulating among critical ministers and growing stronger with every revision.

Hardinge's warning letter, described by Mrs Simpson as 'an impertinence', completely undermined the King's faith in his private secretary. After its receipt, he was ignored and Walter Monckton became the King's conduit to the Cabinet and the Prime Minister. Monckton was prepared for the task with the assurance that marriage with Mrs Simpson should be regarded as beyond doubt and, if it was unacceptable to the Cabinet, the King would abdicate. He, too, chose to hope for a change of heart and mind.

Hardinge's démarche had at least the effect of convincing the King that he must make his position clear to ministers. He suggested a meeting at which Baldwin would be accompanied by Lord Halifax and Neville Chamberlain. Baldwin, the model of constitutional propriety, said it was impossible to involve two members of the Cabinet before the rest had been told anything about the King's dilemma. It was agreed that they would meet tête-à-tête. In preparation for their conversation, the King telephoned Lord Beaverbrook.

It is by no means clear what the King hoped to achieve by asking Beaverbrook for help. He certainly did not want to incite public opinion. Hopes of immediate personal advice were dashed as Beaverbrook was on his way to America, where he hoped the dry Arizona air would cure his asthma. Lord Camrose, another press baron sailing on the same boat, advised him not to return home. 'He's not worth it.'[33] But on the day he landed, while having lunch with the *Daily News* in New York, he was astonished to receive a telephone call from the King. He agreed to sail home at once. On his return he was driven straight to Fort Belvedere.

Baldwin prepared for his meeting with the King by taking advice from the Attorney General, who was equivocal about the constitutional consequences of the sovereign choosing a consort of whom his ministers did not approve. He was, however, absolutely clear that an abdication had to be legalised by an Act of Parliament and that the King's Proctor might investigate the divorce, but could not prosecute the monarch.

It is unlikely that Baldwin would have passed on the information to the King. In any event, the conduct of the meeting was taken out of his hands. In an icy prologue – 'I understand that you and several members of the Cabinet have some fears of a constitutional crisis developing over my friendship with Mrs Simpson' – the King made his intentions plain. 'I want you to be the first to know that I have made up my mind and nothing will alter it. I have looked at it from all sides. I mean to abdicate and marry Mrs Simpson.'[34]

To confirm his determination, the King confided in his family for the first time. 'It can be simply stated that Queen Mary greeted her son's decision to give up the throne with consternation, anger and pain.'[35] The Duke of York was 'speechless' and terrified by the prospect of succeeding his brother as he had 'never even seen a state paper'. Louis Mountbatten consoled him with the assurance, 'There is no more fitting preparation for a king than to be trained in the Navy.'[36] The Duke of Kent claimed to be 'reconciled', but complained that his brother was so 'besotted by that woman' that 'one cannot get a word of sense out of him'.[37] Then an alternative to abdication was put into his head. The idea was promoted, if not conceived, by the *Daily Mail*. Perhaps he was so popular that the Cabinet could not afford to let him go.

On 17 November, the King set off on a visit to South Wales. According to *The Times*, 'the crowds gave him a welcome, the warmth of which there was no mistaking'.[38] But it was the *Daily Mail* which ensured that the visit was recognised as a triumph all over the United Kingdom. Its front page glorified 'THE KING BEHIND THE DOLE COUNTER' and published interviews with 'Workless miners [who] tell him their troubles'. And not only the miners. Outside the derelict Bessemer steel works in Dowlais he met the men who once had been employed there. That night, 'by his command, there dined with him', on the royal train, the recently resigned Chief Commissioner for Special Areas and his successor. According to the *Daily Mail*, the King was categoric. 'These works brought these people here. Something must be done to find them work.'[39] On a housing estate in Pontypool he told the tenants, 'You may be sure that all I can do for you, I will do.' There were only two blemishes on the whole two-day visit. On his way to visit a family at Boverton, 'a man stepped forward and touched the King on the arm'.[40] Restrained by a policeman, 'the intruder explained that he only wanted to remind the King that he was a member of his guard of honour in France during the war'.[41] And, just as he was about to board the royal train for home, the King remembered that he had left in the car the petition presented to him by the Blaenavon Unemployed Men's Committee. That notwithstanding, the *Daily Mail* contrasted his vitality and compassion with Baldwin's callous inertia. Commentators wondered if Harmsworth hoped for the creation of a 'King's Party' – according to *The Times,* 'a wholly mischievous suggestion' designed to drive a wedge between monarch and ministers.*

The article guaranteed Esmond Harmsworth's access to the King. They met at Balmoral, where Harmsworth renewed his promise of discretion and asked if any thought had been given to a morganatic marriage. The King was non-committal but reported the conversation to Monckton, who assured him that the Cabinet would not agree and that the necessary legislation would be unacceptable to Parliament. Harmsworth was not, however, easily discouraged. He put his idea to Mrs Simpson over lunch at Claridge's and, after he learned that the King had floated the idea with the Prime Minister, sought and obtained a meeting at Number 10. Baldwin later claimed to have told Harmsworth that 'he and his filthy paper did not really know the mind of the British people'.[42] The Prime Minister certainly said that Parliament would not accept a morganatic marriage. The meeting convinced Baldwin that inaction would be political suicide. The time had come to rally his forces.

The Cabinet was unanimous in its opposition to a morganatic marriage. Their minds were concentrated on the reality of the idea by the Attorney General, who reported that the preamble to the bill that sought to legalise the innovation would begin, 'Whereas the present King desires to marry a woman who is unfit to be queen . . .'[43] Clement Attlee, the Leader of the Opposition, was consulted and reported that 'all the Labour Party – with the exception of a few of the intelligentsia who could be expected to take the wrong view on any subject – were in agreement with the Cabinet'.[44] That was not completely the case. Ernest Bevin, not then an MP but the General Secretary of the Transport and General Workers' Union and a figure of profound influence, was tempted by the thought of revenge. 'We cannot forget that Old Baldwin "did us" over the Trade Union Act, Abyssinia, over rearmament and over peace.'[45] Attlee persuaded him and the *Daily Herald* to back the government against the King as a matter of principle. Two days later the storm broke.

---

*Politically, Baldwin was at his lowest ebb. He had just made the 'appalling frankness' speech in the House of Commons. See Chapter 16.

When Dr Alfred Blunt, Bishop of Bradford, addressed his Diocesan Conference on 1 December, he meant only to censure the Bishop of Birmingham, who had suggested that the Coronation should become a secular event. 'It is,' Dr Blunt intoned, 'a solemn sacramental rite . . . The benefits depend, under God, upon two elements. First on the faith, prayer and self dedication of the King himself . . . We hope he is aware of this need. Some of us wish that he gave more positive signs of such.' He was later to explain that nothing he said was intended to be a commentary on the rumours surrounding the King and Mrs Simpson. 'I did not know of them.' The newspapers did, however, and, although the national press discreetly overlooked the address, the provincial morning dailies saw it — or pretended to see it — as a comment on the King's relationship with Mrs Simpson. Naturally they thought it was their duty to report Dr Blunt's strictures and to interpret them as a rebuke to the King. The *Nottingham Journal* was typical. Comparing the reputation of the monarchy to the ruins of the Crystal Palace (which had burned down the night before Dr Blunt's address), it wrote that 'a great monument of Victorian tradition lies shattered in a smoking ruin'. But it was the *Birmingham Post* which most influenced the King. After he read its editorial he told Walter Monckton, 'They don't want me.'[46]

The royal depression was increased by a telephone call from Beaverbrook, which warned the King of what he should have realised. The national press was certain to take up the story. Beaverbrook asked to be released from his vow of silence in order to advocate the King's cause. The request was refused on the grounds that nothing was to be gained by the creation of rival campaigns which split the country. The next day the *News Chronicle* raised the possibility of a morganatic marriage, by which Mrs Simpson would become the King's wife but not his queen. That was impossible under British law and anathema to the royal family. Edward VII, the King's grandfather, had forbidden the Countess of Torby to sit on the Duchesses' bench at Buckingham Palace balls because of her morganatic marriage to the Grand Duke Michael of Russia. However, the suggestion encouraged such false hopes in the King that he asked Baldwin's agreement to him leaving England while his subjects considered his future. His plan was to guide their thoughts with a broadcast address to the nation. The Prime Minister's response was simultaneously paternal and magisterial.

What I want, Sir, is what you told me you wanted: to go with
dignity, not dividing the country but making things as smooth as
possible for your successor. To broadcast would be to go over the
heads of ministers.[47]

The King – genuinely anxious not to divide the nation – accepted
Baldwin's advice. Some of his supporters, most notably Winston
Churchill, did not behave with such good sense. On 3 December, half
an hour before a 'Rally for Collective Security' was due to begin in
the Albert Hall, 'all [the speakers] had assembled in a private room
behind the platform except Winston . . . A few minutes later he rushed
up' to Walter Citrine (General Secretary of the TUC and chairman of
the meeting) and told him, 'I must speak to you about the King.'
Citrine warned that, if Churchill mentioned the subject at the rally, he
would be challenged, adding, 'If nobody else does it, I will.' He then
added the threat that he would walk off the platform. In *The Gathering
Storm*, Churchill sets out the statement which he proposed to make as
if he had actually made it. It began with the prediction that, at the end
of the meeting, he would sing 'God Save the King' with more heart-
felt fervour than he had 'ever sung it in his life'. In fact, he accepted
Citrine's advice, left the statement unsaid and issued it to the press later
that evening. It called for the government to allow the King time to
make up his mind.

The next evening Churchill dined at Fort Belvedere, according to
his own account, after receiving an invitation at five o'clock on the
same day. In his biography Roy Jenkins expresses surprise that
Churchill was in London so late on a Friday afternoon, implying that
the invitation must have arrived much earlier and that the Albert Hall
démarche was made to impress the King in anticipation of their meeting.[48] The alternative explanation is that the invitation was issued
after the King read Churchill's statement and that Churchill immediately abandoned his weekend plans. Whatever the details and reasons,
it was the product of a romantic royalism which was to lead Churchill
very near to self-destruction. The dinner was followed by a letter to
the King, which Jenkins attributes to a good lunch. 'News from all
fronts. No pistols to be held at the King's head. No doubt that the
request for time will be granted.' Churchill was wrong about that. His

final sentence showed that his judgement was as faulty as his information about the government's intention. 'Good advance on all parts giving prospects of gaining good positions and assembling good positions behind them.'[49] Churchill was very near to calling for the formation of the 'King's Party'.

It was all too late. The newspapers not only felt free to report and speculate, they felt entitled (indeed obliged) to take sides. Monckton kept in touch with *The Times* in the hope of guaranteeing accuracy if not sympathy. J. C. C. Davidson, Baldwin's parliamentary private secretary, did the same with the *Daily Telegraph* in order that 'one respected newspaper should be properly informed so that it could give the nation a lead'.[50] Both, naturally enough, supported the government. So did the *Morning Post*, the *Manchester Guardian*, the *Sunday Times*, the *Observer*, the *Herald* and all the provincial papers except the *Western Morning News*. *The Times* described the notion of a morganatic marriage in language which was as savage as it was accurate. 'The Constitution is to be amended in order that [Mrs Simpson] may carry, in solitary prominence, the brand of unfitness for the Queen's Throne.' Harmsworth and Beaverbrook ensured that their titles supported the King.

There had been rumblings in Parliament since 17 November, when Ellen Wilkinson, the Member for Jarrow, had asked about American magazines being sold in London with two or three of their pages torn out. It was a lurid gloss on the truth. British editors simply omitted stories about 'Wally and the King', knowing that, if they were included, London wholesalers would not handle them. Attlee limited his interventions to polite requests for information and accepted, with grace, Baldwin's inability to give substantive replies. Churchill exercised no such restraint. On 8 December — after a particularly good lunch at the French Embassy — he once more asked the Prime Minister for an assurance that no irrevocable decision would be taken before Parliament and public had fully considered the issue. He was howled down. Harold Nicolson thought that he had 'undone in five minutes the reconstruction work of years'.[51] Leo Amery said that Churchill was 'staggered by the unanimous hostility of the House'. Robert Boothby, who shared with Brendan Bracken the role of Churchill acolyte, was provoked to such fury that he put his anger on paper. 'This afternoon you have delivered a blow to the King, both in the House and in the Country, far harder than Baldwin ever conceived of . . . What happened this afternoon makes me fear that it is almost impossible for those who are most devoted to you to follow you blindly . . . They cannot be sure where the hell they are going to be landed next.'[52]

Neither he nor Churchill knew that the King had already given up the fight. Four days earlier, Monckton had told Baldwin the King's decision to abdicate was formal and final. The concern at Fort Belvedere was that the throne might be sacrificed for nothing. The King's Proctor, although unable to prosecute the King, could invite the courts to invalidate the divorce if he judged it to be collusive. Monckton asked for two bills – one to confirm the abdication and the other to make Mrs Simpson's divorce immediate. Baldwin seemed to agree, but the Cabinet was adamant in its objection. Of all the ministers, Neville Chamberlain was the most strongly opposed. The whole situation must, he said, be speedily resolved. It was affecting the Christmas trade in Birmingham.

Baldwin made one last 'humble and sincere' attempt to change the King's mind – and persisted in his pleas after the King, speaking too quietly to overcome the Prime Minister's deafness, asked him to desist. Edward VIII would not be 'crowned with a lie on his lips' – the bogus promise not to marry. On the other hand, if he deserted Mrs Simpson he would be 'forever bowed in shame'. The lady herself, anxious to preserve her reputation for selfless devotion, suggested that she make clear her willingness to withdraw her divorce petition. She was easily persuaded by her lawyer that to do so might result in the King's Proctor instigating a case for collusion. There was nothing left to do except perform the obsequies.

The King asked the Prime Minister to leave the House of Commons in no doubt about two issues. First, that he had always been on the best of terms with the Duke of York, his brother and his successor.* Second, that 'the other person most intimately concerned

---

*Lady Soames (née Churchill) told me that, on his return to government in 1940, her father had feared that George VI would express his disapproval of the way in which the campaign against abdication had been conducted. At his first audience, the King thanked Churchill 'for his loyalty to my brother'.

has consistently tried to the last to dissuade the King from the decision he has taken'.[53] Baldwin spoke from notes written on scraps of paper – some of which had to be retrieved by his PPS from where he had left them in Downing Street. Harold Nicolson thought the speech a triumph – 'tragic in its simplicity'[54] – despite its faltering delivery and the Prime Minister's need to confirm facts and dates with the Home Secretary sitting by his side. Unfortunately, he forgot to absolve Mrs Simpson of blame.

A financial settlement was negotiated – and then improved on his brother's behalf by the new King. It was agreed that the old King should be created Duke of Windsor after the coronation of George VI. So when – no longer obliged to accept the advice of his ministers – he made his farewell broadcast he was introduced by Lord Reith, the Chairman of the BBC, as Prince Edward. His explanation that he 'found it impossible to carry the heavy burden of responsibility and discharge my duties as King in the way which I would wish to do without the help and support of the woman I love' was not accepted with universal sympathy. The Archbishop of Canterbury broadcast two days after Prince Edward left for France aboard HMS *Fury*, setting the scene for his views on the abdication with the undoubted fact that 'in darkness he left these shores'. The Primate of All England then continued,

> Strange and sad it must be that he should have disappointed hopes so high. Even more sad is that he should have sought happiness in a manner inconsistent with the Christian principles of marriage and within a social circle whose standard and way of life are alien to all the best instincts of his people.[55]

During what Osbert Sitwell called 'rat week', Mrs Keppel complained that the Duke of Windsor had 'shown neither decency, wisdom nor regard for tradition' and Louis Mountbatten, his erstwhile best friend, wrote to the new King to report 'the profound satisfaction that the Navy expressed of once more having a Sailor King'.[56] An officer of the Royal Fusiliers said that the regiment 'would have drawn swords for him' and added, 'By God, didn't he let us down'.[57] Beaverbrook echoed that opinion to Churchill. 'Our cock won't fight.'

Beaverbrook had wanted the King to battle on because he had 'tramped the outer marches of the Empire he loved' and as a way of expressing his 'long-standing enmity for Mr Baldwin'.[58] That enmity prompted him, twenty years after the abdication, to accuse the long-dead Prime Minister of conspiring with Dawson, the editor of *The Times*, to drive Edward VIII from the throne. The allegation was nonsense. Baldwin was reluctant to take any action and, in the end, was driven to force the King to face reality by the overwhelming judgement of Parliament and press that the constitution could not be rewritten for Mrs Simpson's convenience. The King, on the other hand, had no strategy except to hang on to 'the woman he loved'. As he left Britain, he told Monckton that he had 'always thought that he could get away with a morganatic marriage'[59] – even though the idea had only been put to him less than a month before the abdication.

The hard fact of King Edward's abdication was that – outside the louche set whose company he enjoyed – most British people either felt unmoved by his predicament or thought that he should go. Despite his arrogant insensitivity, he recognised how small the demonstrations on his behalf were. And most of the men who worked with him thought that he was temperamentally reluctant to discharge his onerous duties and incapable of performing them well. Yet, during his years as Prince of Wales, he had seemed to possess such promise. Classicists quoted Tacitus' *Capax imperii nisi imperasset*. Had he never been emperor, no one would have doubted his ability to reign.

# PART II

# Human Habitation

The world was changing but Britain was slow to adapt and accommodate the change. The old industries – steel, coal and shipbuilding – were beginning to die and their death was felt most painfully by the poor. It was the miners – always the shock-troops of the trade union army – who fought the valiant, and most obviously doomed, rearguard actions against reality. The leaders of the TUC knew that a strike in support of the old rates of pay and hours of work could not be won. And the coal owners were determined to starve the strikers into submission. But it was neither betrayal nor brutality which beat the Miners Federation. It was the passage of time.

Ramsay MacDonald was against the General Strike from the start. But loyalty compelled him to give it his formal support. Solidarity with the working class is not a virtue normally associated with MacDonald. He is condemned in Labour folklore as the traitor who deserted his party and led a 'national' government. But perhaps he was less a villain than a victim of the belief that only he could save the nation from financial disaster. Unhappily, he had no idea how salvation could be achieved and the authorities on economic survival feared to give him firm advice in case their prescription proved inadequate. He chose to do his duty as he saw it. It required him to abandon both the party and the beliefs which had sustained him for thirty years.

Poverty was, of course, greatest in the areas where once the old industries had flourished. The middle class thrived, but families at the bottom of the income scale endured every sort of deprivation and, as the numerous marches to London discovered along the way, too few people cared. Among those who did were the churches. For the first time, the Church of England discovered its mission to urban Britain.

It was in housing that the Church's campaign was most effective. In towns and cities from London to Leeds the Church of England drew the nation's attention to the horror of life in the Victorian slums. The encouragement of house building – in all its forms – was one of the few preoccupations for which inter-war governments can take credit. It was about the only way in which the Britain of the poor was made more fit for human habitation.

# CHAPTER FIVE

# Not a Penny off the Pay

The rank and file of the trade unions were quite sincere in regarding [the strike] as a trade dispute in defence of the wage standard and had no conscious intention of attacking the constitution.

Canon Spencer Elliott, St Paul's Church
Reported in *Sheffield Independent*, 18 May 1926

R H. Tawney, in a moment of rhetorical exuberance, asked why – if competition was the best guarantee of efficiency – the War Office had failed to distribute the 1914 military budget between the individual members of the British Expeditionary Force and left market forces to defeat the Kaiser. He misunderstood the psychology of the ruling classes. In time of war, public enterprise becomes popular. In 1915 the coal mines were nationalised for the duration of the hostilities.

No attempt was made to reorganise the industry or improve its efficiency. All that concerned the government was the miners' morale. Longer hours and extra shifts were necessary. Such sacrifice could hardly be expected if the result was greater profit for the hated mine owners. Miners – organised coalfield by coalfield but united in a national federation – had to be treated with caution and respect. They made up 10 per cent of the male workforce, enjoyed higher wages and

greater job security than other workers[1] and were bound together by
a solidarity unmatched in any other occupation.

In February 1919 – three months after Armistice Day – the miners'
strength was increased, at least in theory, by the revival of the 'Triple
Alliance' – the partnership in which they made common cause with
dockers and railway workers. At the same time the mine owners began
to ask for the return of their collieries. Lloyd George played for time.
He appointed a Royal Commission.

Miners regarded themselves as the elite of the trade union movement
and were profoundly ambivalent about their jobs. Few wanted their
sons to follow them down the pit, but most of them regarded mining
as a 'real man's' job, which entitled them to feel superior to other
trades. Ironically, the mine owners were far less socially secure. 'Their
status in society and in their communities depended entirely on coal.
If they failed their moderate wealth and power was at stake. The had
nothing else . . . Few had been to the right schools . . . public school
education was an exception . . . Their births, marriages and deaths
were not recorded in *The Times*.'[2] With a couple of aristocratic exceptions, the mine owners were not gentlemen.

The Royal Commission was said to have a 'balanced membership' – three miners, three mine owners, three industrialists and three
radical economists, including R. H. Tawney and Sidney Webb. As a
result it made three conflicting recommendations – including both
permanent nationalisation and an immediate return to private ownership. Lloyd George chose what he thought to be a compromise. The
miners would be guaranteed existing wage levels and a seven-hour
working day. The owners would resume control.

In 1920, just as the government announced its plans to privatise the
mines, the Miners' Federation of Great Britain (MFGB) demanded a
wage increase and prepared to strike if it was not granted. As so often
in their history, the miners chose the wrong moment to challenge
their employers. Both demand for, and production of, coal was slow-
ing down. The owners – parsimonious even in boom times – rejected
the claim out of hand. Despite the revival of the Triple Alliance, the
dockers and railwaymen refused to rally to the miners' cause. The
threat of strike action faded and, emboldened by their success, the

mine owners exploited the apparent weakness of their workers' union. As the slump deepened, their organisation – the Mining Association of Great Britain (MAGB) – demanded a new wage agreement. The basic rate of pay was to be cut and the 'national pool' (which guaranteed a decent wage to miners in less profitable pits) was to be abandoned. Some miners would be paid less than the reduced national rate. The union refused even to negotiate. The owners declared a lock-out. Miners who did not accept the terms would be refused employment.

On 1 April 1921 a million miners accepted unemployment in preference to wage reductions. Delegate conferences of both the Transport and General Workers Union and the National Union of Railwaymen – fearful that their members might also face a wage cut – agreed in principle to strike in the miners' support. As always, the miners were too proud for their own good. Neither the dockers nor the railwaymen were allowed to take part in the negotiations with management until their members were on strike. Even so, when the miners rejected the offer of mediation both unions agreed to call out their members on 15 April. But at a meeting of the National Council of Labour – held on the eve of the strike to encourage wider support for the miners' cause – Frank Hodges, the General Secretary of the MFGB, told journalists that he was prepared to negotiate new wage rates, area by area.

Knowledge of 'Hodges' offer' was received in Downing Street with as much pleasure as astonishment. Lloyd George wrote to Hodges in the early hours of Friday 15 April, inviting him to a meeting at which the terms of a settlement could be clarified and formalised. The railways and transport unions were equally surprised (and, since they were reluctant to call out their members in support, barely less pleased) to read in the morning papers that the strike would be called off almost before it had begun.

The three union executives met at Unity House, the TUC's Eccleston Square headquarters. The miners insisted that the decision on how to proceed was theirs and theirs alone. So they met in private for two hours while their potential allies waited in an ante-room. Ernest Bevin, the transport workers' leader, found out by accident 'that, by a majority of one, they had turned down Hodges' statement' and that the General Secretary had resigned.[3] The miners still refused to discuss the consequences of that narrow majority with the other unions. Herbert Smith, their President, had a simple response even to requests for information. 'Get on t'field. That's thi' place.' Until they were on strike, the other unions had no status in the dispute.

Denied the right to comment on either strategy or tactics, neither the railwaymen nor dockers felt any obligation to follow the miners into the dispute. Bevin urged both unions to 'act with sympathy and understanding'. But the miners had lost the support of the other unions and were left to fight on alone. After ten weeks without wages a ballot still produced a majority of two to one for continuing the strike. It took three months for them to be starved back to work. They then agreed that wages could be negotiated area by area and that some pits would pay wages which were below subsistence level. But it was what they regarded as the other unions' betrayal, not the dire consequences of the new agreement for their families, that made the miners call 15 April 1921 'Black Friday'.

The debacle convinced the whole trade union movement that, in the words of Robert Williams of the National Transport Workers' Federation, 'Unless we can act in the mass, we shall be broken in detail.'[4] Fred Bramley, secretary of the TUC Parliamentary Committee, reflected on the superior organisation of the Federation of British Industries. 'Against powerful combinations of this kind the individual union is as useless as a pop-gun on a modern battlefield.'[5] The TUC began to reorganise. The ineffective Parliamentary Committee was replaced by the General Council – in effect an executive – and Congress was asked to raise a levy which would provide finance for unified action. The proposal was rejected by the major unions, who feared a loss of sovereignty. Central control became the policy of the militants. The Minority Movement – an alliance of syndicalists and Communists founded in 1924 – adopted the slogan, 'All Power to the General Council'.

The miners were fighting on two fronts – against the owners and against history. The terminal decline of the British coal industry had begun. The downward spiral was briefly halted by the problems of competing producers – devastation of the Ruhr Area and the Saar and prolonged strikes in America. But it was only a temporary respite. The industry's net profit of £59 million in 1923/4 turned into a net loss of £2.1 million in the second half of 1925. The choice before the mine owners was change or slow death.

★

In 1925 140 separate companies owned 2,481 pits.[6] Many of the smaller mines only made a profit in the most favourable years. Even the larger undertakings badly lacked modern machinery. The Lewis Committee, which had examined the prospect for rationalising the industry's trading, judged that coal 'on its marketing side, is probably less well organised than any other major industry'.[7] But the employers had only one remedy for every crisis. Labour costs had to be reduced, by either a cut in wages or an increase in hours worked. It was a vain hope. During the temporary export boom, the MFGB had won an agreement that the pits should work a seven-hour day. And in March 1924 they had 'consolidated' – that is to say made permanent – the highest 'standard rate of pay' in the industry's history. Those achievements were sacrosanct to a union which believed, implicitly, in the solidarity of one member with another.

Between 1914 and 1924 coal production fell from 287 million to 267 million tons. There had been a small improvement in productivity during the war, but labour costs remained higher than in other European coalfields. The more realistic trade union officers agreed, 'We have too many men in the industry and we have too many pits'.[8] Their demands for major restructuring were accompanied by promises that they would accept the consequent unemployment – 150,000 lost jobs if all the worn-out pits were closed. While the parties disagreed about remedies the industry continued to deteriorate. During 1925 unemployment in the coalfields increased from 2.9 per cent to 17.5 per cent. Nine out of ten miners in the export fields – Northumberland, Durham and South Wales – were laid off.

In part the government was to blame. On 25 April 1925 Britain returned to the gold standard at its 1914 parity of one pound to four dollars, eighty-six cents. The immediate result was an increase in export prices. Winston Churchill (a Conservative again and back in the Cabinet as Chancellor of the Exchequer more because of Stanley Baldwin's need to unite the Tory Party than because of his suitability for that office) described the consequences of the new policy in a comment on the Bank of England's advice. 'The Governor shows himself perfectly happy in the spectacle of Britain possessing the finest credit in the world simultaneously with a million and a quarter unemployed.'[9] Despite what sounded like doubts, he endorsed the Governor's policy.

John Maynard Keynes, who described the enthusiasm for the gold standard as a 'barbarous relic of a bygone age',[10] attacked the related 'theory of the economic juggernaut', which argued that wages should be determined by supply and demand for labour rather than the level necessary for a decent existence. But the mine owners – in a year when 60 per cent of collieries ran at a loss, two hundred pits closed between January and July and losses rose to £1 million a month – were not in a mood to discuss social justice and equity. Their position was set out by Sir Adam Nimmo, the Scottish representative on the Mining Association's Council.

> The wages of those engaged in the industry cannot permanently rest upon considerations of cost of living or what the men call a living wage. It is of no avail to suggest that the wages received do not permit the miners to have a proper standard of living.[11]

The mine owners at least shared the union's belief that the only short-term remedy was a government subsidy – though they described it as a brief alternative to a reduction in labour costs. Stanley Baldwin, who had become Prime Minister for the second time in 1924 – after a brief Labour interlude – was categoric in his refusal to provide help. Speaking in Birmingham on 5 March 1925, he was explicit. 'What the government will not do is attempt to control the industries of this country . . . The people have repudiated socialism. They have repudiated nationalisation.'[12] His criticisms of the industry were even-handed. Management was ineffective and investment inadequate, but the unions had contributed to the decline by their attachment to restrictive practices. A week later, in Leeds, he was more partisan. The Communist Party, he claimed, was determining the policy of the MFGB through the agency of the Minority Movement which, by 1925, was supported by one miner in four. Perhaps more significantly, A. J. Cook had become the General Secretary of the Miners' Federation.

Cook was what, these days, would be called 'charismatic'. He had been a part-time Baptist preacher and still addressed meetings with the revivalist fervour that he had employed in the pulpit. A Marxist – though not a Communist – he had been elected as General Secretary (replacing the moderate and long-serving Frank Hodges) on the casting vote of Arthur Horner, the Communist leader of the Welsh miners. The Home Office regarded him as 'an agitator of the worst sort'.* Cook was an orator, not a negotiator. Nor was he a realist. Asked for evidence that the miners were prepared for a long battle, he replied that his mother-in-law had been buying an extra tin of salmon for weeks.[13] But the Federation's president, Herbert Smith, was a moderate who realised how catastrophic the consequences of defeat would be and, by his nature, preferred to 'settle' rather than fight. He persuaded the MFGB to co-operate with the owners in an inquiry into the industry, claiming that he wanted to prove that the union was 'not afraid to face the facts'.[14] His real objective was to prolong the agreement which had been negotiated during 1924. The best he hoped for was the continuation of wage rates which most miners thought inadequate.

More militant miners began to prepare for the conflict which they had no doubt lay ahead. In the spring of 1924 the engineers' union had proposed the creation of an 'offensive alliance against the employers'. The Transport Workers' Union had given the idea half-hearted support but the MFGB – always too proud to follow rather than lead – remitted the proposal to its executive and then forgot about it. In early 1925, the MFGB suggested that the idea be revived. Ernest Bevin regretted that the change of heart had come 'at the time of the miners' difficulty . . .We do not think that, simply because we have an instrument like this, we ought to be striking every minute'.[15] He attempted to make long-term sense of the proposal by suggesting that members of the alliance unions should write a commitment to collective action into their constitutions. The miners led the opposition to Bevin's plan. They wanted allies in the imminent struggle, not the loss of their prized independence.

Between March and May 1925 the total volume of coal mined at a

---

*Seventy years after the event, my mother still boasted that she had 'made tea for A. J. Cook' when he visited the Derbyshire coalfield in 1926.

loss rose from 40 per cent to 60 per cent, and between January and June average export prices – forced down by revaluation – fell by 25 per cent. The Mining Association of Great Britain repeated its demands for the traditional remedy. The miners had to choose between less pay and longer hours. The Association's secretary complained that 'the difficulty of drawing up wage proposals . . . has been greatly increased by the refusal of the MFGB to consider an extension of the seven-hour day'.[16] In June the Association gave notice that it would terminate its agreement with the miners and offered a new pay deal which the union calculated would cut average pay by two shillings a shift. The TUC 'agreed to give complete support to, and co-operate wholeheartedly with, [the miners] in their resistance to the owners' proposals'.

Stanley Baldwin, who had insisted that 'interference carries the risks of real harm',[17] changed his policy if not his mind. The owners were urged to withdraw their new offer. They refused. So he adjusted his position a second time and proposed a court of inquiry. Although the miners – grandly announcing that they would only give evidence to a Royal Commission – ignored its proceedings, the report concluded that 'wages at some agreed minimum rate must, in practice, be a charge before profits are taken'. The industry could not be left to the 'unmitigated application of market forces'. The employers rejected the findings.

The TUC, sure that the employers would soon declare a lock-out, invited the Prime Minister to intervene. He advised the employers to begin unconditional negotiations, but told the Cabinet that 'the question of subsidy would in no event be considered except in the remote contingency of it becoming clear that both parties to the dispute had made the largest possible concessions but there was still a gap which might provide the only means of securing a durable settlement on an economic basis.'[18]

The confused syntax made Baldwin's honest intentions difficult to determine. But the unions sensed that, throughout Britain, employers were beginning to flex their muscles. The engineers reported that some of their members had been told that they must accept longer hours and lower wages, and the textile workers anticipated similar demands. Walter Citrine, the acting General Secretary of the TUC, recalled in his memoirs how he reacted to the news that the battle in the coalfield was likely to escalate into a widespread war. 'If the industries fought singly, they would be broken singly. Only if they could get the TUC to rally to the miners now had they any chance of a settlement in other industries threatened with attack.'[19] In preparing for war, the unions hoped for peace. James Marchbank, the President of the National Union of Railwaymen, forgetting that his members had abandoned the miners, claimed that 'on Black Friday, [we] nearly had the government on its knees'.[20] The job begun in 1924 could be completed in 1925. The TUC agreed to an embargo on all coal movement.

The Prime Minister, genuinely anxious to avoid a strike, met both owners and miners. He was consistent in his insistence that the Miners' Federation should reopen talks but, since he refused to discuss a subsidy, accepted that a solution to the crisis almost certainly required a reduction in labour costs. The *Daily Herald* reported that on 29 July he told the TUC that the miners would have 'to face a reduction in wages'. Other papers, which copied the story, claimed that his demand had encompassed the entire economy. 'All workers of this country have got to take reductions in wages to help put industry on its feet.'[21] The infuriated unions escalated their action. The embargo on coal movements due to begin next day would be no more than the prelude to a full-scale strike. It was a bad moment for the miners to choose. The Nottingham union was reluctant to support a strike when their wages were not threatened and coal stocks were high. It was not the last time that the miners' leaders precipitated a strike at a time when defeat was almost certain.

Baldwin urged the mine owners to buy time. They refused. The Cabinet therefore decided, on the unusual basis of a vote, that 'between a national strike and the payment of assistance to the mining industry, the latter course was the least disadvantageous'. The miners' wages would be protected for nine months by a subsidy which was calculated to cost £10 million. It cost almost twice as much, but the Treasury estimated that peace had been bought at a bargain price. A strike would have cost £70 million. The unions declared a victory for solidarity and called 3 July 1925 'Red Friday'.

The *Daily Express* described the subsidy as Danegeld and the *Daily*

*Mail* declared a 'Victory for Violence'. The Mining Association expressed its 'profound disappointment and very serious alarm' and – more surprisingly – Ramsay MacDonald, the Leader of the Labour Party, was more anxious than elated. In the House of Commons he reacted with balanced caution. But a week later, at the Independent Labour Party Summer School at Easton Lodge, he made his true feelings known. The government had

> handed over the appearance of victory to the very forces that sane, well considered, thoroughly well examined socialism feels to be probably the great enemy . . . The Tory government, in . . . the methods it adopted to bring this temporary settlement into being, has sided with the wildest Bolshevik, if not in words, certainly in fact and substance.[22]

The appearance of victory deceived. The government's statement – issued on 31 July – made clear that all the unions had achieved was a postponement of defeat. The strike would have caused damage 'of the gravest character'. What was more, 'it was not fair to require a reduction in wages, with the present cost of living, before an attempt had been made, by means of an enquiry, towards meeting the situation.' Sir Maurice Hankey, the Cabinet Secretary, reported to the King that 'many members of the Cabinet think that the struggle is inevitable and must come sooner or later'. He added that the 'PM does not share that view'. But he also implied that Baldwin sided with 'the majority of the Cabinet [who] regard the present moment as badly chosen for the fight, [and] thought conditions would be more favourable nine months hence'.[23] The suspicion that the retreat was purely tactical was confirmed when the Prime Minister told his official biographer, 'We were not ready'.[24]

In the House of Commons, Winston Churchill said almost as much.

> We considered that, should such a struggle be found to be inevitable . . . it was of supreme importance that it should only be undertaken under conditions which would not expose the nation needlessly or wantonly to perils, the gravity of which

cannot be possibly overstated. We therefore decided to postpone the crisis in the hope of averting it, or coping with it effectively when the time came.[25]

Lloyd George accused ministers of 'being afraid of cold steel' and claimed that, when they were 'herded into the Lobby' in support of the new arrangement, 'the hand which directs them will be the hand of the Patronage Secretary, but the voice which compels them will be the voice of Mr Cook'.[26] Herbert Smith was less eloquent but more wise. He called the battle which ended with Red Friday 'an affair of outposts. It was a mere skirmish. The main battle has still to be fought and won.'[27] His prediction was reinforced by a speech made by William Joynson-Hicks, the Home Secretary.

> The thing is not finished. The danger not over. Sooner or later the question has to be fought out by the people of this land. Are we to be governed by Parliament and the Cabinet or by a handful of trade union leaders?[28]

The final conflict was preceded by what looked like a genuine attempt to find a real solution to the industry's long-term problem. In 'an attempt towards meeting the situation' the Prime Minister set up a Royal Commission – exactly the form of inquiry which the miners had demanded. He wanted its chairman to be 'a statesman of the first rank' who would not propose a compromise which satisfied neither party. Herbert Samuel, who had served Asquith as Postmaster General and Home Secretary, was appointed. Two of its five members, Kenneth Lee (a textile manufacturer) and William Beveridge (the Director of the London School of Economics), also had connections with the Liberal Party. Ramsay MacDonald was right. It was a Commission 'which the Liberals might have appointed to recommend their scheme for coal and power. And that is roughly what happened.'[29]

The Samuel Report was thorough if not wise. It included an analysis of the coal industry's long-term problems throughout Europe and concluded that the fall in demand was likely to be temporary. It was therefore opposed to the mass closure of pits and offered no short-term solution to the problem it had been created to examine – except

an expedient which was most offensive to the miners. 'We see no
escape from giving up the minimum wage of 1924.' Viability required
labour costs to be cut by 10 per cent. That proposal left little opportunity for discussion of the less explosive recommendations.
Nationalisation of royalties, creation of cooperative selling agencies,
the development of by-products and research into new uses for coal
do not command headlines. On the subject of subsidies the report was
trenchant and, to some trade unions, compelling. It could not recommend that low-paid workers – say shipwrights on 56/- a week –
should be taxed to guarantee miners 76/-.

The Prime Minister gave his reluctant approval. 'The conclusions
reached by the Commission do not in all respects accord with the
views held by the government and some of the recommendations contain proposals to which, taken by themselves, the government is known
to be opposed.' Nevertheless, he was prepared to facilitate implementation of the report 'provided that those engaged in the industry – with
whom the decision primarily rests – agree to accept the report and to
carry on the industry on the basis of its recommendations'.[30]

The union continued to press for a subsidy. When he met the
miners Baldwin first explained that he could go no further than the
official statement because 'if I speak and say anything my word
goes . . . And it will be done'. The memory of that assurance must have
heartened Herbert Smith when the Prime Minister replied to his
question about what would happen if the industry was still searching
for a permanent solution when the 1925 subsidy ran out.

> If, against the advice of the Commission, we found that some such
> temporary assistance, say for three months . . . was going to save the
> situation, then I would be prepared to consider a departure.[31]

Perhaps, at the time that the offer was made, Baldwin really believed
a further period of subsidy was possible. In the light of subsequent
events, his comment looks like little more than a calculated ambiguity – playing for time while the government prepared for the conflict
which every party to the dispute thought inevitable.

Although the wiser members of the TUC General Council knew
that Red Friday was more a truce than a victory, very little was done

to prepare for the inevitable resumption of hostilities. Other unions, for the most part in sympathy with the miners, had profound misgivings about calling out their members in solidarity. Walter Citrine voiced doubts about fighting a total war. 'A general strike – is a literal impossibility and behind the reasoning of those who support it, is always present the feeling that, in some imperfect way, services essential to life must be carried on.' That amounted to the surrender of 'a very powerful weapon'.[32] But the TUC would have a moral duty to fight with one hand held behind its back.

The trade unions' official statement, in anticipation of a general strike, echoed his ambivalence.

> National Bodies in conjunction with the Trade Unions should be left to improvise machinery to safeguard the public against unnecessary inconvenience according to the exigencies of the dispute . . . We would recommend that no cut and dried scheme be formulated at the present juncture as . . . Any such scheme [implying] evidence of good will on Labour's part would be ruthlessly exploited by our opponents.[33]

Sometimes the TUC's behaviour was so cautious that the miners called it cowardice. When the question of help for the strikers' families was raised with Citrine, he first expressed his doubts about the ability of the Co-operative Movement 'to deviate its attention to the feeding of the working class'.[34] Then, when the Co-operative Union – fearful of the extent of credit it would be expected to provide – asked the TUC to underwrite its unrecoverable debts the request was twice rejected.[35]

The *Daily Herald* asked, 'Should the workers take up arms?' and John Wheatley, MP – Clydesider, devout Catholic and the only unequivocal success of the first Labour government[*] – told his local party, 'We want ten million men who are prepared to fight rather than see Britain made into a land of coolies.' He was not typical of the Labour leadership. Ramsay MacDonald, fearing the strength of the

---

[*]For an account of Wheatley's record as Minister of Health, see Chapter 8.

Minority Movement and the appeal of the Anglo-Russian Unity Committee, noted with profound apprehension that Harry Pollitt (the Secretary-General of the Communist Party) had achieved the respectable status of delegate to the TUC. His fear of a 'red takeover' – politics in the streets rather than in Parliament – was only partly allayed by the appointment of Walter Citrine, a figure of impeccable responsibility, as permanent General Secretary of the TUC. It was thanks to Citrine that A. J. Cook's proposal that the unions should raise a levy to finance strikers' food supplies during an all-out strike was 'referred back' to the General Council, a procedure which amounted to rejection without humiliation.

The trade union movement was at best ambivalent about supporting the miners. No one openly opposed it. The memory of past betrayals was still too strong. But the Minority Movement's call for the 'mobilisation of the rank and file' was defeated on the grounds that nobody knew quite what it meant and that, if it meant anything, its purpose was unconstitutional. The Minority Movement adopted the slogan 'Don't trust your leaders' and Cook denounced the campaign for renewed government help with the insistence, 'The miners [are] not going to make it a subsidy issue. It [is] a trade union issue and a wage agreement question.'[36] The Miners Federation of Great Britain was not to be deflected from the basic principles of its policy – no reduction in wages, no increase in hours and no interference with the national minimum. Their slogan – now part of trade union folklore – represented both their courage and their intransigence. 'Not a penny off the pay. Not a minute on the day.'

Unlike the unions, the government was united, ruthless and prepared. By August 1925 Joynson-Hicks was able to tell the Cabinet that the Supply and Transport Committee, which had been created to maintain essential services, had already set up a substantial provincial organisation. The Cabinet rejected his proposals that volunteers should be mobilised to break the strike in anticipation of it being declared, but agreed to return to the subject at a later date. They were relieved of the responsibility. The venerable Lord Hardinge of Penshurst – sometime permanent under-secretary to the Foreign Office, Viceroy of India and confidant of King Edward VII – became head of a movement which called itself the Organisation for the Maintenance of

Supply. It began to prepare a 'citizens' response' to the trade unions' 'threat'.

The government's failure to respond directly to the recommendations of the Samuel Commission had in effect, if not intention, left the owners and miners to confront each other face to face. On 1 April, three weeks after the Samuel Commission reported, the mine owners accepted the recommendation for wage reductions and reluctantly agreed to a measure of reorganisation. But a secret memorandum – circulated to Mining Association members on 17 March – had insisted that 'reorganisation would have no appreciable effect' and described the higher prices which would follow the closure of uneconomic pits as self-defeating. The miners themselves, although formally in favour of restructuring the industry, realised that it offered no solution to their immediate problems. They continued to hope for a subsidy despite Cook's insistence that its continuation could not be the basis of their demands. At the same time, they warned the TUC not to be seduced by subsidiary recommendations of the Samuel Commission. 'It gives us three quarters, so we can't accept it,' Cook said.[37]

The miners, at a special conference convened on 9 April 1926, confirmed the rejection of longer hours, lower wages and locally negotiated agreements. Feeling had grown so strong in the coalfields that, even had they wished to shift their ground, retreat would have been impossible. But the General Council of the TUC was not equally steadfast. On the night before the miners' special conference met, the TUC leaders had told the MFGB that they could not promise unqualified support for a resolution that refused even to consider reducing labour costs.

Tentative talks – always clearly distinguished by trade unionists from negotiation and conciliation – dragged on throughout the month. Throughout that time Baldwin, influenced by no authority more substantial than the *Daily Mail*, believed (in the words of that paper) that the 'miners are keener to give way on hours than on wages'. When the mine owners showed Baldwin their new wage proposals – a reduction from 10/4 to 8/3 a shift in Scotland and even bigger reductions in other parts of the country – he was frank about his doubts that the miners would even consider them. The offer was an ultimatum which required the union to fight or surrender. Notices

requiring the miners to accept the new terms or be locked out of the
pits were issued on 30 April. Lord Londonderry was in an emollient
minority. 'I did what I could to press [the owners] to make the best
offer they possibly could. But they do not look very far ahead . . . with
the result that they made an offer which ensured them a profit.'[38]

The Prime Minister almost certainly shared Londonderry's opinion
of the mine owners' lack of foresight. Unfortunately he did not say so.
The TUC was left with no option other than to rally – with some
reluctance – to the miners' cause. Doubts were expressed only in private. A General Council policy paper endorsed the miners' position
towards wages. 'The figures given in the Samuel Commission's report
make clear that to seek any further degradation of the [wage] level is
indefensible.' But when a special conference of executives met in
Farringdon Hall on 29 April there was no enthusiasm for a head-on
collision between unions and employers. Jimmy Thomas of the railway
union spoke of the need for an 'honourable settlement' – which the
miners feared was a euphemism for surrender. Even Ernest Bevin
warned his more bellicose colleagues that talk of a general strike 'puts
a weapon in the hands of our opponents'. Acceptance that a confrontation could not be avoided resulted in a policy document entitled
'Proposals for Co-ordinated Action' and a resolution authorising strike
action being carried on a card vote by 13,653,577 votes to 49,911. But
the General Council reiterated its hope that talks between miners and
employers would continue. More contentiously, it announced that it
would assume primary responsibility for future negotiations.

The hope of a peaceful settlement was savagely reduced by the
miners' refusal to talk directly to the mine owners until the lock-out
notices were withdrawn and the owners' refusal to talk directly to the
miners while the threat of strike action continued. Various peace for-
mulae were proposed by Horace Wilson, Permanent Secretary to the
Ministry of Labour, and Lord Birkenhead, the Lord Chancellor (on
behalf of the government), and by Jimmy Thomas and Ernest Bevin
for the TUC. They were all rejected by the miners on the grounds that
they implied eventual acceptance of wage cuts. From time to time
there were glimmers of hope. Ernest Bevin, who was trusted by the
miners even when they disagreed with him, told Cook as early as 22
April that he saw no alternative to some sort of wage cut. He

proposed the creation of a wages board to decide on the way in which a graduated minimum wage would be applied in the various coalfields. The TUC's hope of persuading the miners to accept Bevin's formula was frustrated by a ministerial diversion.

Lord Birkenhead, with a lawyer's enthusiasm for written agreements, occupied one Downing Street meeting by drafting a 'holding statement' which he believed would satisfy both government and unions. 'The Prime Minister has satisfied himself as a result of the conversations he has had with the TUC that, if negotiations are continued (it being understood that the [lock-out] notices cease to be operative) the representatives of the TUC are confident that a settlement can be reached on the lines of the [Samuel] Report within a fortnight.'[39] The draft had the virtue of predicting success without giving details of the formula on which it would be based and of clearing away the threats with which both sides to the impending dispute menaced each other.

On 2 May the Cabinet met to discuss with the TUC the formula which Birkenhead had proposed. The TUC delegation was late. While irritated ministers waited impatiently the Postmaster General arrived with the news that several unions had already sent telegrams to their branches telling them that official strikes were to begin at midnight on 3 May. Baldwin persuaded his colleagues that the negotiations should continue. But attitudes had hardened. It was agreed that the TUC must soon be presented with an ultimatum. If the miners did not accept the need for wage reductions negotiations would end.

Delegates from both miners and owners met ministers separately later that day. Discursive discussion about the difference between 'accepting' the Samuel Report and agreeing to a solution 'on the lines' of the Royal Commission's proposal was interrupted by the Prime Minister's demand (which Arthur Pugh, the chairman of the TUC accepted) that the union should agree to withdraw its strike instructions when the lock-out notices were cancelled. A meeting of the full Cabinet that night began with an examination of the 'ultimatum' which, it was increasingly believed, must be presented to the TUC. The meeting was still in progress at ten minutes past midnight when Joynson-Hicks interrupted the discussion to tell his colleagues that compositors of the *Daily Mail* had refused to set the type for an editorial entitled 'For King and Country'. The mood of the meeting

changed. Until then there had been 'strong differences of opinion
about whether or not to issue the ultimatum immediately. But, much
to the delight of the Cabinet hawks, the action of the *Daily Mail*
printing staff brought the doubtful people right up against the situation that the [general] strike had begun.'[40]

Nothing of the kind had taken place. The compositors' action had
been entirely spontaneous and it was repudiated by the General
Council of the TUC at a quarter past one in the morning – barely an
hour after it began. That notwithstanding, the Prime Minister told the
House of Commons that, while he was explaining to the Cabinet the
details of his evening discussions with the TUC, 'we learned, by telephone, that the first, active, overt move in the General Strike was
being actually made, by trying to subvert the press'.

That obvious exaggeration forms part of the evidence, advanced by
Baldwin's critics, that – having grown weary of the long negotiations
and concluded that the miners must be beaten rather than placated –
the Prime Minister seized the opportunity to break off the talks and
issue the ultimatum. That theory is endorsed by his behaviour immediately after the fateful decision was taken. The TUC delegation was
brought from the Treasury boardroom into the Prime Minister's presence and was told (in Baldwin's own account to Parliament) 'the work
of the peacemakers had been killed by the action of hotheads'. He then
handed them a prepared document setting out the terms of the ultimatum – 'sincere acceptance' of terms of the Samuel Report, including
the need to adjust hours and wages. Baldwin went to surprising lengths
to convince the nation of his good will. His Parliamentary report to the
King not only refuted the claim that a negotiated settlement was possible but – extraordinarily for such an elevated document – attacked
the character of the MP who made the claim. 'Mr Thomas is one of the
most clever, glib and astute politicians in the House. Yesterday he was
almost Machiavellian in his cleverness.'[41]

In the House of Commons, the Prime Minister polished his emollient image.

I have worked for two years to the utmost of my ability in one
direction. I have failed so far. Everything I care for is being
smashed to bits at this moment . . . But I know that the seeds

which I have planted in men's hearts these two years are germinating . . . We shall pass, after much suffering, through deep waters and through storms for the better land for which we hope.[42]

The breakdown in the talks came a day before the strike notices were due to take effect. But, despite the TUC's pious statements of hope that discussions might be resumed, attitudes (on both sides of the argument) had hardened to the point at which a head-on collision could not be averted. Ernest Bevin, who had been a consistently moderating influence during the early discussions, had no doubt as to how the unions should respond to the challenge. It was the TUC's duty to 'fight for the soul of labour and the salvation of the miners'.

The General Strike began at one minute to midnight on 3 May 1926 and lasted for a little less than nine days. The Ministry of Labour estimated that rather more than one and a half million workers, excluding the miners, took part. The TUC put the figure at two million – though some of the strikers only joined the ranks of protest after the battle had been fought for several days. The folklore which was generated by the conflict is more concerned with celebrity strike-breakers than with the strikers themselves – the 'plus-fours brigade' of Cambridge undergraduates who worked in the docks, the members of the Ranelagh Polo Club who acted as special constables and the various aristocrats who humbled themselves by the performance of menial duties. Lady Astor led a group of female volunteers who helped to deliver the Royal Mail and Lady Curzon supervised a car pool on Horse Guards Parade. It was all tremendous fun. But the work of undermining the impact of the strike, and therefore guaranteeing its failure, was done by the usually reticent middle classes.

About three hundred thousand men and women volunteered to work at jobs which had been previously performed by strikers. There was a shortage of volunteers in the north of England and the south of Wales, but in London there was a surplus of offers. By the day on which the General Strike ended, 114,000 men had offered their services in the capital. Only 9,500 had been employed. In the Midlands there were twice as many offers of help as could be accommodated.[43] Outside the coalfields and beyond the trade union movement there was very little sympathy for the miners and, even within the ranks of organised labour, support was far more pronounced among the leaders than the led.

Public opinion was skilfully manipulated by the government. Churchill had sought Baldwin's permission to order the closure of the *Daily Herald*, a draconian measure which the Prime Minister initially would not support on the grounds that the Attorney General had not certified its legality. The job of suppression was, for a time, done on the government's behalf by that paper's journalists, who insisted on striking in sympathy with the miners. They only agreed to resume the production of their paper when they were presented with written authorisation from the TUC.

The TUC published a newsletter of its own, the *British Worker*, and printed between 25,000 and 40,000 copies on each day of the General Strike. Few copies reached the provinces. On the other hand, the *British Gazette* – the government's propaganda sheet produced from the offices of the *Morning Post* – printed provincial editions in Aylesford, Grimsby and Aberdeen. By the end of the strike it was printing over two million copies a day and had achieved what, at the time, was the largest circulation of any newspaper in the world.

The *British Gazette* was edited by Winston Churchill. His colleagues hoped that his enthusiasm for writing headlines and editorials would divert his attention from more dangerous initiatives. The Prime Minister had vetoed his plan to send food supplies from the docks to London warehouses, escorted by tanks along routes protected by machine-gun posts. Churchill also suggested that he take over the day-to-day management of the BBC.[44] Baldwin rejected the idea, with the explanation (which was an excuse) that a change in control would imply a lack of confidence in the Director General.*

Passions, outside Parliament, were beginning to rise. The London docks were paralysed. 'Even the rats are starving,' boasted the striking dockers.[45] The government drafted in troops to act as stevedores and Churchill's convoys – with armoured cars instead of tanks and

*For full accounts of the behaviour of press and BBC during the General Strike see Chapters 10 and 16.

unprotected by machine guns along their route – were, at last, organised. Soldiers, often with fixed bayonets, became a common sight on
the streets of London. Churchill's view (expressed to the Cabinet
Secretary) that 'We are at war and must go through with it' was fast
gaining ground. One or two major incidents made headlines. In
Middlesbrough a crowd of four thousand union sympathisers
attempted to wreck a train by forcing the level-crossing gates and
blocking the line with stolen motor cars. In Aberdeen strikers attacked
buses after the town council decided to revive services with student
drivers and, on 6 May, the General Strike claimed its first death. A bus,
driven by an inexperienced volunteer, was forced onto the pavement
by protesters and a pedestrian was killed.

In other places the strikers behaved with forbearance and good
humour. When a few hotheads in Plymouth pulled a volunteer train
driver from his platform and manhandled him the tension was relieved
by the arrangement of a football match between police and strikers.
The strikers won 2–1.

On the day of the first death the Prime Minister addressed the
nation in a BBC radio broadcast, emphasising that he remained 'a man
of peace'. He drew a sharp distinction between striking against a
company and striking against the government. A draft bill circulated to
the Cabinet outlawed the provision of funds to finance a strike 'which
is intended to coerce or intimidate the community'. Baldwin suggested that it should complete the whole legislative process in a single
day, 11 May.

The Bank of England rejected Churchill's request to freeze all trade
union accounts. So the Chancellor proposed a meeting of the Privy
Council to authorise the impounding of all union funds. The King
wisely advised against. Then a message sent to the Prime Minister in
the name of his private secretary expressed his more general concern
about the

dangers of the PM being rushed by some of his hot-headed colleagues which might have disastrous effects, especially at the
psychological moment when there is but little bitterness of feeling between government and the strikers and the situation seems
hopeful.[46]

The hotheads were, to some degree, cooled by the Government Chief Whip's discovery that most Tory backbenchers were against precip-itous and provocative action.

Ramsay MacDonald had, as his leadership of the Labour Party and the Opposition required, given local public support to the TUC and the miners. But, from start to finish of the dispute, he had been deeply apprehensive about both the propriety and feasibility of a general strike. On the day before it began he wrote in his diary.

> The government has woefully mismanaged the whole business, but the TUC has been equally blameworthy . . . it really looks tonight as if there is to be a general strike to save Mr Cook's face.[47]

Five days later he had come to the conclusion – with more relief than regret – that the General Council had begun to look for an escape route. His diary for 8 May recorded

> TUC General Council Negotiating Committee reported con-ference with a nameless gentleman who is Herbert Samuel . . . Discussed situation with H. Smith and Cook. They will accept temporary adjustment in wages, provided base and subsidies not lowered. Early conversation shows, with greater force, the crim-inality of the government in handling this situation.[48]

On the same day Herbert Samuel – back in England from a holi-day on the Italian Lakes where he had been working on a book entitled *What is Wrong with the World* – turned his mind to a more spe-cific problem and sent the Prime Minister a memorandum which both analysed the causes of the General Strike and suggested a formula which might bring it to an end. The owners' proposals for wage cuts had, he complained, gone far further than anything the Royal Commission had recommended and the government had failed 'to explain to public opinion'[49] that the state of the industry made radical changes essential. Samuel's proposals for a settlement had been devised, during his absence in Italy, by William Beveridge. They amounted to very little – a national wages board with independent members, an advisory committee on reorganisation and a subsidy extended for a bare two weeks. J. H. Thomas, the railwaymen's leader who wanted peace at any price, arranged for Samuel to meet the TUC's National Negotiating Committee.

Samuel expanded his ideas in a letter to the Mining Association which, wisely, he did not post. They included the retention of the national minimum wage and would therefore – despite the notion that reductions might be made at district level – have been unacceptable to the mine owners. The TUC, on the other hand, were attracted by what they had heard of the memorandum. At a meeting on 10 May there was enough support for Samuel's scheme for the TUC to put his proposals to a full meeting of the Miners' Federation that evening. 'Miner after miner got up and, speaking with intensity of feeling, affirmed that the miners could not go back to work on a reduction in wages.'[50] The meeting was adjourned for the miners' executive to deliver its verdict. They would only accept Samuel's formula as merely a basis for discussion if the TUC made clear 'that there should be no revision of the previous wage rates and conditions'.[51] Samuel, notified of the miners' attitude, drafted a letter to the Prime Minister which concluded that the government had no alternative but 'to continue the contest until assent is secured to the wage reductions on the scale suggested in the Report'.[52] Before the letter could be sent he was told that the TUC had asked to meet him once more. The General Council wanted to work out a settlement which they could endorse, with or without the agreement of the Miners' Federation.

Samuel repeated his suggestions to the Negotiating Committee and accepted enough cosmetic amendments to allow the TUC to argue that it had won changes to the proposals which he had sent to the Prime Minister. There was only one brief disagreement. The TUC wanted the final settlement to include a promise of 'no victimisation'. Such a promise was, Samuel said, beyond his powers to give. The gesture having been made, the request was withdrawn.

The TUC met the MFGB on the same evening. It was some time before the substance of the agreement was discussed as the miners insisted on registering a series of objections to the Negotiating Committee excluding them from the earlier discussions. As a result, tempers were frayed before the real business of the meeting began.

Arthur Pugh of the Iron and Steel Federation, and Chairman of the
TUC, told the miners they could 'have it or leave it'. The MFGB, after
two hours deliberation, decided on the second alternative.

Bevin was still not ready to abandon the miners. He suggested that
their leaders be invited to reconsider their repudiation of the TUC's
scheme. Jimmy Thomas, claiming that, until he had the explicit permission of his union, he could not support any action which
prolonged the strike, moved that Bevin's proposal be rejected. It was
about to be debated when a message arrived from Downing Street.
The Prime Minister wished to know if there was any likelihood of the
TUC wanting to see him during the next couple of days. The clear
implication was that if a meeting could not make progress during the
following forty-eight hours the government would impose a solution.
At the time no one thought – at least no one said – that the timing of
the intervention was suspicious. Only later was it discovered that
Jimmy Thomas had told ministers earlier in the day that 'although he
was encountering formidable obstacles, he had high hopes' that a little
more pressure would have the result they desired.[53] The invitation to
Downing Street settled the TUC's collective mind. The General Strike
must end. The next day they would tell the Prime Minister that it was
over.

The TUC told the miners of their decision the following morning.
In a display of generosity which must have shamed the General
Council the MFGB expressed their gratitude for the help which they
had been given up to that point. They then resolved that, for them,
there could be no return to work before they consulted a special delegate conference. No one had any doubt what that meant. The miners
would fight on alone.

The TUC delegation received a less gracious welcome from
Downing Street than its members had expected. The door of Number
10 was barred until they confirmed that the purpose of their visit was
an announcement that the General Strike was over. Once that had
been made clear Baldwin became the peacemaker again. 'All I would
say in answer to that is I thank God for your decision . . . I shall lose
no time in using every endeavour to get the two contending parties
together and do all I can to ensure a just and lasting settlement.'[54] The

promised process did not begin well. The TUC delegation, socialising with ministers in the garden of Number 10 when the official meeting was over, raised fears of victimisation and asked for at least informal assurances that the mine owners would be asked to act magnanimously. Ministers, like Samuel earlier in the week, said that relations within the industry were none of their business. The TUC did not press the point.

The following day Baldwin broadcast to the nation. 'The occasion,' he said, 'calls neither for malice nor for recrimination, nor for triumph.'[55] Nor did it call for the implementation of the Samuel proposals, which the TUC, though not the miners, had been prepared to support. There could be no extension of the subsidy. However, when he met the miners on 13 May, and Herbert Smith implied that a modified version of the Samuel compromise might be acceptable to the union, the Prime Minister dropped a heavy hint. 'I would be quite willing, if I saw the chance of finality, to give help in the interval.'[56] He did not mean it.

On 14 May the government published its serious proposals – reorganisation and amalgamation, a national wages board, restricted recruitment and a welfare levy on coal royalties to fund the installation of pithead baths. The scheme was put to the miners on 18 May. Cook proposed an alternative. He wanted to 'maintain the present wages in the pits' and 'let those who could not afford it go out of business'[57] even though the result would be two hundred thousand men dismissed and unemployed. The union chose to support Cook rather than Baldwin.

The owners were no more conciliatory. They had not changed their position since 1925. The industry's survival depended on a reduction in labour costs. And they added that many of their problems were the direct result of government interference – particularly the Seven Hour Act and the minimum wage levels which had been imposed on them in 1924. Baldwin 'profoundly disagreed' with the employers' contention that the government was to blame, but accepted – without any evidence to support him – that 'while the Miners' Federation remains exactly where it was last July, the colliery owners have made some advances from their original position'. Ramsay MacDonald – still doubtful about both the wisdom and

propriety of the strike but outraged by the 'wicked' newspapers' treatment of the miners – had no doubt that the 'government [is]
abandoning the position of negotiator and coming down against the
men'.[58]

For Baldwin to retain the position of peacemaker it was necessary
for him to move only slowly towards outright support for the mine
owners. So a Cabinet Committee was set up to examine the way forward. Its chairman, Lord Birkenhead, pressed for immediate
legislation. Neville Chamberlain, Minister of Health, argued for an
extension of the working day so that 'women and children come out
of the picture altogether. The whole burden falls on the man and he
is not going to get a lot of sympathy if he is obliged to work as long
as the railwaymen.'[59] The owners then made the offer that convinced
ministers that working time was the essence – no wage cuts for three
months in the more prosperous fields and smaller than anticipated in
the rest if the Seven Hour Act was repealed.

The bill to implement the mine owners' proposals made slow passage through Parliament. Outside the two Houses, philanthropists and
clergy continued to argue for compromise and conciliation. Inside, the
arguments grew increasingly bitter. George Lansbury read out details
of Baldwin's shareholdings in steel and accused him of having a personal financial interest in the miners' humiliation. Someone on the
Labour back benches cried out that the Prime Minister was a murderer. The Member in question was thinking of the destitute miners'
families. When the Eight Hour Bill – extending the working week –
received its third reading, they had lived on charity for six weeks. But
there was no sign of the miners' will breaking.

In early August Baldwin, suffering from mental exhaustion, told the
King that he proposed to take a holiday. Royal objections were overcome by the demeaning provision of medical evidence. Baldwin went
for a month to Aix-les-Bains. Churchill was left in command and
behaved in a way which caused the absent Prime Minister to observe,
'The way to make Ministers moderate is to put them in charge.'[60]
Most of the Cabinet, believing that the miners were on the point of
defeat, thought that the government should simply wait for them to
surrender but Churchill – advocating for the first time 'defiance in
defeat, magnanimity in victory'[61] – busied himself with continual

attempts at conciliation. It was of no avail. The owners were not prepared to yield and the miners were not ready to capitulate. Indeed
they grew increasingly defiant. At the end of September the government offered to reconsider the need for the Eight Hour Act if work
was resumed immediately. The Miners' Federation did not even reply
to the letter. Instead it applied the miners' ultimate sanction. 'Safety
men', who protected pits from fire and flooding, were called out on
strike. The Federation's true position was represented by Herbert
Smith. 'A fair deal I will put up with, but I will not have it crammed
down me.'[62]

In the coalfield starvation was doing the owners' work. Strike pay
had run out. The *Daily Worker* urged readers to contribute five shillings
a week towards a hardship fund. Few did. The All-Union Central
Council of Trade Unions in Moscow offered the miners two hundred
thousand pounds. They felt unable to accept 'red gold'.[63] By mid-
October Nottingham, largely represented by the 'Scabs Union' which
had been formed as a moderate rival to the militant Federation, was
suing for peace. Throughout the country, over two hundred thousand
miners had drifted back to the pits. Resistance was still sufficiently
strong for a proposal for a wage tribunal, with powers to revise district
agreements regulated individually or on the basis of an eight-hour day,
to be defeated in a union ballot by seven hundred thousand votes. But
when an almost identical suggestion was again put to the Federation
a month later it was rejected by only 460,806 to 313,200. Thousands
of despairing miners chose not to vote.[64]

The miners' strike was effectively over. The MFGB instructed
regions to negotiate the best terms they could get. By the end of
November every coalfield was back in production. The eight-hour day
was accepted in South Wales, Scotland and the North East, together
with wage reductions. In Nottingham miners who had joined the
breakaway union were rewarded with wage increases of four shillings
a week. The price paid by the nation included the loss of twenty-eight
million tons of export coal, forty-two million pounds added to the
imports bill and almost a hundred million pounds of lost output. The
miners – the luckiest merely destitute and the activists victimised –
paid a greater price. Despite the hard and dangerous nature of their
trade they were no longer the wage elite of the working classes. Nor

did they have the strength and confidence to fight their own battles. It was a quarter of a century before the National Union of Mineworkers (as the Federation became) was once again a power in the land.

The tragedy of 1926 was that too few people believed in the righteousness of the miners' cause. Fewer still believed that they could win. Cook complained that he had been 'bullied by certain trade union leaders to accept a cut in wages' with a brutality he had rarely experienced in his dispute with the mine owners. But Robert Smillie, the previously extremist President of the Federation who had been replaced by the moderate Herbert Smith, wrote another epitaph for the dispute. 'There never ought to be a stoppage by our people in our industry so long as they can secure fair terms by negotiation.' The world was moving on – and leaving coal, once a vital ingredient of Britain's industrial supremacy, behind.

## CHAPTER SIX

# A Question of Confidence

Bonar (Law) has resigned . . . Very sad for him. He will have unusual sympathy.
Had a letter from Baldwin. Definitely wants me to stay at C.O. and as a member of the Cabinet. Baldwin got very good press.

Diaries of the 9<sup>th</sup> Duke of Devonshire
20 and 23 May 1923

Twice in less than twenty years Conservative governments – displaying their disagreements about free trade – paid the inevitable price of visible disunity. In 1905 A. J. Balfour, leading a government which enjoyed a majority of 131 seats, was harassed by Joe Chamberlain into accepting what he called 'tariff reform'. Four Cabinet ministers resigned and Campbell-Bannerman's Liberals won that year's general election with a majority of eighty-four. In 1923 Stanley Baldwin, Prime Minister after the brief premiership of Andrew Bonar Law, thought that honour required a general election to legitimise his party's renewed belief in protection. The Conservatives had withdrawn from the Lloyd George coalition after Baldwin had swayed a meeting in the Carlton Club by describing Lloyd George as 'a great dynamic force', a phenomenon he characteristically went on to denounce as 'a very terrible thing'. In the general election which followed Labour won fifty previously

Conservative seats and the Liberals forty. The new House of Commons had 259 Tory MPs, 191 Labour Members and 158 Liberals. Nobody doubted that, as soon as Parliament assembled, the government would fall.

There were various attempts – some of them disreputable, others risible – to cobble together an alternative to a Labour administration. They were abandoned for reasons which ranged from high principle to cynical expediency. J. C. C. Davidson – Baldwin's PPS and friend – argued that 'to deprive Labour of their constitutional rights' would be 'the first stop down the road to revolution'.[1] Asquith reasoned that 'if a Labour government is to be tried in this country, as it will be sooner or later, it could hardly be tried under safer conditions'.[2] Crucially King George V judged it 'essential that [Labour's] rights under the constitution be in no way impaired'[3] and he added, 'their ideas are different from ours and they are socialists but they ought to be given a chance and treated fairly'.[4] The King had learned the importance of respecting the will of the people early in his reign. He had succeeded his father, Edward VII, at the height of the most dramatic constitutional crisis of modern times. The House of Lords had rejected the Liberal government's finance bill and ministers – led by Asquith and Lloyd George – were determined to curb its powers. That could only be done by threatening to appoint enough new peers to overthrow the inbuilt Tory majority in the Upper House. Edward VII was asked to endorse the threat and, after some hesitation, accepted that he might have to agree. When he died, George V was persuaded that he must allow it to be known that he too would bow to the will of the House of Commons. From then on, although never impartial, the King recognised the limitations on his power. And, from time to time, he gave his ministers thoroughly good advice.

So, after the Baldwin government was defeated on the House of Commons motion to approve the King's Speech, he sent for Ramsay MacDonald and asked him to form a new administration. Winston Churchill regarded Labour in power as 'a nation's misfortune such as has usually befallen a great state only on the morrow of defeat in war'.[5] Beatrice Webb, who might have been expected to take particular pleasure in victory, celebrated at a 'jolly party, all laughing at the joke of Labour in office'. Many party members thought that minority government was a poisoned chalice which MacDonald should not accept. And MacDonald himself clearly had doubts. His diary entry for 8 December 1923, in a reference to his dead wife, reveals more anxiety than jubilation. 'Ah! Were she here to help me.'[6] But, with the support of Labour's National Executive and Parliamentary Party – both of which institutions were formally consulted – he kissed hands and accepted the King's Commission.

The government which resulted was highly talented, profoundly dedicated and sadly inexperienced. MacDonald became his own Foreign Secretary. The conspicuously high-minded Philip Snowden went to the Treasury, J. H. Thomas, a trade union official, to the Colonial Office and Arthur Henderson – party secretary and member of the wartime coalition – to the Home Office. It had been MacDonald's initial inclination to leave Henderson out of the administration completely. Seven years later, with the second Labour government in crisis, MacDonald was to pay a high price for his insensitivity.

James Ramsay MacDonald was a paradox. The illegitimate son of a Scottish domestic servant, he had become the intellectual force, as well as the organising genius, behind the creation of the Labour Party. He, perhaps more than anyone else, takes credit for steering Labour away from Marxism. With years and experience his moderation increased. But the old pacifist instinct remained. The real change – which dictated the politics which were to make him anathema to Labour – was the agonising fear that the interests of his party and the class it represented were in conflict with the needs of the nation as a whole. It was a sense of duty, as well as personal vanity, which made him an apostate.

George V was, at least initially, prepared to give his new ministers the benefit of the doubt – particularly Ramsay MacDonald. 'He impressed me very much,' the King wrote. 'He wishes to do the right thing.' But he added, 'Today 23 years ago, dear Grandmama died. I wonder what she would have thought of a Labour government.'[7] There is little doubt that she would have been impressed with the new Prime Minister's insistence that his Cabinet observe strict Court protocol when attending meetings of the Privy Council. But MacDonald was also determined to repair Britain's damaged relations with the Soviet Union. And that policy would have offended Queen Victoria as much as it infuriated her grandson.

MacDonald did not propose the immediate restoration of full diplomatic relations. Initially he did no more than invite a trade delegation to London. Its leader was not afforded full ambassadorial status, but was required to be content in the rank of chargé d'affaires. But even that provoked an outburst from the King, who hoped that the Prime Minister 'would do nothing to compel him to shake hands with the murderers of his relations'.[8] The Tsarina – killed at Ekaterinburg and her body thrown down a mine-shaft – was one of Queen Victoria's numerous grandchildren.

Perhaps, despite his initial call for fair play, the King had always been apprehensive about the election of a Labour government. Certainly by June he was antagonistic to all it stood for and, according to Neville Chamberlain – Minister of Health in Baldwin's defeated government – 'his language about the Labour Party was vicious'.[9] It all added to the general fear that, even though MacDonald could be trusted, the men and women around him would force his government to adopt near-Bolshevik policies. The concern was misplaced. The whole Cabinet, knowing their tenure to be temporary, proceeded with caution. One of the arguments that MacDonald had used to convince the Labour Party that he should form a government was the explanation that a brief period in office would guarantee the status of official opposition. It all added to his instincts for 'responsibility'. Meanwhile the Conservative Party just waited for a return to what it regarded as the natural order of things. It came during the summer of 1924.

The 25 July issue of the *Workers' Weekly*, an unofficial publication of the Communist Party, published an article which called upon soldiers 'to let it be known that neither in class war nor in military war will you turn your guns on fellow workers'. Five days later the Director of Public Prosecutions – who, not being a regular subscriber to the magazine, must have had the offending sentiments brought to his notice – advised Sir Patrick Hastings, the Attorney General, that, in his view, the paper's editor had committed an offence under the Incitement to Mutiny Act. Hastings, a fashionable lawyer but a recent recruit to politics, agreed to prosecute. John Campbell, the *Workers' Weekly* editor, was duly arrested and charged.

The Parliamentary Labour Party was outraged. Jimmy Maxton, the 'Red Clydeside' MP, announced in the House of Commons that the article exactly reflected his position. Calmer opponents of the prosecution pointed out that Campbell was only the acting editor and that he was 'a man who had both feet almost blown off in the war, who had fought through the war from beginning to end and who had been decorated for exceptional gallantry'.[10]

Law officers of the Crown acting in their legal capacity are supposed to be influenced neither by politics nor politicians and Sir Patrick Hastings, in deciding on the prosecution of Campbell, had followed that golden rule. But members of the Labour Cabinet felt no obligation to protect the Attorney General's independent status. When Campbell offered to apologise and retract his call to mutiny ministers persuaded – or coerced – Hastings into dropping the prosecution. He did so before the letter of apology was received and the Opposition, scenting blood, alleged that the Prime Minister had personally perverted the course of justice.

Incompetence combined with arrogance to prevent the government making the clear statement which might have drawn a line under the whole affair. Damaging Parliamentary questions were followed by a motion of censure tabled by the Conservatives, while the Liberals proposed an amendment calling for a Select Committee to inquire into the whole affair. MacDonald decided, from the start, to regard both the resolution and the amendment as votes of confidence – assuming that, the Opposition being split, the government would survive. Towards the end of the debate, on 8 October, Stanley Baldwin announced that his party would vote against its own motion and for the Liberal amendment. The government was defeated by 364 votes to 198. Ramsay MacDonald resigned the next day. The general election was to be held on 29 October. It was to include one of the most contentious episodes in British electoral history.

Early in the morning of Saturday 25 October, Jimmy Thomas – staying the night with Philip Snowden after speaking in his Colne Valley constituency – woke his host with the cry, 'We're bunkered.'[11] That morning the *Daily Mail*'s front page was led by the banner headline

'Moscow Order to our Reds. Great Plot Disclosed'. There followed
the 'revelation' of a 'secret letter of instruction from Moscow to the
British Communist Party' signed by Grigori Zinoviev, the President of
the Comintern. It urged the British proletariat to rise up against the
bourgeoisie's attempt to prevent the ratification of treaties of friendship between Britain and the Soviet Union. Its authenticity was put in
doubt by laughable references to the 'military sections of the British
Communist Party'. But the *Daily Mail* claimed, with apparent conviction, that Ramsay MacDonald and Arthur Henderson had received
copies of the Zinoviev letter 'some weeks ago'.

Copies of the letter had certainly come into the possession of the
Foreign Office shortly after 15 September, the date on which it was
allegedly signed and sent. It had arrived courtesy of the group of
White Russian émigrés who had written it in cooperation with
employees of Conservative Central Office and members of the
Intelligence Service. But, at the time, the Foreign Office, although sus-
pecting that the letter was a hoax, could not be certain that it was not
genuine. For some time they did nothing. Then, realising that sooner
or later it was bound to become public property, they released copies
together with a protest to the USSR's chargé d'afffaires in London.
The decision to announce the letter's existence was taken on 22
October. The *Daily Mail*'s 'scoop' appeared twenty-four hours before
the decision was implemented. The protest note added to the story's
apparent veracity.

Ramsay MacDonald, still Prime Minister, attracted personal criticism by agreeing that the Foreign Office thought the letter genuine,
yet implying that he believed the diplomats to be wrong. The whole
incident enabled the party which he led to convince itself that it had
been cheated out of office. No doubt 'the Red scare' contributed to
the size of Labour's defeat. But the government was doomed from the
start of the campaign. In one respect, Labour triumphed. Its total vote
rose by over a million. The Tories' support increased by twice as much,
giving them 412 Members in the new House of Commons to
Labour's 151.

The years between the first two Labour governments were notable for
three great political events – the return to the gold standard (which

amounted to the revaluation of the pound), the General Strike and the belated achievement of universal suffrage. The voting age for women was lowered from thirty to twenty-one – by mistake. William Joynson-Hicks, the Home Secretary, promised to support 'the flapper vote' (in a moment of uncharacteristic exuberance) during a rowdy public meeting and the Cabinet decided that honour required the fulfilment of his unauthorised change in policy. Five million new names were added to the electoral register. It is assumed, though there is no proof, that they had a profound influence on the next general election.

The campaign, which was to culminate on 30 May 1929, was dominated by arguments about the parties' rival remedies for unemployment – an issue that, despite its crucial importance, rarely set politics alight. Labour polled fewer votes than the Conservatives (8,370,417 to 8,656,225) but won more seats (287 to 261). MacDonald, returning to London from his County Durham constituency, was greeted at King's Cross by a cheering crowd estimated to be twelve thousand strong.[12] On 5 June he became Prime Minister for the second time.

For a few days he thought of becoming his own Foreign Secretary again. But pressure from colleagues convinced him that Arthur Henderson both wanted the job and must be given it. The delay in gratifying Henderson's ambition was to increase the animosity which – when the ultimate crisis came two years later – was to play a major part in bringing down the government. Prime Ministers in trouble need friends, but Prime Ministers in the glow of victory rarely prepare to meet the dark days ahead. MacDonald, having settled the great office of state, turned his mind to placating the left wing of the Parliamentary Party. Despite his success as Health Minister in 1924 there could be no question of John Wheatley – whose house-building programme had been the government's only real achievement – returning to the Cabinet. He was 'too far on the left'. The token radical was George Lansbury, the veteran ex-leader of Poplar Council who had defied the law in order to pay the unemployed a higher rate of benefit than the government prescribed. He became First Commissioner of Works. As well as the usual duties of supervising the Royal Parks and maintaining the fabric of public buildings, he was made a member of the committee which the Prime Minister set up to investigate ways of surmounting the nation's most pressing problem. It was to be chaired by Jimmy Thomas, the Lord Privy Seal, who, the *Manchester Guardian* reported, had

> been placed at the head of an organisation which will survey and tackle with energy the most practical means of dealing with unemployment . . . not merely by relief works but by . . . national reconstruction.[13]

Lansbury was made chairman of a sub-committee which examined two policies that had been promised in Labour's manifesto. Each had been advocated on its own merits. Both had the added advantage of reducing unemployment. Raising the school leaving age would take fourteen-year-olds out of the labour market and require the recruitment of more teachers. Introducing a retirement pension for industrial workers was estimated to create between 220,000 and 310,000 job vacancies. Lansbury's sub-committee calculated that a pension of one pound a week, paid at sixty with an additional ten shillings for a dependent wife, would cost £21.6 million in the first year, gradually falling to £10.5 million in year five. By the standards of the time they were massive sums of money. In the Cabinet meeting which discussed the scheme, Jimmy Thomas – Snowden's ally in the campaign for 'economy' – opposed the recommendations of his own sub-committee. It was defeated.[14]

One member of the Committee – Sir Oswald Mosley, the Chancellor of the Duchy of Lancaster – was not prepared to let matters rest. He had been elected to Parliament as a Conservative in 1918 but had crossed the floor in 1924 and become the advocate of an economic policy which was at least a forebear of Roosevelt's New Deal and Keynes' belief in stimulating investment and extending purchasing to increase effective demand.

Mosley was an unlikely – though for a while an enthusiastic – Labour MP. After Sandhurst he joined the 17th Lancers, a regiment commanded by his cousin, who was also England's premier polo player. But he transferred to the Royal Flying Corps and ended the war with what he called an 'aviator's limp'. He fenced with enthusiasm, hunted with passion and regarded women as created to serve and satisfy men. Attlee once said that Mosley always addressed him in the manner of the lord of the manor rebuking a negligent under-gardener.

Shortly after Mosley joined the Labour Party he had set out (with typical pretension) what he called the 'Birmingham Proposals' and he had argued for its adoption as Labour policy in the Cabinet sub-committee, claiming that his plan would create three hundred thousand jobs at a cost of three hundred million pounds. His scheme – opposed most strongly by Snowden, Thomas and Herbert Morrison, the young rising star who had been made Minister of Transport – was dismissed out of hand when he put it before the Cabinet. Mosley resigned. But he chose to go out with a bang. There was a 'personal statement' in the House of Commons and a long speech in the unemployment debate which followed. At the Labour Party's annual conference in Llandudno he challenged the leadership's orthodoxy and nearly won the day. The Mosley Memorandum was defeated by only 1,251,000 votes to 1,046,000 – after Lansbury, who personally supported its proposals, loyally accepted collective responsibility and urged the conference to endorse the National Executive's rejection of the presumptuous newcomer's unrealistic plan. A party unwilling to reduce unemployment by introducing an industrial pension was not ready for a massive programme of public investment.

With or without an industrial pension, the cost of social security rose inexorably year by year. The cause of the increase was the fast-increasing level of unemployment. In January 1929 the figure stood at 1,433,000 A year later it was 1,533,000. During 1930 the total escalated to 1,731,000 in March, 1,940,000 in June and 2,725,000 by December. In June 1931 it had reached 2,735,000 – almost double the figure which the Labour government had inherited.

A month earlier in Vienna, the Kreditanstalt Bank had collapsed, setting off a wave of speculation against the German, as well as the Austrian, mark. The Allies were about to pay the economic price for the vindictive peace they had imposed at Versailles. The Reich Chancellor, visiting the Prime Minister at Chequers, warned that confidence could not be restored while the German economy was held back by the heavy burden of reparation. MacDonald, who had always believed that the level of the reparations was morally wrong, welcomed the opportunity to argue for their moderation. His letter to

Henry Stimson, America's Secretary of State, suggested no more than some sort of rescue operation to underwrite the German mark. President Hoover responded with the suggestion of a reparation moratorium. The French had other ideas. They proposed that the reparations should be paid and then returned to Germany in the form of a loan. While 'the powers' haggled, the crisis of confidence deepened. The moratorium was not agreed until 6 July. When, on 19 August, the German banks froze foreign exchange there was an immediate run on sterling.

Even before July and August, fears that the cost of rising unemployment would provoke a crisis had raised the thought that, if or when it came, only a coalition government would be able to avert disaster. The precedent was 1916. In times of national disaster politicians should put aside party loyalties and work in partnership. And there were severe doubts about Labour's competence to tackle the crisis alone – even among the Labour leadership. 'Molly' Hamilton, the daughter of a Scottish university professor, who had become the Prime Minister's close, though platonic, friend, was reported as saying that Baldwin had visited MacDonald in March and offered to serve in a national government. But, since the report came from Hugh Dalton – then Under Secretary at the Foreign Office but eventually Chancellor in Attlee's government – it was almost certainly an exaggeration. Dalton was notorious for improving history. However, by the summer, the idea was beginning to be taken seriously by serious politicians. Viscount Stonehouse, the Conservative Party Chairman, told Baldwin that MacDonald 'thought that a national government should be formed'.[15] Neville Chamberlain believed that the Opposition 'did not wish to be forced to vote against . . . the reform of unemployment benefit and a tariff'.[16] Baldwin himself believed that the idea was gaining enough ground to require him to dismiss the notion as both dangerous and fanciful, and he warned Chamberlain that 'the party would not stand it.' He then told a public meeting in Hull on 17 July that a formal coalition 'such as existed during the war'[17] was neither necessary nor possible. But he was ready to support the Labour government if it took the right decisions – a cut in unemployment benefits and the imposition of a tariff on 'foreign' goods.

The pressure – on the pound, on MacDonald and in favour of a

Two prime ministers at a memorial service: David Lloyd George (right), 'a dynamic force'. Stanley Baldwin (left), who thought 'a dynamic force is a very terrible thing'. *Getty Images*

James Ramsay MacDonald leads the coalition government to victory on the slogan 'The Captain who stood by the ship'. *Getty Images*

The Sinn Fein committee on the eve of the Irish Civil War. Éamon de Valéra is in the centre of the front row; Michael Collins is on his left. *Getty Images*

Jawaharlal Nehru (left), the brains behind the Congress movement, needed Mahatma Gandhi (right) to inspire India 'like a beam of light that pierces the darkness'. *Getty Images*

A. J. Cook – General Secretary of the Miners' Federation. An actor not a negotiator.
*Getty Images*

There were many unemployment marches to London. Only Jarrow – untainted by political intrigue – was a crusade. *Getty Images*

King Edward VIII and Mrs
Wallis Simpson. The crowds in
Dubrovnik, having read of the
relationship in American
magazines, cried '*Zivila ljubav*'
– 'long live love'. *Popperfoto*

Winston Churchill in 1939. The long wait was almost over. *Popperfoto*

Henry Moore wanted to break out from subservience to the artistic values of Greece and Rome. *Getty Images*

Jacob Epstein, with a bust of Paul Robeson. He compared criticism of his sculptures with the persecution of Michelangelo in Florence. *Getty Images*

Ezra Pound – according to T. S. Eliot, 'attracted to the Middle Ages by every thing except that which gave them significance'. *Time & Life Pictures/Getty Images*

T. S. Eliot. 'I will show you fear in a handful of dust.' *Popperfoto*

On the advice of the Foreign Office, the England football team gave the Nazi salute. *The Times* applauded their courtesy. *Popperfoto*

Harold Abraham – at the 1924 Olympic Games – wins the 100 metres in 10.52 seconds and becomes the most exulted runner in the history of British athletics. *Popperfoto*

Douglas Jardine leads out the MCC to start the second Test Match of the 'bodyline series'. The Australian batsmen 'made sentimental farewells to each batsman as they made their way out'. *Getty Images*

When Fred Perry turned professional – after three consecutive victories at Wimbledon – his honorary membership of the All England Club was immediately revoked. *Popperfoto*

national government – built up after the publication of three unfortunately timed reports – the Interim Report of the Royal Commission on Unemployment Insurance,* the Macmillan Report on Finance and Industry and (most influential of all ) the May Committee, set up at the instigation of the Liberal Party. The Royal Commission, re-examining eligibility for unemployment benefit, published an interim report on 4 June. Eligibility and cost are indivisible issues. It recommended an increase in contributions and lower benefit payments – both anathema to Labour. MacDonald told the Parliamentary Labour Party that the government rejected both proposals and was equally opposed to reducing the period during which benefit was paid. The Prime Minister demonstrated his sincerity by introducing a bill which, by increasing borrowing powers, liquidated the deficit on 'the fund' without recourse to either of the Royal Commission's expedients.

Nine days later, the Macmillan Report was published. It said little that was new. But it did draw public attention to the fact about the British economy which politicians chose to ignore. Britain's balance of trade in manufactured goods had been in deficit – with three aberrant exceptions – in every year since 1822. The balance of payments had been kept in surplus by 'invisibles' – banking, shipping, insurance and interest on investment. And invisible earnings had been hit hardest by the wartime expedients.

Argument persists about the Macmillan Report's effect on international confidence. Before its publication the Bank of England was increasing its stock of gold. In the fortnight which followed the stock diminished by thirty-three million pounds and as much was lost in foreign exchange before a fifty-million-pound credit,[18] raised in France and the United States, steadied sterling. The sudden run on sterling may have been a coincidence rather than a consequence of the report. Two days before it was published George V's private secretary – without any foreknowledge of the report's findings – thought it wise to prepare the King for a constitutional innovation. 'A minority gov-

---

*The twenty-year argument about the unemployment benefit – level and eligibility – is discussed in Chapter 7.

ernment will hardly be able to deal with the [financial] situation and it is quite possible that Your Majesty might be asked to approve of a national government.'[19]

It was the third report, presented to the Cabinet on 30 July, which did most damage. Back in February Liberals in the House of Commons had sought to amend a government resolution which reiterated the Chancellor's determination to stabilise the economy. The amendment, which demanded the creation of an independent committee to 'examine all possible and legitimate reductions in public expenditure', was accepted as the price to be paid for Liberal support. A committee was set up under the chairmanship of Sir George May, formerly the Secretary of the Prudential Assurance Company. It reported in a bad week.

Bank-rate had been raised to 3.5 per cent on 23 July and on 30 July, the day the report was received, it was increased to 4.5 per cent. Both steps were thought necessary to reinforce the stabilising effect of the Franco-American loan. In between the two adjustments Treasury officials had warned the Chancellor of the Exchequer that 'the gold exodus is unprecedented . . . Unless we take such steps as are open to us to rectify the situation, there is a real danger of our being driven off the gold standard.' Then the May Committee published its calculation that there would soon be a budget deficit of £120 million.

The alternative was devaluation. Although Ernest Bevin – giving evidence to May for the TUC – had half-heartedly advocated a reduction in the value of the pound, the Cabinet had never even considered it. For reasons which ranged from ignorance to timidity, every member took it for granted that it was essential to remain on the gold standard at the pre-war parity. That required foreign creditors to maintain their faith in the pound and in the prudence of a government which regarded the exchange rate as sacrosanct. That, May suggested, could only be achieved by a massive reduction of public spending including a sixty-seven-million-pound cut in unemployment benefit – the glory of Asquith's pre-war government which, being theoretically financed by contributions, was a 'right' which saved men who lost their jobs from the Poor Law and the workhouse.

Ramsay MacDonald consulted Keynes, who answered that 'it is nearly *certain* that we shall go off the existing gold parity at no distant date'[20] – though, as later became clear, he was by no means certain that the government should anticipate what was almost inevitable. The May Committee, he complained, wanted to bring incomes down to the level of prices – deflation followed by depression. He advocated expansion. While MacDonald considered Keynes' advice, the crisis deepened. Between 4 and 11 August the Bank of England spent eleven million pounds of reserves and ten million pounds of the foreign loan attempting to shore up the pound. The Chancellor told the Prime Minister

> The action of the three central banks in arranging the £50 credit has not had the desired effect and the bank is still losing gold and foreign exchange very heavily. At the present rate the point of exhaustion will come very soon with disastrous consequences . . . the most experienced bankers and financiers attribute [the] root cause to the belief of foreigners that our budgeting position is unsound. Until it is remedied or until we are taking drastic steps to put it right this unease abroad will continue.[21]

MacDonald, behaving with the kind of insouciance no modern Prime Minister would dare display, left London for Scotland. He had barely arrived in Lossiemouth when he received, from Snowden, a copy of a letter written to the Chancellor by the Deputy (and acting) Governor of the Bank of England. A 'rapid adjustment of the budgetary position'[22] was essential. Snowden's covering note emphasised the urgent need for action. 'We cannot allow matters to drift into utter chaos and we are perilously near that.'[23] It was agreed that the economic committee of the Cabinet should examine the May Committee's diagnosis and prescription. It met on 12 August and was greeted by the news that the May Committee had underestimated the deficit. The Treasury calculated that it would rise not to £120 but to £170 million.

The press were told that the government was of 'one mind' in its determination to balance the budget, [24] though it is not clear whether it was thought necessary for maintaining irrational international confidence or if, for a time, the Prime Minister believed that, in principle, expenditure should not exceed income. There was a second meeting

on 13 August and a third on 17. By then the disagreements were out
in the open. They included the Chancellor's rejection of the Prime
Minister's suggestion of a 'revenue tax' – a levy on imports, which was
no more than a badly disguised tariff.

After strong advocacy by Snowden the economic committee of the
Cabinet considered adopting what amounted to the full May package.
It included £90 million to be raised from increased taxation (most on
unearned income) and a cut of £99 million in public expenditure.
The main reductions were to be £67 million from unemployment
insurance and £12 million from education. The standard rate of
unemployment benefit was to be cut by 20 per cent, saving £15 million, contributions were to be increased so as to raise an additional
£10 million and £23 million* was to be 'saved' by ending the Treasury
grant towards the cost of transitional benefit – payments which followed the exhaustion of unemployment insurance and postponed the
necessity of national assistance.

The committee accepted the basis of the Treasury's proposals
but made a series of modifications to the figures. Insurance was to
be cut by £43.5 rather than £67 million, the transitional benefit by
£20 rather than £23 million and the rate was to remain unchanged.
Increased contributions were to raise the insurance fund income
by £10 million[†] and the same amount was to be saved by cutting the
period during which benefit was received. Henderson proposed
the introduction of a 'benefit premium' – a cut by a more palatable
name, which required the deduction of a pound a week from all
payments. By the standards of the time, and when measured against
the principles of the Labour Party, it was a tough package. But at first
it seemed that it had been unanimously accepted. Indeed the
Cabinet Secretary's minute reported unanimity. But Henderson and
Graham (the President of the Board of Trade) insisted that they had
agreed to do no more than 'reserve their position' until the full
Cabinet meeting.

---

*For a fuller description of transitional benefit, see page 156.
†These and subsequent figures of cuts – proposed and adopted – are taken from
David Marquand's biography of Ramsay MacDonald.

The Prime Minister believed that the official opposition should be told of the government's determination to avoid the crisis of which May warned. Not all of his colleagues agreed. But MacDonald insisted on talking to Baldwin and Neville Chamberlain, at least in general terms. The two men prepared themselves for the meeting by asking advice from a group of bankers who had already warned them that catastrophe was close. According to the ever-faithful Davidson, they repeated their dire prediction and said

> plainly 1) that we were on the edge of the abyss and unless the situation changed we would be over it directly. 2) that the cause of the trouble was not financial but political and lay in the complete want of confidence in HMG existing among foreigners. 3) the remedy was in the hands of the government alone.[25]

Although MacDonald kept his word to the Cabinet and spoke only in general terms Chamberlain guessed that the deficit was greater than the May Committee had calculated and Baldwin had concluded that the remedies which the government prescribed would be less stringent than those that May had recommended. Chamberlain – writing in the patronising tone which offended his friends almost as much as it infuriated his enemies – claimed that Baldwin 'asked no intelligent questions' and 'made no helpful suggestions'. He excused his chief's inadequacy with the hope that it was the result of a proper determination 'not to be drawn into something'.[26] Davidson, on the other hand, thought that Baldwin 'went out of his way to indicate that the Tory Party would take a helpful line'.[27] The true extent of the help was revealed in a letter which Baldwin sent to Chamberlain before he left for his summer holiday in Aix-les-Bains. It laid down the rules of engagement to be observed in his absence.

> In the long view it is all to the good that the Govt have to look after their own chickens as they come home to roost and get a lot of dirt cleared up before we come in . . . To have the consequences of their finances exposed – and acknowledged to the world – within four months of the budget would be a wonderful

lesson. We must not forget on the platform that the Liberals are just as much responsible for the crisis as the government.[28]

The Cabinet met on 19 August. The official minutes record MacDonald's opening remarks.

> The Prime Minister and Chancellor of the Exchequer explained the grave character of the financial position, the reasons for immediate action and the various measures required to secure budgetary equilibrium which, in the view of the committee, must be taken forthwith if public confidence at home and abroad is to be re-established.[29]

There was no dissent from that proposition. No one questioned the need, one way or another, to remain on the gold standard and to eliminate the budget deficit. Only the methods by which that end could be attained were in dispute. However the Cabinet's first conclusion was unanimously agreed. 'The budget must be balanced by the application of common sacrifices and effort.'

At first, it was taken for granted that unemployment insurance payments must be maintained at their existing level. But, in order to avoid the £20 million saving on transitional benefit, a sub-committee (chaired by Margaret Bondfield, the Minister of Labour) was instructed to examine the feasibility of reducing government spending by the same amount but in other ways. It was specifically asked to consider the consequences of adding twopence to national insurance contributions, and the revenue which could be raised from the 'Henderson premium'. A straightforward cut in benefit rates might be avoided, at least in part, by a cut in benefit rates made more acceptable by a different name.

The Prime Minister remained devoted to the introduction of a revenue tariff and accepted Henderson's proposal that the idea should be put to the vote – a highly unusual Cabinet procedure and proof that MacDonald was not in full command. Ten ministers voted for its imposition on manufactured goods, five against. A motion proposing its application to all imports, including food, was defeated by the same margin. Some of the supporters of import duties made clear that they regarded the assault on free trade as no more than a temporary and desperate expedient. But Philip Snowden said that he would not have 'protection' on any terms, for any purpose or for any length of time. In the febrile atmosphere of a Cabinet desperate to avoid catastrophe, there was always the risk of resignation. And the Chancellor of the Exchequer was a proud man. Ramsay MacDonald could not risk losing him at the height of the crisis. Because of Snowden's effective veto, confirmation of the revenue tariff was postponed until the next meeting which, the Prime Minister announced, would be held two days later.

Snowden's opposition to protection was based on deep conviction. He was a liberal of the old school, to whom free trade was sacred. Any policy which might be described as a palliative rather than a cure he dismissed as immoral as well as inexpedient. Fiscal rectitude was his gospel and he suited exactly his Colne Valley constituency where the Labour Club was teetotal and prohibited card games. He was the first 'iron chancellor' – inflexible as well as strong.

Cabinets facing economic crises almost always behave in the same way. They return, time and time again, to the consideration of remedies they know to be impractical and they avoid, for as long as possible, accepting the unpalatable solution which, in their more realistic moments, they know to be necessary. The weaker members recriminate and dissemble. The stronger behave with intolerable condescension towards their colleagues who have lost faith and nerve. The MacDonald Cabinet was no different in all these respects from any other. But, in one important particular, it faced a problem which was unique in twentieth-century British politics. It was part of a minority government. As well as satisfying the demands of its members' consciences, and international confidence, it had to convince its political opponents that it was doing the right thing. Without the public support of the Conservatives and Liberals all hopes of saving the pound and remaining on the gold standard were doomed. The time for generalities had passed. The rival parties had to be given details of the recovery plan and asked for explicit support.

MacDonald and Snowden, Prime Minister and Chancellor, met the opposition leaders on 20 August and described to them both the extent of the problem and the government's proposed remedies. The Liberals immediately called for 'drastic action'. Neville Chamberlain was more precise. The government's response to the crisis was 'inadequate'. The Conservative Party 'could not possibly contemplate the imposition of new taxes to the order of £100 million'.[30] The necessary cuts were, he estimated, at least £30 million more than the £78 million that the government contemplated.

The Cabinet met again in the hope that Margaret Bonfield's committee had conjured a solution out of a cut in the transitional benefit. They were worse than disappointed. The Minister of Labour was, she explained, personally opposed to the cut since it would result in able-bodied men being forced to live off the Poor Law. However, her committee had faithfully worked through the figures. Means-testing transitional benefit might save £5 million. A flat-rate reduction would produce barely £4 million. Her mandate had been to find savings of £20 million.

It was then that MacDonald came to believe that the savings necessary to balance the budget could only be obtained by a reduction in unemployment benefit payments. What had been unthinkable when it was demanded by the Conservative opposition had become the only alternative to withdrawal from the gold standard. History has made much of the ministers' failure to think outside the terms of a policy which had been introduced, amidst some controversy, only six years earlier. But the real blame lies with the economists of the period. Robert Skidelsky, in his monumental biography of Keynes, speculates that 'perhaps [he] was held back by an ingrained patriotism from actually urging or even possibly wanting devaluation'[31] while Hubert Henderson (an academic economist far closer to the MacDonald government's thinking) judged that the choice was between staying with gold and a 'complete collapse of the currency, after the mark and the rouble'. He recommended staying with gold and MacDonald 'was happy to accept excuses for inaction delivered in a Scottish accent'.[32] Perhaps both men were simply saying that it was necessary to maintain international confidence, even if that required policy decisions which were, in other ways, absurd. Labour governments are always, at moments of crisis, required to repudiate Labour policies. That was the economic advice to the Cabinet in 1976 and was, no doubt, the case forty-five years earlier. Neither Keynes nor Henderson had much sympathy with Treasury orthodoxy. Both had strong connections with the radical wing of the Liberal Party. Since they did not advocate devaluation it is not surprising that the Cabinet regarded it as unthinkable.

Some ministers felt the same about cuts in unemployment benefit. By the time the idea was discussed the dissidents included Arthur Henderson, in effect the deputy Prime Minister, whose mind had been changed by a meeting with the TUC. He was not so much opposed to the policy itself as to the result its adoption would have on the Labour movement. He predicted a split. Ramsay MacDonald was loftily dismissive of such narrow considerations. His duty was to the nation, not to the party.

Despite the bitter disagreements about the whole idea, the Cabinet considered three possible reductions in benefit payments which would increase the savings on national insurance from £22 million to double that amount. A cut of 11.5 per cent would save £15 million and might be justified by the explanation that it reflected the fall in the cost of living since the Labour Party took office. Neither the figure nor the justification appealed to the Cabinet. A 5 per cent cut (yielding £6 million) was clearly insufficient. A reduction of 10 per cent (yielding £12.5 million) was considered and rejected. The Cabinet was in stalemate. The Prime Minister 'told them that their proposals were now impossible but that we should consult the representatives of the Bank of England and of the other two political parties'.[33]

Chamberlain had already told MacDonald that a reduction of £78 million would not be enough, and he was entitled to assume that another call to Downing Street meant that the government had gone at least some way towards meeting his demands. No doubt to his astonishment, his host announced that the figures had been revised down to a total reduction of £56 million. The only response he found possible was a question. What would happen if the adjustment proved inadequate and sterling continued to lose value? Snowden could only reply 'the deluge'.[34] In the decency of a subsequently arranged private meeting Chamberlain – supported by Herbert Samuel representing Lloyd George, who had been restored to the Liberal Party leadership but was indisposed by illness – spoke more frankly. If MacDonald put his modified proposal to the House of Commons the combined forces of the opposition would bring the government down. The Prime Minister was thus left with three options. He could make bigger cuts in public expenditure, allow his government to be driven out of office and replaced by a Conservative–Liberal coalition or form a coalition of his own. There is no doubt that the coalition idea was in his mind. But during the crucial third week in August 1931 he still behaved as if he hoped to avoid both that desperate expedient and the even more unattractive alternative – relinquishing office.

The Cabinet met again on Friday 21 August. The stalemate was not broken so a further meeting was arranged for the following day – increasing the feeling of crisis which frequent Cabinet meetings always engender amongst both ministers and the general public. At the second meeting the Prime Minister again proposed cuts of £76 million – only 2.5 million less than the figure which ministers had already rejected and £20 million more than the total which he was still not sure they would accept. The Cabinet minute which described where the cuts would fall was unusually imprecise – '£12½ million by a 10 per cent reduction in unemployment benefit and £7½ million in other ways'.[35]

MacDonald's proposal was rejected, though Snowden and Thomas (by formally registering their dissent from the Cabinet's conclusion) established their position as the Prime Minister's unwavering allies. Other ministers confirmed their infirmity of purpose by agreeing that the Bank of England should be invited to discover if the cuts which the Cabinet had refused to make would so satisfy international confidence that the Federal Reserve (the central bank of the United States) would offer sufficient credit to stabilise the pound. MacDonald had clearly made up his mind that, until the crisis was conquered, he would remain in government – one way or another. The time had come to see the King.

Fortunately the King was on his way back south from Scotland. He had left Sandringham for Balmoral barely twenty-four hours earlier, after receiving advice from his Prime Minister that a change of plan might precipitate a panic in the markets. However, within hours of his arrival, a message from MacDonald had reached the castle. It might be necessary for him to make a swift return to London. Clive Wigram, the King's private secretary, recalled how George V reacted. He said 'that there was no use shilly-shallying on an occasion like this and he would proceed south that night'.[36] Exhibiting a devotion to duty which, five years later, was to be contrasted with his son's reckless negligence, he was back in Buckingham Palace by half-past eight on the morning of Sunday 23 August. MacDonald had audience two hours later.

There was still no certainty that the Federal Reserve would offer the essential credit and MacDonald warned the King that (even if the facility were guaranteed) Henderson, Graham and possibly other members of the Cabinet might well resign rather than make the necessary cuts in public expenditure. The Prime Minister's own account of the reply which he received, although reflecting the self-esteem which was an increasing feature of his character, correctly conveys the substance of the King's response.

> King most friendly and expressed thanks and confidence. I told him that after tonight I might be of no further use and should resign with the whole Cabinet. He asked if I would advise him to send for Henderson. I said 'No', which he said relieved him. I advised him in the meantime to send for the leaders of the other two parties and have them report the position from their point of view. He said he would and would advise them strongly to support me. I explained my hopeless parliamentary position if there were any number of resignations. He said that he believed I was the only person who could carry the country through.[37]

It was not only the King who had thought it expedient to return to London. Stanley Baldwin – who had resisted the idea of postponing his holiday – had been persuaded by Neville Chamberlain that he must be ready to respond to the government's imminent collapse. Before MacDonald put together his final package of cuts both the Tory leader and his nominated representative were strongly opposed to the creation of a coalition. Chamberlain welcomed, and wanted to deepen, the split in the Labour Party. Baldwin made clear that 'having destroyed one coalition' in 1922 he 'did not want to create another one'.[38] Indeed, on 23 August – when he, like the King, had just

returned to London – he spent much of the day discussing the composition of a new Tory government with Geoffrey Dawson, the editor
of *The Times*. The two men had lunch together at the Travellers' Club.
In consequence the summons to Buckingham Palace did not reach
Baldwin until the early afternoon. So, in defiance of parliamentary
procedure, Herbert Samuel – still representing the Liberals – saw the
King before the official leader of the opposition had audience.

Samuel was categoric. By far the best solution would be the Prime
Minister's continuation in office until the crisis had passed – if necessary with a reconstructed Cabinet. If that was not possible MacDonald
should be persuaded to lead a national government formed explicitly
to save sterling and committed to resigning as soon as that job was
done. The worst possibility, Samuel argued, was a Baldwin administration. There would be little or no support among the working class
for a Tory government put in office to cut unemployment benefit. The
King – who already believed that MacDonald was the only man who
could save the pound – was convinced. Baldwin was persuaded that,
in the national interest, he must both support the idea of a coalition
and agree to serve in it when it was formed.

At seven o'clock on the evening of 23 August the Cabinet assembled again in Downing Street. There was a brief and discursive
discussion. Then the meeting was adjourned to await news from
America. Until the reply was received from the Federal Reserve,
nothing of consequence could be decided. At a quarter to ten Sir
Ernest Harvey, the Deputy Governor of the Bank of England, arrived
at Number 10 with the anxiously awaited response. The Prime
Minister snatched the *aide-mémoire* from his hand and read it to his
colleagues. The Federal Reserve was not immediately able to provide
the hoped-for assistance. It was possible, though not certain, that a
short-term loan of $100 to $150 million would be available, but even
that was contingent on France providing a similar amount.
Consideration of more permanent support would not be possible
until the austerity measures were actually in place. Its availability
would depend on the government being able to demonstrate that its
policy had the 'sincere approval and support of the Bank of England
and the City generally'.

Despite his memories of the French refusal to help rescue the

Deutschmark and his conclusion, at the time, that 'to do good is not in [their] nature',[39] MacDonald was ready to gamble on Paris coming to the government's aid. He was also willing to accept the humiliation of American bankers dictating terms to the sovereign British government. His Cabinet colleagues were less accommodating. As it became clear that the Cabinet was still divided, the Prime Minister 'asked for support but [made clear that] if any senior minister felt it necessary to resign, the government must resign as a whole.'[40]

> When the immediate crisis was over, and before Parliament met, it would be possible to give the Labour Party [a] full explanation of the circumstances which had rendered it necessary for the government to formulate such a drastic scheme . . . and he could not believe that the Party would reject the proposals when they knew the true facts of the position . . . Yet it must be admitted that the proposals as a whole represented the negation of everything that the Labour Party stood for.[41]

The moral justification for accepting the burden of managing the recovery was, he said, the undoubted fact that any government which might follow his administration's resignation would reduce the unemployment benefit not by 10 per cent but by 20 per cent. And he offered a second justification for the cut, which his colleagues found most hard to hear. Since every other section of the community would be asked to make sacrifices in the name of national sovereignty it was unreasonable for the unemployed to be exempt. Equality of suffering was enjoying its finest hour.

Philip Snowden's support was complete and unequivocal. He was the true begetter of the rescue package. He could hardly have taken up any other position. Jimmy Thomas and Tom Shaw, the Secretary of State for War, argued that as the Cabinet had authorised the Prime Minister to negotiate, it had a moral duty to endorse the outcome of those negotiations – a dubious proposition since it had rejected the terms on which the negotiations were based. The original opponents of cuts in unemployment benefit – Henderson, Graham, Lansbury, Greenwood and Johnson – stood firm. They were joined and supported by Clynes, Alexander, Addison and Adamson, who all expressed outrage at the Federal Reserve's presumption. The rest of the Cabinet – Wedgwood Benn and Herbert Morrison, the young Minister of Transport, among them – sided with the Prime Minister without playing much part in the discussion. The division of opinion was twelve ministers (including the PM himself) for the rescue package and ten against. The government was doomed. About that no one had doubt. The Cabinet meeting concluded with the unanimous agreement that the Prime Minister, with their resignations in his hand, should see the King at once. The ministers he left behind in the Cabinet Room, knowing and sharing his view that a divided administration could not survive, assumed that his resignation, and in consequence theirs, would be offered and accepted. The charitable interpretation of the events which followed is that MacDonald left with that intention. As he left Downing Street at ten minutes past ten he passed Sir Ernest Harvey in the corridor of Number 10 and told him, 'I'm off to the Palace to throw in my hand.'[42]

MacDonald's behaviour during the late-night audience seemed to confirm that he thought that he was doomed. Wigram, the King's private secretary, described him as 'scared and unbalanced'.[43] The King, on the other hand, was calm and lucid and, according to his private secretary's note, 'impressed upon the Prime Minister that he was the only man to lead the country through the crisis'. He hoped that the Prime Minister would not persist in the belief that resignation was his only course.[44] On his return to Downing Street MacDonald seemed to confirm the assumption of resignation by insisting that the opposition parties be given the details of the new economy proposals and told of the Federal Reserve's contingent promise of help.

The information was passed on by the Prime Minister himself in a conversation which Neville Chamberlain, one of the participants, recorded in some detail in his diary.

> . . . he would help us to get these proposals through, though it means his death warrant, but it would be no use for him to join a government. He would be a ridiculous figure unable to command support and would bring odium on himself as well as us . . . I then intervened . . . Had he considered that, though not

commanding many votes in the House, he might command much support in the country.

It is at this point that Chamberlain, Baldwin (who said very little) and Samuel (who passionately advocated coalition) should have noticed the sound of a mind changing.

> The PM said that his mind was not finally made up, but that was his present intention. I then suggested that many people would not understand why, if he supported the new government, he refused to enter it.

Both Chamberlain and Samuel left the meeting believing that they had failed and that, in the morning, Baldwin would be asked to form a government which MacDonald would not join.

It was agreed that they should all see the King at ten o'clock the next morning. That night MacDonald wrote in his diary, 'Cabinet decided to resign but to meet at 12 tomorrow to see if any new situation would arise as result of interview with the King, with Baldwin and with Samuel.' As David Marquand writes in his excellent, and generally sympathetic, biography, 'The only new situation which was on the cards was one form or another of a national government.'

On 24 August MacDonald arrived at Buckingham Palace 'with a resignation letter in his pocket'.[45] And there is no doubt 'informed opinion' thought that he had no choice but to deliver it. But the King, at the start of the audience, said that he 'trusted there was no question of MacDonald leaving office' but that he would 'help in the formation of a national government which the King was sure would be supported by the Conservatives and the Liberals. The King assured the Prime Minister that remaining at his post, his position would be much more enhanced than if he surrendered the government of the country at such a crisis.'[46]

It was the advice MacDonald wanted to hear. He had come to the conclusion that his duty to the nation was far greater than his obligation to the Labour Party which, in its modern form, he — more than any other man — had created. So he offered the resignation of the Labour government and, when it was accepted, kissed hands on the formation of a new administration. It was agreed that both Baldwin and Samuel would serve under him. The three men drew up a memorandum which agreed that the coalition which they formed would remain in office only 'until an emergency bill or bills had been passed by Parliament which would restore once more British credit and confidence of foreigners'. The strange syntax was probably the result of the need for speed. The King had insisted that the agreement should be concluded and a public statement drafted before the party leaders left the Palace. And the Cabinet was waiting in Downing Street.

According to Lord Passfield (the Colonial Secretary, better known as Sidney Webb), MacDonald 'made the announcement very well and with great feeling, saying that he knew the cost but could not refuse the King's request and that he would doubtless be denounced and ostracised but could do no other'.[47] He expressed neither affection for the Labour Party nor the hope that it would one day be reconciled to what he had done. But he urged the younger members of the Cabinet to 'save themselves' by refusing to serve in the coalition. The memorandum of agreement had stipulated that once the job of managing the recovery was done and a general election was be called, the coalition partners would campaign independently. But there was no way back for MacDonald. Seaham Harbour, his constituency, disowned him within days. Thomas had been right to warn him that the formation of a national government would make him anathema to the party which he had led.[48]

That was clear to Herbert Morrison, the young and ambitious Minister of Transport who had supported the proposal for cuts in benefit payments. In his own published account of how the Cabinet reacted to the news that MacDonald was to lead a coalition, Morrison becomes a hero of the Labour movement. 'We were all shocked and those of us who had no intention of going along with MacDonald felt badly let down. Perhaps, because I was the youngest member of the Cabinet, I was the first to get my breath and find a voice. "Prime Minister", I said, "I think you are wrong . . . And I, for one, am not going with you."'[49] Others have a different recollection.

The 'ghost' who worked with Morrison claimed that the first draft of the autobiography was explicit. Morrison had 'asked to be taken in' but he later decided 'there is no point in saying so'.[50] A host of authorities confirm that version of events. George Strauss, Minister of Works in the 1945 government, was so devoted to Morrison that he was one of the prime movers in the abortive coup against Attlee in 1945. Yet his diary entry for 25 August 1931 left no doubt about MacDonald's expectations. The Prime Minister told his Minister of Transport 'he would not ask him to join the Cabinet as doing so would ruin his political career. Morrison was young, he was old. He did not mind committing political suicide.'[51]

Ramsay MacDonald comforted himself with the thought that he had risen above party loyalty.

> It was plain that I should be left almost alone with Snowden . . . 'Finis' is being written. [Most of the Labour Cabinet] choose the easy path of irresponsibility and leave the burdens to others . . . The good fellows just bond to what would be a popular cry. The intellectuals talked of their theories of banking and currency . . . The Chancellor was getting pessimistic as the desertions went on and I tried to cheer him up, but indeed it was a dreary matter.[52]

The Prime Minister was entitled to judge that the eight Cabinet ministers who accepted the need for cuts – but wanted someone else to implement them – had taken up a less than heroic position. But, that apart, few diary entries have compressed so much self-deception into a single paragraph. It was true that most of the Cabinet would not have accepted an offer to join the coalition but their definition of desertion would have been different from MacDonald's. And, since the nine-member Cabinet which MacDonald formed was to include three ministers from each party, only Snowden, Thomas and Sankey (Labour's Lord Chancellor) were invited to 'share the burdens' of managing the recovery. The derided 'intellectuals' were proved to be right and Philip Snowden, far from 'growing pessimistic', was rejoicing in his own righteousness. He knew that he was about to become the revered high priest of financial orthodoxy. By mid-September, when the coalition government had introduced its economy measures into the House of Commons, he was near to canonisation by the establishment. John Grigg (sometime private secretary to two Chancellors of the Exchequer) detected 'something really great about him'. He had 'put through the Tories and Liberals the identical budget which he had proposed to the Labour government'.[53]

Budget day was 10 September. The next day the House of Commons was asked to give a second reading to the National Economy Bill. It raised taxes by £80 million and cut public expenditure by £70 million. A 10 per cent reduction in unemployment benefit provided £13 million of the savings. The debate was bitter. The Prime Minister, who spoke first, was almost shouted down and Tom Johnson, who wound up for the Labour Party, announced that the nation's fortunes were in the hands 'not of a national government but a Wall Street government'.[54] But, as is usually the case in Parliament, the rhetoric changed nothing. The government had already demonstrated its command of the Commons by making the resolution which proposed 'that a Committee of the Whole House consider the financial situation' – a vote of confidence. The motion was carried by 309 votes to 249, with twelve Labour MPs supporting MacDonald and five abstaining. The coalition was safe. The pound, however, was not.

The illusive 'international confidence' proved more difficult to capture than MacDonald had at first believed. Winston Churchill and Leo Amery, making what the Prime Minister regarded as 'mischievous' speeches about the need for protection, made clear that not all of the Tory Party was behind the makeshift administration. Then ministers were dealt one of the unexpected blows which so often further incapacitate already crippled governments. The new austerity package had included cuts in public service pay, to which the King and Prince of Wales had contributed by making voluntary reductions in their respective salaries of £50,000 and £100,000. Not all of the Royal Navy was so accommodating. On 15 September sailors serving with the Atlantic Fleet at Invergordon – infuriated by a rating's pay cut of 25 per cent when the admiral's reduction was only 7 per cent – refused to carry out their duties. The 'mutiny' confirmed the impression, even for the least excitable observer, that the government was not the master of events. The more hysterical looked towards Russia and predicted bloody revolution.

★

Sterling was under pressure again. The Bank of England's losses rose from £5 million on 16 September to £18 million two days later. On that day the Deputy Governor told the Prime Minister that it was no longer possible to maintain the fixed exchange rate. On 19 September he formally asked for a repeal of the Gold Standard Act of 1925. His request was accepted the next day and the Gold Standard (Amendment) Bill passed all its stages and became law on 21 September. So the false god, to which the unemployed and the Labour government had both been sacrificed, was at last exposed. The effects of the devaluation were almost entirely beneficial. Tom Johnson, one of the Labour Cabinet ministers who was most opposed to the creation of a coalition government, offered a pathetic, but in many ways justifiable, excuse for failing to apply the remedy which Keynes and Henderson should have advocated more boldly. 'No one told us we could do that.'[55] But politicians learn slowly. When it was necessary a second and third time (in 1948 and 1967) it was damagingly delayed and then greeted as a national catastrophe.

Labour's National Executive Committee resolved that supporters of MacDonald's national government 'automatically and immediately' ceased to be members of the party. MacDonald apologists have always claimed that it was rejection by the movement he had helped to create which forced the Prime Minister to abandon Labour. But as early as 5 September he had written to Baldwin to express his apprehension about the party which, a week before, he had led. 'Were Labour to have a majority or could even form a government after the next election, the country would again be faced with a financial crisis . . .' He went on to ask, 'Can we draw a line between the time of crisis and the normal conditions which follow?' MacDonald did 'not see any such line'.[56] The idea was taken up by *The Times*. 'Is there any reason why the appeal to the country, whenever it may come, should not be made – on a broad programme of reconstruction which includes a tariff – by the national government as such?'[57] At first the Liberals refused point-blank to be parties to protection and the Prime Minister – clearly anxious to carry on – told the King that he 'had failed and had better clear out'. The King persisted in the view that no one else could see the country through the crisis – an argument to which MacDonald was highly susceptible. So the Cabinet – which was waiting to hear Baldwin's valedictory address to the retiring Prime Minister – discovered, to its surprise, that the Prime Minister was not abdicating but believed that his duty lay in abandoning the promise to separate as soon as sterling was stable. Instead the coalition should go, united, to the country with a request for a 'doctor's mandate'.

The general election was held on 27 October. MacDonald fought on the slogan 'The Captain Who Stuck by the Ship'. The Conservatives won 471 seats. National Labour candidates and the faction of the Liberal Party which abandoned free trade gave Ramsay MacDonald a majority of over 500. Forty-six Labour candidates were elected, the same number as in 1918. Herbert Morrison was not among them. So, after the brief leadership of George Lansbury, Clement Attlee took the reins by default and held them for twenty momentous years.

The egregious Tom Jones (assistant Cabinet Secretary and friend of the mighty) voted Conservative for the first time. He reflected (for once) the views of the nation. 'Labour had to be thrashed . . . We could not trust them with the Bank of England – just yet.'[58] George Lansbury, the Minister of Works who had not followed MacDonald into the coalition, gave a more contentious explanation of the bankers' refusal to come to the aid of sterling when the crisis first broke. 'No matter what scheme we prepared for taxing the rich, nothing would get the Bank of England the gold we needed, unless the unemployed were victimised.'[59] Labour governments only enjoy the favours of international finance when they agree not to behave like Labour governments.

# CHAPTER SEVEN

# Tight-Lipped Men in Caps

There was I, on pleasure bent, well dressed and comfortable and a crowd of barefoot and ragged children scampering along beside me . . . There are thousands unemployed in the town today. What will it be like in another ten years?

Captain W. H. S. Hall (Merchant Navy)
Docked in Middlesbrough 5 May 1926

One image, above all others, has come to represent the hard reality of Britain between the wars. It is not the flapper in a cloche hat dancing the Charleston – even though in 1925 the voting register was extended to include young women in their twenties. Nor was it – despite the immense popularity of professional football – the policeman on the white horse holding back the crowds at the first Wembley cup final. It was not even the picture of King Edward VIII broadcasting his abdication message to the nation – the inevitable consequence of his determination to marry a previously twice-married woman, even though, according to Noel Coward, 'divorced couples hob-nobbed with each other and with each other's co-respondents' throughout London society.[1] The changes in the divorce laws – which gave women the same rights as men – had resulted, according to the Lord Chancellor, in the courts being swamped by applications for decrees nisi and absolute.

Despite those signs of changed times, the one picture of life in inter-war Britain which is most deeply impressed on the collective memory illustrates the abiding tragedy of men without work. Sir Keith Joseph – contrasting unemployment in the 1990s with life on the dole sixty years earlier – claimed that redundancy did not produce 'gaunt, tight-lipped men in caps and mufflers'.[2] The men Keith Joseph had in mind were marching to demand jobs.

The National Hunger Marches were a regular feature of the 1930s. In 1931, 2,500 marchers from the Midlands got as far as Hyde Park, where they were held back by a police baton charge. Their petition was never delivered to Parliament. Three years later an even larger demonstration drew support from all over England. It made its peaceable way to Whitehall where Ramsay MacDonald – leading the national government – refused to meet its leaders. But it is the march that set out for London on 5 October 1936 which is embedded in the national memory. It called itself, and came to be known as, the 'Jarrow Crusade'.

Two hundred marchers represented the 75 per cent of the borough's workforce which, when Palmer's shipyard closed, had no jobs and no prospect of any other employment. The idea of a march was opposed by the Labour Party, the TUC and many of the marchers' wives, who feared that their husbands were not fit enough to walk three hundred miles. It went ahead because the organisers, who had little hope of stirring the government's conscience, wanted to boost the town's self-esteem. According to the Mayor, Alderman J. W. Thompson, the men of Jarrow were 'cowed . . . They have no chance of a job, no chance of earning money and the experience broke many of them.'[3] The march was meant to renew their pride.

'There is,' wrote the *Manchester Guardian*, 'no political aspect to this march. It is simply the town of Jarrow saying "Send us work".'[4] The country accepted it for what it was – the honest claim for justice from working men who were not the creatures of any political party. Other protests and demonstrations were organised by the Communist-inspired National Unemployed Workers' Movement. Jarrow was a spontaneous assertion of the dignity of man. Its only sponsors were the churches, the chapels and the general public along its route. And that is why it occupies a place in the history of the 1930s that no other march can match.

Alderman Thompson launched an appeal to cover the cost of the crusade. He raised £1,567 − £183 from collections in Jarrow itself. The march set off after an interdenominational service, seen on its way by 'practically the whole town'.[5] The Mayor and Mayoress marched at the head of the column for the first twelve miles. Henley Henson, the Bishop of Durham, publicly reproved the suffragan bishop who sent his blessing. Nevertheless the miscreant held a service of support in Ripon Cathedral and throughout the three weeks the marchers were on the road churches, no less than trade unions and local Labour parties, provided food, shelter and encouragement. They marched between twelve and nineteen miles a day and, from start to finish, Ellen Wilkinson − Member of Parliament for the borough − marched with them. In the House of Commons she described the march in the language of the petition she presented to Parliament − 'the urgent need that work should be provided for the town without delay'. The government told her that Jarrow must determine its own destiny. The crusade was not completely ignored by officialdom. The men who marched had not been 'available for work'. So their 'assistance' was cut to reflect their absence from the dole queue.[6]

The Jarrow marchers arrived in London on 31 October. It was raining. The lucky ones wore khaki waterproof capes bought from an army surplus store. The rest were soaked to the skin. In the street where the march ended medical students from the Inter-Hospital Socialist Society bandaged blistered feet. It was there that they learned that Mr Baldwin was 'too busy' to receive their petition.

Ironically, the autumn of 1936 was just about the time when the belated programme, announced in that year's budget, began to create the jobs which peace could not provide. In that year unemployment fell to 10.2 per cent of the total workforce. The following year it fell again. At its height in 1932 it had reached, according to published figures, 22 per cent.[7]

The published figures were wrong. They were based on the number of men and women who were in work covered by national insurance schemes. In 1931 that amounted to only 12.5 million out of a working population of 19.5 million. The calculation did not cover agriculture, domestic service, teaching, nursing or local government. As a result the official calculation underestimated the unemployment total but overestimated the percentage of men and women who were unemployed. In 1932 – the worst year for recorded unemployment – the published total was a little under three million. When the uninsured occupations were included in the calculation it was probably half a million greater. However, although the percentage of unemployed workers – calculated purely on the basis of the insured industries – was 22 per cent, the rate for all workers was 17 per cent.[8] The national government's failure to deal with unemployment extended even to an inability to ascertain its true level. Perhaps we should be grateful. Little was done to solve the problem even at its exaggerated rate. At a lower percentage of the workforce the neglect might have been total.

Unemployment was highest in the 'insured occupations' because the Lloyd George Act of 1910 had covered only the staple industries and it was the staple industries which fared the worst when the brief post-war boom was over. In 1918, when the war ended, British shipbuilders possessed enough capacity to meet the whole world's demand. In 1921 the industry built about a fifth of the tonnage of which it was capable. Four years later the closure and destruction of yards had reduced capacity by 25 per cent. In the year before the war began Lancaster Mills had spun and woven 2,178 million pounds of raw cotton. In 1920 – India having built its own mills and China having begun to buy from Japan – the figure had fallen to 1,176 million pounds. It never reached that total again. The decline in those two industries had a disastrous effect on the fortunes of coal and steel – two sectors of the economy which, starved of investment and still following ancient habits, were particularly vulnerable to changes in the pattern of trade.[9] The result was a pattern of unemployment which varied wildly from region to region. It was 67 per cent in Jarrow and 3 per cent in High Wycombe.[10]

Agriculture, like industry, enjoyed a brief post-war boom, but the prosperity of the farms was not the result of the sudden release of pent-up demand, which had increased income in the factories. The

Agriculture Act guaranteed both minimum prices and a minimum wage. But on 7 June 1921 the government announced that it was to be repealed. George Edwards, Member of Parliament and founder of the modern Agriculture Workers' Union, called the decision the 'greatest betrayal of the industry that any government has ever been guilty of'.[11] But the farmers themselves welcomed the return to laissez-faire. Some regarded the abolition of the wages board as an economic necessity. Others thought of it as the reassertion of a basic principle. One agricultural journal rejoiced at the restitution of 'the absolute right to two free-born Englishmen to make a business arrangement with each other'.*[12] At first the farmers' hopes were realised. Between 1921 and the spring of 1923 agricultural wages fell by 40 per cent. But wheat prices fell too. Farmers who had taken advantage of the boom to increase mortgages and increase acreage echoed their workers' accusation of government betrayal.

Prices stabilised in a couple of years but not before a delegation of both workers and owners had made a formal request for the government's help. Andrew Bonar Law, who was said to have received them with great courtesy, was absolutely unyielding.

I cannot see what can be done or what you could expect the government to do . . . I think that the agricultural industry is in a worse position than almost any other industry, but they have all suffered. The question is, is agriculture to be self supporting or is it to be supported by the state? I think the latter is impossible.[13]

The Labour government which took office in 1924 was just as unsympathetic, but for different reasons. Philip Snowden, the Chancellor of the Exchequer, called farmers 'the pampered darlings of the Conservatives' and agriculture 'a parasite upon the general industry of the country today'.[14]

---

*Free-born Irishmen had been denied that right since Gladstone's 1870 Land Act protected tenant farmers from rack-renting.

The fall in grain prices harmed arable farms but helped the dairy industry, which grew increasingly efficient as new breeds were introduced into Britain. The ending of the embargo on imported beef – a concession for Canada promoted by Lord Beaverbrook – depressed prices in Britain. Growing interest in nutritional values increased demand for eggs and vegetables. The giant dairy companies offered guaranteed markets at stable prices. Then the 'dumping' of cheap milk undermined the scheme. In 1929 Neville Chamberlain, in a report for the Conservative Research Department, warned that only government intervention could stop agriculture 'going under'. Gradually the Tory Party changed its view about the importance of preserving the market. The Wheat Act of 1932 began a process which climaxed with comprehensive legislation 'to increase productivity of our own soil with a view to ensuring increased production in time of war'.[15] By the outbreak of war the farm wheel had come almost full circle, though the agricultural labourers who were in work remained underpaid and often underfed.

Unemployment, in farming as in industry, has never spread evenly across the country. In both sections of the economy the south-east was spared the worst of the depression. That was one of the reasons why the government did so little to help industry at all, and was so late in coming to the aid of agriculture. Then sheer lack of vision combined with archaic prejudice to convince ministers that, although some help for agriculture might be possible, industry was beyond assistance.

The significance of pre-Keynesian economic illiteracy should not be underrated. Keynes himself said that more damage was done by ignorance than by evil. Lord Bradbury, serving on the Macmillan Committee's inquiry into unemployment, was firmly of the belief that 'the best contribution which the state can make to assist industry and promote employment is strict economy in public expenditure and lightening the burden of debt by prudent financial administration'.[16] And unexpected voices were raised to suggest that life on the dole was not as grim as the trade unions and churches suggested. Beatrice Webb, after a tour of employment black spots, concluded,

Various people told us that the men and boys benefited from the rest, sun and open air and abstinence from alcohol and tobacco . . . The children, through an ample supply of first class food (eleven meals each week at a cost of 3/6 per child at whole-sale prices) were essentially improved in health and happiness . . . There was certainly no sign of strain.[17]

Webb, the inspiration behind the radical minority report of the 1909 Royal Commission on the Poor Law, was not only suggesting that the consequences of unemployment were less severe than Labour, the churches and the unions claimed. She was arguing that children whose fathers were in low-wage occupations probably suffered even more than the sons and daughters of the unemployed.

Bitterness combined with desperation. After the creation of a Ministry of Reconstruction, Lloyd George had told Labour leaders,

the country will be prepared for bigger things after the war . . . will be in a more enthusiastic mood, a more exalted mood for the big things being . . . In a greater mood for doing big things. Unless the mood is seized, immediately after the war, I believe it will pass away.[18]

The nation had believed that the big things he had in mind were jobs and social justice. Perhaps Lloyd George – who had once insisted that society had a duty to help its most vulnerable mem-bers – believed it too and the convictions that we are all 'members one of another' which had inspired his radical, non-conformist youth still smouldered at the back of his mind. But by 1918 they no longer burned bright. Before the war ended Lord Rhondda, the Chairman of the Local Government Board, had proposed the cre-ation of a Ministry of Health – particularly to deal with maternity and infant care (an anticipated preoccupation of reunited families), the war disabled and, perhaps, unemployment. But during the brief post-war boom it was assumed, apparently with justification, that unemployment would not be a major issue. The 'approved societies' nominated under the 1911 Act to provide unemployment and health insurance mounted powerful opposition to the government, usurping their authority. And the Poor Law Division of the Local Government Board, as always, opposed any change in provision or eligibility. The creation of the Ministry of Health was postponed. And when it was created, in 1919, by the amalgamation of the Local Government Board and the Insurance Commission, there was tacit, if not explicit, understanding that the Poor Law would survive intact.*

During 1918 – when Lloyd George had felt unwilling to make the radical change in the machinery of government – the Ministry of Reconstruction had warned that

> So far as hardship due to unemployment is not met by insurance (as provided by the 1911 Act) the government of the day will inevitably be driven back on 'measures for the relief of distress' – in other words a system of dole. Unless a scheme of general insurance is devised and launched at the earliest possible date, it may be impossible to avoid the disastrous chaos of unorganised and improvised methods of relieving distress.[19]

The torpor which the ministry feared had exactly the result which it anticipated. Many of the unemployed were not covered by the provisions of the 1911 Act – having not paid the necessary contribution. So the government had to cast around for new ways of paying what was still the dole.

The little that was done to mitigate the suffering of the unemployed was more the result of fear than hope. The post-war government was haunted by the terror that the Bolshevik revolution, which had convulsed Russia, would be exported to Western Europe. Thomas Jones, deputy Cabinet secretary and confidant of every Prime Minister he served, told Lloyd George

---

*The Minority Report, signed by George Lansbury, Beatrice Webb and Francis Chancellor (a future Bishop of Birmingham), had proposed a replacement of the system of indoor/outdoor relief with assistance which, through separate departments, provided help for the three distinct categories of need – sickness, old age and unemployment.

Bolshevik propaganda in this country is only dangerous in so far as it can lodge itself in the soil of genuine grievance . . . A definite reiteration, by yourself, of the government's determination to push forward with an advanced social programme, is the best antidote.[20]

Lloyd George responded with a rhetorical question which seemed to support Jones' view. 'Even if it cost a hundred million pounds, what was that compared to the stability of the state?'[21] At the time he was advocating investment in housing.* But the philosophy applied, or should have applied, to the generality of social policy. Instead palliatives (at best) were invented from year to year.

The first expedient was the 'out of work donation' – initially for unemployed ex-servicemen and then made available to civilians. The scheme was not without merit. Although its non-contributory principle meant that payments were 'uncovenanted benefits' rather than an established right, the change of principle did have the advantage of making clear that the government accepted its obligation to provide 'assistance' for the poor. But the new scheme, which in the words of William Beveridge replaced 'the principle of insurance by the practice of largesse',[22] did not provide comprehensive coverage. The 'uncovenanted benefits' were only available for a limited period. Then there were 'gaps' in entitlement when claimants exhausted assistance under one scheme but still did not qualify for another. The only available help was provided by the Poor Law Guardians. In December 1920 the total recipients of 'poor relief' numbered 568,000. By September 1921 it had risen to 1,243,000 and it rose by another 200,000 during the next month. The needs of the men who were forced by 'the gap' to apply for help to the Poor Law provoked the greatest display of popular dissent to explode in Britain between the wars. It elevated the name of a London borough into a policy and a cause. 'Poplarism', which was technically unlawful, attracted the active support of such moderate figures as Clement Attlee, the Mayor of Stepney. 'I have,' he

---

*For a description and analysis of inter-war housing policy, see the following chapter.

told his local newspaper, 'always been a constitutionalist but the time has come when it is necessary to kick.'[23]

George Lansbury, the editor of the *Daily Herald*, had become the first mayor of Poplar on 10 November 1919. His acceptance speech (made without robes, mace or hat) left no doubt about how he believed the new borough should behave. 'Labour councillors must be different from those we replace, or why replace them?' He promised to use 'all the powers of Parliament has given us an order to serve the commonwealth . . .'[24] There was, however, a problem. Parliament had not provided Poplar with the power to raise all of the money that serving the commonwealth required.

Poplar's policy was, in Lansbury's words, 'work or full mainten-ance'.[25] It was a particularly difficult aspiration to make reality. In 1921, out of a total population of a little less than one hundred thou-sand, 15,574 residents were 'registered unemployed'. A quarter of them lived below the official poverty line. The problem was exacerbated by the nature of the jobs which were available in the area. There was a higher incidence of casual employment – docks and transport – than in any other London borough. Many of the men who worked in them did not qualify for 'assistance' during their frequent lay-offs. Lansbury tried to relieve the poverty by expanding municipal employment and paying higher wages than were accepted as the going rate. He also launched a highly subsidised municipal building programme which, he hoped, would create 'a garden city on the Isle of Dogs'.[26] The money that Poplar proposed to spend could not be raised by a conventional increase in rates.

A penny rate raised £3,200 in Poplar. In Westminster it raised £29,000. Poplar, in consequence, levied 22/10 per pound of rateable value, Westminster 11/2. On 22 March 1921 the borough treasurer received notice of the amount of precept Poplar would have to pay as its contribution to the cost of running the London County Council, the Metropolitan Asylums Board, the Metropolitan Water Board and the Metropolitan Police. The precept had increased by 28 per cent on the previous year and required the Poplar rate to increase to 27/3 in the pound, even if borough expenditure remained static.

It had long been the view of the Labour Party that 'equalisation' of the precept should allow the poor boroughs to pay less while the rich paid more. Lansbury decided to implement that policy before it was lawful. On 31 March the borough council agreed to levy a rate of 4/4 in the pound for the first three months of the municipal year. That covered the cost of no more than local expenditure and the work of the Poplar Board of Guardians.

On 20 June, following an application to the High Court by London County Council, a 'writ of mandamus' instructed Poplar to pay its dues. The borough refused to pay and, on 29 July, Labour councillors left the borough in a procession headed by the Mayor. The banner at the head of the column read 'Poplar Borough Council, marching to the High Court and possibly to prison to secure the equalisation of the rate for poor boroughs'. The council lost, but the councillors still refused to pay. Twenty-nine councillors and aldermen were arrested, charged with contempt of court and, after again declining to obey the injunction, imprisoned – the men in Brixton and the women in Holloway. From the two gaols they issued a common manifesto.

> . . . we have taken the action deliberately and shall continue to take the same course until the government deals properly with the question of unemployment, providing work or full maintenance for all and carries into effect the long promised and much overdue reform of the equalisation rate.[27]

Support for Lansbury and his colleagues was immense inside the borough, and amongst the Labour rank and file throughout the country. It was estimated that, on 2 September, when the news of the writs of attachment reached the streets, fifteen thousand Londoners demonstrated in support of the threatened councillors. The Labour leadership was, however, far less enthusiastic. J. H. Thomas, railway union leader and Colonial Secretary in the first Labour government, feared that 'Poplarism' would undermine the party's prospects of ever forming a government again. And, in *The Times*, Ramsay MacDonald wrote, 'It cannot be over emphasised that public doles, Poplarism, strikes for increased wages, limitations of output, not only are not socialist, but misstate the spirit and policy of the socialist movement.'[28] However, in nearby Stepney, the moderate Mayor Attlee prepared for his council to follow Poplar's example.

On 10 November Alfred Mond, the Health Minister, warned his Cabinet colleagues that 'Poplarism' was certain to spread throughout London and perhaps beyond. Herbert Morrison, already the rising star of London Labour politicians, called on the other Labour leaders in the capital to combine in an initiative to end the dispute and arrange the release of the Poplar councillors. The conference which resulted gave a hero's welcome to George Lansbury, who had been released from prison in order that he could take part. The government was willing to do what it called compromise – though the outcome was seen by the extremes of both parties as capitulation. The result was the Local Authorities (Financial Provision) Act. To accommodate the different levels of unemployment in individual boroughs, the cost of outdoor relief was to be met, in total, by the Metropolitan Common Poor Fund – to which boroughs would contribute according to their ability to pay. Poplar was better off by £400,000.

Lansbury might, and perhaps should, have declared a victory and returned to Poplar a free man and a hero. But that was not his way. He and his colleagues had another battle to fight. The Poplar Board of Guardians – dominated by Labour councillors from the borough – had been making 'relief payments' at levels which were far in excess of the official limit. The Local Authorities (Financial Provisions) Act increased the level of payment Guardians could make to destitute families. But the 'Mond Scale', as it was called, did not satisfy Lansbury. They chose to pay above the new limits and, at the same time, asked the government for a loan to cover the deficit on the borough's account.

Mond responded by setting up a 'special inquiry' into the administration of Poplar Council. Its slightly oblique conclusion was that £100,000 a year could be saved by improvements in efficiency. Poplar continued to pay above the prescribed scale. On 1 July 1922 an Order in Council made 'excessive payments' illegal. Poplar contested the Order's legality and the government felt obliged to put the question beyond doubt by introducing new legislation. The Local Authorities (Emergency Provisions) Act of 1923 enabled the government to surcharge councillors who provided relief above the Mond Scale and imprison them if they refused to pay. The Poplar councillors remained defiant and, in the war of nerves which followed, escaped prosecution.

In January 1924 Ramsay MacDonald formed the first Labour government. A month later John Wheatley, Minister of Health, revoked the Order which had been issued under the Act.

Wheatley's defence against the charge of condoning illegal conduct was convincing. Poplar was being punished for making payments which other boroughs were exceeding with impunity. 'I have not surrendered to Poplar . . . I have rescued my department from a state of degradation.'[29] But it was the first of a series of decisions which convinced Ramsay MacDonald and Philip Snowden that Wheatley, although a Minister of the Crown, was still a 'Red Clydesider' at heart. He was certainly still a devout Catholic and, in consequence, refused to allow the Ministry of Health to provide contraceptive advice – however great the medical, psychological or social need.

By vetoing the ministry's plans to move with the times Wheatley was fighting the rearguard action of a lost cause. In 1918 Marie Stopes had published *Married Love*. It is by no means clear how many women directly benefited from its advice. But, thanks to the controversy it caused, contraception was no longer the necessity which dare not speak its name. Lord Dawson, the Royal Physician, defended Dr Stopes' proposals as economically essential, as well as the guarantee of healthy mothers and children. The Church of England, barely less than the Church of Rome, fought a rearguard action. But by 1926, when Marie Stopes published *Mother England*, the battle was won. The Cambridge Union carried a motion in her support, a Birth Control Ball was held in the Hammersmith Palais and the BMA recommended that all its members give contraceptive advice – when it was requested.

By then the first Labour government was out of office and Wheatley, its only undisputed success, was out of favour with Ramsay MacDonald. When the party returned to power George Lansbury was regarded as too popular a radical to keep out and was made Minister of Works, and Wheatley was thought to be too dangerous a radical to be allowed in. Lansbury built the Serpentine – 'the people's lido' in Hyde Park. Wheatley, given the chance, might have left a more substantial legacy.

Despite what were, or were said to be, his radical instincts, John

Wheatley raised no objection to the caution with which the first Labour government – in power only because of Liberal support – approached the reform of unemployment benefit. It made no major changes, though it removed the time limit on the receipt of uncovenanted payments. Even those limited changes were passed through the House of Commons only after a promise, demanded by the Liberals, that they would be reviewed within two years. The Labour government lasted for eight months. Its successor, led by Stanley Baldwin, set up yet another inquiry. Its remit clearly required the acceptance that benefits should be financed on the insurance principle. That was explicit it its title, the Unemployment Insurance Committee.

The remit was ignored. The committee's report proposed that a new scheme would have to be financed in part by men and women in employment. It recommended that 'uncovenanted benefit' be replaced by a 'standard benefit' which, although in theory available indefinitely, was only available to claimants who had made thirty weekly contributions to 'the fund' in three years. However, thirty contributions could not finance the seventy-four payments which the 'standard benefit' provided.

Men who did not qualify for 'standard benefit', or whose entitlement had been exhausted, were to be saved from the Poor Law by the 'transitional benefit'. The committee judged that 'the dislike of most insured persons to resort to poor relief is natural and laudable' and added, 'We should encourage it . . . An unemployment insurance scheme should provide for the great bulk of unemployment in a manner honourable to those it benefits.'[30]

All improvements in unemployment benefit are assailed by welfare's instinctive opponents with the accusation that they are open to abuse. The new proposals were particularly susceptible to that charge. In previous schemes the ratio of payments to contributions had been so low that a man who made claims to which he was not entitled risked denying himself benefit when he was genuinely unemployed. In 1921 that protection had been reinforced by the rule that required a claimant to prove that he was 'genuinely seeking work'.

To placate critics of benefit increase and to confirm its financial probity the 1924 Labour government applied the rule with particular severity. The number of rejected claims increased from 10 per cent to 17 per cent. The Tories who followed MacDonald's brief tenure tightened the rule even more. In some areas a third of claims were rejected and in the decade between March 1924 and March 1934 almost three hundred thousand applications were disallowed.[31] Labour – although it had contributed to the process when in government – promised abolition of the 'availability for work test' in its 1929 election manifesto.

Labour – back in power as a minority government in 1929 – inherited a new Local Government Act. It was motivated, at least in part, by a desire to curb the 'excessive generosity' of those Guardians who, following Poplar's example, had paid benefit above the prescribed rate. After the general strike in 1926 action had been taken to curb the 'excesses of West Ham, Chester-le-Street and Bedwelty'. But Neville Chamberlain, the Minister of Health – although unbending in his opposition to fiscal irresponsibility – was also, by instinct and upbringing, a believer in the healing powers of elected local government. He believed that the time had come to abolish the Boards of Guardians and replace them with Public Assistance Committees of borough and county councils. In part and in effect he was implementing the basic proposal of the 1909 Royal Commission on the Poor Law – an idea of 'assistance' which had been extended, in the minority report, to encompass the notion that unemployment was a disease which might be cured, rather than a plague whose worst effects could only be mitigated.

The abolition of the Boards of Guardians marked a turning point in the progress of unemployment policy. The Poor Law of 1834 was intentionally punitive. To qualify for 'relief' a pauper had to suffer 'first the loss of personal reputation (which is understood by the stigma of pauperism itself) second the loss of personal freedom (which is secured by detention in the workhouse) and third the loss of political freedom (which is secured by disenfranchisement)'.[32] The clear implication of that attitude was that the unemployed were responsible for their own unemployment. The pre-war Liberal government had taken a more benign approach. They regarded the unemployed, more often than not, as the victim of circumstances. But with few exceptions – Winston Churchill at the Board of Trade had urged public works – ministers did not believe that a reduction in unemployment was within their power. Between the wars social policy gradually evolved into economic policy. It was the Liberal Party which gave intellectual force to the hope that Labour and the trade unions had harboured for half a century. In 1929, the Liberal Party's election manifesto had promised, 'We Can Conquer Unemployment'. It based that belief on the conclusions of a working party which produced what came to be called the Yellow Paper.

The paper was the work of two great economists, Hubert Henderson and John Maynard Keynes. Their ideas were seized upon by Lloyd George – back in favour with the Liberal Party – as a platform from which he could clamber back into power. He aspired only to mount a massive public works programme to mop up 'abnormal' unemployment. Keynes wanted to do much more. He set out his ideas in an article in the *Evening Standard*, 'How to Organise a Wave of Prosperity'.[33] It was written in Keynes' usual combative style. The economy needed 'a programme of national development' – public works to prime the pump.

> When we have unemployed men and unemployed plant . . . it is utterly imbecile to say that we cannot afford these things. For it is with the unemployed men and the unemployed plant and with nothing else that these things are done.[34]

Keynes – having declined an invitation to become the Liberal candidate for Cambridge – had become a member of the party committee which drew up its economic policy document. It became the manifesto and Keynes – momentarily a politician rather than a scholar – recklessly endorsed Lloyd George's dubious claim that it was possible, by a programme of public works, 'to reduce the terrible figures of the workless in the course of a single year to normal proportions'.[35]

The Conservative government responded with a series of 'Memoranda on Certain Proposals Relating to Unemployment'. They all demanded 'fiscal responsibility'. Keynes, continuing the battle of ideas, published, with Hubert Henderson, an essay entitled 'Can Lloyd George Do It?'. Since the Liberal plans were based on Keynes' ideas, the essay came to the conclusion that Lloyd George could. His certainty was expressed in the language which so infuriated the establishment. Keynes – Eton and Cambridge – was regarded as a class traitor.

> There is no reason why we should not feel ourselves free to be open to experiment, to take action, to try the possibility of things. And over against us, standing in the path, there is nothing but a few old gentlemen tightly buttoned up in their frock coats, who only need to be treated with a little friendly respect and bowled over like ninepins.[36]

The ninepins did not fall. But at least the idea of demand management and the cumulative effects of the multiplier had become a subject of public debate.

> The fact that many work people who are now unemployed would be receiving wages instead of unemployment pay would mean an increase in effective purchasing power which would give a general stimulus to trade. Moreover the greater trade activity would make for further trade activity. The forces of prosperity, like those of trade depression, work with cumulative effect.[37]

Keynes and Henderson were not alone in their advocacy of an expansionary economic policy. Ernest Bevin at the TUC argued for state financial investment paid for by a general levy on everybody in work and Tory mavericks – Leo Amery, Robert Boothby and Harold Macmillan – all argued for attacking the causes, as distinct from mitigating the worst consequences, of unemployment. But the Labour government, in the form of Ramsay MacDonald, remained stubbornly in opposition to the idea that public policy could change the economic weather. Some doubted if spending would have the desired effect. Others feared that it would brand the Labour government as 'socialist'. In 1924 MacDonald had told the House of Commons, 'I want to make perfectly clear that the government has no intention of drawing from the normal channels of trade large sums for extemporising measures which can only be palliatives.'[38] Nothing that Keynes or Henderson had written had the power to change his mind.

★

In fact, the second Labour government – before it was swept away by the crisis of 1931 – reverted to the policy of making unemployment less painful, rather than trying to reduce the number of men who were out of work. As the total rose, the rules governing the receipt of assistance were relaxed. The number of transitional benefit recipients increased from 140,000 to 300,000 within the space of two months.

There was, however, one minister in the second Labour government who favoured a direct attack on unemployment. He was the Tory renegade Oswald Mosley. On 23 January 1931 the Chancellor of the Duchy of Lancaster – who had been instructed to help J. H. Thomas, the Lord Privy Seal, evolve a long-term economic policy – broke out from the constraints which limit the conduct of a junior minister and sent, on his own initiative, a plan of action to the Prime Minister. The 'Mosley Memorandum' made three main assertions. Unemployment could at least be reduced by a public works programme of the sort proposed by the Liberal Party. The machinery of government should be changed in a way which made possible direct ministerial intervention in the management of the economy. That was an indication of the way in which Mosley's mind was already working. He was impressed by Mussolini's achievements. He was advocating Keynesianism as employed by the corporate state. To succeed, the change in policy and administrative structure would have to be accompanied by 'a mobilisation of national resources on a larger scale than has yet been contemplated'.[39] Mosley summed up his proposals in language which illustrated why he was so personally unpopular. His proposals, he insisted, 'at least represented policy . . . it is for those who object to show either that the present policy is effective for its purpose or to present a reasoned alternative which offers a greater prospect of success'.[40]

The challenge was not accepted by Mosley's colleagues. None of them supported the memorandum. But the objections were all technical and administrative. MacDonald himself rejected the third proposal – which no doubt Mosley hoped would win the Prime Minister's support for the whole scheme – that he should take personal charge. He endorsed the judgement of the Cabinet's unemployment committee (which met under the chairmanship of

Philip Snowden, the Chancellor of the Exchequer) that Mosley's initiative 'cut at the root of the individual responsibility of ministers, the
special responsibility of the Chancellor of the Exchequer in the sphere
of finance and the collective responsibility of the Cabinet to
Parliament'.[41] Herbert Morrison, the Minister of Transport, was irrevocably opposed to assuming 'national responsibility for building roads
of a certain class'.[42] Arrogant and disillusioned, Mosley resigned office
and, after a doomed attempt to win over the Labour Party rank and
file, set up a political organisation of his own. The government was
unable to expand its ideas beyond the borders of orthodox economics. So it foundered on the proposal to reduce public expenditure by
cutting benefits by 10 per cent.[*]

The national government, which was formed under MacDonald's
leadership during the last week in August 1931, implemented the cuts
which a majority of the Labour Cabinet had judged to be necessary
but were unwilling to put into effect. Insurance benefits were cut by
the 10 per cent that the bankers had demanded – down from the basic
17/- to 15/3. The right to relief was exhausted after twenty-six weeks
and 'transitional benefit' (renamed 'transitional payments' to emphasise
that they were charity not an entitlement) were to be paid only after
a rigorous 'family means test'. No item or aspect of social policy – not
even the Poor Law itself – has ever been so hated.

The objection to means testing involved its attack on the dignity of
the working man as well as its assault on his standard of living. The
means which were tested included the income of the whole family. So
a small increase in the wages of a working daughter who lived at
home with her parents resulted in a reduction in the dole payment
which her father received. The result was the break-up of families and
bitter recriminations, both against the system and the officials who
operated it. By its nature, a scheme based on the assessment of
'household needs' – necessary expenditure compared with a capacity
to meet its costs – required constant investigation of a recipient
family's circumstances. George Orwell set out some of the family

---

[*]For a further account of the crisis and the creation of the national government,
see Chapter 6.

means-test consequences in the cold-blooded style in which he described every aspect of life on *The Road to Wigan Pier*.

> It is very strictly enforced and you are liable to be refused relief on the slightest hint that you are getting money from another source. Dock labourers, for instance, who are normally hired by the half day, have to sign on twice daily . . . Old people, sometimes bedridden, are driven out of their homes . . . An old age pensioner for instance, if a widower, would normally live with one or other of his children, his weekly ten shillings going towards household expenditure, and not badly cared for. Under the means test, however, he counts as a lodger and if he stays at home his children's dole will be docked.[43]

During the first seven weeks of the means-test operation it had the effect of reducing or refusing benefit to 53 per cent of claimants. By the end of 1931, seven hundred thousand households who had received benefit in early November had been either granted payments at a reduced level or completely disqualified.

Even allowing for a percentage of malingerers and frauds, seven hundred thousand households denied benefit or paid it at a reduced rate could only mean that one million men, women and children were living in abject poverty. George Orwell tells a bitter joke about a man who failed the means test because he was seen 'carting firewood'. He had been evicted and the firewood was his furniture.[44] Many of the families in deepest poverty remained destitute for years because the one-time bread-winner numbered among the long-term unemployed. In previous generations the men who set the levels of Poor Law payments and relief could, like the beadles and 'relieving officers' who denied the receipt of benefit, claim that they were unsure about the full extent of the hardship they were causing. They saw the hovels and the barefoot children. But it was only between the wars that reputable studies into the medical consequences of unemployment and associated poverty provided irrefutable evidence. From the early 1930s onward, inquiries great and small came to the same conclusion. The Gradgrinds knew – should have known and could have known – what they were doing.

Evidence of poverty's consequences was all around. The influenza epidemic which swept across the country during the winter of 1918–19 – killing 150,000 men, women and children – did not distinguish between the social classes. David Lloyd George, the Prime Minister, was struck down by the virus while in Manchester and spent two weeks in a bedroom set up for him in the town hall.[45] But the poor, having contracted the contagion, had few resources with which to combat its worst effects. The deaths were most common in the slums.

Among the victims were some of the six million elementary school pupils who, according to the survey carried out in 1913 by the Chief Medical Officer to the Board of Education, included many children whose medical needs were being damagingly neglected. More than 50 per cent suffered from 'injurious tooth decay', 10 per cent from 'serious defects in vision' and 8 per cent from 'defective hearing or suppurating ears'.[46]

The health care of those children was not much improved and the housing needs of their families were more often recognised than remedied. But a real attempt was made to improve their prospects of a basic education. The 1918 Education Bill was promoted by H. A. L. Fisher – academic historian and President of the Board of Education – with the dire warning that, as a nation, we had 'overdrawn our account with posterity'. The debt was to be repaid by legislation to 'increase the value of every human unit in the whole of society'. The bill, when it was presented, almost lived up to its author's rhetoric. The school leaving age was to be raised to fourteen. Continuation schools would offer a further two years of part-time education to whoever wanted it. Nursery schools were to be set up throughout the country. Sadly, neither the pre-school nor further education proposals survived the 'Geddes Axe' which followed the economic crisis of 1931. But the seed was planted. The Labour government of 1924 had made a not-very-determined effort to raise the leaving age to fifteen and in 1926 the pattern of education was changed to meet the demands of a Labour Party policy document – *Secondary Education for All*.

A. J. Balfour's 1902 Education Act had given reality to the 1870 promise of universal elementary education. It had also proposed the creation of 'secondary schools' for pupils who warranted, and wanted, something better. The Hadow Report of 1926 – *The Education of Adolescents* – proposed the creation of a two-tier system in which all pupils, at the age of eleven, twelve or thirteen, should move on from primary to secondary school. The notion of 'elementary education' should, it suggested, be abandoned.

The semi-private sector responded to the idea more quickly than the local education authorities. Few new grant-aided schools were created, but the number of pupils in grant-aided schools rose by a hundred thousand in ten years – mainly because the schools increased in size. Between 1924 and 1937 the number of grant-maintained places taken up by pupils from elementary schools increased from 68 to 77 per cent. But it seems that every education initiative needs a second stimulus to promote its work.[47] Just as the 1902 Act fulfilled the promises of 1870, the 1944 Act implemented the division between primary and secondary education which Hadow had proposed.

Physical deprivation remained. But, after the great depression, the pattern of poverty changed. From then onward the principal cause was not low wages but unemployment – although, despite the extension of the number of occupations covered by statutory wage regulations, low earnings remained a significant factor (as did old age). In the summer of 1932 a survey of family budgets in the south of England compared the diets of the unemployed with Ministry of Health recommendations. It found that they were all deficient in protein in extents that varied from 8 to 56 per cent of the basic requirement and the energy intake was 20 to 25 per cent below the recommended standard. The romantic myth about rural poverty being moderated by home-grown produce was exploded by Widdowson and McCance, who studied the Lincolnshire unemployed in 1930. The men's energy intake was 90 per cent of that of the employed workers. Their wives made the sacrifice that poverty requires and lived on 70 per cent.

> Her husband *must* be fed as upon him depends the first of all necessities, money. The children must or will be fed and the

school will, if necessary, supplement. Equally husband and children must be clothed, not only fairly warmly, but for work or school, fairly decently. She need not be.[48]

Definitions of poverty differed.* One, developed on the pattern of the study made in York by Rowntree before the First World War, defined poverty as the inability to maintain 'bare physical efficiency'. Even when measured against that exacting criterion, poverty in five towns which he believed to be typical of industrial Britain in 1923/4 ranged from 11.3 per cent in Reading – through 7.9 per cent in Warrington, 7.5 per cent in Stanley, County Durham, and 4.9 in Bolton – to 4 per cent in Northampton. At the end of the decade Jones and Owen – working on a modified version of Bowley's definition – calculated the extent of poverty in three other typical areas. On Merseyside in 1929/30 the level was 16 per cent. In Sheffield in 1931 it was 15.4 per cent and in Southampton in the same year 21.3 per cent. The great depression marks the great divide. In what came to be called the 'depressed areas', poverty levels more or less doubled.

The relation between the figures for 'bare physical efficiency' – before and after 1930/31 – is more significant than the figures themselves as an index of personal suffering. The Rowntree survey revised its definition of poverty in a way which was said to make it suitable for the twentieth century. Basic items like stamps, writing paper, bus fares to work and a newspaper were included. By that definition 31.1 per cent of the population of York was still below the poverty level in 1936 – the year when war production gave the boost to the economy which was said to mark the end of the depression. To complete the picture, poverty was calculated, by both definitions, for the whole of Britain. In 1937, while 6.9 per cent of the population could not maintain 'bare physical efficiency', 10.7 per cent were unable to meet what the survey called 'basic human needs'.

Poverty was, of course, most frequent among the long-term unemployed. And the incidence of long-term unemployment was highest in

---

*The figures which follow are taken from *Poverty in Britain 1900–1965* by Ian Gazeley (Palgrave Macmillan, 2003).

the traditional industries, which were suffering not from cyclical fluc-
tuations but from long-term decline. A study of Brynmawr, a town in
the South Wales coalfield, illustrated the pattern of unemployment to
be expected in a community in which work had been provided by the
mines, steelworks and tin-plate factories. Of the 1,202 unemployed
men in the survey, 19 per cent had been out of work for less than two
years, 54 per cent between two and five years and 20 per cent for five
years or more – leaving 7 per cent who, for reasons of health or
inclination, had never worked at all.

With long-term unemployment, as with poverty, the pattern
changed with the slump. 'Apart from (a) small stagnant pool (less than
5 per cent of the long-term jobless), we must think of pre-depression
unemployment as a pretty, rapidly moving stream.'[49] But, 'In the
middle of 1933 when the last of the men thrown out by the depression and not reabsorbed had passed into the long-term class, 25 out of
every hundred unemployed had not worked during the last year.'[50]
The Pilgrim Trust, the authors of a long-term unemployment study,
came to the blindingly obvious conclusion that it was a 'social problem of the first order'. In fact it was a greater problem, numerically,
than the Trust realised. Once again the statistics were based on 'registered unemployed' who signed on for benefit and, by definition, the
men who had been out of work for a year or more were likely to
receive transitional payments or Poor Law relief and therefore could
not be counted.

The geographical pattern of long-term unemployment matched
the incidence of poverty. In 1938, the average period an unemployed
man spent on the dole in the northern region was 71–2 weeks. In the
south-east it was seventeen weeks. In Wales and Scotland one in three
unemployed men had been out of work long-term. In London, the
ratio was one to five hundred. Although the risk of unemployment
was similar in all age groups the highest incidence of unemployment
was among men of sixty or more who, once having lost a job, could
not find another.

Men who were out of work for years were, by definition, medically
vulnerable. Their nutritional standards, like their living conditions,
were likely to be lower than those of men and women in full-time
work. Long periods 'on the dole' resulted in either deteriorating health

or – what is very much the same thing – the illusion of deteriorating health. A 'senior Ministry of Health official', conscious that 'going on the sick' left a family worse off than 'signing on for assistance', came to a solemn conclusion about the rising number of claims for sickness and disability benefit which accompanied increasing rates of unemployment. The willingness to accept a standard of living even lower than unemployment benefit suggested that the sickness was real and desperate. It was also 'inconsistent with the claim . . . that the general health of the nation is generally improving'.[51] The idea that unemployment created its own traumas seems to have escaped him. The mental stress that long-term unemployment created was, in a world still coming to terms with psychological medicine, rarely the subject of consistent scientific study. But few people who witnessed the consequences for the unemployed man's morale would doubt that 'the victim's reaction . . . passes through a series of phases. There is a rough progression from optimism to pessimism [and then] from pessimism to fatalism.'[52] The governing classes – by always making the adjustments to benefits which were necessary to avoid open conflict – achieved one certain result. In William Beveridge's words, they 'produced demoralisation rather than revolution'.[53]

# CHAPTER EIGHT

# My Father's House

I was to sleep in the middle bedroom upstairs in the big bed with Alice, Winnie and Ernie. The first night we were there Winnie and Ernie were put to bed early. Then, later, when Alice and I went up to bed, looking at the sleepers, we found that they were all over in spots. Alice brought the lamp to have a closer look and saw all the spots were bugs.

Doris Gooderson's 'memoir' describes moving house in
Tottenham in 1918

Charity survived, but faith and hope were both casualties of the First World War and the Churches suffered accordingly. Even some of the clergy, returning from the trenches, found the old idealism hard to sustain. The triumph of grace and the perfectibility of man were difficult doctrines to reconcile with Passchendaele and the Somme. Some Christians within the Church of England turned to a theological version of 'modernism', a creed which could be reconciled with the harsh realities of science.

Traditionalists were scandalised by the conclusion of the Conference of Modern Churchmen (held in Cambridge in 1921), that Christ was the Son of God 'only in a moral sense'. But a year later William Ernest Barnes, an avowed modernist, became Bishop of

Birmingham, allowing Lord Balfour to write, in the introduction to *Science, Religion and Reality*, that the three subjects embraced in the title were being reconciled to each other. The Anglo-Catholics did not agree and published a polemical *Essays, Catholic and Critical*, espousing what they regarded as traditional values.

Perhaps the Church of England suffered from the weakness of trying to embrace too many strands of faith. For it was estimated that the Catholic Church between the wars grew in numbers by something like eleven thousand a year – by no means solely the result of a higher-than-average birth rate. The list of converts was headed by such notable figures as G. K. Chesterton, Compton Mackenzie and Ronald Knox.

The Church of England's 1927 attempt to embrace its Anglo-Catholic members by revising the *Book of Common Prayer* – including the acceptance of the reserved sacrament – was frustrated by the House of Commons which, in 1928, twice defeated the motion to accept the revision. Nonetheless Convocation approved its use in dioceses where the permission of the bishop was obtained – at least 'during the present emergency'. The emergency, whatever it was, turned out to be prolonged, but few Anglicans protested. The reserved sacrament had been a feature of some Churches for years. There were sporadic complaints about the 'reformed' text, but they too were ignored by the 'modernists'.

The Church of Wales – disestablished in 1920 by the 1914 Act – was free from parliamentary interference. So, of course, were the Nonconformists. The largest Methodist Churches came together in 1932, three years after the Church of Scotland and the United Free Church become one. But neither the Church of England's attempt at liturgical reform, nor the institutional changes in other denominations, did much to bring the Churches up to date. By 1939 five of the twelve thousand Anglican clergy were receiving salaries of less than four hundred pounds a year, and some were living on annual stipends of no more than 240 pounds. There was no fear of the Church becoming a profession rather than a vocation.

There was, however, great apprehension about the world in which Christianity had to survive. In July 1929 Cosmo Gordon Lang (Archbishop of Canterbury) and William Temple (Archbishop of York) sent a joint pastoral letter to the Church of England. 'We are more enclosed by a material civilisation, great in its achievements, confident in its self-sufficiency, in which no place is found for God or even for the spiritual life of man.' Similar fears had been expressed by Princes of the Church since its foundation. However the Church of England was about to take a giant leap into the modern world by becoming an agent of social change as well as moral and spiritual instruction. That huge step was personified by Temple – a priest whose theological views sometimes seemed out of step with his opinions on temporal issues. As his theology gradually evolved he became a profound opponent of the modernists' determination to find rational explanations for all things around them. 'The world as we see it is strictly unintelligible. We can only have faith that it will become intelligible when the divine purpose, which is the real explanation of it, is accomplished.'[1] Yet that was the opinion of an archbishop who believed in the absolute obligation of the Church to combat the social evils of the age.

Temple's belief in the close relationship between the spiritual and social obligation was epitomised by a visit he made to Newcastle in 1929. During the service, at which the Archbishop preached the sermon, Henry A. Mess presented his report on the life and work in the area. It was blessed, laid on the altar and became an affirmation of the Church's determination to fight the sin of neglect. All denominations contributed to its production. The Free Churches contributed to the cost of the research and a Congregationalist layman paid Mess's salary. But the endorsement by the Archbishop of York made at least the local establishment take notice of the conditions it revealed.[2]

By October 1926 unemployment in the Tyneside shipbuilding industry had risen to 61.3 per cent. Miners were 'working longer hours than at any time during the last sixty years' and earning just three pounds a week. Thirty-three per cent of the families in the region were living in overcrowded conditions. While the national average of infant mortality was fifty-seven per thousand, in Newcastle it was eighty-six. In Jarrow (included in the survey together with Gateshead), where infant mortality was 114 per thousand, the living conditions were the worst in the whole deprived area.

Since that time, and thanks to its famous 'march for jobs', Jarrow –
until then an anonymous north-eastern shipbuilding town – became
synonymous with the waste and misery of unemployment. As the
Mess report made clear, it might well have become the symbol of a
more general cause of inter-war suffering – the shortage of decent
homes. It was to that particular form of deprivation that the Church
of England turned its attention. The success of its endeavour very
largely depended on the enthusiasm of the local clergy. The Jarrow
example illustrated both the magnitude of the problem and its
consequences.

The census, which was required by the 1935 Housing Act, identified the number of houses – both rented and owner-occupied –
which were overcrowded. In 1936 the national total amounted to 4
per cent of the country's housing stock. In Oxford the figure was 1 per
cent. In Jarrow it was 17.5 per cent. The Greenwood Act of 1930 had
encouraged and subsidised slum clearance. So the 1936 housing census
came at the end of Britain's first serious attempt to demolish and
replace property 'unfit for human habitation' and must have revealed
a far smaller number of overcrowded houses in the town than would
have been discovered in a census held ten years earlier.[*3] Then, something like a quarter of all Jarrow houses were overcrowded. The
borough paid the inevitable price – in 1925 infant mortality rates
were twice as high as the national average and four times as high as in
well-housed Oxford.

In city after city, town after town, the consequences of bad housing
were tragically evident. In Leeds, during 1931, a deputation of clergy
told the city council,

In many houses in this city, the birth of a child takes place in the
living room downstairs, for there is no spare bedroom where the

---

*The 1936 census based its conclusions on a very limited definition of over-
crowding. The criteria laid down by the National Housing and Town Planning
Council in 1920 were 'a bedroom for parents and sufficient sleeping rooms to
separate the sexes of the children as they grew up . . . Separate sanitary accommodation for each family.' Separate bathing facilities for each family were regarded
as 'too lavish' for inclusion.

mother may lie for her confinement. When death enters the house, the body is frequently laid out in the same living room. The clergy who have to visit such houses are accustomed to the sight of the family sitting down to meals . . . in the room where the corpse is laid out.[4]

The national assault on overcrowding – which was, in effect, the drive to clear the slums – did not begin until after the Second World War. Figures for the years before Lloyd George promised 'homes for heroes' show that more than half of the houses in Salford and Glasgow did not have a fixed bath. In Bootle and Hull, two out of every three families had to manage with a zinc bath which they kept under the kitchen sink and brought out into the living room when needed.

In Scotland the quality of housing in general and the problems of overcrowded slums in particular were even worse than in industrial England. In the cities, most low-income families lived in 'apartments', which were better described as tenements. The rural poor still inhabited crofts that holidaymakers found romantic but which, in and out of season, usually lacked basic amenities.

Between the end of the First World War and the great slump of 1931 the growth in the number of families almost exactly matched the number of new houses – leaving virtually no new accommodation for slum clearance. Almost 23 per cent of the entire stock of working-class houses – throughout the country – were overcrowded. In rural Lancashire the total was 86.79 per cent.[5] In Clydebank it was 44.9 per cent. Almost all of Scotland suffered in the same way as the industrial areas of northern England.

The pattern of bad housing, like the map of unemployment, showed that the hardest-hit areas were the towns and cities which had depended for their nineteenth-century prosperity on the basic industries of coal and steel, shipbuilding and shipping. The frontier between the 'two nations' of Great Britain still separated the rich and poor. But, to a degree, the boundaries could be drawn on a map. The one partial exception to that geographic rule was those boroughs in which housing had been improved by local exertions. Often, as in Sheffield and Stoke, the energy and enthusiasm came from recently elected Labour councillors. Sometimes – and more dramatically – it came from the Churches which, in the upheaval of post-war life, began, perhaps belatedly, to accept their mission to urban Britain.

The accusation that the Church of England was the faith of the countryside had been a common complaint ever since the growth of the new industrial towns had changed the parochial map in the late eighteenth century. John Wesley and William Booth had both, in their different ways, been a response to the claims that the urban working class were 'sheep without shepherds'. There is no doubt that, in Victorian England, the Anglican Church's conscience was stirred and its mission to the city slums began. But between the wars a new incentive turned the Established Church towards the towns. A report, under the chairmanship of Cyril Garbett, then Bishop of Southwark but destined to become Archbishop of York, concluded that rural England was no longer the Church's natural preserve.

> We regard the Church's association with the land as out of date. The parson is no longer a landed proprietor or a farmer. Tithe was superseded by the Tithe Rent Charge and the Tithe Act almost completed the process of cutting the Church adrift from the land. In spite of the financial loss suffered, we are glad that a fruitful source of friction between parson and people has been done away.[6]

Necessity, as well as compassion, altered the Churches' focus. Part of their purpose was to proselytise for their beliefs. Another part was the determination to improve the living conditions endured by the men and women who they hoped would find God. And theologians increasingly argued that the two objectives were impossible to distinguish. Church numbers were beginning to fall. Part of the evangelical attraction of industrial Britain was the prospect of parishes which teemed with life.

The marriage of missionary zeal and social conscience was symbolised by the amalgamation, in 1918, of the Navy Mission (a purely

evangelical organisation) and the Christian Social Union, which studied social policy and argued for reform. Together they became the
Industrial Christian Fellowship. Its work was typified and encouraged
by William Temple, who was able to express his convictions about the
Church's obligation to promote 'the common good' with unique
authority.

In 1924 Temple initiated a series of conferences during which
churchmen could consider how Christians should respond to the
social challenge of the time. The mood of the meeting was exemplified by Charles Gore, Bishop of Oxford, founder of the Christian
Social Union, one of the influences behind the creation of the
Community of the Resurrection at Mirfield, supporter of women's
suffrage, advocate of equality and friend of T. H. Green, the Victorian
philosopher of social democracy. He told the first of Temple's gatherings in Birmingham,

> This conference will be judged by its practical work and for
> that I tremble. We need tremendous courage to ask ourselves
> frankly whether we are really prepared to accept these funda-
> mental principles and to apply them whatever the effect upon
> our party politics.[7]

It was not the most stirring appeal made to the Churches between
the wars. The most dramatic call had come from Frank Weston, Bishop
of Zanzibar, who told the Anglo-Catholic Congress of 1923 that 'it is
folly . . . to suppose that you can worship Jesus in the Sacrament and
Jesus on the Throne of Glory when you are sweating Him in the
bodies and souls of His children'. But Temple's Birmingham conference and those that followed were far more influential – though the
influence was oblique and indirect.

At the beginning of the Second World War Temple – conscious of
the allegation that his conferences 'have said similar things for a very
long time and nothing happens' – brushed aside the complaints of
impotence which were made against the Churches by 'people who
want utopia tomorrow'. Christians, he claimed, had contributed to a
national change of mood. 'The whole penal system was reformed in a
wholly Christian direction. There was a vast extension of secondary

education. And the proper housing of the people was at last under-
taken on a great scale.'[8] The Churches were not always as conscious of
social necessity as that bold claim suggests. In July 1929 the Labour
government announced that it proposed to raise the leaving age to fifteen for all pupils who left school after April 1931. A bill was promised
to increase the grant to local authorities and provide maintenance
grants for the children of the poor. The Churches – Catholic no less
than Anglican – protested that they could not meet the building costs
required to extend the size of their voluntary schools. The government
promised a new 'religious settlement'. But it had not been negotiated
by the time the bill reached the House of Commons. John Scurr, a
Roman Catholic Labour MP, moved an amendment to delay its passage until the voluntary schools received new building grants. The
amendment was carried and the bill mortally wounded. The House of
Lords administered the *coup de grâce*. But in the case of housing,
Temple's claim could certainly be sustained. In city parishes the
Church was turning militant.

On 13 February 1930 the Convocation of Canterbury passed a
unanimous resolution.

> This House regards the overcrowded and unsanitary conditions
> under which so many are compelled to live as a menace to the
> moral and physical welfare of the nation. It therefore calls upon
> all churchmen to do their utmost to remedy these evils in their
> own parishes and elsewhere, and it urges the government to
> introduce as soon as possible legislation which will facilitate the
> abolition of the slums.[9]

The debate was opened by Cyril Garbett, then Bishop of
Southwark, in a speech which was built around the failures of housing policy in his own diocese. In Bermondsey, there were ten
thousand houses officially designated as unfit for human habitation
and 2,763 families were living in designated 'overcrowded accommodation'. He made the comparison which was to dominate the housing
debate – quality of housing measured against infant mortality rates. In
Bermondsey, Deptford and Paddington it was eighty-five in one thousand. In Chelsea it was forty-five in one thousand.

Other bishops described the position in their own dioceses. In Bristol twenty-five thousand men, women and children lived in 'insanitary conditions'. The tally of 'back-to-back' houses still in use was seventy-two thousand in Leeds, forty thousand in Birmingham and thirty-three thousand in Bradford.

It was the era of subsidised housing for 'general need'. Garbett summed up the debate with his conclusions on how far the increases in building had helped the families in most need of improved accommodation.

> In two test districts, one near Manchester the other near London, private surveys have been carried out with certain intervals between them to see how far those slum districts had been affected by large building schemes carried out in or near the neighbourhood. The surveys showed that the results have been negligible.[10]

The bishop's conclusion was that the Church must press for a change in national policy. It was a Christian's moral duty to act directly to clear the slums by creating societies which owned and managed housing improvement schemes. But 'if there were thirty or forty times as many public utility societies at work, they would only touch the fringe of the slum problem'.[11] He especially commended Fulham Borough Council (which had bought vermin-ridden blocks of flats without sanitation or running water, rebuilt them and rented them out at a weekly rent of 8/6) the Church Tenant Association in Bristol and the COPEC Housing Society in Birmingham. His greatest praise was reserved for the St Pancras House Improvement Society, which had become the inspiration of all the housing schemes which followed.

In 1921 Basil Jellicoe – soon to be ordained a deacon of the Church of England – had been sent to Somers Town in the borough of St Pancras where Magdalen College, Oxford, ran a 'settlement'. The settlement had been created to keep young working men off the streets and – at the same time – bring them to God. In Jellicoe's opinion the settlement was meeting neither of those objectives. So he closed it down with the announcement that, since it was beyond improvement, there would have to be a fresh start. In preparation for that task he began to familiarise himself with the area. He found the slums. They had, he concluded, been 'produced by selfishness, stupidity and sin and only Love Incarnate can put it right. The slums produce something much more terrible than mere discomfiture and discontent. They produce a kind of horrible excommunication, a fiendish plan by the Powers of Evil to keep people from the happiness for which God made them.'[12]

The result of his righteous passion was the St Pancras House Improvement Society – largely composed of Magdalen graduates, augmented by Miss Edith Neville and Miss I. N. Hill of the Charity Organisation Society. It took some time for the Society to decide what to do and even longer to accumulate the funds with which to do it. But by 1925 they had raised enough to buy the leasehold of eight slum houses. Six months later, largely as a result of a supportive letter sent to *The Times* by Viscount Cecil of Chelwood, the Society was rich enough to buy the properties outright. The result was eight reconditioned houses, which saved eight families from the conditions which Edith Neville found as incredible as intolerable. 'How little most people knew or cared that a family of fifteen lived in two smoky little attics with rain pouring through the roof, that babies born healthy died after a few months of life in a damp cellar, that young men and women were starting families in conditions which should have shamed our great-grandparents.'[13]

In the following year the Society, offered the chance to improve sixty-nine houses and an adjacent open space of ten thouand square feet, decided to buy the properties even though it did not even possess the deposit to guarantee the deal. The money was raised after another appeal by Viscount Cecil was endorsed by Neville Chamberlain, the Minister of Health, and a clutch of celebrities. John Galsworthy wrote about the Society for the *Observer* and donated his fee to the building fund. Fifty-two flats were built in fifteen months.

The Society grew increasingly ambitious. In 1930 it held a ceremony which it called the 'Solemn Dynamiting of Sydney Street' and began to build houses where the demolished slums had once stood. The 'Year of the Rubicon' was 1932, when it crossed to the other side of Sydney Street. Because its success became so well known, it was regularly offered land which it could not afford. It always borrowed, bought and built. By 1933 the St Pancras House Improvement Society had built 170 new flats and renovated eight more. Jellicoe decided that the time had come to spread the word beyond Somers Town. He began to travel the country evangelising for better housing and affirming the duty of the Church to provide it. By then the bishops of the Established Church had begun to follow the lead of the diocesan clergy. It chose a good moment at which to make their call. The Greenwood Housing Act had just become law.

Arthur Greenwood, one of a long line of inter-war Health Ministers who introduced housing acts which bore their names, was different from the rest in that his legislation sought to encourage building for the replacement of property 'unfit for human habitation'. The others – although promoting construction – sought to meet the needs of the increasingly prosperous artisans and lower middle classes. They were the families who had benefited from terms of trade which reduced the cost of imported raw materials to the point at which price stability, or sometimes even reduction, improved the living standards of families whose wages barely increased. Their needs were met – or partially met – in a series of housing acts.

Between 1919 and 1922 Lloyd George's coalition government built 213,000 homes for war 'heroes' to live in. Over 170,000 of the new houses were built by local councils and were, in part, financed by the provision of the Addison Act. Dr Christopher Addison, the first Minister of Health – head of a new department formed, belatedly, on the advice of the Committee on Post-War Reconstruction – gave his name to a scheme that provided a subsidy of £260 on every modestly sized house built for sale or rent and his legislation guaranteed local authorities recompense for any loss incurred on the housing revenue account which could not be liquidated by a penny rate. Generous though the scheme was, it did not stimulate enough house-building to meet the nation's needs. Thanks to the post-war marriage boom, demand increased faster than supply. So the slums remained virtually untouched. Addison was first demoted and then sacked from the government, though not for failing to build enough houses.* On the day of the enforced resignation Lloyd George apologised to the House of Commons for not disposing of him a year earlier. The Prime Minister was specific about the justification for Addison's removal. His failure was not building too little. It was spending too much. Houses which should have cost less than four hundred pounds had – because of a total subsidy of almost that amount – cost over eight hundred.

When Neville Chamberlain became Minister of Health in the Baldwin government (following Bonar Law's brief succession to Lloyd George) there was no risk of Addison's profligacy being revived. Chamberlain's (1923) Housing Act provided a flat-rate subsidy of six pounds a year for twenty years and ended the system of controlled rents which, although begun as a wartime expedient, had been carried on for four years after the end of the war. The result was a boom in house building which greatly benefited the middle classes and better-off working families – more than 200,000 houses were built under the provisions of the Chamberlain Act. But only seventy-five thousand were built by borough and county councils. The slums remained virtually untouched.†

The first Labour government – which took office in 1924 as a minority administration with only 191 Members of Parliament accepting its whip – achieved very little. The one undoubted ministerial success was John Wheatley, a Catholic businessman and 'Red Clydesider'. The Wheatley Act of 1924 increased the government subsidy to nine pounds a year for forty years and empowered local authorities to add four pounds a year of their own if the additional subsidy was necessary to build houses that were, once again, let at controlled rents. The Wheatley Act was suspended in 1931 when

---

*He proved remarkably resilient. On the collapse of the coalition in 1922 he joined the Labour Party. He was Minister of Agriculture in Ramsay MacDonald's second Labour government, Leader of the House of Lords in Attlee's post-war administration and in 1951 (the year of his death) still, as Lord Privy Seal, a member of the Cabinet.

†When Iain Macleod, himself a former Minister of Health, wrote Chamberlain's biography in 1962 he did not think his housing programme worth a mention.

austerity became the government's first priority. And its provisions were completely abandoned in 1934. But, during its lifetime, county and borough councils built over half a million houses. Wheatley was not found a place in the 1930 Cabinet. His constant support for 'left-wing causes' disqualified him from membership of an administration which the Prime Minister – to some degree correctly – thought would only survive if it continually demonstrated its political respectability.

The assault on the slums had to wait until 1930 when Arthur Greenwood required every local authority to draw up a plan for clearance and rehousing. His scheme paid a subsidy which increased with the number of families which were rehoused and the escalating cost of rehousing them. The Treasury grant for each house built was £250 and the local authority annual subsidy £3.15.0. The result of the combined capital and revenue payment was a reduction in the rent to about £0.9.0 a week. But the Greenwood Act – like the Wheatley Act which it augmented – was a casualty of the 1931 economic crisis. It was not until 1934, when Sir Ernest Hilton Young, Health Minister in the national coalition, revived some of the Greenwood powers, that there was any attempt to mount a major assault on the thousands of 'unfit houses' – most of them terraces of 'back-to-backs' which lacked both sanitation and running water – that were the legacy of the Industrial Revolution.

'Back-to-back' houses consisted of one room on the ground floor, with a door or window opening directly on to the street, and another single room above. Identical houses, built behind and each side, shared three unavoidably windowless walls. Water was usually obtained from a communal pump. Middens – earth closets – were shared by up to a dozen families. The 1934 assault was both temporary and half-hearted. The slum clearance subsidy was reduced in 1935.

The pattern of inter-war housing policy provides a political parable. In 1918 there was a net shortage of homes in England and Wales of over six hundred thousand houses. There was still a deficit in 1934. But five years later there was a surplus of more than half a million. The Chamberlain building boom had met the needs of the articulate clerks and artisans who had been given the vote in 1918. The only remaining demand came from the slums, which were thought to have little

influence on the outcome of elections. Only twenty-six thousand
houses, out of a grand total of almost four million, had been built to
relieve overcrowding and allow the demolition of 'unfit' property. A
few families escaped the slums by obtaining tenancies in council
houses which had been built for 'general need'. Some moved into
slightly better property which had been left vacant during the great
switch from renting to owner occupation. Yet in 1935 almost a quarter of a million houses officially condemned as 'unfit for human
habitation' were still occupied.

The slum clearance programme which, at least in theory, followed the 1936 survey proposed that 266,851 houses should be
demolished in England and Wales and that 285,189 should be built in
their place to provide accommodation for 1,240,182 men, women
and children. The unconvincingly precise estimate was obtained by
aggregating individual local authority calculations – most of which
were based on what councils thought to be within their power to
achieve rather than what needed to be done. Manchester proposed
thirteen thousand demolitions – half the number of unfit houses
within its boundaries. There were thirty-nine thousand back-to-
back houses and fifty-one thousand houses without lavatories in
Birmingham alone – ninety thousand slums, in one city, out of a
national total which was said to be a quarter of a million. London,
Leeds, Liverpool, Manchester and Sheffield accounted for over 40
per cent of the total demolition plan. All those boroughs – being
overwhelmed by the magnitude of the task they faced – failed to
meet their targets.

In Scotland the crisis was even deeper and more widespread than it
was in England. And the assault on the slums was even slower to start.
Of the sixty thousand slum houses identified by local authorities in
1919, only 12,500 had been demolished and replaced by 1930. In
1934, operating legislation parallel to the 1931 Greenwood Act in
England and Wales, Scottish local authorities proposed the demolition
of sixty-three thousand slum properties. By 1938 fifty-five thousand
had been demolished and forty thousand replacement houses had
been built. But when war broke out there were still sixty-six thousand
slums in Scotland and at least two hundred thousand new houses
were needed to end overcrowding.

Although the Conservative Party – in power for most of the inter-war years – could not have been expected to make slum clearance a priority, by 1934 it at least acknowledged that a problem existed. But the real leap forward had been the Greenwood Act of 1931. However, the action which it encouraged (or perhaps only permitted) required a local agency to implement the powers and claim the financial help that the permissive legislation allowed. In consequence the map of slum clearance, like the pattern of unemployment, showed wide vari-ations in different parts of the country. And the Acts which made slum clearance possible were so short-lived that councils had barely the time to put them into action before the slum-clearance incentives were snatched away. The towns which made most progress were those in which an individual or institution organised what amounted to hous-ing crusades. Nowhere was the power of local persuasion more effectively employed than in Leeds, where the Reverend Charles Jenkinson, vicar of the combined parishes of St John and St Barnabas in Holbeck, regarded the clearing of the slums as his vocation.

The houses of Holbeck were unfit for decent human habitation even when they were built, in the middle of the nineteenth century. Little or nothing was done to improve them during the eighty years which followed. Indeed they deteriorated. The lathe and plaster walls had proved ideal breeding grounds for rats, mice and bugs. The com-munal pumps had rusted. And the middens – always insanitary – harboured generations of germs. The final report of the National Unhealthy Areas Committee – a well-intentioned but powerless group of altruists – published in 1919, described the extent of Leeds' problem.

The City of Leeds is perhaps confronted with the most difficult problem to be found in any of the provincial towns owing to the enormous number of back-to-back houses, the building of which continued up to a comparatively recent date . . . There are altogether 72,000 of these houses in the city . . . About 27,000 are built in blocks of eight which open directly on to the street and have their sanitary conveniences provided in the open spaces between each pair of blocks. These conveniences can only be reached by passing along the streets . . . The remaining 33,000 are the oldest and worst.[14]

Although Jenkinson recognised the state of housing in his parish immediately he arrived in Leeds in 1927 – and accepted his moral duty to campaign for improvement – he moved carefully, perhaps even cautiously, towards making the public demand that the slums be cleared. He began his ministry with attempts to stir the public conscience by use of the methods which Bishop Temple had employed. Both priests were sure that, once the nature of the crisis was understood, men and women of good will would demand that it was ended. So public meetings were arranged in Leeds to discuss the Christian obligation to improve life in this world as well as to prepare for life in the next, and a 'parliament' met each Thursday evening in the Sts John and Barnabas Sunday School Hall to discuss how a Christian obligation to society could best be met. On Sunday afternoons a 'forum' discussed more technical details of what the other gatherings had agreed. Without the need of much prompting from Jenkinson, there was general agreement that Leeds's first call on the Christian conscience was the slums.

Jenkinson prepared background material to enable the forums to gauge the extent of the dilapidation and consequent suffering. It proved that life in his parish was almost always brutish and short. The infant mortality rate was 13.5 per thousand for Leeds as whole, 9.5 for healthy areas and 23.6 for the slums. Tuberculosis deaths were 1.28 per thousand in the entire city, 0.63 in most healthy areas and 3.31 in the least. There is no clear evidence to demonstrate the effect such figures had in stimulating reforming zeal among those who heard them. It is, however, certain that they convinced Jenkinson, who had prepared the figures, that it was necessary to take practical action. He decided to stand for election to the Leeds City Council. He had no difficulty in deciding where his allegiance lay.

> My contention is that the essential principles of the social and political movement known as Socialism correspond more closely than the principle of any other social and political movement to the principles of the Christian religion.[15]

Jenkinson was not a natural party man. He never felt it necessary to support items of policy with which he was in personal disagreement and admitted that he held a Labour Party membership card 'for reasons much less satisfactory than [he found] for being a socialist'.[16] But he became a Labour candidate and was elected a Labour councillor.

By the time Jenkinson was elected to the City Council, clearance plans for the borough had already been sent to the Ministry of Health. They proposed the demolition of four hundred slum houses a year for five years, but included a codicil that it was by no means certain that the target would be met. Jenkinson's response was a proposal that the Medical Officer of Health prepare a report on the full extent of the Leeds slum crisis – numbers, location and consequences. The defeat of the proposal by thirty-nine votes to forty stimulated, or perhaps provoked, him into greater efforts. The speech in which he moved the rejected resolution was published in his parish magazine and reprinted as a pamphlet. Twenty thousand copies were distributed throughout the city. Local clergy rallied round in what became a remarkable partnership between religion and politics. In June 1931 the Leeds Ruridecanal Chapter passed a resolution which was more or less identical to the one that the City Council had rejected.

> In the opinion of the Chapter, housing conditions in considerable areas of this city call for urgent attention on moral grounds as on other grounds. The Chapter therefore represents to the City Council that, with a view to arousing the public conscience on this matter, it is highly desirable that a precise statement of the situation and the possibilities under the Slum Clearance Act of 1930 should be prepared and at least a summary of the facts published.[17]

The resolution ended with a familiar call for the issue to be 'removed from the sphere of party political controversy'. But what little doubt there was about the partnership between the Labour Party and the Church was removed by the organisation of a mass protest meeting in Leeds Town Hall. It was organised by the Leeds Christian Social Council (well known for its radical agenda) and, recalling William Temple's national conference on the Church's social obligation, it invited the Archbishop of York to be the principal speaker.

Temple was a socialist. Before the war he had regularly preached at John Bruce Glasier's Labour Church on the subject of Socialism and Christianity. In the early months of 1918 Temple had formally notified the Lower House of the Canterbury Convocation that he had become a member of the Labour Party.[18] He left in 1925 but a year later – during the miners' strike that dragged on throughout the year – there was no doubt where his sympathies lay. The Archbishop of Canterbury had been overtly critical of the miners when their demands were debated in the House of Lords. But his disapproval of their conduct was nothing as compared with the denunciation thundered from the Westminster Cathedral pulpit by Cardinal Bourne. He called the strike 'a direct challenge to lawfully constituted authority and a sin against the obedience which we owe to God'.[19] It may be that Temple had been lucky to be out of Britain during the days of the General Strike itself. He was spared the danger of feeling an obligation to take sides publicly. On his return, he did no more than take part in an always-futile attempt to persuade the Church of England to act as a mediator between the intransigent mine owners and the immovable miners. And he engaged in that limited exercise with some doubts about its propriety. But, because of his history, he was accused of being the miners' friend and, when he proposed that the Ecclesiastical Commission should voluntarily forgo its income from mining royalties, all doubts about where his emotional allegiance lay were removed.

In fact Temple's first loyalty was to the Church – but his own vision of the Church with a social conscience. And he never feared to leap to its defence when it was assaulted. In 1931 the Ecclesiastical Commissioners had been accused – certainly accurately, but perhaps unfairly – of obtaining income from slum rents, as well as living indirectly off the prostitutes who inhabited some houses on their land. Temple took the dangerous step of explaining – accurately but equally disingenuously – that the Commissioners owned no more than the land on which the slums were built and leased it out to the hated landlords on terms which could not be altered.

By the time of his visit to Leeds Temple was increasingly emphasising his detachment from party politics. But that did not prevent him from being invited by the editor of the *Daily Herald* to 'write a 1,000

word article supporting Labour'. Nor did it prevent Professor Harold
Laski – political philosopher and party activist – from writing to him
with the earnest plea that he would accept the invitation and, by so
doing, 'counteract [the] tragic effect of Canterbury's tragic pro-
nouncement of the church's position in the Labour Movement'.[20]
Temple's appearance on the platform in Leeds, far from elevating the
occasion 'above party politics' as the clergy of the diocese had claimed,
confirmed the radical nature of the gathering. It was not an impression
which caused Jenkinson much concern.

The campaign which the rally launched convinced the ruling
Conservatives of Leeds City Council that ignoring demands to clear
the slums would be political suicide. So when Jenkinson moved a resolution 'to set up a housing committee to enquire into, and report
upon, the present position and future policy on housing' it was carried, despite its similarity to the defeated motion of three months
earlier. Churches of every denomination gave evidence to the inquiry
which followed. All of them emphasised the moral corruption as well
as the physical suffering that was inevitably endured by many of the
families who lived in the slums. The report did not attempt to minimise the size of the problem. Indeed, it judged it to be so great that
it estimated that at least a quarter of a century would pass before a
serious inroad could be made into the ranks of slum dwellers. Twenty-
five years was far too long to satisfy Jenkinson. He decided that, with
the help of two other committee members, he would write a minority report. The three men visited London, Birmingham, Manchester,
Sheffield, Wakefield, Amsterdam, Cologne and Frankfurt, as the report
made clear, 'specially though privately'. There could be no suggestion
that public money had been used in the enterprise.[21]

It took two years to complete the report and, by the time that it was
finished, the Labour Party had taken control of the City Council.
Jenkinson was made chairman of the recently created housing committee and set about the task of creating a housing department for it
to supervise. Its first task was to prepare a new slum clearance plan for
presentation to the Ministry of Health.

The 1931 plan had proposed the demolition of four hundred houses
a year. Only twenty-five had been demolished in each of the first two
years of its operation. The revised plan proposed to demolish three

thousand houses a year and to eventually rehouse 110,000 men, women and children – almost a quarter of Leeds' total population. The total cost to the city was estimated to be twelve million pounds, supplemented by a government subsidy, under the Greenwood Act, of ten million pounds. Nothing like it had ever been seen, or even contemplated, in Britain before.

Many of the slums which were to be cleared away under Jenkinson's scheme did not qualify for compensation payments. Houses 'unfit for human habitation' were marked red on the redevelopment map and, since they were deemed to be worthless, were to be acquired by the Leeds Corporation at no more than site value. Jenkinson also insisted that every house in the development area – particularly houses which were shoddy from the day when they were built – had only a limited life. After eighty years they were, in his judgement, worthless and therefore their acquisition by the council did not attract compensation.

The limits that Jenkinson imposed on compensation payments aroused the usual cries of legalised theft and the hackneyed stories of widows – who had invested their life savings in the property – being left in poverty. It was not, however, the vilification that he received which made him consider his position – one foot in the parish church and the other in the council chamber. It was the fear that he could not do justice to both his callings. He chose to devote himself to housing and the council. In November 1933 he published in his parish magazine a list of the 'City Council's position which [he was] occupying immediately' and asked his parishioners to agree that it was not possible for them to be conscientiously 'continued with the vicarage of the parish'. For once his powers of persuasion failed. A letter, signed by several hundred residents of the Holbeck area, wrote to the bishop urging him not to accept Jenkinson's resignation.

The new houses were not to be built in the parts of the city which had previously been occupied by slums. The country as a whole was in the mood to move out to the suburbs. Jenkinson had no doubt that what was good for the southern middle classes was good for the poor of the north. The policy of building high-quality accommodation in the most desirable areas was self-evidently right. But inherent within it were almost insurmountable problems.

In 1918 the Local Government Planning Board described the sort of homes that should be built for the returning heroes. Its recommendations included the minimum size for a three-bedroom house, electricity or gas (as distinct from a coal-fired oven) for cooking and a building density of no more than twelve houses an acre. Desirable though the higher standards were, they complicated the task of rehousing the very poor. Unfortunately, even in the years when the government's fluctuating subsidy was highest, the cost of a 'Planning Board quality house' was more than the rent affordable by a low-income family could bear. The net weekly income, estimated as the necessary minimum for paying council rent without constant struggle, was between £3.10.0 and £4 a week. In 1934, the total income of 78 per cent of all Birmingham families (earned, or received in 'dole money') was less than that.[22]

The problem of matching tenants on low incomes with houses which possessed essential amenities had been complicated by what was known as the 'Overcrowding Bill'. It was to become illegal for local authorities to own, manage or rent out properties which did not conform to the Local Government Planning Board's standards. That required separate bedrooms for adolescent siblings of different sexes. In Leeds thousands of families were still sleeping five or six to a room. Jenkinson asked the Housing Committee to consider, 'Is it a fact that the larger families are the most capable of paying the highest rent?' Knowing that the answer to his rhetorical question would be 'No', he 'decided to face precisely those problems which the country as a whole will face when the Overcrowding Bill becomes an operative Act'. One solution would have been to build cheaper (though sufficiently large) houses for low-income tenants. He dismissed that option with the explanation that, 'We in Leeds hold that such attempts are sociologically pernicious and on every ground reprehensible.'[23] Leeds 'totally rejected all attempts to build down to the economic position of the poor or poorest families'. His solution was to set every rent at the sum necessary to service and repay the debt incurred in its erection and cover the cost of its maintenance. Then, citing the justification that the slum clearance subsidy was calculated on the number of persons rehoused rather than the number of houses built, he proposed to use both the government and local authority grants to offer 'rent relief' to families who were not capable to paying the full market price.

Thus in Leeds what was later called a 'differential rent scheme' was born. But in 1930s West Yorkshire the rent relief Jenkinson proposed was more often referred to as a 'means test'. However, it was, despite a leader in *The Times* suggesting the opposite, entirely legal. Most housing authorities welcomed either the scheme itself or Jenkinson's audacity in breaking such new ground. Archbishop Temple was more cautious. His message concluded, 'I am extremely interested in the scheme you are adopting for the poorer families. To put it at its lowest, it will be a social experiment of the very greatest value.'[24] Jenkinson, despite his loyalty to the Church and to its hierarchy, must have read the guarded endorsement with the fear and feeling that, if he ever strayed beyond the boundaries of legal propriety and popular support, he should not expect to be rescued by the Princes of the Church.

Jenkinson was not a man to be deterred by absence of support from faint hearts who might have been expected to become his allies. In any event, he still had one more great bequest to make to the future of municipal housing. It was not a legacy which, in retrospect, is universally regarded as beneficial. But, in its way, it was more influential in the development of public sector housing than any other of his innovations. Charles Jenkinson was the pioneer of what, twenty years later, was called 'multi storey development'.

In 1934 he had organised, with the help of International Tramping Tours, a parish holiday in the Rhineland. It included a number of visits to German municipal housing estates. The German example stimulated his interest in 'high-rise' flats. He pursued that interest with a visit to Vienna to witness first-hand 'the miracle that, right at the heart of central Europe, which had been shaken by the economic crisis more perhaps than any other part of the world, the finest building ever erected for the working class could spring up almost overnight'.[25] The miracle had, unhappily from Jenkinson's point of view, the name of Karl Marx House.

Jenkinson asked professional advice from the West Yorkshire Society of Architects. It was, in its reaction to Karl Marx House, ecstatic.

. . . to those who associate barrack–like monotony drabness with tenements or flats what has been done in Vienna comes as a revelation . . . The whole unit is welded into one building scheme of extraordinary quality, inexpensively but architecturally designed for large mass effects.

The scheme which the architects commended had 'a frontage of about half a mile by 120 yards wide'. Jenkinson decided to build something which he hoped would be as good, and would certainly be as big. The result was the Quarry Hill Flats – originally designed as a 'decanting centre' at which families rescued from the slums could take temporary shelter until they moved into workmen's cottages with a front door and a garden at the back. But they proved so popular – at least in part because they were approached by lifts (a symbol of inter-war modernity) and contained the Garchey system of waterborne waste disposal which allowed residents to flush away refuse, from potato peel to tin cans, down a hole in the sink. In the years before the war high-rise building was rare. After the six years' pause for hostilities, local authorities returned to the Leeds model which had become so popular in the 1930s. But society – and the definition of the good life – had changed. By the 1970s the multi-storey development had lost its charm. Thousands were built, but gradually demolished thirty years later.

The multi-storey housing development became the worst example of the soulless housing estate – in which families felt lost and crime flourished. But other, more traditional, slum clearance schemes combined with houses built for general need to create – though it was not realised at the time – unavoidable social problems. The Kingstanding Estate in Birmingham eventually housed thirty thousand citizens – about the same number as the nearby city of Shrewsbury. In Shrewsbury there were thirty churches and fifteen church halls. In Kingstanding there was one of each. The problem of the 'soulless and friendless' estate was exacerbated by the speed with which, once building began, the new 'communities' were created. Becontree, on the edge of Dagenham in East London, was begun in 1921. By 1924 3,286 houses accommodated 14,564 people. By 1930 there were 17,874 houses and 82,689 residents. In 1932 22,117 houses were home to 103,528 families.[26]

Very clearly the decision to move at speed was right at the time. Indeed, it is possible to argue that the authorities – national and local – should have moved even more quickly. But, looking back, it now seems that slum clearance was no more than one step towards the creation of a better-housed nation. Quarry Hill's status as 'transitional accommodation' was probably its proper role. But that is the judgement of those who are wise after the event. The imperative of the time was clearing the slums. The Church of England, by not rendering that duty to Caesar alone – and illustrating in Leeds how Caesar should discharge his duties – made life more tolerable for thousands of families.

# PART III

# The Shape of Things to Come

Most of the changes in daily life that were enjoyed between the wars had been pioneered in Edwardian Britain. But it was only when Europe had returned to an uncertain peace that the marvels and miracles became part of everyday life. Motor cars were on sale at a price which travelling salesmen could afford. Flight was evolving from a weapon of war or a five-shilling thrill at an air show to a popular form of passenger transport. The 'cats' whiskers' – which hissed and moaned as they broadcast a barely comprehensible message – were superseded by 'wireless sets' which broadcast music, drama and news. Most important, 'the pictures' learned how to talk.

The cinema encouraged transatlantic attitudes as well as American accents, and made the years between the wars the age in which the cult of the refrigerator and the vacuum cleaner was born. But it provided entertainment for millions of men and women and broadened their horizons as it gave them pleasure. It became the favourite night out for families who would have felt lost at the theatre. And they went home with new hopes and dreams.

Sport became a great deal less patrician. The age of the gifted amateur was coming to an end, though the MCC, as always struggling to beat Australia, thought it might best achieve its aim by appointing 'gentleman' captains who behaved like 'players'. Olympians paid for private coaching and football teams bought success on the transfer market.

Only one institution stoutly defended the need to put 'improvement' before amusement. The British Broadcasting Corporation was founded as a public institution and became, at least in theory, answerable to the men and women who listened to the radio. The BBC was accused of patronising the public it was created to serve. John Reith, its Director General, responded with the assertion that few 'knew what they wanted'. The arrogance guaranteed his downfall. But he, like the men who built cars, designed planes and directed films, helped to shape the Britain of the future.

# CHAPTER NINE

# Few Know What They Want

| | |
|---|---|
| WIRELESS SET (McMichael 135) | 15-15-00 |
| Loudspeaker | 2- 9- 6 |
| Stand | 2- 2-00 |
| Ariel | 9-00 |
| Fitting | 1-00 |
| Less for old set | 1-15- 6 |
| | 19-00-00 |

Family accounts for 1935
William Hartley, LMS Railway Co. manager, Warrington

The story of broadcasting in Britain confirms each theory of human progress. It began with men of genius – Guglielmo Marconi, who took all the credit, and Sir Oliver Lodge and Alexander Muirhead who certainly replicated and perhaps even pre-dated his work – developing an idea which generated its own irresistible momentum. Then economic pressure moved the story on. Electrical engineering companies realised the profit that could be made from the manufacture and sale of 'wireless telegraphy receiving apparatus' – but only if a national network of 'signals' extended the potential market throughout the country. And finally – to gratify historians who claim that progress is only possible when 'men of action' impose their will on lesser mortals – British broadcasting passed into the hands of a genuine, if highly flawed, hero. His name was John Reith.

Reith was not, either by training or inclination, a 'broadcaster'. Such people did not exist in 1918. He was an engineer – a profession which (to his regret) he followed because his father, a minister of the Presbyterian Church, had doubts about the value of an academic education. During the Great War he had initially served in France with the 5$^{th}$ Scotland Rifles – the territorial battalion into which he had been commissioned in February 1911. But he thought of himself as a Royal Engineer and agitated for a transfer. On 7 October 1915 – three weeks after his wish was granted – he was badly wounded in the neck and face. After his recovery Reith spent the rest of the war in America ensuring that Enfield rifles, which were mass produced by the Remington Corporation of Delaware, were of the quality expected by the British Army. At the end of the war, at the age of thirty-nine, he returned to Britain without a job and, like thousands of other demobilised men, began to look for work. His prospects were not improved by his overbearing personality, which his huge frame seemed to emphasise.

In 1918 radio in Britain was still largely the hobby of devoted amateurs – men who made their own receiving and transmitting apparatus and sent signals to each other. On the insistence of the War Office their activities had been severely restricted to ensure that the broadcasts would not interfere with the messages which were being sent and received from the front line. The Wireless Telegraphy Board, representing the official view of the Armed Forces, produced dramatic stories of a Vickers Vimy pilot, lost in the fog, whose attempt to establish his location was interrupted by a concert of classical music. A recital by Lawrence Melchior was said to have 'jammed [all] aircraft communications'.[1]

However, in October 1919, despite the opposition of the chiefs of staff, enthusiasts were once more free to use 'wireless apparatus' and the ever-resourceful Guglielmo Marconi opened station MZX at Chelmsford. He began to broadcast recitals by 'the world's best artists'. Dame Nellie Melba was a regular performer. 'Listening to the wireless' became increasingly popular. The immediate result was conflicting pressures on the Post Office, radio's regulating authority. On one hand, the Wireless Telegraphy Board, reflecting the view of the naval and military establishment, continued to complain that 'wireless entertainment' would interfere with broadcasts of national importance. But the demand for an extended service was irresistible. Popular newspapers sensed that radio was the entertainment of the future. The *Daily Mail* was fortunate in that it employed Tom Clarke (a signals officer in the war) as Lord Northcliffe's assistant. He persuaded the paper's proprietor to send reporters to Hampstead Heath to pick up clear broadcasts and to London railway stations to hear the public's opinion of the innovation. Radio was becoming popular. By August 1921 *Wireless World*, originally the magazine of the amateur enthusiast, claimed to detect a mood of

national resentment that services such as wireless and telephony should be left to our neighbours to provide and that permission to transmit weather reports, news and music by wireless telephony should be refused to companies competent and willing to do so without interfering with the defence services of the country.[2]

During the war the United States of America had restricted broadcasting even more severely than Great Britain. In 1917 Radio America, a nascent commercial broadcasting company, was taken over by the federal government. But the USA was quick to release the wartime shackles and to realise the commercial potential that radio broadcasts represented. The Radio Corporation of America was founded, on the initiative of the General Electric Company, in October 1919 and in August 1921 RDK Pittsburg (in association with the Westinghouse Corporation) broadcast live commentaries from a baseball match, the Davis Cup competition and a prize fight. In between, sales of radios boomed. The impulsion to do more and better came from manufacturing companies. In 1922 sales averaged twenty-two thousand a month.[3]

The American radio boom had created a cacophony of conflicting stations. But a nation emotionally committed to free enterprise was instinctively opposed to legislation which regulated the conduct of one section of the economy. In Britain a succession of Postmasters General – empowered by the Wireless Telegraphy Act of 1904 which

forbade any person 'to install or work any apparatus for wireless telegraphy'[4] without permission – recognised the danger of a free-for-all
but were even more worried about the creation of a broadcasting
monopoly. In early 1922 F. J. Brown, the Deputy Permanent Secretary
at the Post Office, visited America to see if the development of broadcasting there suggested ways in which both evils could be avoided. In
April of that year the government's Wireless Sub-Committee – with
the results of Brown's research to guide it – set out the rules which
should constrain widespread broadcasting. The Committee of Imperial
Defence had argued for exacting restrictions and the proposals which
were eventually agreed reflected the Armed Forces' anxiety. There
was to be one wavelength (440 metres and no more than one and a
half kilowatts), no news except that which had already been published
in newspapers (except by special permission) and a rigid limitation on
broadcasting hours. Advertising was to be prohibited and the
Postmaster General would be empowered to require stations to broadcast government communiqués.

Initially, the government favoured what it called 'the two company
solution' – dividing the franchise between the Marconi Company
and Metropolitan Vickers. But within weeks it accepted that progress
depended on cooperation rather than competition. On 4 May 1922
the Postmaster General told the House of Commons that he proposed

> to ask all those who apply, and the various firms who have
> applied, to come together at the Post Office and cooperate so
> that an efficient service may be rendered and that there shall be
> no danger of monopoly and that each service shall not be inter-
> fering with the efficient working of the others.[5]

There were other modifications to the original plan. The permitted
broadcasting band was widened from 350 to 425 metres and it was
stipulated that every broadcast must begin 'Hello! Hello! I have a
message from all stations . . .' The words of the introduction emphasised the limitations of technology. A single company could be
enfranchised to broadcast to Britain. But, if its signals were to cover the
whole country, it would have to transmit from a number of stations
throughout the United Kingdom.

The Marconi and Metropolitan Vickers companies accepted the government's change of mind with remarkable good grace and met with the Western Electric Company, the Radio Communications Company, the General Electric Company and the British Thomson-Huston Company to draw up a plan for a single-enterprise solution. At the suggestion of the Postmaster General, two representatives of small companies were invited on to the board before the formal inauguration of the new company on 15 November 1922. One of them was Sir William Bull, who had been nominated by the British subsidiary of Siemens. Bull had been a National Liberal Member of Parliament and a supporter of Austen Chamberlain and the Lloyd George coalition which was dissolved in 1922. He had persuaded an unemployed officer of engineers – John Reith – to become his honorary assistant.

Reith had left the army in the spring of 1919 and resumed his career as a mechanical engineer without much enthusiasm. He had hoped to become the Glasgow Corporation housing manager, but the job had gone to a sanitary inspector. After six months of temporary employment with the Ministry of Munitions, winding up small arms contracts, he was appointed chief engineer at Beardmore of Coatbridge – one of the companies which had sponsored Ernest Shackleton's first expedition to the South Pole and had, in consequence, given its name to an Antarctic glacier. However, by the time of Reith's arrival, the days of glory were far behind and soon after he left – disappointed and disillusioned – the factory was, according to him, 'virtually closed down'.[6]

Perhaps in desperation, Reith contemplated a political career. J. R. Clynes, trade union leader and Labour Member of Parliament, gave him no encouragement. So he transferred his attention to the National Liberals and agreed to work without payment for Sir William Bull in order to gain experience. He found politics barely more congenial than engineering. But, if his diary is to be believed, as he struggled to find even suitable employment he never lost faith in his own destiny. On 3 October 1922 he went, as he went each Sunday, to evensong in the Regent Square Presbyterian Church. The minister took his text from Ezekiel. 'Thus said the Lord . . . I sought for a man among them that should make up the hedge, and stand in the gap before me for the land, that I should not destroy it . . .' To Reith it seemed like a message from on high. That night he wrote, 'I still believe that there is some great work for me to do in this world'.[7]

It must have taken a great leap of the imagination to conclude that the destiny to which Ezekiel had pointed him was revealed in the advertisement columns of *The Times*. 'The British Broadcasting Company (in formation)' needed a director of programmes, a chief engineer, a company secretary and a general manager. Reith applied for the post of general manager and was interviewed on 13 December 1922 by three of the directors. He was lucky. The favourite candidates withdrew. And Sir William Bull undoubtedly used his influence on Reith's behalf. On 18 December the chairman of the company telephoned with the news that the board had agreed, unanimously, that he should be appointed. Reith asked for £2,000 a year but accepted £1,750. His letter of acceptance made clear the style of management he would adopt. 'The general manager will have the full control of the company and its staff and will be responsible to the directors.'[8] Reith began as he meant to go on – the servant of a higher cause than a company board could represent. His diary made his obligation plain. 'I am profoundly grateful to God for his goodness in this matter. It is all His doing.'[9]

By the time of Reith's appointment the eight foundation directors had already decided how the British Broadcasting Company should be financed. They asked for a share of the licence fee which, they assumed, everyone who owned a receiver would be required to pay, and a percentage of the profit earned on the sale of sets. They offered in return – partly as a reciprocal gesture and partly because of their genuine patriotism – to approve, and therefore encourage for sale, equipment made in Great Britain. A grateful industry – desperate to promote the development of nationwide broadcasting – offered to pay the BBC 10 per cent of the net wholesale price of every set sold. The House of Commons had to be convinced that it was right to lease broadcasting in the hands of one conglomerate and, even if it was proper, to place the contract to broadcast in the Postmaster General's legal gift. The parliamentary wrangle went on until the end of the year. The BBC's licence to broadcast was not issued until 18 January 1923.

The BBC could not wait. Operating under the existing limited licence, it began daily broadcasts from Marconi House, London, on 14 November 1922. It preceded each news bulletin with a thoughtful preamble. The information would be 'read twice, first of all rapidly and then slowly, repeating on the second occasion wherever necessary details about which listeners may want to make notes'. The broadcasters were as anxious to allay the newspapers' fear of unfair competition as they were to meet the needs of serious listeners. The programme which broadcast the results of the general election of 15 November 1922 ended at one o'clock on the following morning – so as not to pre-empt their publication in the national dailies of 16 November. At the same time it issued an obsequious statement. 'We want to act in such a way that broadcasting may be an incentive to the public to buy more newspapers.'[10] The piety reflected an agreement which had been made between the BBC and the newspaper proprietors on 11 November and came into force on 23 December 1922. There was to be a daily news bulletin of between twelve and twenty-four hundred words. It would always begin with the announcement, 'copyright news from Reuter, Press Association, Exchange Telegraph and Central News'.

The newspaper proprietors were not satisfied. In January 1923 they announced that as 'the Broadcasting Company is a commercial institution with, it is understood, favourable financial prospects' it would have to pay advertising rates for the publication of broadcasting wavelengths and schedules. The announcement amounted to an ultimatum. Unless the BBC negotiated a deal with the Newspaper Publishers' Association (NPA), none of its members would publish programme details. The BBC board was ready to capitulate and pay. But the new general manager was made of sterner stuff. With some difficulty Reith persuaded the directors to ignore the ban and it was duly imposed. Help was, however, at hand. There had been broadcasts from a rooftop studio at Selfridge's Store and Gerald Selfridge had become a wireless enthusiast. He offered to include broadcast schedules in the advertisements he placed in the *Pall Mall Gazette*. The BBC gladly agreed and, much to Reith's delight, that newspaper suddenly enjoyed a dramatic rise in circulation. It was the turn of the NPA to lose its nerve. Its members were told that they must decide for themselves whether or not to publish programme details. They all decided that they would. But, in the meantime, Reith – always in favour of the BBC standing on its own feet – had come to the conclusion that the company should have a publication of its own. He thought of calling it the *Radio Times*.

Reith's first weeks at the BBC were not wholly taken up by controversies. Between 23 December 1922 and 18 January 1923 the BBC broke acres of new ground. The broadcasts, for the first time, of lectures, orchestral concerts, religious homilies and opera all encouraged excitement, enthusiasm and the sale of wireless sets. The new programmes were heard by an increasing number of listeners. By December 1922 almost six hundred thousand radio licences had been issued. By the end of the following year the total had risen to 1,129,578 – justifying the chairman's claim that the BBC had become 'a going concern'.[11] But no one was sure how many listeners were 'tuning in' without payment. A March 1923 report to the governors had suggested that, although the number of licence payers had increased to eighty thousand, four times as many listeners did not regard the possession of a licence as necessary.[12]

Two months after his appointment John Reith travelled to Birmingham to discuss the problem with Neville Chamberlain, the new Postmaster General, and suggested that, as well as pursuing listeners who had no licence, the government should 'except in very special cases refuse all amateur licences' – which were issued free for 'experimental receivers', loosely defined as wireless sets constructed from parts rather than bought ready for use. According to Reith, Chamberlain was 'entirely unhelpful' and 'scoffed at it being worthwhile to enforce licences'.[13]*

Chamberlain's successor, Sir William Joynson-Hicks, was equally sceptical. He was particularly dismissive of the suggestion that he should act against those companies which were importing radio parts in increasing quantities and openly advertising their purchase and

---

*Chamberlain's biographers do not even mention the part he played in the development of broadcasting. The biographies of the three Prime Ministers who were in office during the period when the BBC was established are equally silent on the subject.

assembly as a way of avoiding the licence fee. 'I am not,' he told the House of Commons, 'going to be party to compelling any British manufacturer to join any particular combine.'[14] But he went on to say that, with the long-term future of broadcasting still in doubt, he proposed to set up 'the strongest committee I can to consider the whole question'. The inquiry under the chairmanship of Major-General Sir Frederick Sykes, sometime Chief of the Air Staff, included John Reith in its membership. He also gave evidence. The result was the most blatant confusion of partisan witness and prejudiced interrogator since Joseph Chamberlain sat on the House of Commons select committee which investigated the origins of the Jameson Raid.

There is no doubt that Reith – with some justification – regarded the Sykes Committee's conclusions as all his own work. In *Broadcast over Britain* – his discursive account of the BBC's early years – he suggests that when the deliberations began 'the whole fate of broadcasting hung in the balance'. He was 'profoundly grateful that a BBC representative was on the committee'. As a result, its conclusions were 'not only an unequivocal commendation for that which had been accomplished already, vindication from any charges which had been advanced and explanations of objections, but in addition the Company was given many additional and highly important facilities and an extended licence'.[15] Reith did not think it necessary to describe what those facilities were.

The inquiry dragged on for longer than Reith would have wished – partly because Sykes himself was distracted by the terminal illness and consequent resignation of Andrew Bonar Law, his father-in-law. But its eventual conclusions – the introduction of a unified ten shilling licence, the ending of subvention from the profit on wireless sets and the sterner approach to 'constructors' who thought licences unnecessary for their home-made sets – put the BBC on a firm footing. Despite Reith's panegyric it was a less generous settlement than the company had hoped. And it was only obtained after the general manager had made bitter complaints about the less generous proposals in the draft report. But it solved the BBC's financial problems. Within days of its publication licence numbers increased from 180,000 to 414,000. The general public accepted that radio had come to stay.

★

Much of the committee's discussion concerned the rights and responsibilities of what (the BBC was not allowed to forget) was a monopoly. Ironically, it was Viscount Burnham, a newspaper proprietor, who represented the libertarian point of view and complained that the restriction on independent news-gathering and the broadcasting of controversial material amounted to a 'censorship far more severe than was exercised during the war by the Censor's Department'. Reith chose to argue not for the BBC's freedom from censorship but in favour of it being allowed to censor itself. The Postmaster General could, he insisted, rely on the fear of the licence not being renewed to prevent broadcasters from causing offence. And he substantiated that claim with an assertion which modern programme makers would regard as both ludicrous and demeaning. 'The Broadcasting Company has never, I think, broadcast anything controversial and, of course, they are taking great care not to do so. Whether or not they are prevented from doing it, they would not do it.'[16] Sir Charles Trevelyan (another member of the Sykes Committee) told him, 'If you are going to exclude anything which anybody thinks is doubtful, you are going to make yourselves very dull.'[17] But Reith had some sympathy with the view that controversy is not quite respectable. And he knew that the accusation of partiality was the strongest weapon in the armoury of those who wanted to break the BBC monopoly.

The Newspaper Society openly expressed its suspicions that broadcasters might disseminate 'certain social, political and religious ideas which suited the company and which could not be answered'.[18] Its real objection was that 'a monopoly set up by the government should compete, unfairly compete, with businesses which are established, or may be established'.[19] The alternative view was supplied by Herbert Morrison, then leader of the London County Council. 'Instead of a partially controlled, but otherwise irresponsible, private monopoly, [broadcasting] should be publicly owned and controlled.'[20] But it was a member of the Sykes Committee, Sir Henry Bunbury, who made, at least by implication, the most revolutionary suggestion. What if the BBC was controlled not by manufacturers who made sets but by a 'body of people who receive the news'?[21] Years later John Reith claimed that Bunbury's question had created the opening which enabled him to advocate and coin the phrase, 'public service broadcasting'.

However the idea was conceived and developed, its immediate result was a proposal by a majority of the Sykes Committee that a 'broadcasting board' should be established by statute to assist the Postmaster General in the administration of broadcasting and to advise him on important questions concerning the service. The government approved the innovation and the board was created, with Sykes as a member alongside what was thought to be a representative sample of the whole community – press, trade unions, radio industry and radio enthusiasts among them. It rarely met. For Reith regarded it as a burden rather than a support. When, in 1952, he spoke in the House of Lords debate on commercial television, he insisted that 'the brute force of monopoly' was necessary for progress. He was expressing a philosophy of life, not just his conviction that the BBC must dominate the airwaves. He had no doubt that for the company to prosper he must have a monopoly of power, and acceptable ideas within the institution. The broadcasting board, if it was allowed to think itself important, might well stand in his way. The BBC's probity, integrity and aesthetic standards would be underwritten by the probity, integrity and aesthetic standards of John Reith. Who could ask for more?

So, in those early days, he constantly described the damage which would be done to society if broadcasters did not appreciate and share his own exalted view that the radio had been devised by providence to act as an agent of human improvement. His comments on the subject were always *obiter dicta*. 'Incalculable harm' would be done – the implication was to the whole nation as well as to the future of broadcasting – if the British Broadcasting Company was 'content with mediocrity, with providing a service which was just sufficiently good to avoid complaint'. Broadcasting was meant for a 'more intelligent electorate' and as an 'integrator for democracy'.[22] The rejection of the most common criticism was not so much magisterial as regal – whatever the context in which he used the royal plural.

It is occasionally indicated to us that we are apparently setting out to give the public what we think they need and not what they want. But few know what they want and very few what they need . . . In any case it is better to overstate the mentality of the public than to underestimate it . . . As we conceive it, our responsibility is to carry into the greatest possible number of homes everything that is best in every department of human knowledge, endeavour and achievement.

And, of course, the only way to secure that happy outcome was to make sure that broadcasting was run by the right sort of people. 'The possibility of the doctor himself turning patient can only be prevented by securing a high and conscientious type of man or woman for the profession.'[23] Fortunately the BBC was, for the time being, safe in the hands of John Charles Walsham Reith.

It would be wrong to say that Reith was either intolerant of criticism or attempted to stifle it. He knew his view to be self-evidently correct. So he was admirably sympathetic, in a patronising way, towards those unfortunate individuals who could not recognise the truth – as long as they were not in a position to impede his progress to broadcasting perfection. When the Newspaper Publishers Association had threatened to charge full advertising rates to publish programme schedules, Reith had recruited George Newnes – the founder of *Titbits* – to help in the creation of a BBC periodical. Even when the NPA relented, plans for the *Radio Times* went ahead. The first edition, in September 1923, included a letter which, as well as typifying the criticism of broadcasting down the age, continued Reith's habit of listening to, but not accepting, criticism.

Do they really think that a majority of the listeners are really interested in such lectures as the decrease of malaria in Great Britain, how to become a veterinary surgeon etc? Why is it thought not appropriate to repeal the request nights which are so popular? Would it not be appropriate to have one classical night a week? Frankly, it seems to me that the BBC is only concerned with catering for listeners who own expensive sets and pretend to understand and appreciate highbrow music and educational snob stuff.[24]

For the couple of years after the Sykes Committee reported – and the licence was extended until December 1925 – the BBC was more eclectic in its choice of programmes than its critics allowed. Reith certainly insisted that the broadcasts met the needs of cultivated minorities. Lewis Casson and Sybil Thorndike appeared in *Medea*. When the first novel was serialised it was Charles Kingsley's *Westward Ho!*, not Ian Hay's *Knight on Wheels*, Jeffrey Farnold's *The Amateur Gentleman* or any other example of the period's popular fiction. More time was spent on the transmission of serious music than was devoted to all other forms of broadcast. But listeners were also offered Albert Sadler from the Palm Court of Eastbourne's Grand Hotel. George Robey told jokes, but he was not a success, and Tommy Handley, destined to be one of radio's greatest stars, was allowed the occasional performance although no one thought he would go far.

It was in Reith's nature to want to extend the frontiers of broadcasting. And it was equally inevitable that the inhabitants of the lands he proposed to inhabit would attempt to hold back his progress. Concert hall proprietors and theatre managers thought that broadcasting live concerts and plays would put them out of business by reducing box office takings. Newspapers feared being 'scooped' by outside broadcasts. Reith, as always, pressed on. He wanted to broadcast a 'description of the Boat Race repeated into a microphone by a reporter on the scene',[25] live speeches from city dinners and commentaries from the England vs Scotland rugby match and the Epsom Derby. The Postmaster General, whose permission was needed for any deviation from the schedule of studio transmissions, was left to make the judgement of Solomon between the demands of the old and new media. And Reith had to wrestle with a second problem. Broadcasting was proving an expensive business. He was advised that, to maintain the service he thought barely satisfactory, he needed six hundred thousand pounds a year. The Post Office was only providing five hundred thousand – paid monthly in arrears. The government had made no provision for capital investment, though it was generally accepted that new stations would have to be built at Daventry and Belfast to relay London broadcasts to the Midlands and Northern Ireland.

The government's faith in committees of inquiry was inexhaustible.

Another was set up to examine both the BBC's financing and the scope of its future activities. Reith announced – on what authority it is not clear – that although the BBC would not prepare a formal submission to the inquiry, he would make a personal appearance. Reith had already set out his vision of broadcasting in *Broadcast Over Britain*.

> To have exploited so great a scientific invention for the purpose and pursuit of entertainment alone would have been a prostitution of its powers and an insult to the character and intelligence of the people . . .[26]

But when he gave evidence to the committee in December 1923 he did no more than give an account of the company's achievements, which made the chairman wonder why any change in its constitution was necessary. What form of governance did Reith want to see?

> I do not think it would be right for me to give my opinion.
> We will make up your mind for you.
> I do not imply that it is not already made up.[27]

The government's mind was made up too. Sir Evelyn Murray, the Permanent Under Secretary in the Post Office, had begun to consider the idea of the broadcasting monopoly being managed 'in the public interest'. He suggested that the private company should become a public corporation which, despite its ownership, should be detached from the government.

> The Corporation should enjoy a large measure of independence and should not be subject either in its general policy or its choice of programmes to the detailed control of the PMG, from which would follow the corollary that the PMG would not be expected to accept responsibility or to defend the proceedings of the Corporation in Parliament.[28]

The Crawford Committee published its report in March 1926. It received virtually no attention, even though it contained the unanimous recommendation that the British Broadcasting Company should become the British Broadcasting Corporation, a public monopoly. What little argument there was concerned the powers which the new institution should possess and whether or not it should be prevented, by law and regulation, from competing with newspapers and live entertainment. Both the creation of the new BBC and the provision of new powers depended on the safe passage of a bill through Parliament. That required the good will of the government. It was the BBC's misfortune that, before the law could be changed, events took place which required the Company to choose between compromising its integrity and causing deep offence to the most powerful – and least emollient – Cabinet ministers.

On 3 May 1926, at a quarter past eleven at night, the BBC broke into its scheduled programmes to announce, 'The negotiations have failed and the General Strike is fixed for midnight.'* Two days earlier the General Council of the TUC had announced that it regarded the BBC as an arm of the government and, for what it was worth, black-listed all broadcasts. It urged its members to ignore all that they heard on their wireless sets. In fact, the Cabinet was divided about what the role of the BBC should be. Winston Churchill, the Chancellor of the Exchequer, was for taking it over completely. Sir William Joynson-Hicks, the Home Secretary, saw advantages in maintaining its neutrality. At a meeting of the Cabinet's Strike Committee on 6 May, which Reith attended by invitation, Joynson-Hicks reported that Stanley Baldwin, the Prime Minister, shared his view. Churchill, in Reith's words, 'emphatically objected and said it would be monstrous not to use every instrument to best advantage'.[29] The Home Secretary immediately retreated and noted that the disagreement between min-isters could only be resolved at a full meeting of the Cabinet. The BBC remained in limbo until the day before the strike ended, when the Cabinet endorsed Baldwin's view that the neutrality of the BBC – or what was left of it after the events of the previous five days – should be preserved. Reith regarded Churchill's defeat as a 'negative decision' which left 'things to go on as they were. The BBC [was]

---

*For a full account of the causes, conduct and outcome of the General Strike, see Chapter 3.

neither commandeered nor given full liberty. Not quite fair.'[30] Fortunately the following day brought him, if not the miners, a new sense of security.

When Stanley Baldwin told the BBC that he wished to broadcast to the nation Reith had neither the power nor the inclination to stand in his way. The Prime Minister was, on 11 May, exercising a right which was enshrined in legislation. And Reith's lofty view of broadcasting, as well as his general views about the maintenance of good order within society, left him in no doubt that, in times of emergency, the radio should be central to the search for a solution. A cable was laid to Reith's house in Barton Street. But before the broadcast began the host had some comments to make about the speech's contents. They were made not in his capacity as general manager of the BBC, advising a new contributor on the demands of the media – even though contributors were usually issued with a notice which warned 'the most experienced speaker will realise, if he has not broadcast before, [that] he is about to experience something which is quite different. If you will cough you will deafen millions'.[31] Reith instead spoke to the Prime Minister as a man of conscience and concern for the public good. His presumption proved effective. At Reith's suggestion, Baldwin agreed to say, 'I am a man of peace. I am longing and working for peace. But I will not surrender the security and safety of the British constitution.'[32]

From then on Reith walked a tightrope between preserving what he could of the BBC's neutrality and maintaining enough of the government's good will to at least reduce the prospect of legislation being introduced further to limit its freedom. The balancing act was complicated by Reith's genuine probity. As well as deciding what was expedient, he also felt an obligation to do what he thought right.

Some of the difficult decisions were taken for him. The government refused permission for leaders of the Trade Union Congress to explain why they believed a general strike was justified. Ramsay MacDonald, the leader of the opposition, intervened. But the government had remained adamant. Reith, with much justification, wrote in his diary, 'I do not think they treat me altogether fairly. They will not say that we are to a certain extent controlled and they make me take the onus of turning people down.'[33] His embarrassment was compounded when Viscount Grey of Fallodon, the former Liberal Foreign Secretary, was allowed to broadcast a philippic against the miners who, on his analysis of events, wanted to hold the nation to ransom.

Reith later claimed that he had received an assurance that Grey would speak in general about the futility of conflict. But when he was told that the elder statesman was to be collected from 11 Downing Street he must have realised that the ever-partisan Winston Churchill had recruited his old Liberal colleague as an ally. Inside Number 11, drinking coffee while his contributor composed himself, Reith was accosted by Churchill who – failing to recognise him, or pretending to do so – asked if he was 'from the BBC'. Reith replied, 'Yes, until the strike I ran the place.'[34] They began, at once, to argue about the BBC's conduct. As Grey and Reith left, Churchill's tone changed. 'He came to the car with us and said that he was glad to have met me. He had heard that I had been badly wounded during the war. "In the head wasn't it?"' Perhaps Churchill did not intend to make an offensive implication. Reith's reply accommodated that possibility. 'I said yes but my present attitude was not traceable thereto.'[35]

Reith's embarrassments multiplied. On 9 May he was forced to write to Dr Randall Davidson, the Archbishop of Canterbury, explaining why he could not agree to the Primate broadcasting an appeal for peace which had been composed 'after full conference with leaders of the Christian churches'. The task was made more delicate by the nature of the two men's relationship. Reith had convinced the Archbishop that broadcasting was the means by which, in the modern world, the good news of salvation would be spread. He had visited Lambeth Palace to supervise the installation of the first wireless set, assured Mrs Davidson that opening the windows was not essential to good reception and, when told of her husband's love of piano solos, telephoned the BBC with the instruction that one must be broadcast – immediately. He took refuge in a letter of almost, but not quite complete, frankness.

Although it might appear that we are neglecting to do right in this respect, I am sure you will see that it would be unfortunate to do right if it led to what we consider a great wrong being

imposed upon us . . . We are in a position of considerable delic-
acy at the moment. We have not been commandeered but there
have been strong recommendations to the effect that this should
be done . . . It would therefore be inadvisable for us to do anything that was particularly embarrassing to the government, by
reason of the fact that it might lead to other decisions which we
are hoping to obviate.[36]

Reith did not think it necessary to add that he had been warned
that Davidson's broadcast might be the opportunity for which
Churchill had been waiting. A word of sympathy for the miners or of
criticism of the government would have been followed by the insistence that the BBC be completely taken over by the government. Later
in his life he was to write, 'A nice position to be in between Primate
and Prime Minister . . . bound to vex one or the other. And me only
thirty-six years of age.'[37] And 'when it was all over [he] wondered if it
would have been better had the BBC been commandeered'.[38] He
concluded that it would have been better for him, but worse for the
BBC. In fact, the BBC had enjoyed one undoubted benefit. The
prohibition on news-gathering had been lifted when strike action
prevented the publication of national newspapers. The Archbishop of
Canterbury, with remarkable generosity, pronounced that 'broadcasting is now a well-assured feature of national life — a uniquely
widespread influence'.[39]

Ramsay MacDonald, the Labour Party and the TUC found it hard
to forgive Reith for what they believed to be his partisan behaviour.
And the government — denied the unequivocal support which it
believed it deserved — was more resentful than grateful. The problem
was exacerbated by the contempt in which Reith held Sir William
Mitchell-Thomas, the new Postmaster General, and the dislike that
Mitchell-Thomas felt for him. Paradoxically, the doubts and reserva-
tions resulted in the creation of an institution which each of the
major political parties hoped would have the independent power to
resist pressure from their opponents. Weeks after the General Strike
ended, the government announced that it was to accept the advice of
its most recent committee of inquiry. A Corporation was to be established by Royal Charter. Lord Clarendon, parliamentary under

secretary in the Dominions Office, was to be chairman, supported by four other governors nominated by the Postmaster General.

Nothing explicit was said about the BBC's funding. Reith believed that the income had to be large enough to finance continual expansion. 'The service cannot stand still . . . if it does not go forward it must decline . . .' But it seemed that Mitchell-Thomas did not agree. The argument went on all summer, although new recruits to the board took the BBC's side against the minister who had appointed them. It ended, as such arguments usually do, with victory for the government. When Mitchell-Thomas called their bluff by threatening to make new appointments in their place the governors immediately capitulated.

The licence fee was fixed at ten shillings. After 12.5 per cent was deducted to cover collection costs the BBC was to retain 90 per cent of the total revenue from the first million licences, 80 per cent from the second million, 73 per cent from the third and 60 per cent from the rest. The BBC's borrowing powers were increased to five hundred thousand pounds – more than had been originally proposed but, in Reith's opinion, not enough. The government was empowered 'from time to time, by notice in writing' to instruct the Corporation to refrain from sending any broadcast matter (particular or general) specified in the notice. government announcements were to be transmitted as instructed. But the restrictions on collecting and broadcasting news were permanently abandoned. Reith tried, without success, to insert a clause which enabled the Corporation to broadcast advertisements. He also objected, without the governors' support, to what he regarded as excessive remuneration for governors.

Three days after the charter was published the Postmaster General told the House of Commons of his pleasure that terms had been 'agreed'. Reith described the statement, in a letter to his chairman, as 'unfair, arbitrary and quite dishonest'.[40] The wound had not healed by December when Reith – now director general rather than general manager – received a letter from the Prime Minister notifying him that Baldwin was, in the official jargon, 'minded to recommend' him for a knighthood. A more informal note from the principal private secretary added that 'Mr Baldwin has submitted no name to the King with greater satisfaction'.[41] Reith himself was far from sure that he should accept. He canvassed a wide variety of opinions – including Ramsay MacDonald. Eventually he concluded that the honour was not to him but to the BBC and so he became Sir John. Reith's view of the unacceptability of honours gradually changed. According to his diary, he thought it 'monstrous' that the success of the Jubilee Celebration broadcast in 1935 had not resulted in his becoming a Knight Grand Cross of the Royal Victorian Order.

The BBC went from strength to strength – alternately stimulated and inhibited by the restless, didactic and arrogant, but always powerful, personality of the director general. His exertions were augmented by improved reception and a reduction in the cost of radio receivers, which made possible an explosion in the number of listeners. Between March 1930 and March 1931 licences increased at the rate of one thousand a day. In 1932 the overall increase was 20 per cent. The five millionth licence holder was identified (and rewarded) by the *Radio Times* in November 1932. Six years later there were eight million licence holders. By then, 98 per cent of the population were in reach of a high-quality signal and six hundred makes of radio set were in mass production. The Philco People's Set cost five guineas. Seven years earlier the Marconiphone S3 had cost twenty-eight.

The quality of programmes improved and their diversity increased in step with the growth in the number of licence holders. Saturday schedules for the national service were built around fixed points – the *Morning Service, Band Wagon* (a variety show), *In Town Tonight* (a magazine) and *Children's Hour*. Music continued to fill most air time – Promenade Concerts, virtually rescued by the BBC in 1927, the BBC Symphony Orchestra (founded in 1930) and opera, which was subsidised by the 1931 Labour government. Concessions were made to popular taste, particularly by the broadcasting of dance music. Henry Hall was the first star conductor. Then came Billy Cotton, Sydney Lipton, Joe Loss, Oscar Rabin and Ray Stone. New plays were written for the BBC by L. du Garde Peach.

The Corporation moved into its own specially designed building in Portland Place in May 1932. It was decorated with a stone relief of Ariel – a pun sculptured by Jacob Epstein. The Corporation adopted a motto which presaged its future expansion. 'Nation shall speak peace unto nation'. The time had come for the BBC to send its signals to the world.

Broadcasting to the Empire and Commonwealth was a natural extension of Reith's vision for the BBC – it was necessary for the fulfilment of his ambitions for the Corporation and absolutely consistent with his view on the importance of Britain's place in the world. A trial broadcast had gone out in November 1927 and, had it not been for the financial constraints which constantly held back plans fo expansion, 'overseas' would have been attempted even before the Corporation received its charter. The BBC hoped that the government would find some political attraction in the idea. A memorandum of August 1929 suggested that the King's distant subjects would welcome the chance to 'participate in great occasions and exciting events'. The King's political enemies also had to be borne in mind. It was not 'impossible to conceive of a situation in which deliberate recourse to propaganda might be desirable'.[42] The government did not respond. In November 1931 the BBC decided to go ahead without either government encouragement or extra investment. Six months later the broadcasts began.

The timing could hardly have been better. The Ottawa Conference had (or was hoped to have) forged new links between the Dominions turned Commonwealth. So, in his Christmas broadcast of 1932, King George was able to say, 'I take it as a good omen that wireless should have reached its present perfection at a time when the Empire has been linked in a closer union, for it offers immense possibilities to make the union closer still.' But it was three years before the government – enthused by the Empire broadcasts of the Silver Jubilee – agreed to provide the capital essential to the provision of a worldwide service.

Until 1937 a foreign-language service had not simply been regarded as beyond the BBC's capacity. It had been ruled out as positively undesirable. In March of that year it was still the BBC's official view that 'to introduce foreign languages into the Empire service would . . . inevitably prejudice the integrity of the service'.[43] But the Italians had begun to broadcast in Arabic from Bari and pressure for the BBC to defend British interests in the Middle East began to build. Reith agreed, as long as impartiality could be maintained and the

Corporation could make its broadcasts 'in its own way'. He went on to demonstrate his independence by giving extensive coverage to the execution, on British orders, of two Palestinian Arabs who had been convicted of the illegal possession of firearms. The broadcasts were aimed at what are now called 'opinion formers'. They were described by S. H. Perowne, the first Arabic service organiser, in a way which made no concessions to class sensitivity. He did not prepare programmes 'for the man under the palm tree . . . He may, and probably does, listen to the news if he is lucky enough to be near a receiver . . . Our listening body is drawn almost entirely from the executive class. That is to say government officials, school teachers, students and men and women of leisure and means.' It was not just Reith's innate elitism which made the BBC carry that target audience in its mind. Nor was it simply acceptance of reality. 'It is in the hands of this class that the future of their countries must lie for some time to come.'[44]

The Arabic service opened on 3 January 1938. By then the call for the BBC to provide an objective worldwide news service was being made by all the opponents of the European dictators. A House of Commons resolution, tabled in February 1938, drew the government's attention to the need to counter anti-British propaganda, not by responding in kind but by the 'widespread dissemination of information and news'.[45] Herbert Morrison, back in the House of Commons after running the London County Council, wanted the BBC to broadcast news bulletins in German. But the next extension of the service was into Spanish and Portuguese, following a report that 'countless Brazilians, Argentines and Chileans . . . friendly to this country' were finding it hard to 'stand by and watch [sic] damaging propaganda on all fronts without Britain lifting a finger'.[46] At last the Foreign Office provided a 'grant in aid'.

The technical progress which made overseas broadcasts possible created a challenge for the BBC which ministers were in a mood actively to encourage. The Corporation had a monopoly of broadcasting from Britain. But broadcasts to Britain from France and Luxembourg were received in more than a million homes. They were proving particularly popular on Sundays, when the BBC's sabbath solemnly matched Reith's Presbyterian instincts, not the mood of the people. Kingsley Wood, yet another new Postmaster General, told Reith that he was 'not averse to commercial broadcasting from inside Britain'.[47] The pattern had been established. Politicians – particularly politicians in government – were simultaneously proud of and dissatisfied with the BBC.

Relations between the government and the Corporation were constantly imperilled by ministers' diverse reactions to Reith's personality. Some thought him to be a difficult genius. Others regarded him as just difficult. Lord Halifax, the Foreign Secretary, embroiled in an argument with Reith about the incompatibility of wealth and virtue, feared he was a socialist.[48] In 1934, when the application for the BBC's licence extension was in doubt, Reith had found it necessary to speak to the 1922 Committee in order to convince the Tory backbenchers that he was not the head of a spendthrift and subversive organisation. The charter negotiation had ended very well for the BBC, with the government agreeing that 'if broadcasting is to present a reflection of the time, it must include matters which are in dispute'.[49] But Reith realised that, while he remained, the BBC would never be at peace with the government. In November 1937 he offered his resignation to a meeting of the Board of Governors.

Speeches, which combined astonishment, admiration and anguish in equal measure, convinced him that he should stay on. But the doubt about his value to the BBC remained in his mind. However, when it became clear that the government wished him to leave he had nothing but regret about accepting what he knew to be inevitable. He was invited to Downing Street on 10 June 1938. Horace Wilson – the Ministry of Labour civil servant who had become the Prime Minister's confidant – disclosed his fate. 'He said he had been authorised to instruct me to go [as chairman] to Imperial Airways, tomorrow if possible.'[50] Reith was only prepared to accept an instruction from Chamberlain's own lips. A hasty meeting was arranged, and the Prime Minister explained that Reith should have been invited rather than instructed to move on. In his own explanation of what followed, 'monstrous pusillanimity'[51] prompted him to accept what he knew was less an offer of one job than the dismissal from another. He was not asked to advise on the choice of his successor. F. W. Ogilvie, the vice-chancellor of Queen's University, Belfast, was appointed. 'Not the right man for the job,' said Reith.[52]

John Charles Walsham Reith had left the BBC by the time that television became a viable medium. The first issue of the *Radio Times*, back in 1922, had predicted its eventual popularity. And by 1928 enthusiasts were attacking the BBC for doing too little to pioneer its development. But Marconi himself had pronounced, 'While convinced that television will have a definite place in the future, I do not think any purpose would be served by discussing the service at the present time.'[53] Acceptance and adoption was not encouraged by a demonstration, organised in September 1929 by John Logie Baird, for Reith and the Postmaster General. *The Times* reported that the event had been marred by a 'slight technical hitch'.

By August 1932 the BBC was sufficiently provident to set up an experimental television station in the basement of Broadcasting House. But the real breakthrough came in 1933 when the Corporation's engineers discovered that Baird's home-grown equipment was inferior to the apparatus produced by the Westinghouse Electric and Manufacturing Company. By 1934 EMI was making Emitron Tubes. The BBC's contract with Baird Television Limited was ended.

Broadcasting in Britain has always progressed by way of public inquiries stimulated by the success of foreign competition. And so it was with television. The Germans moved further and faster and the Berlin service, established in March 1935, broadcast pictures from the Olympic Games in the following summer. A committee of inquiry, under the chairmanship of Lord Selsdon, had produced an indecisive report. But a select committee of the House of Commons, which reported in January 1935, recommended the 'ultimate establishment of a general television'[54] service and the immediate creation of a station in and for London. It urged the rejection of general advertising but accepted the possibility of sponsored programmes. The government did not just accept the report. It set up a Television Advisory Committee to push the work along. Unlike radio, progress was not hampered by the fears of the live entertainment industry, most of which agreed with the judgement of Sir Charles Carpendale, the BBC's Deputy Director. 'If television had come in before the movies, I might think otherwise but the cinema today is so cheap and so perfect and so universal in its appeal that I doubt if it could stand up to it.'[55]

Carpendale lived in a world in which television expanded slowly. There were only four hundred television sets in Britain at the beginning of 1937 and no more than two thousand by the end of the year. Sales might have been boosted by a live broadcast of the Coronation in May. But although eight miles of cable were laid from Hyde Park Corner to television's home at Alexandra Palace the transmission was limited to the procession to Westminster Abbey. The solemn scenes inside were not regarded as suitable for screening. What might have been continual, if gradual, expansion ended with the outbreak of war. And it was left to the next Coronation, in 1953, to give television the impetus that enabled it to dominate the life and change the culture of the whole nation.

# CHAPTER TEN

# As Quick As I Can

There now passes an average of 250 passenger and 300 goods trains per day through Warrington . . . It is in road motor transport traffic however that the most spectacular increase has taken place.

W. H. Hartley
LMS Railway Co. manager for company magazine, 1931

Edward Elgar, Master of the King's Musick, Theo Goddard, solicitor to Mrs Wallis Simpson, and Neville Chamberlain were three men who had very little in common. But, during the 1930s, each one of them was congratulated by friends and commended by the press for the same act of exemplary heroism. In their declining years, they all flew for the first time – Elgar (in 1933) to conduct a concert in Paris, Goddard (in 1936) to consult his client in Cannes and Chamberlain (in 1938) to meet Adolf Hitler at Berchtesgaden. Flying was still an adventure. That was how it was represented in the headlines of newspapers which, on more obscure pages, emphasised the aeroplane's commercial and military potential.

The news was made by daring young men – some of them competing in their flying machines for cups and trophies, others who wanted to beat the record for journeys across continents and over oceans. In the 1920s most of them were veterans of the Great War. The years of battle had whetted their appetite for adventure. Having learned to fly in France and Flanders, they had come to believe that nothing else in life was worth doing. And when the peace came they were able to fly a new generation of aircraft which had been designed and developed at a speed which would have been unthinkable without the stimulus of war. Less than six months after the Treaty of Versailles was signed Henry Hawker and Kenneth MacKenzie Grieve attempted to fly the Atlantic in a single-engine Sopwith biplane. They were forced down and given up for lost. The assumption was wrong. They had been rescued from the sea by a Danish steamer which, possessing no radio, could not send the news to England. The great adventure had begun.

The Americans, who believed in the economics of scale, planned for three Curtiss NC4 flying boats to make the crossing west to east. One of them, captained by Lieutenant Commander A. C. Reed, made it to Lisbon after two stops in the Azores. Then Captain J. Alcock and Lieutenant A. Whitten Brown – flying a converted twin-engined Vickers Vimy bomber – made the first non-stop Atlantic crossing, 1,890 miles from coast to coast in three minutes under sixteen hours. Once the first flights had been made, the adventure came from beating previous times and competing against rival crews and aircraft.

The competition which has commanded the most attention down the years was the Schneider Trophy – a speed trial for light seaplanes. Its place in British affections was secured by the knowledge that the planes which had been developed for that race evolved into the Spitfire and, by contributing to victory in the Battle of Britain, played a crucial part in preventing invasion after the fall of France. Like so many British achievements in both peace and war, the chance to surge forward was almost missed.

Britain won the Schneider Trophy in 1922 with a Supermarine Sealion at a speed of 122 miles per hour. By 1927, when Britain won again with a Supermarine S5, the winning speed had almost doubled and by 1929 (the year of yet another British victory) it had risen to 328 mph. There was no race in 1930, but the British industry looked forward with unlimited confidence to the following year when the Royal Air Force 'high speed squadron' – equipped with the Supermarine SB6, complete with new Rolls-Royce engine – would again demonstrate Britain's supremacy in the skies. No allowance had been made for the Labour government and the economic crisis from which it was attempting to extricate the country.

In September 1929 an Air Ministry communiqué announced that the government 'had decided that an RAF team would not again be entered in the Schneider Trophy Race', thus leaving British participation to private enterprise under the auspices of the Royal Aeronautical Club. It gave two reasons to justify its decision. 'The contest has assumed a character not in accordance with the intentions of M. Jacques Schneider' and 'in the present financial situation, the expenditure of public money (not less than £80,000) would not be justified.'[1] The change in character to which the Ministry referred was the evolution from chivalry to chauvinism. Some countries regarded winning the competition as essential to national prestige.

In Britain, the outcry was loud and instantaneous. The Royal Aeronautical Club – as well as making the usual point about promoting British exports – pointed out that the participating planes had all been government property. Without them it was impossible to take part in the race. Ramsay MacDonald, the Prime Minister, first reinforced the Air Ministry's policy with a robust statement of support for its decision, and then overruled it. He was, he said, 'strongly averse to perpetuating these contests between rival government teams'.[2] But he was 'prepared to authorise defence of the trophy by the RAF' provided private sources raised the extra costs which the defence budget would incur. He estimated that one hundred thousand pounds would be needed.

The *Daily Telegraph* promoted a public appeal. But before it had really begun Lady Lucy Huston put up the whole amount. Her accompanying statement was a model of its kind. The government's chief aim, she wrote, was 'to down anything that extols or glorifies the wonderful spirit' of the British people. 'Down with the Army, down with the Navy, down with the Air Force, down with our supremacy in India, but up with Gandhi and up with strikes.'[3] The government hit back. Frederick Montague MP, the Under Secretary for Air, attacked 'wealthy industrialists [who] demand stringent economies at the cost of the desperately poor'[4] while demanding extra spending on projects

which caught their fancy. More woundingly, the government refused
to authorise the RAF's participation until Lady Huston's cheque had
been underwritten with a banker's guarantee. A scandalised Lady
Huston provided it and the RAF entered the competition and won
with a speed of 340.6 mph. It was the RAF's third successive victory.
The Schneider Trophy was Britain's to keep.

The Supermarine SB6 had been designed by R. J. Mitchell – an
aircraft designer with no formal training in aerodynamics. At the
RAF's suggestion it was adapted into a single-seat land monoplane
according to Air Ministry specifications which were thought to make
it a military 'fighter' rather than a sporting aircraft. The new plane was
not a success. Mitchell then redesigned the S6, the victorious seaplane
of 1929, with ministry guidance. The result was the Supermarine
Spitfire. Before the job was finished Mitchell was diagnosed as suffering from rectal cancer. He worked on, and the first Spitfire flew a
year before he died, aged forty-two, in 1937. Twenty-three thousand
were produced during the next five years. Together with the Hawker
Hurricane they won the Battle of Britain and, therefore, made it
possible to win the war.

The Spitfire was not the only aircraft which evolved from a com-
mercial design into a Second World War fighter plane. In 1934 the
MacRobertson Air Race from Mildenhall in England to Melbourne
in Australia was won by a specially designed twin-engine de Havilland
Comet at an average speed of 180 mph. The Comet became the
Mosquito.

The 1934 MacRobertson Air Race, and the ten-thousand-pound
prize money which went with it, was won by Charles Scott and Tom
Campbell Black, two pilots from Wilson Airways, in seventy hours,
fifty-four minutes and twelve seconds. Much of the publicity was,
however, devoted to the pilots, also in a Comet, who came third.
They were Amy Johnson and her husband Jim Mollison.

Amy Johnson ('Wonderful Amy' according to the popular song of the
time) was the daughter of a Hull fish broker who, having graduated
from the University of Sheffield, found that the only job on offer was
shorthand typing in the office of London solicitor. Desperate for a
break in the boredom – and still recovering from an unhappy love

affair – she joined the London Aeroplane Club. She began flying
lessons in September 1928 and won an A-licence by early June 1929.
Then, financed by a gift of a hundred pounds from her father, she
worked, without pay, as an aircraft fitter. By December she had
become the first woman to gain a ground engineer's licence. But
even her obvious infatuation with the air did not prepare her friends
for what lay ahead.

On 5 May 1930 she took off from Croydon aerodrome in a second-
hand Gypsy Moth which she had bought for six hundred pounds,
painted bright green and called 'Jason' in tribute to an earlier adventurer. Before she climbed into the cockpit she told the Press
Association duty reporter at the airfield that she was bound for
Australia. 'I have no desire to make a record,' she said. 'I just want to fly
to Australia and I shall be as quick as I can, but I am not out for record
breaking.'[5] Her modesty was understandable. She was twenty-seven,
had never before crossed the Channel and had only ninety solo flying
hours in her logbook.

Amy Johnson almost crashed on take-off. That was not a habit
which persisted through her flying career – she usually crashed on
landing. But she arrived in Vienna without further mishap, then survived a sandstorm on the way to Baghdad and a fractured
undercarriage when she got there. She broke the record for a flight
between Great Britain and India, smashed her undercarriage again
when she landed at Rangoon and then risked running out of petrol by
crossing the Timor Sea in a single flight. Wonderful Amy arrived
(accompanied by a posse of welcoming aircraft) at Darwin after nineteen days – three days outside the record. As she had said at Croydon,
time did not matter. She was a heroine.

There were, of course, critics of her exploits. Charles Grey, always
described as 'the monocled editor' of *Aeroplane* magazine, made it his
business to denigrate her achievement. 'The epochal nature of her
feat,' he predicted, 'cannot long survive as the music-hall turn which
it has inescapably become.'[6] Unfortunately Miss Johnson also provided
ammunition for even less prejudiced detractors than Mr Grey.

During her triumphant tour of Australia Johnson's personal finances
had spectacularly improved. The de Havilland Aircraft Company had
presented her with a new aeroplane and the *Daily Mail* had signed her

up for a publicity tour. The local newspapers calculated that, as a result, she was twelve thousand pounds better off. Then Castrol Oil announced that they were to sponsor her future endeavours. One newspaper headline called her 'Gold Digger of the Skyway'. Others were even less generous. And the reputation followed her home. On 5 May the *Daily Mail* gave a lunch in her honour at the Savoy and presented her with a gold cup and cheque for ten thousand pounds. On the following Sunday the *Observer* reported, 'Miss Johnson has issued a writ claiming £200 against the proprietors of the Palais Royal Dance Hall in Sydney. The sum is alleged to be a fee for her presence at a special ball during her stay.' The *Sunday Express* claimed that, 'Australian papers which criticised Amy Johnson state that when she was guest of honour at a Sydney theatre she received a gift of £100 each time. No £100. No Amy.'

Amy Johnson's flights continued to be interrupted with accidents and miscalculations. But that only made her achievements more heroic. She broke new records, year by year – London to Tokyo in 1931 and London to Cape Town in 1932. In 1934 she established a new record for the flight from London to Karachi. That year she had to share the glory with another pilot – J. A. Mollison, a Scot who had served with the RAF during the war and was employed by Australian National Airlines.

Mollison's ambition was to beat the record for a flight between England and Australia held by Flight Lieutenant Charles William Anderson Scott, a man described by Lord Amulree, the Secretary of State for Air, as 'a high type of all round development, mental as well as physical'.[7] Nobody had ever said that about Jim Mollison who, on the day after Scott landed in England, made his first attempt on the Australia to Europe record. Heavily laden with fuel, his Moth failed to take off and crashed into the aerodrome fence. The plane, though not the pilot, was damaged beyond repair.

At first Mollison's exploits were barely noticed in Britain. The newspapers already had a male aviation hero to compete for headlines with Amy Johnson. His name was Alan Cobham. He had spent most of 1919 touring the country giving joy rides in an army surplus reconnaissance aircraft and graduated to piloting air transport planes with

the slogan, 'Fly Anyone – Anywhere'. In 1924 he had won the King's
Cup (a round-Britain air race organised on the principle of a motor
rally) and was, in consequence, awarded the Royal Aeronautical Club's
Gold Medal. He became a national hero (and was knighted) after a
flight from Australia, which ended with him landing his his seaplane
on the Thames in front of the Houses of Parliament. By July 1931
Cobham was the star of the aviation show and Mollison a member of
the supporting cast. Sir Alan charted new routes over Africa for the Air
Ministry and Wonderful Amy, having flown to Tokyo in seven days,
received the Japanese Medal of Success. On the day of her arrival in
the Far East Mollison, who had lost his way in fog during what
amounted to a local flight from Le Bourget, landed on Pevensey
Beach. As usual, it was a bumpy landing.

The flight – despite its embarrassing ending – made Mollison's
reputation. It was the last leg of a record-breaking journey from
Australia to England which Mollison had completed in eight days and
twenty-one hours, averaging 1,100 miles a day, surviving on two
hours' sleep at night. More records followed. His first attempt to better
the London to Cape Town time ended in failure, though he made the
fastest-ever journey between Britain and Egypt. But his second, with
the benefits of an enclosed cockpit and an extra-large fuel tank, both
established a new record and won the praise of the usually grudging
*Flight* magazine. 'Anyone who has made a flight of even a few hours
knows the almost irresistible tendency to sleep induced by the engine
drone. How Mollison manages to remain awake with so little sleep is,
in itself, a wonder.'[8] His secret was alcohol.

By coincidence Amy Johnson was in South Africa recovering from
both a hysterectomy and a nervous breakdown, which had been more
induced by relentless publicity tours than by the demands of inter-
continental flying. She met Mollison and, after a six-month romance,
they married on 29 July 1932. Their wedding would, in any event, have
made them the undisputed champions of the aviation headline competition. But Cobham had already decided to transfer his enthusiasm
to the less glamorous but more remunerative business of organising
flying circuses. Other pilots attempted, and sometimes broke, records.
But Mr and Mrs Mollison led the news – not always for the best of
reasons.

A month after the marriage, Mollison set out to fly the Atlantic again. He flew the 2,600 miles from London to New Brunswick in thirty hours and thirty minutes, then left the aircraft, on landing, clearly drunk. For the next year records were interspersed between crash landings and aborted take-offs. Mollison flew from Port Natal to Brazil (4,600 miles) in just under four days, extended his flight to Rio Janeiro and then, to general surprise, announced that he would return home by sea via Madeira where he would be joined by his wife. On arrival in Southampton they immediately announced that they would fly together to New York and, on the return journey, carry on over Britain in order to see how long they could remain airborne. They crashed taking off at Croydon. A second flight began successfully but ended when, instead of landing in Maine (as Amy wanted), her husband insisted on going on to New York – where he wrecked the plane on landing. A flight from Toronto to Baghdad was abandoned after their plane (a Seafarer II) had twice failed to take off and then, on the third attempt, had succeeded in leaving the ground by a few feet, followed by a sudden descent which broke the undercarriage. Their journey home by sea was greeted by *Flight* with mock congratulations. 'Mollison will have created yet another record by being the only aviator who has crossed the Atlantic twice in a ship accompanied by a potentially record-breaking aeroplane.'[9]

Controversy was beginning to obscure the congratulations. The Mollisons quarrelled in public, separated and were reunited. Amy Mollison, as she had become – appointed aviation correspondent of the *Daily Mail* – claimed in an interview with the *Daily Despatch*[10] that when she had force-landed in Poland she had been 'molested by peasants who demanded money'. The Polish Embassy complained to the Royal Aeronautical Club, who made clear that it did not believe the story. Jim Mollison, exposed as a drunk, tried to justify his addiction in his autobiography.

With me it was brandy, lots of it. If you ride in baby cars, trams and trains you may sneer at me for drinking on the job. You drink next time you are cold, tired, frightened. Then you will understand why.[11]

By 1934 new – and less flawed heroes – had begun to take to the skies. On 23 May Jean Batten flew from Darwin to Perth in four and a half days fewer than Amy Johnson had taken to cover the same route. And when a new plane was designed to compete in the MacRobertson Air Race it was not the Mollisons who flew the Comet to victory but Charles Scott and Thomas Black. The Mollison era was coming to an end, but they had a lasting legacy. They had made flight glamorous. In the years which followed their fame aeroplanes became just superior forms of transport and an essential element in the preparation for the war which everyone anticipated. But the public, thanks to Jim and Amy, still thought of flying as an adventure.

Commercial flights – passengers rather than freight – began almost immediately after the end of the war. Surprisingly, Germany was first in the field. On 5 February 1919 Deutsche Luftreederei opened a service between Berlin, Leipzig and Weimar. Ten days later France, in the form of the Farman Company, began regular flights between Paris and London. The pattern persisted in the years between the wars. Britain always lagged behind – usually America, but far too often Europe.

In August 1919 the Aircraft and Travel Company Limited opened a two-and-a-half hour service (for both passengers and freight) between London and Paris. It was the world's first scheduled commercial service but, at a fare of twenty-one pounds for a single journey, it failed to attract enough passengers to make the venture viable. It was another five years before Imperial Airways was created – long after KLM in Holland but well in advance of the United States Colonial Air Transport. For once the echoes of empire had been in tune with Britain's modern aspiration. The colonial connection encouraged the development first of long-haul routes and then of planes purpose-built to fly them. The colonial services began with the Handley Page W8, an adaptation of the 6/405 bomber. But it soon began to fly two purpose-built three-engined biplanes – the de Havilland Hercules and the Armstrong Argosy. Britain had become part of the boom in passenger flight. In 1919 – excluding Russia and China where the statistics were unobtainable and the totals almost certainly negligible –

commercial airlines carried five thousand passengers and flew a million 'passenger miles'. Ten years later the figures had increased to 434,000 passengers who had flown, in total, 57,000,000 miles.[12] During the 1920s air travel evolved from an eccentricity into an industry in its own right.

The development of the European transport plane was led by Fokker and Junkers of Germany, until both companies were challenged in their home market by the American development of genuine passenger 'airliners'. It began with the Boeing 247, which first flew in February 1933, and continued with the Douglas DCI. Britain, meanwhile, continued with the caution which led to the suggestion that Imperial Airways had chosen as its motto 'Slow But Sure'.[13] The Handley Page 42 and 45 carried forty passengers at 100 mph. The eight which were in service in the ten years before the war flew over ten million miles (one hundred thousand flying hours) without a major accident. But rival companies offered cheaper and swifter travel.

Britain could at least claim that, side by side with Germany, it pioneered light aircraft. Geoffrey de Havilland hoped that a variety of Moths – including Puss, Tiger and Dragon – would bring pleasure flying within reach of the masses. Alan Cobham, prompted by the Air Ministry, attempted to develop methods of refuelling in flight. The French pioneered the helicopter and the Spaniards, experimenting with the related gyroplane, prepared the way for the vertical landing and take-off aircraft which became an essential part of twentieth-century warfare.

Britain's failure to exploit aeronautic invention and innovation is, however, best illustrated by the official attitude towards the development of the jet engine. Frank Whittle had taken out a patent on the idea in 1930 but it was the Germans who (in August 1939) flew the first turbo jet, the Heinkel HE178. The stimulus of near-defeat prompted the British government to galvanise the aircraft industry into action. So the work of Doctor Hans von Ohain was caught and overtaken by the end of the war. But during the dog-days of the mid-1930s, the prospects of progress were destroyed by ministers who were as out of touch as they were complacent. In 1934 the Under

Secretary for Air exemplified their attitude in a letter to the British
Interplanetary Society.

> We follow with interest any work which is being done in other
> countries on jet propulsion, but scientific investigations into the
> possibilities has given no indication that the method can be a
> serious competition to the airscrew-engine combination. We do
> not consider that we should be justified on spending any time
> and money on it ourselves.[14]

A year later, the impetus to make belated improvements to Britain's
air defences began the drive to design, if not to produce, new war
planes. The names now sound like battle honours – Hawker
Hurricane in 1936 and, in the following year, the Supermarine
Spitfire, the British Blenheim, the Vickers Armstrong Wellington and
the Handley Page Hampden. War became the mother of aeronautical
invention. The Gloster Gladiator, the last of the biplane fighter
aircraft, had a top speed of 250 mph and a practical ceiling of thirty-
three thousand feet. Part of its fuselage was made of wood. The
Spitfire, which replaced it as the RAF's premier fighter plane, was all
metal. It had a top speed of 350 mph and a ceiling of forty thousand
feet. The Second World War was a major stimulus to aviation. But it
exacted a price on the industry which had shown more dash and
daring than development in the years of peace. Amy Johnson
Mollison, who had spent the war ferrying planes across the Atlantic,
was lost in the Thames during what was officially described as 'a
routine flight'.

In comparison to the excitement which kept both aviators and aviation on the front page of British newspapers, the motor industry
made prosaic progress. It had its heroes. Principal among them was
Malcolm Campbell – the son of a broken marriage who, as a youth,
consistently failed to live up to his father's expectations. He rejected
employment in the family diamond business and became an insurance
broker. In 1913 he began to race, first motorcycles and then cars – an
enthusiasm interrupted by war service with the Royal Flying Corps.
Peace did not bring Campbell contentment. Both his private and

professional life staggered from crisis to crisis. He drove his racing cars
and speedboats with the reckless fury of a man who cared for neither
life nor death. And he fitted perfectly into the bogus gentility of
motor sport. The organisers worked hard to make the atmosphere
around the track reminiscent of Ascot and Epsom. Drivers talked of
'stabling their mounts' in the garages and there was a suggestion that
drivers should wear distinctive colours. Campbell, it was assumed,
would wear his clan tartan.

Sir Henry Segrave, who broke the land speed record in 1929, might
have achieved Campbell's success and enjoyed his fame, had he not
been killed a year later on Lake Windermere while trying to beat the
world water speed record. Segrave – an Eton contemporary of
Anthony Eden and Aldous Huxley – volunteered for active service
when he was seventeen. He transferred from the infantry to the Royal
Flying Corps after twice being wounded. In July 1916, after a plane
crash which may have been the result of nothing more heroic than
engine failure, he was judged unfit for front-line duties and served on
the staff in London. As a result, Segrave joined the establishment.
When – with some difficulty – he broke into motor sport, he became
Whitehall's favourite driver. After forcing his way into the Sunbeam
racing team he won the French Grand Prix in 1923 and the Spanish
Grand Prix a year later – and became the bridging passage between
the hardened professional driver and the gifted amateur.

In 1926, the year in which the British Grand Prix was first run, the
Sunbeam Company announced that it could no longer afford to compete. The new form of racing required the construction of specially
built cars with engines too large for use in regular vehicles. Campbell,
Segrave and John Cobb – a City merchant who was still an amateur
at heart – moved on to the pursuit of new land speed records.

In January 1926 Segrave recorded 152.33 mph on Southport Sands,
adding 1.53 mph to the 'flying kilometre' record. As the speeds
increased, the specifications of the cars grew more exacting and it
became necessary to find new locations where the extra miles an
hour were not hampered by the surface or the length of track. In 1928
Segrave reached 203 mph in Dayton, Ohio, and he pushed it up to 231
mph at the same location in 1931. Malcolm Campbell, in 1935,
became the first man to travel overland at a speed of 300 mph and, that

barrier being broken, transferred his interests to breaking the water speed record.

Both the cars and the drivers which made the record attempts only briefly captured public attention. But for a while the excitement of pure speed generated a demand for improved performance. Yet the motor industry – making cars for British roads – was not greatly affected by the derring-do of the record-breakers. Its development, between one war and another, was the story of gradual progress from meeting the wishes of the very rich to responding to the demands of a mass market. Segrave's Golden Arrow was what people read about in their newspapers. Ford's Model-T and the Austin Seven were what they saw on their streets and wanted to own. In a rare expansion into popular motoring, Donald Campbell drove an Austin Seven at 94.03 mph. It was small cars, winning small car races, which made the general public want and hope to become drivers.

The Great War had demonstrated, beyond doubt, that in the modern world motor transport was less a luxury than a necessity. The 'taxis of the Marne' had brought up the reserves which halted the German advance and the Indian Army had travelled across France in AEC-built London buses, on which advertisements for Oxo and Pears Soap were still prominently displayed. But it had also lost the industry five years of development. The Austin and Morris companies had switched from making cars to manufacturing munitions. In the process, they learned something about mass production – but not as much as they would have absorbed from direct competition with the American industry and the growing demand for an affordable car. At the start of the war the British motor industry was five years behind its American counterpart. By the end the gap had doubled.

One wartime regulation had provided at least the illusion of assistance. In 1915 Reginald McKenna – Chancellor of the Exchequer in the dying days of Asquith's government – imposed a 33 per cent tariff on motor imports. Initially, commercial vehicles were excused. But, together with freight and insurance costs, the duty increased the cost of passenger cars imported from America to 54 per cent[16] above their domestic price. When the war was over the tariff was continued as part of the general policy of taxing luxuries. It was briefly repealed by the short-lived Labour government of 1924, but restored – with commercial vehicles included – by its Tory successor and continued under the general protectionist policies of the national government of 1931. As always, there were arguments about the real benefit that protection provided. William Beveridge led a group of economists who argued that the tariff had insulated the industry from market forces which would have encouraged amalgamation and rationalisation. But one thing is certain. The tariff brought real competition to the British motor manufacturers' front door. Ford and General Motors both decided that they would beat the tariff by working inside it. General Motors bought Vauxhall and Ford moved its main production from Manchester to Dagenham where, it rightly believed, it could expand to the point at which it became a major player in the British market.

Whether or not Beveridge was right to argue that the tariff had encouraged the temporary survival of companies which (in the long term) were not viable, there is no doubt that, for one reason or another, the post-war industry was made up of too many small firms. The 'demobilisation boom' (which began immediately after the influenza epidemic and a brief coal shortage) was fuelled by low interest rates and easily available credit. Between 1919 and 1922 forty new types of car were available to British motorists and the total issue capital of the industry rose by fifty million pounds.[17] In 1922 there were ninety-five motor manufacturing companies in business in Great Britain. By 1926 there were forty. The manufacturers had only suffered a slow five-year decline. The workers were not so lucky. In February 1921 21.9 per cent of West Midland engineering employees were on the dole. By June the total had risen to 33.1 per cent.

Employment in the automotive industry was seasonal as well as cyclical since cars were sold most readily in spring and summer and the motor manufacturers were reluctant to store models which had been made in the autumn and winter. The 'linked spell' rule of unemployment benefit allowed car companies to lay off their employees for two days a week in the knowledge that the men would receive local assistance payments and be ready to return to work after the weekend. When they were in employment, the car workers earned high wages. In 1927 they averaged four pounds a week when the middle classes took home no more than five pounds. Ford was regarded as a particularly good employer. In 1926 it had reduced the working week from forty-eight to forty hours without a wage cut. It did however expect its employees to be upright citizens and sent inspectors to their houses to confirm that they were living respectable married lives. Trade unions were regarded as at best unnecessary and at worse a disruptive influence. The Transport and General Workers' Union began to recruit members in the motor plants during the spring of 1927. But for years Ford, Vauxhall and Morris Cowley stayed outside the Engineering Employers' Federation so as to avoid the unpleasant necessity of recognising any trade union. A combination of paternalism and egoism convinced the owners that they and their workers were in the same fight for success and survival.

Herbert Austin – now rightly regarded as a pioneer of efficient inter-war car production – only just survived the slump. His post-war error was to insist on making almost all the parts he needed at his own factory in Longbridge. As a result, the sudden fall in demand during 1920 and 1921 left him with almost two million pounds of debt.[18] Although the company was still making a working profit, shareholders rebelled at the news that there would be no dividend. Austin's problems were not all of his own making. By 1921 every car maker was feeling the effect of a sudden recession. But as he had expanded more quickly than the others the slump him hit particularly hard. The company had a thousand unwanted cars parked on wasteland at Longbridge. The receiver began to examine the possibility of the whole business going into liquidation. But a local draughtsman and a debenture issue saved the day. The long-term future of the company was gambled on an act of admirable daring. Herbert Austin changed company policy.

Having inspired his board of directors with the injunction, 'We have lost everything except our good name and we must not lose that,'[19] Herbert Austin went on to astound them with the proposal that future production should be based on 'a small family car within the reach of modest purses in regard to both first cost and more important, running expenses'.[20] The first reaction was entirely unfavourable. But Austin was alternately persuasive and insistent. The design, he announced, would be in the hands of a young employee who would work in his house, at his own expense. Stanley Edge was taken out of the Longbridge drawing office, installed at Lickey Grange in Bromsgrove, and, under close instruction from his chief, produced what was to be affectionately called 'a bath on wheels'. Its official name was the Austin Seven.

The first experimental model was ready for public view on Whit Monday 1922. It was unveiled at a carnival on the Austin sports ground – to the consternation of the salesmen who saw it for the first time. William Rootes – then the biggest dealer in Britain and soon to become a manufacturer in his own right – was typical. 'My dear sir,' he said to Austin, 'the public will never stand for it.'[21] Austin was unabashed. 'My dear sir, I am educating the public.'

Austin's optimism was justified. When the finished product was put on sale at Olympia in November *The Times* was complimentary and *Autocar* was fulsome, though its compliment sounds strange to modern motorists. The Austin Seven was, the enthusiasts' magazine proclaimed, 'remarkable'. At last there was a 'small car intended to compete with a motorcycle combination'.[22]

The Austin Seven was specifically aimed at the motorcycle market. Sales of 'combinations' (sidecars as well as the cycle itself), facilitated by manufacturer-sponsored 'easy payments' schemes, reached their inter-war peak in 1929, before compulsory third-party insurance (introduced in the following year) ended one of the advantages which they enjoyed over cars. Until then a comparison of running costs was always in the motorcycle's favour. An 4hp combination was on sale for something like £135 and cost 1 36d a mile to run. A 11.9hp car cost about £325 and could be kept on the road at 2.29d per mile.[23] The Austin Seven cost £195.

Any doubt that Austin was trying to capture the market was dispelled by his claim that the new car could fit into a motorcycle garage and easily pass through a gate wide enough to accommodate a cycle with sidecar. His second claim, which became the slogan by which the car was promoted, was clearly aimed at the same potential customers. It was, however, more difficult to substantiate. The Austin Seven, its manufacturer proclaimed, cost 'a penny a mile' to run. Had that been true, its petrol consumption would have been seventy-eight miles to the gallon.

False claims apart, the creation of the Austin Seven was an act of entrepreneurial genius. Herbert Austin's talent was not so much recognising what the public wanted but making it want what he had to offer. Edge, the car's creator, offered his own explanation for the success of the model he had designed. It was a version of Austin's promise to change the nation's attitude towards motoring. The success of the Austin Seven was a victory for 'supply creating demand and filling it to the last ounce and penny piece'.[24] By that he meant that the new model had created the hope of owning a car in the minds of thousands who had never before thought car ownership was for people like them.

To make and popularise a 'people's car' Austin had to weather a financial storm. Even in 1923, after the Austin Seven was in production, the company had debts of almost two million pounds and, although it had a working profit of £351,000 in the first three months of the year and the receiver was discharged, there was no hope of a dividend being declared and distributed. The surplus on the year's work had to be paid to the debenture holders whose loan had rescued the company during the previous year.

Austin thought that long-term salvation might lie in a merger with Morris Motors. Morris rejected the idea without even pausing to consider what Austin regarded as its merits. The General Motor Company of the United States might well have been willing to consider an amalgamation (which, in effect, would have been a takeover) but the Austin board was not prepared to see its company absorbed. With a highly marketable car in production, Austin chose to take the only route to a guaranteed future which was open to him – an improvement in production methods.

William Morris had, like every other motor manufacturer, been perilously close to bankruptcy during the 1921–22 slump. His liabilities included a contract to buy forty thousand engines from Hotchkiss of Coventry. It seemed unlikely that any of them would ever be put into car bodies. That one debt amounted to £137,000. Morris was saved by his friends. The Earl of Macclesfield and Arthur Gillett, a retired banker, gave personal guarantees to secure a bank loan. But there were still books to be balanced.

Morris' mistake had been almost identical to the error which Herbert Austin had rectified with the bath on wheels. He was making a car which cost (and was therefore priced) at a figure far too high to attract sales. In October 1920 the Morris Cowley sold for £465. Sales figures reflected the market's resistance – 235 complete cars and chassis (for bespoke body work) in October 1920 and 74 in January 1921. The first price cut was announced the following month. By November the Cowley retailed at £225 – £20 less than its production cost. The works was kept in business, the Hotchkiss engines were all used and, by improving the efficiency of the company, Morris was able within three years to reassert his authority within the engineering industry. When the Hochkiss management expressed reluctance to concentrate production on his needs Morris bought the company. In 1921 Hotchkiss produced one hundred complete engines a week. After Morris took it over in 1923 the figure increased to three hundred. By 1925 output had escalated to 1,250.

In the years which immediately followed the war the whole automotive industry had found it difficult to adjust to the new world in which it existed. Many of its leaders were sceptical about the merits of mass production, arguing that the British market could never replicate the vast demand enjoyed by American companies and that the smaller percentage of families who aspired to own a car would, unlike motorists in the United States, want something which was individual rather than standard. Morris was quicker than most to realise that the opportunities for expansion were boundless. 'Until the worker goes to his factory by car I shall not believe that we have touched more than a fringe of the home market.'[25] To tap that market it was necessary to exploit the benefits of standardisation.

It was not only the post-war slump which forced the motor manufacturers to face reality. Between 1924 and 1939 eighty carmakers went out of business and, thanks to the benefit of Morris' example, prices fell on average by 25 per cent. The fifty firms which survived were only able to remain in production because they changed. Slowly, very slowly, the British motor industry began to adopt the philosophy of Henry Ford – twenty years after he had laid down the principle on which he operated during a conversation with one of his investors.

The way to make automobiles is to make one automobile like another, to make them all alike, to make them come through the factory all alike. Just as one pin is like another pin when it comes from the pin factory, or one match is like another match when it comes from the match factory.

You need not fear about the market. The people will buy them alright. When you get to making the cars in quantity you can make them cheaper and when you make them cheaper you can get people with enough money to buy them. The market will take care of itself.[26]

On the basis of that philosophy fifteen million Model T Fords were made and sold. The Austin Seven – in a smaller market and a less propitious climate – sold three hundred thousand. It was a considerable achievement, which would not have been possible without production methods which approached the quality of the engineering and design. Austin's success was measured in the figures of man–hours and output which calculate production. In 1922 there were 3,500 employees at the Longbridge factory and it took fifty-five 'man-weeks' to build a car. By 1935 the labour force had grown to almost twenty thousand and production time had fallen to nine 'man-weeks'.[27]

Even as factory floor efficiency was being increased, the limits of the Morris/Austin vision were becoming clear. Two self-made men – one who had made bicycles, the other sheep-shearing machinery – were not impressed by all the American methods. Morris refused to employ graduates. Leonard Lord, one of the few professional managers to be employed by either company – he worked for each in turn – subscribed to the prejudices of his employers by not training apprentices.

That is not to say that they did not struggle for better performance within their own empires. William Morris had learned, when his Coventry factory switched from car production to making explosive 'mine sinkers', that specialisation and the division of labour pays. Made from start to finish on the premises, a mine sinker cost between forty and fifty pounds. Assembled from bought-in parts, they could be produced for less than thirty pounds.[28] In Morris' own estimation, one of the reasons for his inter-war success was 'methods learned during the war which I have adapted'.[29] 'Buying in' offered manufacturers another bonus. There was no need to stock components worth thousands of pounds. The capital outlay was financed by the companies which made and held the parts. But buying in only improved efficiency if the components – often acquired daily – were there when they were needed. Relying on outsourcing was an incentive to greater efficiency in internal organisation.

Some of the pre-war insistence that a car maker made every part of the car themselves was related to the belief that, in a limited market, high-quality cars had to be the work of individual craftsmen. The situation was typified by the production of car bodies. Until the late 1920s they were, almost invariably, made from wood and fabric. During the brief boom which followed the war, bodies could not be made quickly enough to meet demand or to keep pace with the production of chassis and engine. A letter in *Motor Agent* [30] illustrated the production technique of the period. It called for motor manufacturers to launch a major campaign to recruit joiners and cabinet makers. When the woodworkers had done their job the bodies were attached to the chassis by hand-forged metal flanges and brackets. Then the painting began – forty or fifty coats for expensive cars, twenty or thirty for cheaper models. Each coat was applied by hand and given several days to dry.

The American answer was all-metal bodies which, as well as being cheaper to produce, allowed cars to be designed with more elegant lines. But it did rely on the acceptance of a limited number of body shapes and therefore a limited number of basically different cars. Morris visited America in 1924 to see if the technique would travel. He was so impressed that, together with Edward Budd (the owner of a Philadelphia car body plant who held the patents for the process), he set up the Pressed Steel Company on land adjacent to his Cowley factory.

Morris, increasingly determined that he should control his component manufacturers, bought SU Carburettors to guarantee supplies at his own price. But some of the subsidiary companies were either too big or too stubborn to be absorbed into his empire. Joseph Lucas – the lamp manufacturer – was a beneficiary of the First World War. It had already evolved from hollow-ware wholesaler to pioneer of electricity-powered motor lighting systems. But it was the belated discovery, in 1914, that British car makers were dependent on German magnetos which allowed it to expand to a point at which it dominated the industry. Lucas acquired Bosch's British assets and, from that position of strength, absorbed a number of smaller companies and became Morris Motors' principal supplier. When it expanded, with the acquisition of C. A.Vandervell and Rolax, Lucas virtually monopolised the supply of lamps and electrical components to all the high-volume car makers. In 1931 it signed an agreement with Bosch, by which the two companies shared the result of research but agreed not to trespass on each other's territory. Autolite of America was paid not to export to Britain. Lucas's domination of the market – although not the result of the competitive forces which are supposed to promote efficiency – was complete.

Dunlop began as a manufacturer of pneumatic safety bicycle tyres – the invention of its founder, a Belfast veterinary surgeon. During the Great War it perfected the production of a rubberised material which would bear the weight of a motor vehicle. Until 1926 it withstood the competition of foreign imports. Then, ironically, when import duties were extended to tyres, it faced the stern challenge of Goodyear-Firestone (from America), Michelin (from France) and Pirelli (from Italy). All three companies decided to establish British plants inside the 'protective' tariff.

Britain was at least abreast, perhaps ahead, of the United States in the development of tyres and electrical lamps. But America continued to innovate. In 1926 Henry Ford – involved in a car crash – was badly cut by broken glass. The next day he received a telegram, 'Fit Triplex and be safe'.[31] Seven months later Triplex signed a contract with Ford to provide shatterproof glass for all the cars that the company made. Britain followed suit. Austin began to fit Triplex glass windscreens a year later. Morris, believing that he had been outsmarted, acquired a controlling interest in the company and sold himself glass at so low a price that Triplex ran at a loss. As cars improved, demand expanded.

A survey conducted by the Society of Motor Manufacturers and Traders (SMMT) in 1926 had aimed at making an estimate of the total number of potential motorists. Families with annual incomes of less than £130 were not even included in a survey which assumed that nobody who earned less than £450 a year could afford to own and run a car. Of the 4,700,000 families examined, 3,940,000 were thought to be incapable of sustaining ownership, while 87,700 were judged (since they had incomes of more than £2,000 a year) to be in the 'two-car bracket'. That left 660,000 one-car families and a home market ceiling of 835,000.[32] The SMMT made the crucial error of imagining that the pattern of demand, and the way in which cars would be acquired, would never alter.

Over the next ten years attitudes – as well as the pattern of personal income and car prices – changed. Hire purchase became more generally available and more acceptable. Cars were offered to an increasing number of employees – salesmen in particular – as part of their incomes. Most important of all, working-class incomes increased and those who received them showed themselves willing to postpone or abandon other pleasures and purchases in the interest of buying a car.

The continual determination to improve the product was certainly a contributing factor in the expansion of the automotive industry. But the great incentive was, as always, increasing demand. It is possible to argue about how much of the new desire to own a car was spontaneous and the achievement of that aim the satisfaction of a long-felt want. Men like Austin and Morris carefully promoted the notion that the good life included motoring. That is the way of the successful entrepreneur. What is beyond doubt is that during the years between the wars the ownership of a motor car changed from the privilege of a few to the aspiration of the whole population and the achievement of the middle classes. At the same time – as both the cause and effect of that process – the nature of car production changed from craftsmanship to mass production. For some people it remained a status symbol. But, for most drivers, it became a practical convenience which swiftly turned into a necessity.

The change is clear from the statistics of production. In 1926 the British automobile industry produced 153,500 cars. Ten years later output had more than doubled, and at its peak in 1938 it totalled 341,628.[33] At the same time, the real cost of a car fell dramatically – reflecting both the car makers' increased efficiency and the ruthless competition in the retail market. The index price (taking 1924 as 100) had fallen to 49.8 in 1935. Cars were becoming within the means of families who had previously hoped for no more than a motor cycle and sidecar. Ford's prediction and Austin's aspiration had both become reality.

The advent of 'family motoring' encouraged (and was itself encouraged by) a whole series of innovations. In 1925 front-wheel brakes became standard on the Morris Oxford. In that year the 'bull-nose' Morris became Britain's most popular car. The 54,000 models sold accounted for over 40 per cent of the market. Windscreen wipers and five-point lighting were available, though charged as optional extras. Five years later more expensive makes of cars – led by Sunbeam – were offering synchromesh on some forward gears, shock absorbers and four-wheel braking. Radio receivers were advertised inside the back cover of *The Romance of the Road*.[34] Cars, easier to drive and more of a pleasure for passengers, became both fashionable and a protected species.

That was not because the motor car was in danger of extinction. In 1918 160,222 were on the roads of the United Kingdom, which then included what is now the Republic of Ireland. That was a lower figure than in 1912, but by 1921 there were 478,538 registrations – an increase of almost 300 per cent. Private ownership rose from 77,707 to 245,882 while the number of lorries increased from 40,700 to 134,549. Every sort of vehicle was obliged to observe a speed limit of 20 mph, laid down in the 1903 Traffic Act. Those who chose not to do so were rarely prosecuted. The 1930 Road Traffic Act – which also created traffic commissioners to regulate bus routes throughout Britain and imposed tentative obligations to insure all vehicles – abolished the speed limit completely. There was no driving test or driving licence. Drivers were essentially self-regulating and at legal risk only from specific offences of dangerous and careless driving.

The anecdotal evidence suggests that the courts were not over-severe in their application of the law. The West Middlesex coroner, conducting an inquest into an 86-year-old accident victim, warned that 'old ladies who go about like this may cause any amount of danger to other people. In trying to avoid them, motorists and cyclists may find themselves in other difficulties.'[35] In 1934, ninety-one motorists were prosecuted for manslaughter. Fifteen were found guilty – despite a Home Office circular urging the judiciary to take motoring offences more seriously. That year, a new Traffic Act was passed through both Houses of Parliament – despite the predictable protests of the motor industry, led by the Automobile Association and the Royal Automobile Club. It introduced the 30 mph speed limit in built-up areas (defined as streets with local authority lighting), tightened the regulations which required all vehicles to be covered by comprehensive insurance, established controlled 'pedestrian crossings' on urban roads and limited licences, previously available to anyone who paid the fee, to drivers who passed a test. Sixty-nine years after the Locomotive Act required a motor car to be preceded by a man with a red flag, it was officially recognised that the way in which a vehicle is driven is as important to the protection of life and property as its speed.

There was talk of a vast national programme of trunk-road build-ing – inspired in part by the German example and encouraged by the experience of America's New Deal, which had demonstrated that investment in public works was a sure and certain method of reduc-ing unemployment and made a direct and immediate contribution to national prosperity. A National Road Improvement Fund – created in 1909, when it was clear that tarmacadam must replace cobblestones – had been expropriated by the Treasury during the war as a contribu-tion towards the cost of victory. However in 1918, special grants were made towards the reconstruction of roads which had deteriorated because of wartime neglect. But the licence was bringing in more revenue than the government could, or was willing to, spend. So in 1925 Winston Churchill, the Chancellor of the Exchequer, raided the Road Fund again in order to balance the national budget. From then on a fund, exclusively devoted to road improvements, was a Treasury fiction.

In the year before the outbreak of war the glamour of flight and land speed records was briefly superseded by the glittering achievement of a more ancient form of transport. On 3 July 1938, *The Mallard*, travel-ling south from Grantham to King's Cross on the LNER line, reached a speed of 126 mph – beating the world record and adding to the romance of railways that its illustrious predecessors, notably *The Coronation* and *The Flying Scotsman*, had done so much to preserve. Motor cars and aeroplanes had begun to change the way in which the world both worked and played. But a voice echoing out of the 1920s had already warned of the dangers which would follow the rejection of rail in favour of roads. 'There is little doubt that a halt will have to be called to the national expenditure on roads. Great Britain absolutely cannot afford to discard the finest railway system in the world and build roads to take its place.' The prophet of potential doom was Sir Henry Segrave.

## CHAPTER ELEVEN

# Taking Part

Daddy quietly passed away . . . Dads looked so lovely like a wonderful marble statue. Kissed him goodnight. Gloucester 69 all
out. Yorkshire 98 all out. Yorks second innings 18 for 3.

(Elizabeth) Daphne Thompson, aged 16
cricket enthusiast
12 May 1924

Seventy-nine British rugby internationals were killed during the
First World War – more than five whole teams. Other sports could
not quote such a spectacular example of service and sacrifice. But
there is no doubt that losses among cricketers, association footballers
and athletes were just as great. It was for that reason that survivors
deeply resented the couplet with which Rudyard Kipling began a
poem strangely entitled 'Russia to the Pacifists'.

*God rest you, peaceful gentlemen, let nothing you dismay,*
*But – leave your sports a little while – the dead are borne this way!*

Kipling – who had a low opinion of 'flannelled fools and muddied oafs'
in both peace and war – argued in vain for a postponement of sporting
hostilities. Having done their patriotic duty in full measure the athletes,

cricketers and footballers wanted no let or hindrance to prevent a swift return to the track, pitch and field. Some expressed their desire to re-create the world which had passed in stunningly insensitive language. *Bailey's Hunting Directory* for 1919 described the consequences of the four-year slaughter which, when compared with the British casualty figures – 750,000 dead, 1,500,000 seriously wounded – seemed embarrassingly trivial.

> It is a very sad state of affairs, and one for which the war is entirely responsible, but it is nevertheless a fact that the prices of horses, of saddles, clothes, forage, hounds, meal and every commodity that is used in the hunt establishments have risen at least 100 per cent and the wages have gone up in similar fashion.

Cricket reacted to the challenges of peace very differently. A few radicals feared that the returning warriors would find the pace of the game too slow. They proposed 'reforms', which ranged from shorter boundaries to the prohibition of left-handed batting as a way of eliminating the *longueurs* of field changes. Some traditionalists – who had feared that the pre-war game had been made dull by the rise of dour professionalism – called for a limit on the number of 'players', as distinct from 'gentlemen', in county teams. But Lord Harris – doyen of county chairmen and sometime captain of Yorkshire – had no doubt that the game was indestructible. His faith was vindicated. Big matches at Lord's, before the war, had attracted crowds of seven or eight thousand. After the war they averaged twenty-six thousand and sometimes rose to thirty thousand. The 'Roses Match' between Yorkshire and Lancashire, played at Bramall Lane, Sheffield, in 1919 was watched, on the Saturday, by forty-five thousand spectators. The 1920 *Wisden* 'cricketer's almanac' applauded Lord Harris' prescience.

> In the days of the war, he expressed his conviction that, when peace came back, cricket would have all its old charm for the English people. Everything he said was amply justified.[1]

The undoubted charm of the English game was not matched by its success. A series of 'gentlemen' captains were appointed and arbitrarily dismissed. J. W. H. T. Douglas lost five-nil in Australia and (after losing two more matches in England) was replaced by Lionel Tennyson, who lost one and drew two. A. W. Carr drew three Test Matches, was ill during the fourth and replaced by A. P. F. Chapman for the fifth. Chapman triumphed in Australia and the cricket establishment assumed that the English game was on the brink of a renaissance. They had, however, underestimated the influence of a new phenomenon – a young Australian batsman from the backwoods town of Bowral. His name was Donald Bradman.

There has always been a disagreement about the nature of his genius. According to one theory, a peculiarity of brain or eye allowed him to see the ball more quickly and clearly than was possible for other human beings. The alternative – and more likely – explanation of his talent was his capacity for concentrated hard work. As a boy, he spent hours hitting a tennis ball, as it bounced off a wall, with a cricket stump. As a man, he applied himself to the task of making runs with ruthless determination. In a careeer which ended with a Test Match average of only a fraction below 100, no one could remember him ever deliberately hitting the ball in the air.

England felt the full force of Bradman's genius during the summer of 1930. He made 131 in the second innings of the first Test Match. In the second Test, at Lord's, he scored 254 out of an Australian total of 729 for six. At Leeds a month later he scored 300, in five hours and thirty-six minutes, on the opening day before he was eventually bowled for 334. At the Oval, in the last Test, he made 232 in a match which Australia won to regain the Ashes. No one – players, spectators or commentators – had ever seen anything like it.

The MCC's determination to bring the Ashes home after the winter tour of 1931–32 was reinforced by the personal antagonism towards Australian cricket and cricketers which was felt, and sometimes expressed, by the MCC establishment. The chief complaint concerned the status of the Australian players. Although they received barely disguised payments they were classified as amateurs. There is no doubt that the English gentlemen resented what they regarded as the pretensions of jumped-up colonials. But they also felt an obligation, in the words of A. W. Carr, to express their indignation that Australians 'were made a great fuss of and given privileges denied to our own professionals'.[2] Carr was allergic to green baggy caps and antipodean accents.

I know plenty of professionals whom I would be delighted to have as guests in my own home, but I am afraid that I cannot say the same about many of the Australians I have met.[3]

As it turned out, Carr was the man in command of the heavy artillery which, the strategists of Lords decided, would be brought up to breach the walls of the Australian defences. Two bowlers, fresh from the Nottingham coalfields, opened his county attack. Being players rather than gentlemen, their names appeared on the score cards as Larwood, H. and Voce, W. To employ them to full effect, England needed to be captained by a man of ruthless dedication.

It was, of course, inconceivable that the job should be offered to a professional. Jack Hobbs, perhaps the greatest English batsman of all time, had taken over the captaincy for the fourth Test in 1926 when A. W. Carr contracted tonsillitis on the first morning of the match. But although it was thought necessary to replace Carr for the final match in the series, Hobbs – being a player – was not considered. It was thought at the time that, even if the offer had been made, he would have refused it. Herbert Sutcliffe, the other half of the exalted opening partnership, had already declined a package deal which would have provided him with sufficient private income to change from player to gentleman and thus enable him to captain Yorkshire.

Sutcliffe was a complex character who was accused, by 'gentlemen' cricketers, of having ideas above his station. I. A. R. Peebles of Cambridge and Middlesex explained (or perhaps complained), 'He emerged from the First World War an officer, convinced that he could take his place in any society and to this end took pains to acquire the accents of Mayfair and Oxford rather than the broad vowels of Pudsey.' This attracted a certain amount of ridicule which might have disconcerted a lesser man but – his mind made up – Sutcliffe was never deflected from his chosen course.[4] And he possessed a fierce pride in his status as a *professional* cricketer. He not only rejected the offer of bogus employment and the Yorkshire captaincy as a 'gentleman', he also turned down the chance to captain the county as a player.

He was on tour with the MCC in South Africa when he received a letter from the Yorkshire Secretary.

Dear Herbert,

At the Committee Meeting yesterday you were appointed captain without your status being altered. It is hoped that this will be
agreeable to you and that you will accept the same and will be
happy and successful in your new and honoured position.[5]

Sutcliffe's reply was telegraphed not to the secretary but to Lord
Hawke, the president.

Official invitation received yesterday. Great honour regret to
decline. Willing to play under any captain elected.[6]

Whether or not Hobbs would have reacted in the same way, Surrey
never made a similar offer. The qualifications which the MCC
regarded as essential for the discharge of a captain's responsibility were
thought most likely to reside in a man who played the game for love
rather than money. But, faced with Donald Bradman and the possibility of humiliation at his hands, they selected a captain who played
cricket as if his life, not only his income, depended on it.

Douglas Jardine was educated at Winchester and Oxford. He was a
man of patrician appearance, aristocratic demeanour and a pathological dislike of the way in which cricket was played in Australia. He
particularly disapproved of the Australian spectators.

To take the most charitable view of the position, the behaviour
of Australian crowds at its best (when judged by the standards
accepted by the rest of the world) is not naturally good . . . Here
was democracy arrogating to itself the right to demand, in full, a
pound of flesh for which it had paid the princely sum of a
shilling or two at the gate.[7]

In short, Jardine did not like barracking. And the barrackers did not
like him. When he toured Australia in 1928–9 they took particular
exception to the Harlequin cap and silk cravat which he always
wore.

It was P. F. 'Plum' Warner, recently reappointed chairman of selectors, who picked out Jardine as the man to win back the Ashes. The news of his appointment caused Rockley Wilson – who taught Jardine at Winchester and occasionally bowled for Yorkshire – to predict, 'We shall win the Ashes, but we may very well lose the Dominion.'[8]

Warner – later Sir Pelham – was one of cricket's great survivors. As a young man he had earned his living as a journalist – often reporting matches in which he played – and, as a result, always maintained his amateur status. As England captain, he had been neither ruthless nor successful. Nor had he, either as captain or administrator, been notable for original thinking about the game. It seems most likely that the idea of developing a form of bowling which would bring Bradman down to the level of mortal Test cricketers was Jardine's, not Warner's.

Jardine was appointed with no more specific instruction than to fight hard and to tell Larwood and Voce to bowl fast. He decided on the way in which the battle should be conducted after observing Bradman's technique.

> Though I did not take part in the Oval Test Match of 1930 I have been told that Bradman's innings, impressive though it was in the number of runs scored, was far from convincing on the leg stump.[9]

He concluded that Bradman's supremacy could best be challenged by bowling at his leg stump at a speed which made it difficult for the batsman to defend both his wicket and his person. The idea was not new. Indeed Warner – in one of his more sanctimonious moments – had put on record in the *Morning Post* his distaste for Yorkshire's display of what was then called 'leg theory'.

> Bowes bowled with five men on the legside, and sent down several very short pitched balls which repeatedly bounced head high or more. Now that is not cricket and if all the fast bowlers were to adopt his methods the MCC would be compelled to step in and penalise the bowler who bowled the ball, less than half-way up the pitch.[10]

Four months later, Plum Warner – in his capacity as chairman of selectors, as distinct from journalist – selected Bill Bowes to augment Larwood and Voce in the employment of leg theory against the Australians in general and Bradman in particular.

Warner and Jardine set about their task with a deliberation which was out of keeping with the cavalier amateur tradition. Jardine sought advice from F. R. Foster, the Warwickshire and England bowler who had pioneered a benign form of leg theory during England's 1911–12 tour of Australia.* And Carr brought Larwood and Voce to London to hear what would be expected of them in Australia from Jardine himself.

In the first Test Match of the 1932–33 series Larwood – bowling with six close fielders on the leg side – took ten wickets for 124 runs. But Australia still mustered a respectable 360 in the first innings – and lost. In the second, Bowes bowled Bradman first ball and Australia won. Jardine, who had failed in all four innings of the first two Tests, offered – with proper patrician dignity – to stand down from the third. He left the room while the selectors deliberated. On his return, he was met with an equally patrician decision. '*Non possumus.*'[12] Had the decision been otherwise, the history of cricket would have been different. G. O. 'Gubby' Allen, the vice-captain and Jardine's putative replacement, disapproved of leg theory.

On the opening day of the third Test there were thirty-seven thousand spectators in the Melbourne ground. England, batting first, made a number of minor complaints about Australia's conduct. Resin, they claimed, had been rubbed into the ball. They accepted the bowler's protestations of innocence when he turned out one pocket, even though he did not empty the other. They then claimed that fielders were moving behind the bowler's arm. Before the second day began Eddie Paynter – the Lancashire all-rounder – was assaulted by hooligans on his way to the ground.

The early wickets in the Australian innings fell to orthodox fast bowling. Larwood was not bowling leg theory when he hit W. M. Woodfull over the heart. Although he batted on, medical opinion (at

---

*Foster subsequently apologised that his 'experience was put to such an unworthy cause'.[11]

least as reported in the Melbourne newspapers) claimed that, had the pericardium been full, Woodfull would have been killed. But the crisis which followed did not result solely from the Australian captain being only half a heartbeat away from death. The English captain's reaction to the incident was equally to blame.

Before it was clear how badly Woodfull had been hurt, Jardine called out, 'Well bowled, Harold.' Then, according to his critics, when the batsman was ready to receive the next ball, he stopped Larwood in the middle of his run up to the wicket and indicated that he wanted the field to move into its leg theory positions. The obvious intention was intimidation. That is why Bill Johnson, an Australian selector, called the England captain's behaviour 'the most unsporting act ever witnessed on a cricket field'.[13] Canon Hughes, the president of the Victoria Cricket Association, went further. He proposed that the rest of the matches in the series should be 'cancelled . . . let England take the Ashes for what they are worth'.[14] Woodfull batted on. Bradman, the last man out, was so disoriented that, at the end of his innings, he walked away from, rather than towards, the pavilion.

After stumps were drawn 'Plum' Warner went to the home side's dressing room to enquire about Woodfull's health and to commiserate with the shaken, but not injured, Australian captain. Their conversation was subsequently quoted, in many different forms, by a variety of eye-witnesses. The most plausible account begins with Woodfull, normally the mildest of men, rejecting Warner's peace overtures.

> 'I don't want to see you, Mr Warner. There are two teams out there. One is playing cricket. The other is not.' Warner then replied, 'Apart from that, we sincerely hope that you are not too badly hurt.' Woodfull mellowed a little. 'The bruise,' he said, 'is coming out.'[15]

Jack Fingleton – opening batsman and journalist – insists that the conversation continues with Woodfull adding, 'This game is too good to be spoilt. It is time that some people got out of it.' Another account of the confrontation suggests that the Australian captain's valedictory words were, 'The matter is in your hands, Mr Warner, and I have nothing further to say. Good afternoon.' An alternative version has Woodfull issuing what amounted to an ultimatum. 'If these tactics are persevered with, it may be better if I do not play the game.'[16]

The actual words which Woodfull used are less important than the use to which they were put. The next day various versions of his snub to Warner appeared in the newspapers. Warner, totally unequipped to deal with such a situation, issued a statement which claimed that the Australian captain had apologised for the public revelation of a private conversation and added, 'We are now the best of friends.' Woodfull felt honour-bound to repudiate the claim that he had been the source of the leak. His denial carried the strong implication that the claim of friendship was equally untrue.

In those distant days there was no play on Sundays. The Australian Board of Control (ABC) used the rest day to make formal representations to 'Plum' Warner. Jardine, they insisted, must abandon leg theory. Warner replied that team tactics were a matter for the captain. The ABC then considered approaching the MCC at Lords with an official request for Jardine to be instructed to change his tactics or be recalled. Meanwhile, the Test Match continued.

On the third day Australia fought back. But halfway through the afternoon Larwood – bowling fast and on the leg stump but to a conventional field – made Bert Oldfield, the Australian wicket-keeper, change his mind in mid-stroke. The cut, which became a pull, deflected the ball on to his temple. As he fell he cried, 'It wasn't your fault, Harold.' At the time he did not know that his skull was fractured.

Oldfield issued a statement exonerating Larwood but the Australian press was, naturally enough, less interested in intentions than in consequences. W. J. O'Reilly – known, because of the aggressive way in which he approached the game, as 'Tiger' – made no secret of their apprehension.

We made sentimental farewells to each batsman as he made his way out to bat. We had a genuine feeling that they were making a journey from which they might be brought back on a stretcher.[17]

Four members of the Australian Board of Control were in Adelaide. All of them believed that an official protest must be made. Other members were consulted by telegram. A majority of eight to five voted to cable Lord's. The message read,

Australian Board of Control to MCC 18 January 1933

Bodyline bowling assuming such proportions as to menace the best interests of the game, making protection of body by batsmen the main consideration. Causing intensely bitter feeling between players as well as injury. In our opinion it is unsportsmanlike. Unless stopped at once likely to upset friendly relations existing between England and Australia.

Immediately after it was dispatched a press conference was held in the Australian dressing room. Woodfull and Bradman refused to be associated with what they regarded as an unnecessary escalation of a dispute which should have been resolved in Australia.

Cricket correspondents at the press conference cabled their stories at the 'urgent rate'. The ABC sent its telegram by a slower route. As a result English newspapers reported the Australian protest before it was received by the MCC. That did nothing to make the Lord's committee more sympathetic to the ABC's complaint. Some days after the Adelaide Test Match had been comprehensively lost by Australia they condescended to reply. The response, constructed in less than perfect English, contained a challenge. Was the ABC so concerned about the state of play that it was prepared for the MCC touring party to return home at once?

We the Marylebone Cricket Club deplore your cable. We deprecate your opinion that there has been unsportsmanlike play. We have full confidence in captain, team and managers and are convinced that they would do nothing to infringe either the laws of cricket or the spirit of the game. We have no evidence that our confidence has been misplaced. Much as we regret accidents to Woodfull and Oldfield, we understand that in neither case was the bowler to blame. If the Australian Board of Control wish to

propose a new law or rule, it shall receive our careful consideration in due course. We hope the situation is not as serious as your
cable would seem to indicate, but if it is such as to jeopardise the
good relations between English and Australian cricketers and
you consider it desirable to cancel remainder of tour, we would
agree with great reluctance.

The national government in general – and J. H. Thomas, the
Colonial Secretary, in particular – were fearful that the row over nothing more than a game would escalate into a major conflict with the
whole Australian nation. There was even wild talk of the risk that
Australia would leave the Commonwealth. But the MCC
Committee – largely composed of aristocrats with military experience
to stiffen their backbone – held its collective nerve. On 30 January
1933 another telegram from the ABC played for time.

We the Australian Board of Control appreciate your difficulty in
dealing with matter raised in our cable without having seen the
actual play . . . We are deeply concerned that the ideals of the
game shall be protected and have therefore appointed a committee to report on the action necessary to eliminate such
bowling . . . from the beginning of the 1933–34 season.

The gentlemen of the MCC knew how to turn victory into the
enemy's complete rout. The second ABC cable received a reply within
twenty-four hours of its arrival.

We the Committee of the Marylebone Cricket Club note with
pleasure that you do not consider it necessary to cancel the
remainder of the programme and that you are postponing the
entire issue until after the present tour is completed. May we
accept this as a clear indication that the sportsmanship of our
team is not in question? We are sure you appreciate how
impossible it would be to play any Test Match in the spirit we all
desire unless both sides were satisfied that was no reflection upon
their sportsmanship.

After much soul-searching, the ABC capitulated. It did not go quite as far as Jardine demanded. The English captain wanted a full and public apology to the whole team. But the MCC were assured that, 'We do not consider the sportsmanship of your team to be in question.' The tour continued. Bradman, whose batting average for his whole Test career was 99.94, was reduced to human proportions and averaged only 56.57. England won the series by three matches to one. Australia retained its Dominion status.

Martindale and Constantine gave England a taste of its own body-line medicine when the West Indies toured England in the summer of 1933. But the MCC were adamant that the laws of cricket should not be changed, even though persistent bowling at the batsman's body 'would be against the spirit of the game'. In fact, Lord's felt in a position of such moral superiority that there was some talk of cancelling the 1934 Australian tour of England. In the end it went ahead – without Larwood or Voce in the home side. Australia regained the Ashes. The pendulum had swung again. There were personal triumphs – Len Hutton scored 364 against the Australians at the Oval in 1938 – but England did not win a series against the old enemy for the next twenty years.

Impatience with the amateur ethic – playing being more important than winning – spread far beyond Lord's and the MCC. Between the wars, the Olympic Games became as much a battle for national prestige as for personal excellence. The history of the Olympics has been confused in the public mind by *Chariots of Fire* compressing several Olympiads into one tournament. But the moral and message of the film holds good. Britain wanted above all to win gold.

The amateur ethos survived the war. At the Antwerp Olympics of 1920 Bevil Rudd of the Achilles Club won the 4,000 metres, narrowly beating Guy Butler (also of Achilles) into second place. And Philip Noel Baker – destined to become a Member of Parliament and Minister – stood aside from the 1,500 metres to allow Albert Hill, a working man, the chance to win a medal. Hill came first and went on to win the 500 metres. He repaid Noel Baker's sacrifice by turning professional immediately afterwards. Athletics, as a whole, was moving in the same direction.

Sam Mussabini, the coach of Polytechnic Harriers, accepted payment for providing personal training. Although his conduct broke no rules it was in conflict with the spirit of amateur athletics. But a new breed of runner was less concerned with the proprieties of competition than with the hope of glory. Mussabini was able to improve technique enough to gain the extra yard that was the difference between victory and defeat. He insisted on bent elbows and arms held low, and urged his protégés to grasp corks in their clenched fists as an aid to concentration. Most important of all, he made them concentrate on their first stride – which he measured, and marked during practice at what he regarded as the optimum length. His ruthless professionalism had a particular appeal to Harold Abrahams of Repton and Cambridge, who had won his heat in the 100 metres of the Antwerp Games but came nowhere in the final.

Abrahams was not just a sprinter. He had broken and still held the British long jump record. When the Amateur Athletics Association announced its team for the 1924 Games in Paris Abrahams was entered in the 100 and 200 metres, the long jump and the sprint relay.

In the *Daily Express* 'A Famous International Athlete' wrote that it was folly to stretch Abrahams' talent so thinly.

> H. M. Abrahams is chosen for four events, which is unfortunate. From the point of view of the Olympic Games this athlete should leave the long jump severely alone. The authorities surely do not imagine that he can perform at long jumping at two o'clock and run 200 metres at 2.30 on the same afternoon. Let us hope that Abrahams has been told by the authorities to concentrate his efforts on the 100 metres.[18]

'A Famous International Athlete' spoke with particular authority. It was the pseudonym of Abrahams himself. Whether or not the AAA executive knew of the connection, they paid heed. Abrahams' name was withdrawn from the long jump.

Abrahams was to run against the best sprinters in the world – Charles Paddock (the reigning Olympic champion), Jackson Scholz, Loren Murchison and Chester Bowman. The hotly anticipated showdown in the final might never have taken place. Abrahams was almost knocked out in the semi-final.

> I did a very stupid thing which nearly lost me the race. I saw a runner on my right move slightly. The pistol went off (I thought it might be a recall) and I took my mind right off the work in hand and I started badly as a result.[19]

He was behind until the last yard and a half. But he scraped through. In the final, he won in 10.52 seconds, two feet clear of Scholz. It was perhaps the greatest victory in British Olympic history.

The next day Abrahams came last in the final of the 200 metres. It did nothing to change his permanent place in the pantheon of athletics. Nor did the silver medal that he won in the 100-metres relay. One victory – perhaps one race – had made him the most exalted runner in the history of British athletics until Roger Bannister ran the first sub-four-minute mile. The following year – as if to confirm the wisdom of the advice which he had given himself before the Paris Olympics – Abrahams injured his leg while long jumping and never again took part in either track or field events. But on 25 July 1924 he had beaten the three best sprinters in the world and became the authentic hero of British amateur athletics – the dedicated gentleman.

Eric Liddell, the other British sprint gold medallist of the Paris Games, was a hero of a different sort. That he was an amateur of the purest kind was never in doubt. But he was more dedicated to what he believed to be his religious obligations than to bringing Olympic medals back to Britain. The all-conquering faith was the product of his upbringing. He was the son of a Christian missionary in the Tientsin province of China. At Eltham College in Blackheath – to which he was sent when he was five – teachers discovered that he was fast. Religion left little time for training. But, just before his twentieth birthday, and despite having received no formal coaching, Liddell won the 100-yards sprint in the Ireland-Scotland-England triangular tour-nament. In 1922 he won the first of his seven Scottish rugby caps and in the following year (with Abrahams injured and out of the compe-tition) he won the 100- and 200-yard titles at the Amateur Athletics

Association's annual championship – the 100 yards in one tenth of a second slower than the best time that year.

He had made clear from the start that he would not compete in the 100 metres heats in Paris. They were to be held on a Sunday and Liddell believed that to participate would be to defy the command to keep the day holy. He was more criticised for his refusal to run than he was praised for his piety – especially in Scotland. But the Olympic Committee of the AAA agreed to enter him for the 200 and 400 metres – races in which, because of the shortcomings of his technique, he was thought to be far less likely to win. He won the bronze medal in the 200 metres which, when he was drawn in the outside lane of the 400 metres final, was assumed to be the only trophy he would take home to Scotland.

The pessimism seemed justified when he ran the first half of the race at a pace which no one believed he could sustain. He won the race in 47.6 seconds, one fifth of a second outside the world record – or so the crowds in the stands were told. The Olympic Committee decided differently. The record was for 440 yards – run by Ted Meredith in 47.4 seconds. Since it was two and a half metres *longer* than the 400 metres it was said not to qualify as a world record. Liddell was awarded the crown.

It was four years later that Lord Burghley – who had won fame in Cambridge by running a full circuit of the Great Court of Trinity College while the clock chimed noon – won the 400-metres hurdles. Douglas Lowe came home from Amsterdam with the 800 metres gold medal. Tom Hampson won it for Britain again in Los Angeles four years later when Tommy Green – a railwayman and therefore not typical of the traditional Olympic athlete – came first in the 50-kilometre walk. But the sun was setting on the bright day of the genuine amateur athlete. The Olympic Committee had agreed that competitors could receive payment for 'broken time' – as long as it was paid by the employers from whom they have taken leave. The Soviet Union and the United States had begun to establish 'sports scholarships'. The devoted amateur was not quite extinct. But the age of the casual genius was over.

In association football the amateur ethos was in terminal decline. Even the Corinthian Casuals – a team which had once been synonymous with playing purely for pleasure – began to compete against professional teams. The Corinthians refused to take part in the FA Cup before the war but they agreed to enter the competition in 1922. In the same year Max Woosnam (once their most illustrious player) illustrated the shortcomings of the amateur game by winning a full international cap – a distinction he would have been unlikely to enjoy had he not signed on, first for Chelsea and then for Manchester United.

By then the Football League had begun to 'modernise' the structure of the game. Both the first and second divisions were expanded to include twenty-two teams. One beneficiary of the reorganisation was Arsenal – 'elevated' to the First Division although its position in the second did not justify promotion. It established the Gunners' reputation as fortune's favourite. It was to become the dominant club of 1930s football.

Much of Arsenal's success was due to the work of Herbert Chapman – attracted to the club by a salary of two thousand pounds a year. Under his management the club won the FA Cup in 1930 and the League in 1931 and 1933 – identical to the success he had achieved at Huddersfield, where he won the Cup in 1922 and the League in 1924 and 1925. Chapman was given credit for inventing the 'W-M formation', which became the strategic basis of the game for half a century. His scheme – centre half in line between the full backs with the two wing halfs playing ahead of them and the inside left and right playing just behind the centre forward and wingers – was designed to accommodate the first of regular changes to the rules of the game which were introduced to make play more exciting and therefore likely to attract bigger crowds. After 1925 a player was offside if only two players – rather than three – were between him and the goal when the ball was kicked. Chapman helped to change the game but, in football, tactical genius had to be augmented with hard cash. During Chapman's first two years as manager, Arsenal spent twenty-five thousand pounds on transfer fees – a fortune by inter-war standards. Two signings accounted for four-fifths of that total – David Jack from Bolton Wanderers for eleven thousand pounds in 1928 and Alex James from Preston North End in 1929 for nine thousand. But in other clubs the most popular heroes were home-grown. When it was rumoured that Stanley Matthews would leave Stoke City, three thousand men and women packed a protest meeting and another two thousand were locked out.

Huddersfield and Arsenal dominated the twenty years between the wars, but the manager who made them was lucky to survive in football long enough to guide them on to glory. In 1919, when he was in charge of Leeds City, the Football Association suspected that he was attracting players with the offer of illegal payments. The club refused to open its books and was, in consequence, evicted from the FA and expelled from the Football League. The best players were sold off to other clubs. The rest were auctioned with the furniture. Chapman was suspended, in the phrase of the time, *sine die*. But then the FA decided to announce the date on which for ever would end. The suspension lasted for one year.

In 1921 the third division was formed out of the old Southern League – only Grimsby Town (from just south of the crescent of rivers which Harry Hotspur said divided Britain) played anywhere in the north. A year after its foundation, the third division became the third division (south) and a third division (north) was created. There were forty Football League clubs in 1918. By 1921 there were eighty-six. The following year John Moores, a telegraph clerk from Liverpool, confirmed – if confirmation was needed – that football had become an industry as well as a sport. He established, on the strength of £150 capital, Littlewoods Football Pools. Ten years later Vernon's and a number of smaller companies were competing for custom with Littlewoods and ten million men and women (though mostly men) were 'filling in' a 'coupon' each week. By the time that the Second World War began pools companies, with thirty thousand employees, had an annual turnover of £50 million and were spending £20,000 a week on newspaper advertising.

The churches in general (and the Nonconformists in particular) were horrified by the explosion of what was – despite the small sums involved – a benign form of gambling. They campaigned with such success that even the Football Association, in its evidence to the 1933 Royal Commission on Lotteries and Betting, argued that the government should make football pools illegal. The Royal Commission disagreed. The FA's attempts to persuade the clubs not to advertise the pools in their programmes and to stop the pools companies from printing the fixture lists failed. But it maintained its policy of lofty disapproval. When, as a conciliatory gesture, the pools promoters offered to make an annual grant to assist in the development of the game, it was rejected.

Respectability, lost by the vicarious association with the pools, was – to a degree – restored by the patronage of the BBC. On 22 January 1927 the first live radio commentary was broadcast from Highbury. It was the radio – describing matches with the aid of a diagram which divided the pitch into numbered squares – which finally convinced the League that players would be identified by numbers. An experiment was begun in the season which followed the first broadcast commentary. Several permutations were tested. In the 1933 Cup Final Everton wore numbers one to eleven and Manchester City twelve to twenty-two. For the next sixty years both teams were always one to eleven. The goalkeeper, always number one, never wore a number.

In 1931 Sheffield United tried, unsuccessfully, to persuade the League to amend rule thirty-three so as to permit the unemployed to be admitted for half the usual price. It was a gesture of pure altruism. Each Saturday they filled their Bramall Lane ground at full price. Most first-division matches were played in front of packed stands and terraces. The crowds were largest in Scotland. In 1937 a crowd of 146,433 watched Celtic play Aberdeen at Hampden Park and the official attendance at the 'Old Firm' match between Celtic and Rangers at Ibrox in 1939 was 118,567.* Even in England, 'gates' were the highest in football history. After 1925 (when a count was first made) they never exceeded eighty thousand. But the best years were almost certainly before the count began. In April 1923 over two hundred thousand would-be spectators converged on Wembley Stadium in the hope of watching Bolton Wanderers play West Ham in the first Cup Final to be staged in the shadow of the twin towers.

The Cup Final was a preview. Wembley Stadium was built – at a cost of £750,000 – as part of the Empire Exhibition of 1924. Its total

---

*International matches attracted even bigger crowds. There were 149,547 spectators at the England/Scotland game at Hampden Park in 1937.

capacity was 127,000, counting both the stands and the terraces. There were some anxieties among the company's directors about the long-term profitability of so ambitious an idea. So they looked for an extended guarantee against bankruptcy. One was a deal negotiated with the FA. Wembley would host twenty-one Cup Finals – beginning in 1923. It was finished and ready just four days before kick-off.

Confident that all would be well, Wembley sold tickets for the stands. But in those days the men who stood on the terraces were expected to pay at the turnstiles. More than an hour before the game was due to begin it was clear that most of the crowd outside the ground would not be inside by three o'clock. Pressure from the back of the queue and panic at the front resulted in the turnstiles being stormed and broken down. The surge forward was too great for the terraces to accommodate. Men and boys tumbled over the barriers on to the pitch. By a miracle nobody was killed. When King George V arrived at two forty-five there were ten thousand spectators still on the pitch. They were gently pushed back by the first of the many Wembley legends – not a man but a white horse called Billie. It was ridden by Constable George Scorey.

Football, Britain's national game, was becoming the favourite sport of the entire universe. In Amsterdam in 1928 the first Congress of the Fédération Internationale de Football (FIFA) proposed an international competition to be called the World Championship. The four British national teams declined to take part. It was widely assumed that each 'home nation' – and England in particular – felt that the tournament was beneath their dignity and that play was likely to be below the quality to which their players were accustomed. But, if that was the real reason for the four nations' self-imposed isolation, their public explanation was very different. After the war, the home nations had joined with Belgium, Luxembourg and France in calling for the exclusion of Germany, Austria and Hungary from international competition. When the proposal was defeated on the traditional grounds that football transcended politics they withdrew from FIFA membership. Their return in 1924 was followed by an argument about the status of Olympic footballers who, like track and field athletes, were to be allowed to receive broken time payment from their employers. The

British Football Associations withdrew again in 1929. For the next ten years England, Scotland, Ireland and Wales chose not to compete in the World Cup, but they did play individual 'friendly' matches against continental opponents. If it really had been a feeling of superiority which kept them out of the World Cup, the results suggested that it had been unjustified.

In 1931 Scotland lost five-nil to Austria in Vienna – the first defeat inflicted upon them by a continental team. The following year England beat Austria at Stamford Bridge and Italy at Highbury, but in 1934 lost in Prague, Brussels and Budapest. In 1936 Austria avenged its Stamford Bridge defeat in a home tie. By 1938 the Foreign Office thought it necessary to warn the FA of 'the embarrassing situation created as the result of visits abroad by poor teams'.[20]

The embarrassment was alleviated by a conclusive victory – by three clear goals – over Germany in Berlin on 15 May 1938. But triumph was marred by a humiliation for which the Foreign Office should have prepared the Football Association. The world had witnessed Hitler's attitude to sport during the Olympic Games, held in the same city two years earlier. Hitler's attempt to turn the Olympiad into a festival of Aryan supremacy had been frustrated by the triple victory of Jesse Owens, the black American sprinter, but his intention had been clear from the start. However, Britain had justified its participation with the argument that its concern was sport rather than the persecution of the Jews. Harold Whitlock won the 50-kilometres walk and Britain came first in the double sculls and the 4 × 400 metres relay. The men who thought sport all-important regarded it as a satisfactory outcome.

The problem at the 1938 Berlin football international – which the Foreign Office should have anticipated, and perhaps did – was the pre-match ceremony. The Germans made clear that the England team would be expected to give the Nazi salute. The FA was doubtful about whether responding to the request would be the best way of fulfilling its traditional determination to keep politics out of sport. But His Britannic Majesty's Ambassador to Berlin – Sir Nevile Henderson – insisted that good manners required the guests to respect the wishes of the hosts. By one version of events, Eddie Hapgood, the England captain, argued against accepting the German Chancellor's diktat right until the moment at which the teams ran out onto the pitch. But

diplomacy prevailed and – according to Stanley Matthews – the players took sentimental refuge in concentrating their gaze on a lone
Union Flag in the crowd.[22] They gave the Nazi salute. The Foreign
Office was delighted. 'The splendid game played by the English team
was thoroughly enjoyed by a huge crowd.'[23] And *The Times* was even
more ecstatic. 'The English team made a good impression by raising
their arms in the German salute.'[24] The following day Aston Villa did
something to redeem England's honour when it beat a German Select
XI by three goals to two – having refused, point-blank, to give the
Nazi salute at the start.

Whatever the typical football supporter thought of Germany – and
the likelihood is many of them thought very little – the Fatherland
was held in high esteem by tennis enthusiasts. Baron Gottfried von
Cramm had lost (6–1 6–0 6–0) to Fred Perry in the 1936 Wimbledon
men's singles final without revealing that he was suffering from a
groin strain. Members of the All England Club were susceptible to
exhibitions of aristocratic chivalry. And they were profoundly dubious
about Fred Perry, who only became a national hero long after his playing days were over.

Perry had come out of park tennis. He was the son of a Labour and
Co-operative Member of Parliament. Worse still, he was a ruthless
competitor who made no secret of his passion to win. When he won
his first Wimbledon title in 1934 Jack Crawford – his defeated, but still
relaxed Australian opponent – was given the larger ovation. Crawford,
being rich, was indisputably an amateur. Perry, although still within the
All England Club's definition of that status, was earning money from
the game. After he won the American and Australian championships in
1933 Perry accepted employment with the Slazenger sports company. Technically he was the firm's Australian representative. Work for
them in London would have broken the All England Club's rules. But
everyone knew that his influence was worldwide.

Within weeks of winning at Wimbledon Perry was invited to join
the Bill Tilden professional tennis 'circus'. Despite the huge rewards
which Tilden offered, Perry turned him down. His determination to
win a second Wimbledon title and keep the Davis Cup in Great
Britain had been reinforced by appeals to his patriotism from both his

father and the Foreign Secretary. He also declined an offer from Daks to endorse the company's ready-made tailored trousers and receive a shilling for every pair sold. So he played again and won at Wimbledon in 1935. The third consecutive victory was Perry's last. He turned professional in the autumn of 1936 and his honorary membership of the All England Club – the privilege of all champions – was instantly and automatically withdrawn.

In golf, while the rapid distinction between professionals and amateurs remained, the disparity between the quality of play was so much greater than the differences in social background that the men who teed off for money became popular heroes. The British professionals won the Ryder Cup in 1933 (four years after its foundation) and in 1934 Henry Cotton broke an American monopoly which had lasted for more than a decade by winning the Open Championship. But Cotton was a gentleman who had left Dulwich College to risk all as an assistant golf professional in the way that public schoolboys, down the ages, had abandoned quad and dorm to find fame and fortune in the colours and colonies. And Cotton had proved the British could produce a golfer to match the apparently invincible Ben Hogan – a man whose American habits were as objectionable as his success. He refused to share the changing rooms with other professionals and ate lunch on the back seat of his Rolls-Royce.

Golf – always the people's game in Scotland – was gaining a wider appeal south of the border. London County Council, which still prohibited football in its parks on Sundays, had owned and managed a public golf course in Hainault Forest since before the war. When it suggested that a second be built in the Royal Park at Richmond the *Daily Mail* launched a campaign to persuade the Crown Estate to agree. After some doubt and delay, the Comptroller of Works offered to lease ninety-six acres at an annual rent of two hundred pounds. The creation of England's second municipal golf course was quickly followed by a third in Birmingham. By the outbreak of war there were thirty courses, which were open to the public on the purchase of a daily ticket rather than available only to members of the club.

★

Christopher Isherwood (left) and W. H. Auden, about to change trains. Their friendship, begun at prep school, lasted until Auden's death. *Getty Images*

James Joyce. *Finnegans Wake* ended with an unfinished sentence to illustrate that time is a circle not a straight line. *Getty Images*

Laurence Oliver planned, with Tyrone Guthrie, to play a Henry V who did not glorify war. 'But neither of us had the guts to go through with it.' *Topfoto*

Peggy Ashcroft. When she played Desdemona at Stratford, critics asked if she found kissing Paul Robeson (who played Othello) offensive. *Getty Images*

George Bernard Shaw. *St Joan* was a polemic against nationalism, the cause which had swept through his native Ireland. *Getty Images*

Edward Elgar. One of the few English composers to stand comparison with the continental masters. *Time & Life Pictures/Getty Images*

Amy Johnson and Jim Mollison broke records and attracted scandal in equal measure. *Getty Images*

William Morris points at the special features of the cut-price car which he taught the motoring public to love. *Getty Images*

John Reith, appointed Director General of the BBC, was 'profoundly grateful to God for His goodness in this matter. It is all His doing.' *Getty Images*

Geoffrey Davison: twice editor of *The Times*. Faith that he would stand up to his proprietors was justified. He took his instructions from the government. *Getty Images*

Noel Coward. Sensing the mood of the time, he abandoned exposés of scandalous conduct in favour of stories of old Vienna. *Getty Images*

Stanley Spencer painted angels in suburban houses and cherubs in tweed suits. *Getty Images*

Lord Rothermere used the *Daily Mail* to support Oswald Mosley's Blackshirts and undermine Baldwin's leadership of the Tory Party. *Topfoto*

Lord Beaverbrook: 'The foodstuffs we need in this country could all be raised either in our own soil or in British Dominions.' *Getty Images*

Neville Chamberlain returns
from a meeting with Adolf Hitler:
'I believe it is peace for our time.'
*Popperfoto*

Samuel Hoare. After he resigned from the Foreign Office, King George V told him, 'No
more coals to Newcastle and no more Hoares to Paris.' *Getty Images*

The 'sport of kings' – true to the paradox of its claim – remained immensely popular among both the working classes and aristocracy. There was, however, some concern that the social changes which followed the war had lowered the tone at Ascot. In 1921, some ladies wore the same dress on consecutive days and in 1924 some even wore sleeveless dresses, which exposed vaccination marks.[24] Increases in unemployment prompted some commentators to wonder if such a conspicuous display of idle wealth was wise. *The Times* would have none of it. 'The dislike of other people's pleasures, which has been an active force in English life for nearly three centuries, will always become vocal at such provocation as Ascot.'[25]

Winning jockeys had been popular heroes since racing began. They won money for their fans. And despite their usually humble beginnings they were able to dictate to the wealthy owners and aristocratic trainers for whom they rode. When Steve Donoghue won the 1922 Derby, he was paid a five-thousand-pound bonus. At the time, four pounds a week was a good wage. The grateful owner was not solely motivated by patrician generosity. Donoghue played notoriously fast and loose with stables. He accepted retainers and then deserted owners and trainers when he was offered a better ride. The 1922 bonus did not secure his loyalty.[*] In 1923 he accepted a ride from a rival stable and won the Derby on Papyrus – to the usual chorus of, 'Come on Steve.' Popularity as well as technique made Donoghue his own master.

Donoghue's successor as champion jockey was a man of less flamboyant disposition. Gordon Richards left school at thirteen to work in a warehouse – good, steady employment which his parents were desperately reluctant for him to leave. But, after much persuasion, they agreed to an apprenticeship with a respectable stable. Five years later he was champion jockey. In 1926 he was diagnosed as suffering from 'a tubercular infection'. But he was back in the saddle within a year and champion again in 1927. By then he was riding for Lord Glanely, a self-made millionaire with none of the virtues that are said to accompany noble birth. In 1930, in an effort to cut costs, Glanely

---

[*]He was, however, admirably loyal to winning horses. He won the Queen Alexandra stakes six times on the ex-steeplechaser Brown Jack.

proposed to reduce Richards' retainer by one thousand pounds a year. After negotiations, the reduction was halved. But an unhappy Richards lost the championship in 1931. So he moved on. The result was unparalleled success. He rode 4,870 winners in 21,843 races and was champion jockey twenty-six times in a career that spanned almost forty years.

Other sports had more exotic heroes. The Empire, as it was still called, was gradually achieving a supremacy in rugby union. Great Britain lost four of its five test matches during the 1930 tour of Australia and New Zealand and, during the return matches in 1931, the New Zealand All Blacks beat each of the home nations. But in 1936 England had its revenge when the White Russian émigré, Prince Alexander Obolensky, scored two tries to secure victory for his adopted country. His fame was guaranteed by his achievement being recorded on the newsreels which were shown before the big picture in every cinema. Rugby league, although attracting average gates of twenty-five thousand in the north-west, could not compete for glamour with the public school amateur game.

But the working class was on the march, bringing with it essentially working-class sports and pastimes. Tommy Farr, a miner from South Wales, kept half of Britain awake when the BBC broadcast a commentary on the New York fight in which he got near to beating Joe Louis, the Champion of the World. The Greyhound Racing Association was established in 1925 when – thanks to C. A. Munn's development of the electric hare – competitions could be run efficiently and free from the attentions of the animal welfare lobby. Belle Vue Stadium in Manchester was opened in 1926 and, after a slow start, confirmed the popularity of 'the dogs' to the satisfaction of entrepreneurs. New stadia were opened at Hall Green in Birmingham, the White City in London and Powder Hall in Edinburgh. William Hill, anticipating the popularity of the sport, made a book at the first White City meeting.

The popularity of motorcycling – and Britain's brief domination of the world market in motorcycles – encouraged both the extension of road racing (most famously on the Isle of Man) and the introduction of an Australian innovation called dirt-track racing. It soon adopted the Anglo-American name of 'speedway'. By 1939 there was a professional team in every city and, in the south of England, crowds of twenty thousand watched evening 'floodlight meetings'.

In the north of England the passion for 'coarse fishing' was undiminished. The platforms of Sunday tram-cars were regularly crammed with wicker baskets owned by men on their way to sit on the banks of canals and rivers while their floats bobbed in the grey waters of industrial Britain. But they were happy in the cold and rain – just as the spectators were content waiting for play to be resumed during bad light at county cricket matches and football fans gladly swayed up and down the Spion Kops and Bunker Hills as they concentrated on the great battles of Cup and League.

In *Brave New World* the Director of Hatcheries and Conditioning expresses his surprise that, 'even in Our Ford's day most games were played with no more apparatus than a ball or two, a few sticks and perhaps a bit of netting. Imagine the folly of allowing people to play elaborate games which do nothing to increase consumption.' He had failed to notice that during the dismal days between the wars sport was not only the opiate of the people. It gradually became big business.

## CHAPTER TWELVE

# Private Daydreams

We had local cinemas called flea pits. You came away with fleas, so decrepit were they. Some supplied a cup of tea at the interval. Later we had a few large new cinemas built. They seemed so luxurious then.

> May Hopper (née Cracknell)
> Born Walworth Road, London, 1919

The cinema (or 'the pictures', as it was called by the working class) took inter-war Britain by storm. In 1919 half a million men, women and children visited a cinema twice a week.[1] Five years later, according to the Conference on Christian Politics, Economics and Ethics, an evening at a picture house had become 'solidly established as the pastime of millions'.[2] Nine hundred and eighty-seven million cinema tickets were bought and sold in 1938 – making the cinema, in terms of crowd appeal, twenty-five times more popular than association football.[3] And the numbers continued to grow. By 1939 the weekly cinema audience was well over twenty-three million.[4] The cinema had become the entertainment of men and women who regarded a night out as an opportunity for relaxed and unselfconscious pleasure. Their carefree attitude – a feature of the abandon which followed the war – had, the establishment feared, cheapened and coarsened the previously elevating experience of attending the theatre.

Before 1914, an evening at a West End theatre was a social event. Patrons of the pit and gallery did not put on evening dress, but looked for this courtesy from the stalls and dress circle.[5]

Traditional theatre critics believed that theatre-goers from the lower middle class – 'perfect tweenies whose terror is to fall into the class below and ambition to rise into the higher class'[6] – would drag drama down to their own level. And the same people had become a major part of the rapidly increasing cinema audience.

Before 1914 films had often been shown in church halls, drill halls and assembly rooms, which were rented for weekend picture shows. Few of the temporary premises held more than a couple of hundred people and most were locally managed and owned. They were often affectionately, though appropriately, known as 'flea pits' and 'bug huts' – not at all the sort of accommodation for the products of the 'dream factories' that were to develop on both sides of the Atlantic.

As films – both their storylines and their production techniques – grew more sophisticated the buildings in which they were exhibited improved in design and construction and qualified for the name which their owners chose for them. Cinemas became 'picture palaces'.

The buildings themselves became escapist fantasies, their decor and accoutrements – sweeping marble staircases, silvery fountains, uniformed staff and glittering chandeliers – providing a real life extension of the glittering world on the screen.[7]

The architecture – mock Moorish palaces, ersatz Egyptian temples and bogus Spanish haciendas – was execrable. But it all contributed to the fancy which the pictures aimed to provide.

The improvement in comfort and the superficial opulence combined with the increased technical (and sometimes artistic) quality of films gradually to make 'going to the pictures' a middle- as well as a working-class occupation. By 1935 it was 'becoming distinctly rare to find an educated person who does not know something about the outstanding films of the last year or so. The cinema is acquiring prestige.'[8] What was more, it was acquiring an almost hypnotic hold over its devotees.

There is more to cinema going than seeing films. There is going
out at night. There is the sense of relaxation combined with the
sense of fun and exaltation . . . It is to be expected that success of
this sort will breed a habit and a habit will build a fashion . . . the
name picture palace is far from inapt.[9]

Thinking people began to wonder what effect the new phenomenon would have on the life of the nation. In 1938 Mass Observation –
which claimed to assess public opinion – examined the cinema goers'
motivation. The answer to the questions they asked was almost always
the same. It was escapism that drew people to the pictures. Seventy-
eight-year-old Lillie Williams was explicit. 'I go to the films to be
entertained, to be amused and to forget everything.' Thomas Wetherall,
a manual worker almost sixty years her junior, said much the same. 'I
like Western films because there is plenty of excitement, action,
killing . . . When you have spent a dull dreary day in the spinning
room you need to see some open air, like you usually get in Western
films.'[10]

Escapism was sometimes the product of desperation. George
Orwell described the power of the cinema to provide a moment's
insulation from the troubles of the world.

You may have three halfpence in your pocket, not a prospect in
the world and only the corner of a leaky bedroom to go home
to, but . . . you can stand at the street corner indulging in a private daydream of yourself as Clark Gable or Greta Garbo which
compensates for a great deal.[11]

It is important to note that Orwell's fantasists were 'wearing new
clothes'. The man had bought himself a suit 'for two pounds ten on
the hire purchase' and the women could 'look like a fashion plate at an
even lower price'. The dream world of the cinema could be inhabited
by the poor, but not by the very poor. The destitute could not afford
the price of a ticket.

A woman in Sheffield who is very poor, lives in a slum house
and has four children is in constantly bad health. She says that she

must rest sometimes during the day and sometimes plays cards or ludo. 'It's cheaper than the pictures. I have no money for the pictures.'[12]

The cinema was, however, the greatest single leisure occupation of the unemployed. Most of the out-of-work men attended matinée performances in order to take advantage of the lower admission price. Harry Hardcastle, the hero of Walter Greenwood's *Love on the Dole* – who bought a 'threepenny seat in a picture house twice a week' as well as attending a 'ninepenny or shilling dance on a Saturday night' – was almost certainly a member of the afternoon audience. During the great depression 43 per cent of all seats cost sixpence or less and another 37 per cent sold for no more than a shilling. There was a fear that – lumped together at the two o'clock performance, without the leaven of men in work to counteract their resentment – the unemployed would combine and foment dissent or even subversion. It was one of the reasons why, for twenty years, films shown in British cinemas were subject to the most rigorous – though politely ignored – censorship. It all came about in the most gentlemanly way.

When films first came to Britain only a tiny radical minority saw anything wrong in the Lord Chamberlain possessing the power to refuse a licence for the live performance of a play. So it was taken for granted that the cinema must accept parallel restrictions. In 1912 the industry itself created the British Board of Film Censors (BBFC) in the hope that, by accepting self-regulation, the production companies would prevent the government from interfering with the content of their films. In a sense, the tactic worked. Between the wars, numerous Acts of Parliament specified cinema opening days and times, imposed minimum safety regulations and limited the hours in which children and young people could be admitted. But subject matter, like the obligation to respect 'good taste and decency', was left to the discretion of the film-makers. Unfortunately, as often happens with self-regulation, independence was only preserved by the voluntary acceptance of limitations and prohibitions which were at least as restrictive as anything that ministers would have imposed. And they were not limited to avoiding the production of films which might deprave, corrupt or offend against the accepted canons of decency.

Between 1917 and 1929 (under the presidency of T. P. O'Connor, once a Parnellite in the Imperial Parliament) the Board set out forty-three basic rules which film-makers were required to obey if a 'licence to exhibit' in public was to be issued. They remained in force until 1945. Thirty-three of the rules concerned 'morality' – defined as references to sex, bodily functions and coarse language. Ten were entirely and overtly political. All 'subjects . . . which dealt with relations between capital and labour'[13] were banned. Lord Tyrrell, who became president of the BBFC in 1935, had no doubt that the political prohibitions were essential. 'Cinema,' he insisted, 'needs the constant suppression of controversy to stave off disaster.'[14] The Board was not just fearful that films dealing with industrial disputes would encourage social unrest. It was equally afraid that films about poverty would both demoralise the nation and provoke agitation. As a result, the first application to make *Love on the Dole* was rejected on the grounds that it portrayed 'too much of the tragic and sordid side of poverty'.*[15]

Some films which dealt with controversial subjects did slip through the net. But they invariably had happy endings and confirmed the superiority of the established economic order over all possible alternatives. They usually starred Gracie Fields as the ebullient mill girl who triumphs over adversity and, more often than not, illustrates the common interests of all classes by marrying a gentleman. Such a film was *Sing As We Go*, screenplay by J. B. Priestley.

Priestley's screenplay did not escape unscathed. The film's story began with the closure of Graybeck Mill, the catastrophe from which the rest of the action flowed. Priestley wanted the scene to be set by an elderly woman who 'tearfully and wearily' accepts her 'cards' in return for a very small pay-off. He was 'persuaded' to abandon the idea. On general release Graybeck Mill went out of business without much show of emotion from the redundant employees. The blame was laid explicitly on escalating production costs and the son of the owner heroically went down with the ship. Then the development of a new spinning technique enabled the whole labour force to be re-employed.

---

*The film was eventually made in the more socially relaxed atmosphere of wartime Britain. Deborah Kerr played the unlikely role of 'downtrodden' – as distinct from 'irrepressible' – mill girl.

Gracie Fields led the workers back into the mill – in a chorus of the title song. The film was a huge financial success.

Gracie Fields – on film if not in life – always conformed to the standards of behaviour which the censor thought should be reflected on the screen. Those standards required the rejection of *The Blue Circle* because 'the whole story centres around the drug traffic. The language and morals are impossible. Under no circumstances could the BBFC pass a film based on that play.'[16] Gracie Fields, on the other hand, represented virtue.

> In her own way, she has done a tremendous amount of good. In the cinema there is an absence of healthy amusement. There is too much sex appeal. But in the performance of Gracie Fields we get a breath of fresh air and the opportunity for some real laughter. This helps to keep the right spirit of England together – clean living with total absence of anything unnatural.[17]

If some films did influence the character of the nation, the result was not a new enthusiasm for revolution. A visit to the cinema made picture-goers want to live the dream.

The theatre was, in its own way, a dream factory too. But between the wars it tackled subjects which the cinema would not have dared examine. And it dealt with them in a way which the bright young things of the period accepted as daring rather than dull. Noel Coward's *The Vortex* led the vogue for entertainment dealing with topics which were previously not discussed in polite society. The subject's sensational impact on West End audiences was increased by the suspicion that Nicky Lancaster – drug addict, 'up in the air effeminate' and consumed by affection for his promiscuous mother – represented attributes which, to a lesser degree, Coward shared. The young John Gielgud – chosen to play the part in America because he could play the piano! – described his lines as 'so extraordinarily characteristic that when you had heard [Coward] deliver them himself, it is almost impossible to speak them on stage without giving a poor imitation'.[18] Neither the plot nor the characters made *The Vortex* a twentieth-century *Oedipus Rex*. But it did make audiences think –

although the pleasure it provided to those who liked to shock the easily shockable was, in its way, an escape from the more prosaic problems of everyday life. Coward had sufficient theatrical ingenuity to enable him also to play a part in providing the more conventional forms of escapism. Between the wars much of it was set to music.

Much of Coward's success was the result of his ability to judge the mood of the times. So he moved on from the risqué examination of social scandals to uninhibited nostalgia and romance. *The Vortex* and *Private Lives* – a frivolous examination of divorce and adultery – gave way to *Bitter Sweet*, a romance of Old Vienna. But it was America, not Europe, which colonised the popular theatre, as it was colonising the cinema.

The enthusiasm for musicals was long-standing but in the 1930s – partly due to the export of American productions – the escapist magic of good songs and plots which ended with the heroine and hero living happily ever after was in greater demand than ever before. The Cinderella story, in which virtue triumphs and love conquers all, was particularly attractive to a nation in economic distress. It took on a new and unusual lease of life with Bobby Howes starring in *Mr Cinders*, a male version of the rags-to-riches story. Every year throughout the 1930s he played in a new heart-warming story of victory over adversity. For theatregoers who wanted something more rumbustious there were three adaptations of German operettas – *The White Horse Inn*, *Waltzes from Vienna* and *Casanova* – while Drury Lane revived its fortunes with two Ivor Novello extravaganzas – *The Dancing Years* and *Glamorous Nights* – which even James Agate's review could not destroy.

> The first glimpse of Krasnia consists, quite rightly, of twenty-four Hussars lined up in front of a curtain and singing a rousing song entitled 'Her Majesty Militza'. This is strange since Militza is King Stephen's mistress and not his Queen and irony in Hussars is misplaced.[18]

No one ever suggested an Ivor Novello musical, as distinct from Ivor Novello himself, was sophisticated. And, at least in spirit if not in setting, his work was far more English than Ruritanian. 'Englishness' was an essential ingredient of the early post-war musical theatre, with Jack Buchanan and Jack Hulbert specialising in a character – elegant in white tie and tails and insouciant in the face of both danger and romance – who was thought to be the epitome of the upper-class English gentleman. Often the genteel elegance of the male lead was in sharp contrast to the cheerful indomitability of the working-class heroine – usually played by Jessie Matthews. But after the transatlantic cultural invasion began, white tie and tails became the prerogative of Fred Astaire dancing in American with his sister Adele before she left the stage to marry into the aristocracy.

Jessie Matthews had to compete for stardom and popularity with Dorothy Dickson, who came to London to star in a Cochrane revue and stayed to play the lead in three Jerome Kern musicals – *Sally*, *The Cabaret Girl* and *The Beauty Prize*. English additions to the cast were not always an unqualified success. *Show Boat* – a commercial sensation which, along with *Rose Marie* and *Desert Song*, helped to rescue the fortunes of Drury Lane – had, as the actor-manager of the paddle steamer which brought music hall to the Mississippi, Cedric (later Sir Cedric) Hardwicke. According to Agate he played the part 'in his well-known Devonshire manner'.[19] Vincent Youmans' *No, No Nanette* opened in London and then transferred to New York. But the description 'Broadway musical' had acquired a cachet which London productions found hard to match. Even the title of Cole Porter's *Nymph Errant* suggested that the audience would be transported into the glamorous world of cocktails and polo tournaments. The best musicals became movies, with real desert in the *Desert Song* and convincing cardboard Rockies in *Rose Marie*. They were made in Hollywood.

Some quintessential English productions bloomed amid the exotic transatlantic imports. *Me and My Girl* was cockney to its core and *The Crazy Gang* exhibited a peculiarly British humour. Throughout the 1920s stage thrillers remained stubbornly loyal to heroes in the trench coats they had worn in France and Flanders. But as the memories of the war faded 'whodunnits' conformed to the 'modern' desire to shock and scandalise. Emlyn Williams' *Night Must Fall* was the story of a young Welshman with an Oedipus complex. It was inspired by the story of a German murderer who ate his victim's flesh – a crime which so fascinated Williams that he visited the scene. Cannibalism was apparently more acceptable on stage than lesbianism. *Night Must Fall* was passed for public performance. *Children in Uniform*, which was thought to have Sapphic overtones, was certified as suitable for production only 'on the proviso that the setting remains German'. But the mood of the time did not favour the sort of outright challenge to Grundyism that Shaw and Granville-Barker had mounted in Edwardian Britain. When Noel Coward's *Design for Living* was refused a licence the playwright just waited for the Lord Chamberlain's office to grow up and change its mind.

On the evidence of *When We Are Married* J. B. Priestley – who enjoyed a popular triumph with *The Good Companions*, a picaresque novel of theatre life – could have become the great comic dramatist of the 1930s. He chose instead to attempt experimental theatre – a strangely fashionable preoccupation for a man who, in other respects, made a profession of despising fashion. Priestley's philosophic mentor was P. D. Ouspensky, who believed that time moved in a circle rather than a straight line. The best-known result was *Johnson over Jordan*, made famous by a film version in which Ralph Richardson played Johnson – whose corpse is displayed as the curtain rises. At the end of the play he declaims into the storm a speech in favour of love and remorse.

Women – who always made up a large proportion of cinema patrons – were, thanks to the tentative moves towards emancipation, beginning to attend the theatre in larger numbers and increasingly influencing the sort of plays which were produced in the West End. The traditional critics were not sure that they welcomed the innovation.

> There were gallery boys before the war. After the signing of the Armistice, they had almost disappeared and in their place came the gallery girls, whose capacity for emotional excitement was almost inexhaustible.[20]

St John Ervine was not alone in treating the new female theatre-goers as if they were all mindless 'bright young things'. Some critics were explicit. 'Flappers in the stalls wanted to see flappers on stage.'[21] Others just described, with undisguised regret, the new phenomenon.

'Not only did two thirds of a typical London audience judge plays from a female angle, but a goodly proportion of them judged them from the standpoint of very young women.'[22] All that is surprising about that revelation is that some apparently reputable critics were surprised.

Naturally enough, women's views of films were also influenced by their age, experience and hopes. Middle-aged women showed a clear preference for romance. Young middle-class women liked films which starred actresses who specialised in playing strong and successful female characters with interests and careers which kept them well away from the kitchen sink. Claudette Colbert and Joan Crawford were particular favourites. Working-class housewives admired a quite different type of screen personality. A survey of attitudes in Bolton showed that the wives of mill workers were drawn to films about sensitive, long-suffering, self-sacrificing women tied to ungrateful and unworthy husbands and children. On the other hand, the mill workers themselves were attracted by stories of 'tough macho men who are good in a fight, stand up for what is right and love their country'.[23] The survey may have revealed more of what Bolton thought about itself than what it thought about the cinema. But it confirms that the men and women in the sixpenny and shilling seats identified with their celluloid heroes and heroines. In consequence, they adopted their mannerisms and habits. And, halfway through the two decades between the wars, the great leap forward in film production intensified the process. As a result, proud Welshmen complained that in the Rhondda Valley, 'The delightful local accent was broken up by such words as "Attaboy", "Oh yeah?" and "Sez you".'[24]

In March 1919 the *Spectator* had heralded the arrival of an innovation which guaranteed that most films would be all-singing and all-dancing. A technique had been discovered by which the cinema could 'supply the human voice simultaneously with the spectacle of human beings in dramatic action'. The *Spectator* gave the invention only a cautious welcome.

> We cannot foresee the effects on the methods of the film star. If the appeal is to be not only on the eye, there will be a slump in the value of facial contortion.[25]

It was another ten years before the first 'talkie' was screened in London. Then *The Singing Fool*, starring Al Jolson, made history at the Regal Cinema, Marble Arch. The film was almost as notable for its sentimentality as for its sound. The hit song – 'Sonny Boy' – was a father's lament for his dead child which ended with the lines, 'The Angels were lonely/Took you because they were lonely/Now I'm lonely too, Sonny Boy'. When the film was released in the provinces publicists supplied local newspapers with information about the number of damp handkerchiefs found in the auditorium after the end of performances and details of the distraught members of the audience who had needed the help of the St John Ambulance Brigade officer who was always on duty at the back of the stalls.

The talkies could hardly have got off to a better commercial (as distinct from artistic) start. But it did not need what came to be called a 'weepie' to guarantee that the cinema was about to achieve new heights of popularity. The critics were unanimous in their celebration of the achievement. 'I have just seen my first talking picture, *The Singing Fool*, and was impressed by the possibilities of the new. It is uncanny the way that almost a soul is breathed into the characters' performance.' But every cloud has a grey lining. It was also 'a bitter disillusionment to hear the half-mumbled elocution of the otherwise beautiful women'.[26]

There is a continuing debate about how much blame the British motion picture industry must accept for the American domination of the inter-war market. At the peak of production British studios made only 30 per cent of what was on offer to British cinemas. But there is a good deal of evidence to suggest that the American invasion met with only token resistance – even though, initially, the natives were far from friendly. 'The public at first found the American accent bewildering and missed much of the dialogue.'[27] Instinctive resistance was, naturally enough, strongest outside London. 'The English working class and the northern working class in particular exercised a strong suspicion, not to say hatred, of the American idiom.'[28]

Some British producers attempted to capitalise on what they hoped was anti-American sentiment. British International Films advertised its productions as 'Spoken with the charm and purity of English vowel sounds'. Gradually the cultural chauvinists were won over. By 1935, when Winifred Holtby wrote *South Riding*, the working class had actually absorbed the idioms they heard at the cinema. Elsie, the *South Riding* housemaid, was 'like most of her generation and locality . . . trilingual. She talked BBC English to her employer, Cinema American to her companions and Yorkshire dialect to old milkmen like Eli Dickson'. She, no doubt, subscribed to the ideas advanced by a working man in the Bolton survey.

> British films are tame. The actors are self-conscious and wooden, the settings easily recognised as the work of novices. The man in the street likes pictures which advertise an American cast. One often hears the remark, 'It's a British picture, let's go somewhere else.'[29]

That was not how the American industry saw the British attitude towards British-made films. Hollywood, where the United States' industry had settled, thought that it sold fewer films in Britain than the quality of its films deserved.

> The outstanding fact of the British film of 1932 was the complete stranglehold that home-made pictures established on the local box office. No one could suggest that the studio output as a whole anywhere approached Hollywood in originality or quality . . . The huge success of the British film can only be described to temperamental affinity to the home audience.[30]

The truth is that the cinema in Britain had its ups and downs. But by the end of the 1930s, Hollywood was irresistible. The home-grown stars whose names sold British films began to cross the Atlantic. First C. Aubrey Smith (who captained the Hollywood cricket team), George Arliss and Edna Best. Then Charles Laughton and Diana Wynyard, followed by Vivien Leigh and Leslie Howard. In the end even 'Our Gracie' left home in order to earn what her publicist called 'the highest salary ever paid to a human being'.

The cinema's influence on at least serious drama was not in every respect malign. Audiences were drawn to the live theatre by names which they had read in film credits. Tyrone Guthrie – a brilliantly inventive director at the Old Vic – was able, because of his reputation, to attract and retain actors who were undoubtedly film stars. His first recruits were Charles Laughton, Elsa Lanchester (then Laughton's wife), Athene Seyler and Flora Robson. Robert Donat, Emlyn Williams and Laurence Olivier followed. As their fame developed, Guthrie's direction was sufficient to keep them working in Waterloo Road rather than accepting more lucrative offers. As early as 1929 Gielgud had chosen ten pounds a week at the Old Vic rather than fifty pounds in the West End. By 1937 Olivier could command five hundred pounds a week in Hollywood but turned down film offers in favour of working under Guthrie's direction for about a tenth as much.

Shakespeare and the Old Vic apart, the 'star system' – like every other cinema innovation from talking pictures to Technicolor – worked strongly in favour of the United States. The ethos of American business, perhaps even the American way of life itself, encouraged the conscious creation of 'personalities' who could be guaranteed to fill cinemas. Douglas Fairbanks was the star among stars. *The Iron Mask*, *The Black Pirate* and *Robin Hood* were all huge box office successes. But he was by no means alone in enjoying a status which the movie moguls called 'banker' – certain to fill cinemas in whatever film they appeared. A dozen American actors were as big draws in Britain as in the United States. Gloria Swanson and Bebe Daniels (an early convert to plastic surgery) had huge followings on both sides of the Atlantic. Fatty Arbuckle, Harold Lloyd and Mack Sennett competed with Charlie Chaplin (working by then exclusively in America) in the comedy markets. Westerns, in which Britain did not even compete, made stars of Hoot Gibson, William S. Hart and Tom Mix, whose popularity was enhanced by his horse. Rin Tin Tin, the first dog to be featured in a major motion picture, was American. So was Lon Chaney who, in *The Hunchback of Notre Dame*, created the first in a long line of characters who were irresistible in their ugliness.

In the early years of the century the City had been far slower than Wall Street to recognise the potential of the new medium. And between 1914 and 1918 – although the industry did not lie fallow – it produced, by necessity, a limited crop. When, in the couple of years which followed, film-making was swept up in the temporary boom, optimism was irrationally unconfined. Lord Burnham – the proprietor of the *Daily Telegraph* – told the 1920 Dinner of the Cinematograph Exhibitions Association what its members wanted to hear.

> The high finances of the world are flocking into the cinema industry. Formerly it was difficult, I believe, to raise even a small sum of capital for a cinema enterprise. Today, if you ask for a million, you get half a million over subscribed.[32]

According to contemporary estimates, investment in the industry increased, from £15 million in 1914 to something between £30 and £50 million by 1927. Most of it went to 'cinema enterprises' – not making films but building new picture palaces in which they could be shown. The developers did not care where the films were made.

By 1930 the British industry was still only producing, at best, about two hundred films a year. America's annual production ran to several thousand. The belief that quality would always transcend quantity ignored the basic fact of film-making. The creative talent of writers, directors and actors is only one element of the achievement of both commercial and critical success. The technical capabilities of the studios and the time (which is money) spent on each production were just as important. Those ingredients were most readily available to companies with a secure and extensive capital base of backers who were willing to invest in making, as well as exhibiting, films.

The American companies, exercising the power which comes with size, sought to make their domination complete by practices which were, by any standard, 'in restraint of trade'. In 1922 a 'block-booking' system was introduced. First it required British picture houses and the companies which owned them to buy a variety of second-rate films, with limited public appeal, in order to obtain films which would be undoubted box office sell-outs. Then the United States companies began to invest in British picture houses so that they could control the distribution of their own product.

At first the fight-back was ineffectual. The Prince of Wales inaugurated a British Film week, during which – it was hoped – the domestic product would be given preference over foreign imports. Virtually nothing changed. Then in 1927 the government – still in agonies of indecision about whether or not to end its traditional commitment to free trade – decided that, in one particular, protection was essential. Some sort of barrier had to be erected around the film industry.

The Imperial Conference of 1926 considered the recommendations of a sub-committee appointed to examine 'the need for the production within the Empire of films of high entertainment value and sound educational merit and their increased distribution throughout the Empire and the rest of the world'.[33] There were, the sub-committee concluded, three ways in which that result might be achieved – customs duties on foreign films, the prohibition of blind- and block-booking and the introduction of a system by which cinemas that exhibited a minimum quota of domestically produced films were given priority when the blockbusters were distributed. The Conference – with the support of such eminent statesmen as Mackenzie King of Canada and Stanley Bruce of Australia – endorsed what amounted to a hybrid of the second and third options. The result was the Cinematograph Film Act of 1929.

The 'long title' of the Act (which described its purpose) was absolutely and unequivocally explicit. Its purpose was to restrict the block-booking systems and guarantee the renting and exhibition of a minimum number of films produced by British (rather than Empire) companies. The proportion of British films which were to be shown in British cinemas was to rise, during the lifetime of the Act, from 7.5 per cent to 20 per cent. Opposition to the Bill, as it passed through Parliament, was less concerned with the crude and overt restriction on free trade than with the likely effect on the quality of films to be shown in British cinemas. Bernard Shaw told *Bioscope*, 'My contempt [for the proposals] deprives me of speech,'[34] and the Beaverbrook press – normally the champion of imperial preference – denounced it as an admission of the domestic film industry's weakness.

Proponents of the Act claimed that it had an immediate beneficial effect on the film industry's fortunes. Even before the quotas were legally enforceable both investment and output increased. But between 1932 and 1936 exhibitors constantly booked more British films than the quota.[35] That may have been because the existence – or anticipation – of the Act set off a chain reaction. Or perhaps, for a brief period, the domestic industry produced films that the film-going public wanted to see. The causes of the subsequent problems are more easily described. It may well be that the decline – which preceded the Second World War – was a direct result of the 'Quota Act'.[36]

In 1935 United Artists decided to produce a picture which was British, within the meaning of the Act, by hiring Alexander Korda's London Film Company to make *The Private Life of Henry VIII*, starring Charles Laughton. It was a commercial and artistic triumph on both sides of the Atlantic. Other American companies had begun to operate as domestic producers but, according to the Report on the Cinematograph Film Act, prepared for the government by Lord Moyne,

> In order to . . . satisfy the renter's quota, the majority of foreign-controlled renters appeared to have made arrangements for the production of British films at the minimum expense, regardless of quality.[37]

*The Private Life of Henry VIII* seemed to demonstrate that quality paid. The result, in an industry which lived by exaggeration, was another sudden and massive injection of capital.

Again it was spread too wide. And, when the investment in production failed to show a short-term gain, there was no solid base of either funds or confidence to see the production companies through hard times. Capital Films and Twickenham Films went out of business. Associated British Pictures failed to get into the export market and cut back production. Gaumont closed its Shepherd's Bush studios. Alexander Korda, his reputation enhanced by the success of *Henry VIII*, was, for a time, backed by Prudential Insurance and, with Charles Laughton again in the starring role, made two more successful historical films – *The Life of Catherine the Great* and *Rembrandt*. Then he spent far more than he could afford on *The Shape of Things to Come*. Like *The Ghost Goes West* – directed by René Clair – it flopped in America and Korda, without enough capital to see him through a temporary setback, decided that his future lay in Hollywood.

*Pygmalion* (starring Leslie Howard and adapted by Bernard Shaw from his own play) won an early Oscar. *The Citadel* (A. J. Cronin's romance of medical ethics with Robert Donat as the doctor who spurns Harley Street) and *The Lady Vanishes* (early Hitchcock, in which British espionage and British eccentricity combine) were both classics of their kind. *The March of Time* series (short, 'explanatory' films which began life as radio features) educated the nation about subjects as diverse as cancer research and the football pools. Much that was good came out of the British film industry. But it was overwhelmed by the size of its American competition in both numbers and quality. And, as a result, Britain changed much of its language and some of its habits.

PART IV

# Today the Struggle

There have been times when the description 'modern' was a dubious compliment. The years between the wars were not one of them. It was not only the bright young things who believed in the importance of moving with the times. Poets of the period called themselves modernists – though they often disagreed about what the term meant. But the best amongst them represented the spirit of the age by composing the poetry of doubt, disillusion and, sometimes, despair.

The serious theatre prospered. A new galaxy of stars was sufficiently attractive to West End audiences to ensure that seats were sold for productions which did not simply aim to accommodate the lowest common denominator of public taste. There was little sympathy or support for productions which drew attention to social injustice. But although the theatre of conscience had been a casualty of the war, new dramatists attempted, not always successfully, to combine entertainment and the examination of serious ideas.

Sculptors defined the great leap forward in a different way. They broke out of the constraints of the classical inheritance and insisted that it was part of a tradition which knew no barriers of time or place. Their work was strange. So it was excoriated. Like the conceptual painters of the inter-war years, their work was denounced as immoral as well as unattractive.

The popular press was almost unanimously on the side of the philistine – as it was in support of the appeasers and, on some notable occasions, the Nazis abroad and the fascists at home. Auden, in the last of his political poems, spoke for the writers and artists who recognised the threat ahead. 'Yesterday the prayer to the sunset and the adoration of madmen. But today the struggle.'

# CHAPTER THIRTEEN

# Into the Wasteland

The older pupils sometimes went to the Old Vic Theatre to see a Shakespeare play as it was not far away . . . The adventure of getting on the tram to go there meant more to us than the actual Shakespeare.

May Hopper (née Cracknell)
Born Walworth, East London, 1919

The Old Vic had been created to fight poverty and disadvantage by offering the poor a better distraction from their condition than the saloon bar of the nearest public house. Its charter required its cheapest seats to be no more expensive than a pint of beer and its repertoire to be 'suited to the recreation and instruction of the poorer classes'. Lilian Baylis, its director, fulfilled her mandate by running a three-weekly repertory company which specialised in Shakespeare and, in her own words, 'met the crying needs of working men and women who want to see beyond the four walls of their offices, workshops and homes into a world of awe and wonder'. May Hopper and her classmates were not typical of the East-Enders. Lilian Baylis's faith in the working classes was vindicated when John Gielgud's sensational 'shell-shocked' *Hamlet* transferred from the Old Vic to West End. The cheaper seats sold out. The more expensive remained empty.

The 'shell-shock' was not the attraction. Most audiences in the

1920s wanted to put the hard realities of war behind them. At the end
of the decade R. C. Sherriff left audiences in little doubt about the sin
of wasting young lives in the hope of capturing a meaningless strip of
ground. But his *Journey's End* was not typical of the period's plays.
Osborne, the elderly second-in-command, is steady under fire.
Raleigh, the recently commissioned subaltern, overcomes fear and
disappointment. Even the butcher, risen from the ranks, does his duty.
And there was little enthusiasm for the message that there was a nobility even in pointless sacrifice. But playwrights, as playwrights will,
interpreted the slaughter in whatever way they thought dramatically
effective. On the eve of the Second World War Terence Rattigan's
*After the Dance* included a young woman who attributed the reckless
hedonism of the previous decades to the four years of carnage which
it followed. 'You see, when you were eighteen, you didn't have anybody of twenty-five or thirty-five to help you. They'd all been wiped
out . . . The spotlight was on you and you alone . . . You did what any
child would do, you dance.'

   Her bitterness was wholly unconvincing. One of the extraordinary
features of serious literature between the wars – prose, poetry and
drama – is the nature of the disillusion that runs through much of the
best work. It was not the result of righteous anger about the dead of
the Somme and Gallipoli. It was the product of a general despair
about mankind and it was typified in the plays and poetry of T. S.
Eliot, who could write with personal conviction.

> *I have seen the eternal Footman hold my coat, and snicker,*
> *And in short, I was afraid.*

Eliot set the tone with *The Waste Land*. Twelve years after it was published Evelyn Waugh took the title for his novel of rejection and
disillusion from the text, 'I will show you fear in a handful of dust.' Not
that Waugh represented much about the years between the wars
except the froth and the waves which battered society. His genius is
beyond dispute. But the same can be said, with even greater conviction, of E. M. Forster, who published *A Passage to India* in 1924. Forster
did not represent the spirit of the literary age. He wrote of urbane
moral doubt. Eliot was the poet and playwright of disillusion.

*The Waste Land* was published in 1922 when Eliot was already an established poet. 'The Love Song of J. Alfred Prufrock' had defined his self-consciously erudite style. Like Edmund Burke, he was 'a classicist in style, a Tory in politics and Anglo-Catholic in religion'. Yet *The Waste Land* owed nothing to any of those guiding principles. The modernists – a sufficiently eclectic group to include Eliot – were inspired by the ideas of the time, particularly Freud's *The Interpretation of Dreams*, J. G. Frazer's *The Golden Bough*, an anthropological study of the legends that shaped western civilisation, and Jessie Weston's *From Ritual to Romance*, which argued that all the myths of the Holy Grail had a common origin. Frazer and Weston confirmed Eliot's theory of progress. 'The mind of Europe . . . is a mind which changes . . . This change is a development which abandons nothing en route, which does not superannuate Shakespeare, Homer or the rock drawing of the Magdalenian draughtsman.'[1]

Henry Moore's view[*] of the proper development of sculpture was much the same. The future had to be built on the experience of all, not part, of the past. Moore interpreted the theory as a spring of hope for what was to come. Eliot saw it as the well of despair about current moral and aesthetic failures. Modernists believed that a new beginning had to be built on an understanding of, and respect for, the past. Precedents and conventions were not rejected. A new beginning did not require a repudiation of the past.

Jessie Weston had written that 'a prototype containing the main features of the Grail story – The Waste Land, the Fisher King, the Hidden Castle with its solemn Feast and mysterious Feeding Vessel, the Bleeding Lance and the Cup – does not, as far as we know, exist.'[2] In *The Waste Land* Eliot, true to his theory of artistic progress, set out to fill the vacuum. *The Waste Land* was followed by 'The Hollow Men', a poem of outright despair. But 'Ash Wednesday', commissioned as a chorus to accompany a religious pageant, shows that Eliot's mood changed with his conversion to High Anglicanism. Like 'The Journey of the Magi' ('A cold coming we had of it'), it was the work of a pilgrim who believed in the necessity – no matter how painful – of

---

[*]For Henry Moore and sculpture, see Chapter 14.

rebirth and rededication – a conviction which W. H. Auden believed was the result of 'a few intense visionary experiences which probably occurred in very early life'.[3] 'Ash Wednesday' was the testimony of a lost child who, when he was found, wrote the *Four Quartets*. 'Burnt Norton', the first of them, emphasises the passion for continuity. 'Time present and time past/Are both perhaps present in time future'.

Judgements of Eliot's poetry were often influenced by two essentially unliterary criteria – dislike of his misanthropic temperament and disagreement with his view that religion in general, and Christianity in particular, were essential to the progress of civilisation. And he wrote plays – perhaps better generically described as dramas – of fearsome complication. But everything about him was complicated. 'Sweeney Agonistes' – described in the 'unfinished poems' section of his collected works as 'fragments of Aristophanic melodrama' – was said to be much influenced by Eliot's morbid interest in Dr Crippen's murder of his wife, a theory which seemed to be confirmed by the poet's appearance at a fancy dress party masquerading as the homicidal dentist.[4] It was a strange preoccupation for the author of the twentieth century's greatest religious drama, *Murder in the Cathedral*.

The celebration of Thomas à Becket's martyrdom was commissioned by the Canterbury Festival to be performed in the Chapter House of the Mother Church of England. Use of phrases only common in the twentieth century provided an anachronistic link with the modern world. *Murder in the Cathedral* was meant to be accessible. Its objective – wholly consistent with the modernist aspiration – was to rehabilitate poetic drama, which Eliot believed once did, and should again, reflect the language of the people.

> What we have to do is bring poetry into the world in which the audience lives and to which it returns when it leaves the theatre; not to transport the audience into some imaginary world, totally unlike its own, where poetry is intellectual. What I should hope . . . is that the audience should find, at the moment of awareness . . . that it is saying to itself, 'I could talk poetry too.'[5]

That object he meant to achieve by requiring the audience (which is often treated like a congregation) to participate in paying homage to a saint who often exhibited highly unsaintly characteristics. To encourage the audience to relax, the verse has grating homely moments. After the Chorus has speculated about the prospect of Thomas 'bringing death to Canterbury', the Second Priest assures the Archbishop, 'Your Lordship will find your rooms in order as you left them' and his Lordship, anticipating death, promises, 'And will try to leave them in order as I find them.' A man often regarded as the greatest poet-playwright of the twentieth century adapted, for his poetic use, a notice which used to be common in public lavatories.

*Murder in the Cathedral* is a morality play which, Eliot hoped, the audience would find an improving experience. 'The greatest treason, to do the right deed for the wrong reason.' The knights who step forward in turn to justify the assassination blame Becket for his own murder in the manner of public house hooligans excusing an assault on an offensive outsider. 'When he had deliberately exasperated us beyond human endurance, he could have easily escaped'. Eliot was incomprehensible to a large proportion of the inter-war population not only because he wrote 'difficult poetry' – something which, in one his most famous critical essays, he refused to believe existed. His attempts to be accessible patronised his audience in a way which alienated the men and women who sensed his feeling of superiority. Ezra Pound dealt *Murder in the Cathedral* a devastating blow by complaining, 'Oh them cawkney voices!'[6]

Eliot himself was not wholly satisfied with *Murder in the Cathedral*. *The Family Reunion* was meant to bridge the gap between the devout minority and the mass of unbelievers amongst whom they lived. It has the plot of a stage thriller. But Eliot had higher aims. 'Not a story of detection [or] of crime and punishment, but of sin and expiation.' He was no happier with *The Family Reunion* than he had been with *Murder in the Cathedral*. The story of death and martyrdom had, he feared, come to a 'dead end'. The examination of desertion, loss and culpability was, in his view, an even greater 'failure of adjustment between the Greek story and the modern situation'. He had relied on Aeschylus again. But the result was an unhappy compromise. 'I should have either stuck closer to the text or taken a great deal more liberty with the myth.'[7] The result of the acknowledged failure was the mortal injury, if not the death, of poetic drama.

Whatever his doubts about his success as a dramatist, Eliot knew himself to be the master of the elegant insult. He described Ezra Pound as 'attracted to the Middle Ages by everything except that which gives them significance'.[8] But he also regarded him as 'more responsible for the XXth century revolution in poetry than any other individual'.[9]

Pound, like Eliot, was an American. He arrived in Europe in 1908, proclaiming that the United States was 'a half savage country' and 'out of date'. England, on the other hand, was decadent but capable of regeneration. He proposed to achieve that goal single-handed – partly by founding small-circulation magazines and partly by passionately, but briefly, embracing the artistic vogue of the moment. He was successively an imagist and a vorticist – first rejecting romanticism and then celebrating violence, energy and mechanisation. He finally became a modernist.

England failed to meet Pound's exacting demands. So he left. Touring continental Europe, he published, in 1920, *Hugh Selwyn Mauberley* – a collection of poems in two parts which tells the story of a disenchanted poet who struggles to survive in a world which does not recognise his merits. The anti-hero is more unpleasant than the world he despises. He is openly anti-Semitic and particularly jealous of more successful writers. And he rejects democracy. 'We choose a knave or a scoundrel / To rule over us.' Pound's contempt for the common man down the ages was boundless. 'The Greek populace was PAID to attend Greek tragedies and darn well wouldn't have gone otherwise, or if there had been the cinema.'

*Hugh Selwyn Mauberley* – with its obscure references and passages of intentional pastiche – anticipated *The Waste Land*. And its arrogant disenchantment, reflecting the pessimistic strain within the modernist movement, struck a chord with a disillusioned continent. But Pound was more than fashionable. He was a poet of distinction. For the next thirty years he worked on the *Cantos*,* by his own description 'poems

---

*Cantos LXXXV – XCV are entitled 'Rock Drill' – also the title of an Epstein sculpture.

which include history'. Their quality should not be obscured by the unattractive ideas they contain – the admiration of 'strong rulers' and the need to subjugate private happiness to the public good. Pound had settled in Rome and come to regard Mussolini as the leader who would purge Italy of its sloth and decadence. In *Jefferson and/or Mussolini*, he wrote, 'I assert again my own firm belief that the Duce will stand not with the despots and the lovers of power, but with the lovers of order.' Mussolini was the modernists' Caesar, come to build a new nation out of the values of the old city-state. It was an infatuation which persuaded Pound to broadcast during the war on behalf of the Axis powers. At the end of the hostilities the living embodiment of Hugh Selwyn Mauberley was arrested by the occupying American forces and indicted for treason. Four psychiatrists judged he was of unsound mind.

During the second year of Pound's detention T. S. Eliot acknowledged the poetic debt that he owed to the unhappy inmate of an American psychiatric institution. 'I placed before [him] the manuscript of a sprawling, chaotic poem called *The Waste Land* which, left in his hands, [was] reduced to about half its size and the form in which it appears in print.'[10] Ruthlessly pruned, it was published in the *Criterion*, a magazine which Eliot had founded. In the same year James Joyce's *Ulysses* reached the bookshops of Paris – via *The Little Review*, a Chicago monthly. The extracts which the periodical had chosen were judged so obscene that the New York Post Office put *The Little Review* on its index of material which it would neither deliver nor collect. The cause of complaint was the frank treatment of the characters' sexual conduct – particularly in the last chapter which consists entirely of Molly Bloom's thoughts while in bed. The real significance of *Ulysses* was its style – though style, in the singular, is perhaps the wrong noun. For Joyce meant *Ulysses* to be a maze of styles and literary conceits which elaborate 'internal monologues'. The technique of setting out a character's thoughts was not original, but Joyce took the practice to new extremes by including half-thoughts, associated ideas, ruminations and peripheral worries. He portrayed the moral anarchy of the inter-war world in a process which came to be called 'stream of consciousness'. Joyce – using the language which had made *Ulysses* unintelligible – offered his own definition of modernism in the last line of *Portrait of the Artist as a Young Man.* 'Welcome, O life! I go to encounter for the millionth time the reality of my experience and to forge the smithy of my soul . . .'

Stephen Dedalus, the hero of *Portrait of the Artist as a Young Man*, was Joyce in all but name, down to the details of the astigmatism which affected both author and character. Joyce's education was interrupted first by his parents' inability to pay his school fees and then by his own doubts about the Canons of Faith. However he learned enough to enrol in University College, Dublin – Cardinal Newman's 'Catholic Balliol on the banks of the Liffey' – with the intention of becoming a doctor. He chose instead Paris and writing. The *Irish Homestead* magazine commissioned a series of articles, which Joyce proposed should appear under the name of Stephen Dedalus. But the alter ego had a long and painful birth. The articles were rejected. Dedalus eventually came to life in *Portrait of the Artist as a Young Man*. He reappeared in *Ulysses*, Joyce's mock heroic account of a Homeric Odyssey through Dublin on one day, 16 June 1904 – as Telemachus to Leopold Bloom's Ulysses and Molly Bloom's less-than-chaste Penelope.

The result – combined with the Homeric parallels and constant parodies – was 'a baggy monster, fluid pudding of a novel'.[11] But that was exactly what Joyce intended. There is no doubt about his power of formal plot construction. It is displayed, close to perfection, in *Dubliners*, the story of one day in the life of the city.

What T. S. Eliot called the 'combination of contemporarity and antiquity' in Joyce's writing is only fully appreciated by readers who possess a substantial knowledge of earlier literature and it is most easily understood by those who know something about the author's personal history – two characteristics which Eliot's own work shares. The complications of Joyce's texts reflect the working of his mind. Some of the characters in *Finnegans Wake* (published in 1939) have multiple personalities. The language is equally convoluted. The Liffey is described as 'leaning with the sloothering slide of her, giddygaddy, grannyma, gossipaceous Anna Livia', and the last sentence of the book is left unfinished to illustrate that time is a circle, not a straight line. But Joyce's writing was less surreal than both his critics and admirers claimed. 'His characters are all going about their business like the characters of any other novelist.'[12] But modernist characters go about their business in a variety of different ways and their business may be only tangentially related to normal experience. Virginia Woolf – combining aristocratic hauteur and genuine originality – observed the rule by writing of men and women who had a special relationship with time. She sets out her ambition in a review of Dorothy Richardson's *The Tunnel*, which she wrote in 1919. 'We want to be rid of realism, to penetrate without its help into the regions beneath it.'[13]

Virginia Woolf pursued (and sometimes achieved) her goal in a series of novels which genuinely broke new ground. *Mrs Dalloway* (1925) describes twenty-four hours in the life of the wife of a middle-aged MP as she prepares to give a party in honour of an old lover who has returned from India. Her memories are interposed with the thoughts of a shell-shock victim. Ingenuity increased with the years. *To the Lighthouse* (1927) records two days – separated by ten years. During a pre-war summer the Ramsays are prevented, by bad weather, from visiting a lighthouse on Skye. They return again when peace is restored and examine the anatomy of disappointment. In *Orlando* (1928) the hero/heroine, whose lives are followed through several centuries, changes sex. Its clear lesbian association was, friends assumed, the result of such a relationship between the author and Vita Sackville West, the wife of the MP, diplomat and diarist Harold Nicolson. *The Waves* (1931) dispenses with plot completely. Six characters who were childhood friends meet at a reunion and talk and talk and talk and talk – a common failing of modernist characters.

Modernists – even those who, like Virginia Woolf, lived in high-minded prosperity – were never wholly at ease with the world around them. Ford Madox Ford, founder of the *English Review* and author of *Parade's End*, the 'Tietjens tetralogy', 'was nature's expatriate, his country was the novel, he left his baggage in every hotel room'.[14] The image reflects the reality of his life as well as his work. In common with writers between the wars, he never felt at home. Like Pound, Eliot and Joyce, in their different ways, Ford was alienated from his physical and intellectual environment. D. H. Lawrence – a protégé of Ford's *English Review* and another sort of modernist – was alienated from his country, his class and his origins.

By the outbreak of the First World War Lawrence had abandoned his teaching career, and Frieda Weekley (the wife of his old professor in the University College at Nottingham) had abandoned her husband in order to live with him. Lawrence was unfit for military service and spent the war years developing literary tastes and making literary friends. At first the genius which created *Sons and Lovers* deserted him. *The Lost Girl*, which he abandoned in Germany when he left at the outbreak of war, was retrieved and published in 1919. It was a comedy of lower-middle-class manners – not a genre in which Lawrence excelled. And he regarded his work in hand, *The Sisters*, as such a failure that he would not even send it to his publisher. Eventually he split it in two, publishing the first half as *The Rainbow* in 1915, and was once again at the centre of controversy for his explicit treatment of (this time lesbian) sex. The second part was totally rewritten, but for four years he could not find a publisher for what he called *Women in Love*.

*Women in Love* is the story of the Brangwen family. The sisters, Ursula and Gudrun, are both 'spoken for' – one by a young school inspector, who is detached and cold, except for his hatred of industrialisation, and the other by a mine-owner's son who, despite his business acumen, seems to lack all feeling. The story becomes an assault on urbanisation and material progress with occasional diversions to attack the intellectualism which stifles emotion. The quality of life depends on living at peace with the physical environment. William Cobbett would have agreed with the conclusion that the world has deteriorated since the factories came.

*Aaron's Rod* (published in 1922) has probably been subject to more interpretation (and misinterpretation) than any of Lawrence's novels. The Aaron in the Book of Numbers was the brother of Moses, whose authority as a priest was confirmed by the miracle of his flowering rod. So there is much supposed imagery about impotence and castration.

Lawrence's life and work always invited such irritating speculation. At least the autobiographical significance of *Kangaroo* (1923) is not in dispute. It reflects lessons learned during Lawrence's travels in Australia. There can be arguments about the plausibility of the political disputes between the socialists and the 'Diggers', a particularly Australian type of fascist. But Richard Lovat Somers, the footloose writer, *is* Lawrence. Like him, he suffers what was to both of them the profound humiliation of a military medical examination. *The Plumed Serpent* (1926), written after Lawrence had moved on to Mexico, is the story of Kate Leslie, an Irish widow who, hoping for a mystical rebirth, meets and falls in love with the leader of an ancient cult of which she becomes the fertility goddess. Yet this farrago of phallic nonsense was written by a man of undoubted sensitivity – as witness *The Widowing of Mrs Holroyd* and *The Odour of Chrysanthemums*, a play and short story which tell – with compelling understanding – the tortured relationship between a miner and his wife.

Inevitably, when *Lady Chatterley's Lover* was published it was excoriated because it was misunderstood. Lawrence was a prude. 'I would censure genuine pornography, vigorously . . .You can recognise it by the insult it offers invariably, to sex and to the human spirit.'[15] *Lady Chatterley's Lover* is a love story which tries, with mixed success, to describe a loving physical relationship in a way which is not prejudiced by language and, at the same time, expresses outrage at the industrial destruction of the English countryside. The dialogue is what Lawrence – rightly or wrongly – believed to be a response to Ford Madox Ford's cry for the 'actual talk of real people'. Its problem was the obscurity of its symbolism. The easy, and no doubt correct, assumption is that Sir Clifford – Connie's cuckolded husband – represents, because of his incapacitating war wounds, the impotence Lawrence dreads. Perhaps. But he is much more than that. The land-owning aristocrat – paralysed from the waist downwards – embodies all the decaying power which Lawrence feared and despised. Sir Clifford defiles the England that he owns. The proof is in the landscape, which is sacrificed for his greed. Mineshafts and pit-heads rape the countryside.

All that *Lady Chatterley's Lover* stands for is encapsulated in the last pages of the novel. Connie has left Sir Clifford, who has refused to divorce her. Mellors is working on a farm in Old Heanor, preparing to become owner of a smallholding at which Connie, and their baby, will join him. He writes to her with the latest news of crops planted and reaped but the letter turns into a manifesto. 'The young ones get mad because they've no money to spend. Their whole life depends on spending money and now they have none to spend. That's our civilisation and our education: bring up the masses to depend entirely on spending money and then the money gives out . . . If you could only tell them that living and spending isn't the same thing.'[16] *Lady Chatterley's Lover* is a novel for puritans – particularly those who, like the modernists of post-war Britain, believed that the golden age, whenever it was, had passed but had bequeathed a heritage which made it easier to face an uncertain future.

Between the wars was a time when the puritan virtues, properly defined, flourished. Writers argued for the adherence to moral codes which came from personal conviction not external pressures. Chief among them was George Bernard Shaw. His writ ran further than might first be imagined. Writing about *Murder in the Cathedral*, T. S. Eliot surprisingly suggested, 'I may, for all I know, have been slightly under the influence of Saint Joan.'[17] The Saint Joan of which he wrote was Shaw's creation. *Saint Joan*, the play, was not Shaw's only excursion into religious controversy. *Back to Methuselah* – not a single play but five 'playlets'– is a medieval mystery play, which begins in the Shavian Garden of Eden when Eve reacts with an 'expression of overwhelming repugnance' at the serpent's revelation of the 'secret' by which the lately created human species can be reproduced. But her final words to Adam give hope of a world which is free of the repugnant facts of procreation and absolved of the material desires which have prompted Cain to cry, 'I revolt against the clay. I revolt against the food.' The paradise on earth to which they all aspire is, in its sexless vegetarianism, Bernard Shaw's personal vision of heaven on earth. In the aesthetic paradise,

> *Man need not always live by bread alone.*
> *There is something else. We do not yet know*
> *What it is, but some day we shall find out*
> *And then we will live on that alone. And there*
> *Will be no more digging nor spinning nor*
> *Fighting nor killing.*

Shaw, being Shaw, could not let the play end on such a sentimental note. The final stage directions read, 'She spins resignedly. He digs impatiently.'

Shaw was at his worst attacking religion, which his temperament did not allow him to understand, and at his best examining political ideas in which his intellect exalted. *Saint Joan* is a polemic against nationalism, the cause which had swept though his native Ireland and was creating new states in Europe. Its dangers are exposed with the help of allies on whom Shaw rarely relies. 'The Catholic Church knows only one realm, and that is the realm of Christ's kingdom. Divide that Kingdom into nations and you will dethrone Christ. And who will then stand between our throats and the sword? The world will perish in a welter of wars.' Saint Joan is accepted by Shaw as a saint even though he does not believe in sanctity. She is a practical, down-to-earth country girl who is impatient with the decadence of the French court and chooses to fight the English with whatever weapons are available to her. To Shaw she possessed two saintly qualities – her singleness of purpose and her sexless personality. She exists to achieve only one objective, which she describes herself in the play's most memorable line – 'Nothing counting under God, save France free and French.' And she makes her way through the French lines without one licentious soldier threatening her virginity. Indeed she exacts such respect that, in front of her, they moderate their language.

The audience is told, 'There hasn't been a word that has anything to do with her being a woman.' And when Foulmouth Frank blasphemes in her presence he is struck down by a seizure and collapses, fatally, into a well. Shaw was notoriously sceptical about the pleasures of the flesh. But Joan's strength does not lie in their rejection. The androgynous quality which he admires is not simply an absence of femininity. It is the assertion that she does not exist as an individual but only as an instrument of God's will for France. Joan is a thunderbolt.

As was usual with Shaw, the preface to the play set out its purpose. *Saint Joan* had three distinct themes – 'the romance of her rise, the tragedy of her execution and the comedy of posterity's attempts to make amends'. The romance – the acceptance of her divine mission by the French court and her victories over the English – occupies five of the six scenes and includes the 'miracles' which confirmed her right to canonisation. Shaw dramatised them more because of their theatrical value than because of any belief in their veracity. She changes the direction of the wind in order to allow Dunois to sail against the

English and identifies the Dauphin even though he is disguised and, furthermore, she has never previously seen him. All that is the work of Shaw the playwright. So is the sixth scene, which encompasses her trial and 'the tragedy of her execution'. The 'attempt to make amends' – written by Shaw the polemicist – is left to the epilogue. Joan dead, but making a ghostly visit to the Dauphin-turned-King, is also the product of Shaw the polemicist. The aristocrats of both England and France who have betrayed Joan are ridiculed as cowardly and self-seeking. Ascending to the throne of St Louis has not ennobled the Dauphin. Urged by the spectral Joan to expel the English, who triumphed after her burning, he replies in comically feeble language. 'If you are going to say "Son of St Louis, gird your sword and lead us to victory" you may well save your breath to cool your porridge, for I cannot do it.' The language is one point at which the work of Shaw and Eliot touch. Uncommon people speak common English – with a dramatic success which remains in doubt. Shaw's great achievement – not altogether in tune with the spirit of 1924 when *Saint Joan*, which had opened in New York, was published – was to portray the pathos which goes with heroism. The death sentence is commuted to life imprisonment, but Joan prefers the flames to the prison. 'I could let the banners and the trumpets and the knights and the soldiers pass . . . if only I could have the wind in the trees and the larks in the sunshine.'

By 1918, Shaw was not an 'Irish playwright' in the sense that W. B. Yeats was a born-again 'Irish poet' writing in and about the Irish tradition. That role was occupied by Sean O'Casey, who typified 'the most distressful country' school of literature in three plays. He too wrote about nationalism. But his subject was the penalties it exacted. *The Shadow of a Gunman* (1923), *Juno and the Paycock* (1924) and *The Plough and the Stars* (1926), although undoubtedly moving, were little more than collections of unrelated tragic incidents associated with 'the troubles'. In *Juno and the Paycock*, Johnny is executed by Unionist irregulars, Juno's legacy proves to be an invention and Mary 'the fallen woman' is abandoned by Jerry, her wayward lover. The characters in *The Plough and the Stars* fare even worse. Nora loses her baby and is driven mad by her husband's death, while Bessie is accidentally shot and killed. No one should have doubted O'Casey's support for the cause of Irish nationalism. But it was not an uncritical commitment. The more histrionic supporters of independence, who postured rather than acted, were lampooned in *Juno and the Paycock* in the character of Captain Baylis and *The Plough and the Stars* – although it contained a passage in homage to Padrick Pearse, one of the Martyrs of the 1916 uprising – so outraged nationalist opinion that there were riots inside and outside Dublin's Abbey Theatre on the opening night. O'Casey moved to England and in 1928, on the advice of Yeats, the Abbey refused to stage *The Silver Tassie*, an 'anti-war play' about an injured footballer's attempt to adjust to a new life. Yeats claimed that his criticism had been purely artistic. O'Casey believed it to be political. The isolation from Ireland was complete.

O'Casey turned from Irish nationalism to socialism of a sort and, like Bernard Shaw, fell briefly in love with the Soviet Union. In 1939 he took it upon himself, in a letter to the Writers' Union of the USSR, to comment on the contemporary British (or perhaps English) attitude towards William Shakespeare. 'One theatre in London – called the Old Vic – gives performances of Shakespeare's plays constantly. Some of these are done very well and many of them are done badly . . . As for the workers, it may be said that they never come in contact with Shakespeare from the cradle to the grave.' In fact a good deal of Shakespeare was being produced in the West End – most of it, with the exception of exports from the Old Vic, was acted in the overblown style of a past era. Theatre-goers of the 1920s got a Shakespeare which, according to Tyrone Guthrie – making his name at Waterloo Road – had 'nothing to it but ranting and raving'.[18] Even as late as 1932 one reviewer complained that Julius Caesar was played by actors 'mesmerised by the sound of their own voices'.[19] But help was at hand. Barry Jackson at the Birmingham Repertory Theatre and Harcourt Williams, who took over at the Old Vic, began to innovate. They moved forward by returning to the traditions of the distant past – or at least the interpretations of ancient style with which Granville-Barker had experimented before the war. John Gielgud described Harcourt Williams' work as 'Elizabethan productions which preserved the continuity of the plays by means of natural and speedy delivery of the verse and imaginative settings allowing a quick change of scene'.[20]

Williams' methods were not, initially, a commercial success. But the stars of the Old Vic – principally Gielgud – had acquired such a reputation that almost anything in which they appeared would attract an audience. The dawn of the new decade witnessed a Shakespeare revival of a sort, with three *Hamlets* running simultaneously and Peggy Ashcroft playing Desdemona in an *Othello* which attracted audiences for a variety of reasons – including Paul Robeson in the role of the Moor of Venice. Reaction to his performance is a sad commentary on British society between the wars. Two years earlier Robeson had been lionised in London when he appeared in Jerome Kern's *Show Boat*. Even James Agate, whose reputation had not been built on over-generous reviews, had written ecstatically about the performer if not the play. 'It is,' he wrote, 'typical of this piece that Mr Robeson – magnificent actor, exquisite singer and man cut out in such a pattern as Michelangelo might have designed – should be given nothing to do except dodder about with a duster.'[21] But the reaction to Robeson working as a slave on the Mississippi was quite different from the response he attracted when he became a black general married to a white woman. The attitude of the general public was reflected in Peggy Ashcroft's brave attempt to be rational. 'Ever so many people have asked me if I mind being kissed . . . by a coloured man and it seems to me so silly. Of course I do not mind. It is just necessary for the play. For myself, I regard it as a great privilege to act with a great man like Paul Robeson.'[22] A more typical reaction to what the *Observer* called 'a tragedy of racial conflict'[23] was reported by the drama critic Hannen Swaffer in *Variety*. 'One London editor walked out because there were negroes around him in the stalls.'[24] The critics reflected various degrees of prejudice – subconscious and overt. Herbert Farjeon was impressed by Robeson's authentic 'thick lips' but insisted that he was the victim of miscasting since 'Shakespeare wrote the part for a white man'.[25] Agate described the production as 'nigger Shakespeare' and regarded Desdemona's decision to 'choose a darkie' as confirmation of her 'fragile intellect'.[26]

More progressive ideas were flourishing under Tyrone Guthrie at the Old Vic and in Old Vic exports in the West End. Guthrie was accused by traditionalists of inventing 'stunts' to make Shakespeare more accessible to an audience in search of escapism. In fact, as the

1930s made their depressing way to the inevitable second war, Guthrie was reflecting the spirit of the time, both in his casting and in his interpretation of the plays. Guthrie's technique was controversial, intellectual and, in many aspects, Freudian. The three witches did not appear in his production of *Macbeth*. 'Surely the grandeur of the tragedy lies in the fact that Macbeth and Lady Macbeth are ruined by precisely those qualities which make them great . . . All this is under-mined by any suggestion that the Weird Sisters are in control of events.'[27] Emlyn Williams' Richard III was a sexual deviant, Olivier's Iago a homosexual and his Hamlet shared a mother complex with Oedipus. It was largely due to the Old Vic and its stars that Shakespeare had infiltrated the West End in the 1920s. During the 1930s – with Gielgud in command – it established a permanent place in Shaftesbury Avenue and the Haymarket. *Hamlet* in 1934, *Romeo and Juliet* in 1935 and *Richard II* alternating with the *Merchant of Venice* in 1938.

In 1933 the Open Air Theatre was opened in Regent's Park with Robert Atkins again seeking to produce Shakespeare as Shakespeare himself would have wanted it to be produced. In Stratford the Memorial Theatre – gutted by fire in 1926 – was rebuilt and reopened in 1932 after five years in which the summer season (then the full extent of what was essentially a festival) had been staged in a converted cinema. The first director of the new theatre, W. Bridges Adams, wanted all sorts of modern innovations – behind a proscenium arch. The design was condemned from the start as destroying 'all contact between actors and audience'.[28] Seventy years later plans for rectify-ing the mistakes of the 1930s were approved by the governors of the Royal Shakespeare Company.

Only one Shakespeare venture completely failed. Lilian Baylis built a brand-new theatre at Sadler's Wells. Both its design and location proved unsuitable for the plays which she wanted to produce and unacceptable to the audiences she hoped to attract. But Shakespeare had returned to its proper place at the heart of the nation – reflecting the mood of the people as well as representing the timeless values which embrace every generation. In 1931 (at the height of the depres-sion) the Old Vic revived *King John* as a study in bad leadership, and followed it with an essentially unheroic *Henry V*. Ralph Richardson played both parts. Six years later, in the same theatre, Guthrie wanted a new production of *Henry V* to be an attack on jingoism. Olivier agreed. 'I fought against the heroism by flattening and getting underneath the lines. No banner waving for me.'[29] But both actor and director were swamped by the wave of patriotic emotion which swept the country in anticipation of George VI's coronation. The plan was to cast doubts on the idea of kingship as well as condemn the glorification of war. 'But when the bunting went off [*sic*] neither of us had the guts to go through with it'.[30]

Olivier was reflecting the growing politicisation of all the arts – which extended far further than the overtly political writers. The politics of Britain between the wars are, in their most direct form, represented by Eric Arthur Blair, a natural radical known to posterity as George Orwell. These days Orwell is remembered, and to a limited extent revered, for *Animal Farm, 1984* and a series of biographical excursions – *The Road to Wigan Pier, Down and Out in London and Paris* and *Homage to Catalonia*, the accounting of his experiences in the Spanish Civil War which were considerably more extensive than Auden's. But before the works of lasting value there was a series of novels which are not only forgotten but which Orwell wanted to forget. *Keep the Aspidistra Flying* (1936), written while he was working in a bookshop, is the story of an unhappy shop assistant who is forced to marry against his will. He blames his troubles on Christianity and poverty. Parodying Chapter Thirteen of St Paul's Letter to the Corinthians, he concludes, '. . . And the greatest of these is money.' He becomes prematurely impotent. 'How can you make love when all you have is eight pence in your pocket and can think of nothing else?' Orwell's purpose was not so much didactic as evangelical. 'The novel would somehow warn against war, demonstrate the decency and commonsense of ordinary people and show some faint hopes for the future.'[31] In the author's own view, it failed. Orwell refused to have it reprinted.

Orwell's essays succeeded where his novels failed because they were overtly polemical. Their appeal – greater after the war, when the social revolution had begun, than when they were written – was always to an influential radical minority. Orwell's natural audience wanted a direct assault on the society of which they disapproved. 'When I first saw unemployed men at close quarters, the thing that horrified and amazed me was to find that many of them felt ashamed of being unemployed . . . The middle classes were all still talking about "lazy, idle loafers on the dole" and saying "these men could find work if they wanted to". Naturally these opinions percolated to the working class themselves'[32]

Orwell wrote his own epitaph for the period in his review of Malcolm Muggeridge's *The Thirties*. 'What a decade! A riot of appalling folly that suddenly becomes a nightmare, a scenic railway ending in a torture chamber.'[33] That is an even more depressing judgement on the jazz age than W. H. Auden's gloomy conclusion that Britain in the 1930s was 'a country where nobody was well'.[34] Auden's attack on the failings of the established order was more oblique. He came to represent that young group of poets who – initially at least – were 'political' both because they were associated with parties of the left and because they wrote about the condition of society.

Most of the radical poets were children of prosperity. It was at Gresham's School, Holt, that Auden had his moment of poetic Pentecost. 'One afternoon in March at half-past three when walking in a ploughed field with a friend. Kicking a little stone, he turned to me and said, "Tell me, do you write poetry?" I never had, and said so, but I knew that very moment what I wished to do.'[35]

Auden went to Gresham's from St Edmund's preparatory school in Hindhead, where he had met Christopher Isherwood. Although they went their separate ways at fourteen, they remained friends for the rest of their lives. At Cambridge Isherwood ended his undergraduate career by spoiling his examination papers. At Oxford, after some confusion, Auden chose to read English. Christ Church did not boast an English tutor. So he sat at the feet of Neville Coghill in Exeter College and told him, with typical perversity and in contradiction to the story of his boyhood epiphany, 'I never meant to be a poet.'[36] The judgement on Auden's undergraduate years was pronounced by A. L. Rowse. 'Wystan's cleverness was verbal, pyrotechnical – not intellectual. It did not enter the realm of thinking.'[37] The impatience with ideas – whether or not it characterised his poetry – was revealed in Auden's almost flippant attitude towards great causes. Only posterity has made him a political activist.

In 1926 Auden drove a car for the TUC, by his own admission, 'out of sheer cussedness'[38] rather than conviction. By then his friendship with Stephen Spender had begun, completing with Isherwood the trio which was to symbolise (though not wholly embody) English poetry in the 1930s. Spender was a more contemplative man than Isherwood, whose intellectual admiration for Auden befitted his emotional attachment.* His judgement that Auden's 'life was committed to an intellectual effort to analyse, explain and dominate his circumstances'[39] is open to a variety of meanings. One is explained by Auden's own insistence that 'No man can be a writer without devoting himself to it. He must order his whole life and reading to one end.'[40] That is a reflection of T. S. Eliot's view that 'the progress of an artist is continual self-sacrifice, a continual extinction of personality' – a belief Auden quoted and endorsed.[41] But there is another explanation of his driven personality, which is perhaps revealed in a letter to his brother. 'As a bugger, only three courses are open to one. Middle aged sentimentalism . . . The London bugger, sucking off policemen in public lavatories . . . pursuing the life of aestheticism.'[42] The letter ended with the assurance that he would try to devote himself, exclusively, to the third option. We know that he failed.

There has been much speculation – most of it pointless – about how Auden's sexuality, and that of the other poets with whom he associated, affected his writing. Auden himself looked for other influences to explain his views on literature and life. 'It is impossible to understand modern English literature unless one realises that most English writers are rebels against the way they were educated.'[43] For most of the novelists the problem was school – Orwell desperately regretted that he was an Old Etonian and Waugh desperately regretted that he was not. Even those who loved their schooldays were marked indelibly by them. Cyril Connolly wrote that after Eton 'all is anti–climax, dust and ashes'.[44] But for Auden the defining influence was Oxford. It was there that he began to find his literary feet. And there is no doubt by whom they were guided. He told Coghill, 'I have

---

*We lunched together quite often after meeting at a Foyle's Literary Lunch. On every occasion he urged me to read Auden's *The Shield of Achilles*.

torn up my poems because they are no good. Based on Wordsworth. I've been reading Eliot. I now see what I want to write. I've written two poems this week. Listen!'[45]

Auden identified different inspirations at different times – partly because his views on the nature of poetry changed over the years as different influences bore in on him. But his comments on his mentors reveal indisputable facts about him. His views on society do well as literature. Writing about Yeats in 1947 he complimented him for facing 'modern problems of living in a society in which men were no longer supported by tradition . . . And in which therefore every individual who wishes to bring order into the stream of sensations, emotions and ideas entering his consciousness . . . is forced to do so deliberately by himself.' Many old certainties died in the years between the wars and the poets who marked their passing spoke for their modernist age.

The romantic assumption has always been that the greatest influence on Auden's early work were the years spent with Isherwood in Berlin. There is no doubt that he enjoyed the decadence of the time and place. He wrote to Spender in 1928, 'I am incredibly happy spending my money on strumpets and white slave traffic'[46] – pleasures which he increased in December of that year by moving his lodgings from a middle-class suburb to an undoubted slum. The days of wine and roses ended in April 1930 when the allowance, which he received from his parents for two years after he came down from Oxford, ended. Perhaps it was only by coincidence that, in the same year, T. S. Eliot (who had rejected, on behalf of Faber and Faber, Auden's first collection of poems) found a new anthology acceptable. In 1936 – the year of 'Funeral Blues' – he published a volume of poems dedicated to Erica Mann, his partner in a marriage arranged to enable her to leave Germany on a British passport. He called the anthology *Poems, 1936*, which Faber and Faber thought gave the impression of complete works to date. So, taking advantage of Auden's absence in Iceland, they called it *Look, Stranger!* – according to the author, a title only suitable for 'the work of a vegetarian lady novelist'.

It was while he was in Iceland that Auden learned that General Franco had landed in Spain with his North African Legion and that the attempt to overthrow the legitimate government had precipitated a civil war. Auden's decision to join the International Brigade was so

out of character that he thought it necessary to explain his reasons. 'I
so dislike everyday political activities that I won't do them, but here is
something I can do as a citizen, not a writer, and I have no depend-
ents. I think I ought to go.'[47] Initially he was self-consciously noble.
'The poet must have direct knowledge of political events . . . I shall
probably be a bloody bad soldier but how can I speak to/for them
without becoming one?'[48] Then he changed his mind. A non-com-
batant could speak for freedom if not for freedom fighters. So he
applied to become an ambulance driver. The republican authorities
thought they had better work for him to do and set him to work
broadcasting anti-fascist propaganda. The routine did not appeal and
the job did not last for long. Auden left Spain after seven weeks. A
poem, 'Spain 1937', is far more heroic than the part Auden played in
the Civil War.

> *Yesterday the belief in the absolute value of Greece,*
> *The fall of the curtain upon the death of a hero;*
> *Yesterday the prayer to the sunset*
> *And the adoration of madmen. But today the struggle.*

The royalties were donated to Medical Aid for Spain.

Auden had found great emotional release not in Spain but in New
York, where he was able to pursue his pleasures uninhibited by either
the conventions of his class or the concern of old friends. He and
Isherwood left Britain for America on 19 January 1939. They only
returned as visitors. Four months after his arrival in New York he met
Chester Kallman. They were partners for the rest of Auden's life.
America and emotional stability changed his poetry and he began to
write about time, not place. 'September 1 1939' was written in Auden's
'English style' and became, in the mythology, comparable with Yeats'
'Easter 1916'. Ten years after it was written Auden told a friend one
reason he left England 'was precisely to *stop* me writing poems like
"September 1 1939"'.

Although Auden had his brief moment of tentative political commitment he was – in heart and head – far too detached to support a
cause for long. The poet of the Spanish Civil War was John Cornford,
the first Englishman to join the republican army. He died on the

Cordoba Front in 1936. But Stephen Spender (briefly a card-carrying member of the Communist Party) did write 'political' poetry. Some of it is disturbingly reminiscent of Soviet social realism. 'Pylons, those pillars / Bare nude, giant girls that have no secret.' But the political poetry of the left had many forms. Cecil Day Lewis – an active Communist in his youth who became Poet Laureate in middle age – spoke for the generation of young men and women who, uncontaminated by the cynicism which breeds despair, looked forward to what Marxists called 'the millennium'.

> *You above all who have come to the far end, victims*
> *Of a run down machine who can bear it no longer . . .*
> *You shall be leaders when zero hour is signalled,*
> *Wielders of power and welders of a new world.*

But the republicans lost in Spain and Soviet Communism turned out to be a brutal tyranny. The idealists of the left were outnumbered by cut-price hedonists of no particular political persuasion. Louis MacNeice is credited with the definitive judgement on a morally lost generation. 'It's no go the Yogi-man, It's no go Blavatsky,/ All we want is a bank balance and a bit of skirt in a taxi.' But serious writing between the wars – poetry, prose and drama – was far more solemn than that. It was not always more uplifting. But it did not drink to drown its sorrows or dance into the night in search of oblivion. The girl in the Terrence Rattigan play had a more intellectual sister. Those who thought about life found it grey as well as grim. Some writers could describe the path to redemption. But few of them expected the world to follow where it led.

# CHAPTER FOURTEEN

# Shaping the Idea

You have had two years in which to develop as a painter. During this time you have not succeeded in making a living out of it. If you can't paint what the public wants, you must give up and take a job. I now wash my hands of you and your so called art which is nothing but 'obscene ugliness' (his words). If you want support go to those who like your daubs, if there are any . . .

Rosamund Lehmann, quoting to a friend a letter in which her husband learned that he had been disinherited by his father.

During the summer of 1919 Ernest Grosnier, a French collector and connoisseur, told René Gimpel, an art dealer with whom he was doing business, that William Orpen was 'England's most popular painter'.[1] The description was undoubtedly justified. Both Orpen and John Singer Sargent – the two great portrait painters of the Edwardian age – had been official war artists. But Orpen – after some argument in the Foreign Office and thanks to the friendly intervention of Lord Beaverbrook – had been appointed to record the Paris Peace Conference. Initially he was offered three thousand pounds to paint one comprehensive picture of the statesmen's deliberations, on the understanding that the sketches of the individual participants were to be given to the Imperial War Museum. Then the commission was extended to three pictures – for a fee of six thousand pounds – in which the heads of state and government would appear in what amounted to a series of personal portraits. The fame which followed brought the rich and famous to Orpen's studio door. Count John McCormack, the Irish tenor, Dame Madge Kendall, the last grande dame of the Edwardian theatre, David Lloyd George, the Prime Minister, and even the Prince of Wales travelled to the Boltons and sat behind the long window on the first floor. Lord Leverhulme argued that because he had been painted sitting down, the portrait was not full length and the price should be reduced accordingly.[2] Most of the gallery-going public – in general the educated middle classes – believed that Orpen's work typified the return to solid respectability which they hoped would follow the war.

In that the nation in general thought about art at all, its preoccupation was with the sculpture of war memorials. Edward Lutyens designed the Cenotaph on Whitehall – first a temporary and them a permanent monument to the war dead – and the sword-embossed cross which was erected on a thousand village greens. The most celebrated memorial was Charles Jagger's monument to the Royal Artillery on Hyde Park Corner. Reliefs, showing the horrors of battle, were surmounted by a great stone howitzer, which represented the engines of war that had brought the horrors about. Roger Fry – as always braving the tide of public opinion – dismissed the whole memorial genre in a single sentence. 'The tradition that all British art shall be crassly mediocre and inexpressive is so firmly rooted that it seems to have almost the prestige of a constitutional precedent.'[3] But Fry was still regarded by conventional opinion as an aging *enfant terrible*. He had been responsible for the Edwardian 'artquake' and, in 1910, had persuaded the Grafton Galleries to exhibit the work of Cézanne, Matisse and Gauguin – a group of artists who, he suggested, should be called the 'post-impressionists'. His theory of art – set out in the numerous magazines to which he contributed, and collected in *Vision and Design*, published in 1920 – was a diametric contradiction of the principle on which Victorian (and still revered) British painting was based. To Fry, 'form' was all and 'content' a minor consideration at best.

The rejection of art as a type of storytelling was anathema to sentimentalists, traditionalists and philistines. Fry compounded his offence by insisting on advancing a 'theory of aesthetics' – to the great irritation of people who 'knew what they liked'. Much of Fry's formalist theory of art was advanced by way of disputation with Clive Bell, a fellow member of the Bloomsbury group – a movement which was held together as much by the emotional entanglements of its members as by a common view on the place of art in society. Fry – whose wife was committed to a mental institution soon after their marriage – had a long affair with Vanessa, Clive Bell's wife and the sister of Virginia Woolf. Long after their affair was over Vanessa decorated the urn which held Fry's ashes in King's College, Cambridge, and Virginia wrote his biography.

Bell chose to 'extend' Fry's thesis by defining what he described as '*significant* form' as 'lines and colours combined in a certain way, certain forms and relations of forms [which] stir our aesthetic emotions'.[4] But although Fry adopted the revised language he never accepted the intellectual tyranny of Bell's approach. He believed that storytelling had only blunted aesthetic sensibilities. Bell insisted that it had rendered the masses totally incapable of making any sort of aesthetic judgement.

Both men wanted to extend the appreciation of art to beyond the boundaries of the Greco-Roman tradition on which all conventional teaching was based. When a cheaper edition of *Vision and Design* was published in 1923 a copy was borrowed from the Leeds Art Reference Library by a young Yorkshire sculptor called Henry Moore. He was particularly attracted by the chapters on African, Bushman and Ancient American art. Moore came to regard *Vision and Design* as a manifesto for artistic liberation. 'Once you had read Roger Fry,' he said, 'the whole thing was there.'[5] Moore's encomium confirmed that Fry had an informal distinction to add to the accolades recorded in *Who's Who* – Slade Professor of Fine Art at the University of Cambridge, founder of *The Burlington Magazine* and curator of paintings at New York's Metropolitan Museum. He had a profound effect on the most important art to come out of Britain between the wars – the sculpture of Jacob Epstein, Henry Moore and Barbara Hepworth.

★

Fry was not alone in breaking new ground. Before the war Jacob Epstein – the son of Polish exiles who moved to Britain via France in 1905 – had already been acclaimed as the man who would provide the antidote to what the vorticists denounced as the 'flat and insipid' traditions of conventional humanist art. His early commissions – the frescoes on the British Medical Association building in Tavistock Square and the tomb of Oscar Wilde in the Père Lachaise cemetery in Paris – all excited as much anger as awe. The explanation that the fresco 'bluntly' depicted every stage of human life and that the tomb combined the mystery of a Mayan god with the strength of the Assyrian winged bull did nothing to assuage the critics.

In 1915, heavily under the influence of Ezra Pound, he had produced what seemed to subscribe to all the canons of the vorticists' creed – the celebration of violence and energy as epitomised in the machine. *Rock Drill* was a robot – an 'armed sinister figure of today and tomorrow [with] no humanity . . . The Terrible Frankenstein monster we have made ourselves into.'[6] The 'monster' was drilling, without care or concern, into the living rock. 'Rock Drill' was also the title of a Pound poem. But it seems likely that, even as Epstein made the sculpture, he had doubts about the vorticists' preoccupation with power and force. The critic Richard Cork noticed that the monster's head is turned away, as if afraid to witness the damage that its work has done. And when the war was over vorticism – perhaps prophetic in its espousal of violence – lost much of its charm. Epstein truncated the figure and deprived it of its drill. It is now on exhibition in Tate Britain – a memorial to Epstein's conversion to belief in a more gentle theory of aesthetics.

The gentler Epstein won new admirers, among them the Royal Society for the Protection of Birds which commissioned him to sculpture a memorial to W. H. Hudson, naturalist and author of *The Crystal Age*, a utopian novel in which the world has achieved peace through the suppression of the sexual impulse. Epstein chose as his theme Rima – the wild female genius of the forest who was featured in Hudson's *Green Mansions*. He depicted her surrounded by birds which no member of the RSPB could have possibly identified. *Punch* dismissed admirers of Epstein's work as followers of a transient minority fashion. 'The allure of Epstein and Oxford trousering has been for the few. The crossword puzzle captivated the many.'[7] Other critics reacted more violently.

The memorial was unveiled in May 1925 by Stanley Baldwin, the Prime Minister. Shortly afterwards it was tarred and feathered by a group of cheerful philistines who endorsed the view of Frank Dicksee, RA, that Epstein had produced 'a bestial figure'. Assaults with green paint – peculiarly appropriate in light of the title of the novel by which the memorial was inspired – followed. They continued sporadically for four years until Epstein provided another target for vulgar assault. In 1929, *Night* – his sculpture over the entrance of the headquarters of the London Underground in Westminster Broadway – was bombarded with home-made tar grenades. Epstein, not a humble man, compared his persecution to the treatment meted out to Michelangelo, whose statue of David had, he claimed, been so unpopular in sixteenth-century Florence that it had only been saved from mutilation by a high protective fence.

Two years later Epstein exhibited his *Genesis* at the Leicester Galleries. It provoked an even greater outcry than had been aroused by *Night*. The *Sunday Express*, always the voice of the lowest common denominator, described it as 'so gross, so obscene and horrible that no newspaper has ever published a full picture of it'. It then added an image that was previously unknown to artistic criticism. 'As a dinner table decoration in ice cream, these atrocities would at least be gone by next morning.'[8] The excoriation continued unabated. *Ecce Homo* (1935), *Consummatum Est* (1937) and *Adam* (1937) were all provocative examples of what polite society regarded as Epstein's unforgivable sin – the overtly pagan treatment of Christian themes.

Epstein's genius was best reflected in his carving. His popular success and prosperous lifestyle were built on an acceptance of the spirit of the age, which became so enthusiastic about personality and portraiture that even Walter Sickert – founder of the Camden Town Group of 'social-realists' who believed that 'all art fades at a breath from the drawing room'[9] – ended his professional life painting celebrities.

Henry Moore, the son of a Yorkshire coal miner, and Barbara Hepworth – a northerner and a woman – shared Epstein's belief that a 'world view' of sculpture must be as much influenced by primitive and pre-classical sources as by the traditional classical foundations of

conventional art. And they were not distracted from their pursuit of a
new theory of aesthetics by diversions into portrait sculpture. Like
Epstein they had both, initially, been influenced by vorticism – particularly a carving by Gaudier-Brzeska called *Bird Swallowing a Fish*
which they thought, true to the vorticist tradition, exhibited great
strength and energy. But their work marks a rejection of vorticism
rather than its adaptation to post-war hopes and apprehensions. By
1918 even Wyndham Lewis – once vorticism's great exponent and the
co-founder of *Blast*, its magazine – could write, 'Vorticism was not so
much the harbinger of a new order as a symptom of the terminal disease of the old. The brave new world was a snare and delusion.'[10]
Moore and Nicholson offered something less destructive and more
optimistic.

Moore's early work was profoundly influenced by prehistoric carvings.
His 'mother and child' – a constantly repeated theme – looked like
fertility figures and were always (in a typical feature of his work) com-
fortingly round, smooth and boldly three-dimensional. Both he and
Hepworth began to bore holes through their sculptures to emphasise
that they were complete and consistent from every angle. Then they
developed the idea of a single form broken up into multiple parts.
Hepworth's *Large and Small Form* and Moore's *Four Piece Composition:
Reclining Figure* were both completed in 1934.

In the same year Moore published, with the support of the Unit
One group of artists, a paper entitled 'The Sculptor's Aims'. It set out
five points which explained his belief in what amounted to the *ethical*
importance of direct carving. First was '"truth in material" . . . If the
sculptor works direct . . . the material takes its part in the shaping of
the idea.' He illustrated the point by reference to *Figure*, a small sculpture which he had completed, in wood, three years earlier. The
prominent grain had influenced the sweep of the shoulders and the
shape of the head and neck. Second, 'full three-dimensional realisation'
revealed the 'dynamic tensions' between the various parts of the work
and allowed it to be appreciated from many different 'points of view'.
Third, the observation of natural objects – pebbles, bones and trees –
encouraged the understanding of various and distinctive 'principles
of form and rhythm'. The fourth and fifth points emphasised the

paramount necessity of 'vision' and 'vitality'. Moore argued that sculptors must both respect 'the abstract qualities of design' and reflect 'a psychological human element'. Purist critics insisted that the two objects were incompatible. But nobody doubted either Moore's genius or the new energy which he and Barbara Hepworth had brought to sculpture.

In 1938, and after a long irregular relationship, Barbara Hepworth married Ben Nicholson, who had 'just moved from post-Cubist paintings to the geometric reliefs in white for which he is best known'.[11] Hepworth believed that the union 'helped to release all [her] energies for an exploration of free sculpture form'. Domesticity had an altogether beneficial effect on her work. In October 1934 (after coincidentally giving birth to triplets) she became 'absorbed in the relationships in space, in size, in texture and in weight as well as in the tension between the forms'. It encouraged her to search for 'some absolute essence in sculptural terms' but at the same time produce work which was also 'a comment on the quality of human relationships'.[12] It added up to a search for a liberating view of sculpture – an art Moore believed should be limited by neither history nor tradition. The world was his studio.

> The world has been producing sculpture for at least thirty thousand years. Through modern development of communication, much of this we now know and the few sculptors of a hundred years or so in Greece no longer blot our eyes to the sculptural achievements of the rest of mankind. Paleolithic and Neolithic sculpture, Sumerian, Babylonian and Egyptian, Early Greek, Chinese, Etruscan, Indian, Mayan, Mexican and Peruvian, Romanesque, Byzantine, Negro, South Sea Island and North American Indian sculpture; photographs of all are available giving us a world view of sculpture not possible previously.[13]

Moore hoped to move art on by example. Nicholson – unusually for a painter – hoped to move British art forward (or at least provide it with an opportunity to advance in the wake of French innovation) by founding or promoting a succession of new pressure groups. His relationship with the conventional artistic establishment had been reflected in the pictures he painted after visiting Paul Nash at Dymchurch in 1923. Nash's pictures looked along the coastline. Nicholson confronted the sea head-on. Group X, Seven and Five and Unit One – each one created to encourage a break with traditional artistic values – all owed either their existence or their survival to him. They were equally abominated by the popular press.

In 1926 the *Daily Express* reviewed the Seven and Five exhibition under the headline 'Weird Puzzles in Paint'. It judged that 'the pictures and sculptures confirm the artists' ability to express what they feel; they proclaim also that it is unnecessary to express these feelings in their present state to a wider circle than the society itself provides'. That judgement could not have been further from the truth. The members of the group were desperate to 'relate' to the society in which they lived and worked and produce pictures which were 'meaningful' in contemporary society. What the *Daily Express* meant was that the artists of Seven and Five felt no obligation to reproduce what they saw with the accuracy of a photograph. 'Mr Ben Nicholson has three muddy nudes against wishy-washy backgrounds. It is obvious that the figures are not meant to be anatomically probable – one woman's ankles are three times the width of her neck. One wonders why he had to paint them.'[14]

Much of Nicholson's work is associated with Bankshead, his home in Cumberland. But during the early 1920s – partly because of ill health – he regularly spent the winters in Switzerland, from where he made occasional excursions to Paris. In 1921 he visited Paul Rosenberg's gallery, where (it is believed for the first time) he saw a picture by Pablo Picasso. Its title has never been identified. But we know that it was a Cubist work painted in or around 1915. To Nicholson it seemed entirely abstract and its impact on him was immense.

In the centre there was an absolutely miraculous green – very deep, very potent and absolutely real. In fact, none of the actual events in one's life have been more real than that, and it still remains a standard by which I judge any reality of my own work.

From then on Nicholson was more than influenced by Picasso. He was Picasso's disciple and apostle within the British artistic community. All of the many societies which he helped to found were aimed at 'modernising' British attitudes to art. More often than not, that meant understanding, admiring, and, where possible, emulating Picasso.

The Seven and Five society was disbanded in 1935 – by which time Ivon Hitchens (who had invited Ben Nicholson to join in 1923) was the only founding member to remain in good standing. Art was moving on. And the surrealists were moving in. In his introduction to the catalogue for the 1936 International Surrealist Exhibition Herbert Read, who was later to edit both an anthology of Barbara Hepworth's work and a biography of Henry Moore, left the general public in no doubt that surrealism had a sterner purpose than bewildering people of a literal mindset. 'Do not judge this movement kindly. It is not just another amusing stunt. It is defiant – the desperate act of men too profoundly convinced of the ruthlessness of our society to want to save a shred of its respectability.' All art is political. Surrealism had decided to become overtly so.

The exhibition struggled to catch public attention by organising stunts. Salvador Dali gave a lecture dressed in a deep-sea diver's suit and holding two Irish Wolfhounds on leashes. Nobody should have been surprised, and the surrealists were probably grateful, when J. B. Priestley – assuming his familiar role as Down-to-Earth-Jack, the Man of the People – denounced them in prose with broad vowel sounds.

> They stand for violence and neurotic unreason. They are truly decadent. You catch a glimpse behind them of the deepening twilight of barbarism that may soon blot out the sky, until at last humanity finds itself in another long night. There are about too many effeminate or epicene young men, lisping and undulating. Too many young women without manners, balance, dignity – greedy, slobbering sensation seekers. Too many people who are lapsing into shaven and powdered barbarism . . . Frequently they have strong sexual impulses that they soon contrive to misuse or pervert.[15]

Outrage, disgust and disbelief were not enough to kill British surrealism stone dead. It struggled on, delighting in causing shudders as well as shock until the beginning of the war. With every month that passed it displayed more and more outré political views as well as increasingly bizarre examples of the nihilism at the heart of its theory of aesthetics. By 1935 it was in open conflict with painters of the Euston Road School (William Coldstream, Claude Rogers and Graham Bell) who, with every justification, contrasted the 'humility and honesty of their realism' with the 'vociferation and pretentious flourish' of its surreal antithesis. But it was not intellectual argument which brought the movement's downfall. It was a combination of political *naïveté* and old-fashioned duplicity – producing a situation to which the term surreal could be legitimately applied.

The surrealist movement's headquarters were the London Gallery in Cork Street. From there, E. L. T Messens edited and issued the *London Bulletin*. During the winter of 1938– 9 Messens published, as a supplement to the *Bulletin*, a manifesto entitled 'Towards an Independent Revolutionary Art'. It was signed by two practising surrealists but it had been written in collaboration with the exiled Leon Trotsky. That turned most independent artists against the movement. Then members themselves rebelled against the edict – more Stalinist than Trotskyite – that surrealists must always work and write as followers of that discipline. Deviation was forbidden.

Inevitably in the time of turmoil which was the 1930s, politics influenced, if not inspired, many of the artists who hoped to break new ground. But faith – or more specifically Christian belief – remained an inescapable theme. The pious public were perplexed and offended by Epstein's religious sculptures but perplexed and encouraged by Stanley Spencer's paintings of the *Last Judgement* and the subsequent *Resurrection*. Between the wars it was still possible to believe that tombs would open and the dead would rise in bodily form – in Spencer's judgement, round, pink and justifiably self-satisfied. And Spencer's pictures possessed a second great attraction to the citizens of an uncertain world. Each one told a story. The narrative tradition in British art had, like the corpses in Spencer's paintings, been reincarnated.

Spencer was born and bred in the Berkshire village of Cookham which, although he left at age seventeen for the Slade, remained a major influence on his painting throughout his life. His father read him bible stories and one theory of his work suggests that he came to believe in an eventual earthly paradise – not unlike Cookham. 'Walls are often used to separate the divine from the everyday. In his painting of *Zachariah and Elizabeth* sacrificing in the temple, a child peeps over a wall expressing Spencer's own sense of the nearness of the spiritual world.'[16] Not even the First World War – in which he served first as a medical orderly and then as an infantryman – shattered Spencer's belief in the possibility of heaven on earth. Neither did two unhappy marriages and the rejection by the Royal Academy hanging committee of what is believed to be one of his greatest works – *Saint Francis and the Birds*.

In 1925 Spencer was invited to paint the murals in the Sandham Memorial Chapel in Burghclere, Hampshire – scenes of army life which were commissioned to commemorate the life of the patron's brother. Spencer chose to ignore the horrors of death and destruction and point instead to what he regarded as the gentle pleasures of army life – washing, cooking, eating simple food. He had been inspired by the confessions of Saint Augustine of Hippo. God was to be found in small and mundane things as well as the great and noble. The angels, witnessing Christ carrying the cross, lean out from windows of a semi-detached suburban house. His cherubs wore tweed suits.

Spencer's work at Burghclere has been compared to Giotto's reverential frescoes in Florence and Padua. But it culminated in an altar-piece – *The Resurrection of the Soldiers* – which bore the unmistakable imprint of the artist's belief that the sacred and profane were inextricably intertwined. To confirm the bodily reincarnation of the Blessed, the risen immediately indulged in the pleasures of the flesh. It was his second great painting with that theme. *The Resurrection at Cookham* had been started before the Sandham commission and when his work on the memorial chapel was done he returned to Cookham to pursue the same idea. His hope was to create a 'Church House' in which his paintings – both spiritual and temporal – would hang side by side. The building was never even begun, but much of Spencer's subsequent work was intended to hang within a gallery, which he hoped would be dedicated to the partnership of God and man.

Spencer's cheerful, homely figures made him, if not a popular favourite, at least accepted by the wider public as a painter whose work was comprehensible. But he was not the artist whose pictures they wanted on their Christmas cards. The prints they wanted to frame – in passepartout as was the habit of the time – and hang on their walls were scenes from the circus and ballet by Laura Knight, horses by Alfred Munnings and rolling English fields and harvest time by Rowland Hilder.

As always the avant-garde was not above forging a remunerative relationship with the proletariat. In 1932 Brain and Company of Stoke-on-Trent, the makers of Foley China, asked Paul Nash, Ben Nicholson and Duncan Grant to offer decorations for their plates. Grant – in many ways the most Bloomsbury of Bloomsbury figures – sent them an 'Old English Rose'. He went on to design border motifs (to complement posies of flowers) for the 'Lustre' tea service manu-factured by Arthur J. Wilkinson and Co. His culinary ceramics went on display at Harrods under the title 'Modern Art for the Table'.[17] Patrons bought tea sets and felt part of the cultural elite.

It is architecture which is said to be the inescapable art which imposes itself on the lives of men and women who are not even aware of its existence as an aesthetic discipline. At the end of the First World War the two men who were thought both to reflect and influence the spirit of the age were the great Edwardians Sir Edwin Lutyens and Sir Giles Gilbert Scott. Lutyens – who designed everything from a castle on Lindisfarne to a block of council flats in Westminster – was most famous as the architect of the Viceroy's House and Parliament Buildings in New Delhi, begun in 1915 but not completed until 1924. Scott, at the age of twenty-one, had won the competition to design the new Liverpool Protestant cathedral in 1901. He too could claim an eclectic choice of commission. For he was also the architect of Battersea Power Station, commissioned in 1929.

By then 'eclectic' – as an adjective to describe style rather than choice of commissions – was, in the language of modern architecture, a term of abuse. It implied a willingness to accept the values of other times and other places – a weakness which romantics claimed could be blamed on the flexible thinking which followed the Reformation.

Lutyens' designs were more or less classical, Scott's by and large Gothic. Neither, the modernists said, was true to the values of the twentieth century.

Most generations of artistic and intellectual activities call themselves and their movements 'modern'. The modernist architects of the twentieth century were exceptional in so much as they could define what they meant by the term. Their buildings were based directly on the new techniques and the new materials that scientific progress had provided for them, their designs were primarily based on the function of the proposed building rather than its appearance and their work was never reminiscent of long-dead schools of architecture and design. During the 1920s the modernists' most notable work was done in America and on the continent of Europe under the influence of Frank Lloyd Wright and Le Corbusier. Their ideas were late to spread to Britain because of the awe in which Lutyens and Scott were held – and because both architects modified their natural styles to accommodate both the new materials and the new ideas of inter-war Britain. Liverpool Cathedral is often described as the last great Gothic building in England, but it is clearly a Gothic masterpiece as designed in the early twentieth century. Had not Lutyens' design for the Catholic cathedral in Liverpool been overtaken by costs and the Second World War there would have been a matching twentieth-century classical edifice at the other end of Hope Street.

Lutyens and Scott take credit for protecting Britain from the worst excesses of the 'Regency Revival' or (as the most bitter critics described it) the 'playboy era' and 'the age of ancestor worship'[18] which followed the rejection of arts and crafts in favour of beaux arts. Lutyens himself, at Britannia House in Finsbury Circus, London, and the Reuter Building in Fleet Street, developed a plain classical style to match the Gothic moderation of Liverpool Cathedral and Scott's almost austere Church of Our Lady at Northfleet in Kent. Others followed suit with 'emasculated Gothic'[19] – most notably the architects Welch, Cachemaille-Day and Lander (in St Nicholas', Burnage, Manchester) and Sir Edward Maufe (in Guildford Cathedral). The designs were simple. The windows were usually square and always plain and there were large expanses of empty walls.

The modernists demanded more than a compromise with antiquity.

And in Britain they were reinforced in their campaign by a group of inspired modern architects from countries which suppressed or discouraged independent artistic thought. Because of their immigration, the situation changed as one decade ended and the next began. During the 1930s, Britain moved from the tail end of the modernist movement to the vanguard. Their inspiration was Walter Gropius, appointed in 1919 the head of the Weimar Art College, which became the Staatliche Bauhaus. Gropius himself came to Britain in 1934 and designed, with Maxwell Fry, the Impington Village College before he left for America. His disciples stayed and changed the face of British building.

Berthold Lubetkin was born in the Caucasus. He studied architecture in Paris (where he was convinced of the importance of pre-stressed concrete, a vital ingredient of the modernist formula) before moving on to England in 1930. On his arrival he formed – with a group of young English architects – the Tecton Group. Together they designed the gorilla house and penguin pool for London Zoo. A feature of the penguin pool were 'flying' steel-reinforced runways along which the birds could promenade.

The Tecton Group's bequest to architectural posterity was Highpoint Flats in Highgate – Highpoint One, as they became. They were designed in strict conformity with the 'Five Points of Architecture' set down by Le Corbusier – pillars supporting the whole structure, a roof terrace which could become a garden, an open floor plan, a façade free of ornamentation and windows designed to let in light rather than to contribute to the appearance of the building.

Highpoint was designed in the shape of a Cross of Lorraine so as to maximise views over London and to retain as much contact with the world outside its walls as was possible. The body of the eight-storey building was lifted on pilotis – essential, in the view of Le Corbusier, to encourage the feeling of space and to allow either the passage of traffic, which would unite the tenants with the wider community, or landscaping, which would make the development a green lung within a grey city. The roof garden was for the communal use of all of the flats and the ground floor was set aside for communal activity. The exterior was white and smooth and plain. Le Corbusier himself described it as 'one of the vertical garden cities of the future'.[20] As was the case with so much modern architecture, it expressed a clear view about how men and women should live in the twentieth century.

Highpoint Two was built between 1936 and 1938. To the disgust of true modernists, it did not conform to the rules of functional austerity which Highpoint One had observed. Indeed the complicated façade, the variety of materials used to give different textures to the external walls and (above all) the appearance of classical caryatids on the canopy caused despair among the architects who had believed that Lubetkin was the leader of the new movement. The *Architectural Review* called it 'an important move forward from fundamentalism'. Anthony Cox, of the avant-garde, disputed the description and suggested in its place 'a symptom of decline'.[21]

Erich Mendelsohn fled to Britain in 1933 to escape Nazi persecution and, in partnership with Serge Chermayeff, almost immediately won the competition to design the seaside De La Warr pavilion at Bexhill in Sussex – particularly important in the story of inter-war architecture because public commissions were so rare. Concrete cantilever terraces and wide horizontal windows gave uninterrupted views of the sea and a semi-cylindrical concrete and glass tower contained a spiral staircase which linked all the floors.

Glass 'curtains', cladding steel or concrete skeletons were the 'functional' order of the day, as exemplified by Boots' warehouse in Beeston, Nottingham, and the Peter Jones store in Sloane Square, London. In both cases the architects chose to emphasise utility rather than appearance. The flexibility in the exterior walls which their design allowed made it possible for loading bays to be cut into the ground floor of the Boots' warehouse and the whole of the Peter Jones frontage to be a shop window. It was this elegant simplicity which united them with Highpoint One and made them – not Guildford Cathedral or the Reuter Building – the architecture of inter-war Britain. Whether or not they influenced the spirit of the time, or the spirit of the time influenced them, it is clear – just by looking at such buildings – that they are the 1930s expressed in glass and concrete.

The serious music of the period is not so easily identified. But Edward Elgar – still generally regarded, despite one or two dissenting voices, as the only British-born composer since Purcell to rank with the continental masters – believed that he could describe the national mood. In a letter dated 30 December 1924 he told Frank Schuster, a loyal friend and generous patron, 'Music is dying in this country.'[22] That gloomy judgement was intended both to confirm and justify the news that Schuster could expect 'nothing more from [Elgar's] pen'. The Master of the King's Musick – appointed only six months earlier – had decided to compose no more. Schuster's hope that Elgar would at last complete his trilogy of oratorios – and that they would become the English rival to Wagner's *Ring Cycle* – was not to be realised. *The Apostles* and *The Kingdom* remained complete in themselves, but denied the promised climax of Christianity triumphant.

For Elgar 1924 had been a year of mixed fortunes. What looked like worldly success was constantly compromised by Elgar's fear that, although he was acknowledged as a great composer, he was not recognised as an English country gentleman. The British Empire Exhibition – which had opened at Wembley Stadium on St George's Day – was to begin with a pageant. Elgar was commissioned to write the music. But the King wanted *Land of Hope and Glory* and the Guards' massed band was apprehensive about learning a new and complicated suite in a few days. So *The Pageant of Empire*, eight songs with words by Alfred Noyes, was performed halfway through the exhibition, after the band had formed up and marched in – playing a march which Elgar had written for Queen Victoria's Diamond Jubilee. Then Elgar conducted *Pomp and Circumstance Number Four* while the crowd sang A. C. Benson's words. On the rostrum he looked magnificent. In private, he found the whole experience intolerable, as illustrated by his comments on the rehearsal.

> Overwhelmed by etiquette and red tape . . . everything seems so hopelessly and irredeemably vulgar at Court . . . No soul. No romance. No imagination.[23]

Less than a week later he was appointed Master of the King's Musick.

Even the pleasure of royal recognition was soured by the circumstances of his appointment. His predecessor, Sir Walter Parratt, was, in Elgar's view, a nonentity – even though he had been a nonentity who had immensely helped Elgar's career by introducing his music to the royal household. The declining status of the appointment seemed to have been confirmed by the King's inclination to abolish the title. Elgar had lobbied for its continuation on the grounds that abolition would imply that the Court had no concern for music. The lobbying had been successful, but Elgar feared that others would feel – and per- haps he felt it himself – that he had argued on his own behalf. The ambivalence was typical of a decade in which he – in common with so many others – never felt quite at peace.

The years of peace had begun well. In 1918 Elgar, who had previ- ously not found chamber music to his taste, returned, more productively, to the complications of sonata, quartet and quintet. The great cello concerto was begun and he was enjoying country life in one of the many houses which he had rented over the years – flying kites, playing billiards, fishing and chopping wood. Hubert Parry – one of the few 'academic' musicians whom Elgar admired – had died in October and Elgar interrupted work and play to travel to London for his funeral. But on Armistice Day a strange sadness engulfed him. He wrote to Laurence Binyon to explain his refusal to set a 'peace poem' to music.

> I do not feel drawn to write peace music . . . The whole atmo- sphere is too full of complexities for me to feel music to it; not the atmosphere of the poem, but of the time, I mean . . . the individual sorrow and sacrifice – a cruelty I resent bitterly and disappointedly.[24]

The cello concerto was finished in August 1919 and the first per- formance arranged for 26 October. Elgar was himself to conduct the London Symphony Orchestra as part of a programme which con- cluded with Albert Coates conducting Scriabin's *Poem of Ecstasy*. The Scriabin needed more time for rehearsal than the organisers had anti- cipated and Coates continued with the preparation for most of the afternoon, intruding into at least two hours which should have been spent rehearsing the cello concerto. The result was a poor perform- ance and lukewarm notices from the critics. Elgar – who should have recalled that the reputation of *The Dream of Gerontius* had

survived a similar fiasco in Birmingham town hall twenty years earlier — retired bruised and bewildered to a friend's house in Worcester.
The Malvern Hills were always a comfort in times of disappointment
and distress.

Throughout all his vicissitudes Elgar's recording contract with His
Master's Voice kept him prosperous, though not contented. The cello
concerto was to be recorded by the youthful Beatrice Harrison — one
of three prodigious sisters whose talents had been obvious at such an
early age that Margaret was enrolled in the Royal College of Music
when she was four and May made her concert debut at the Wigmore
Hall at the age of thirteen. Elgar enjoyed the company of young
women, though the pleasure of his partnership with Beatrice
Harrison — like the recording itself — was interrupted by the death of
his wife. Lady Elgar had been almost indispensable, both to Elgar's
work and his self-esteem. Adrian Boult — a schoolboy at Westminster
when his friendship with Elgar began — described her as 'a small
woman, rather timid [who] spoke so quietly that it was sometimes difficult to hear her, but where Elgar was concerned she was made of
iron.'[25] Being 'a lady', she helped Elgar believe that he was, or should
have been, accepted by 'society'. She also fought, in a way Elgar could
not have fought himself, for his proper recognition by the music
establishment.

Elgar's anguish at the death of his wife was so intense that it almost
certainly accounted for his strange reaction to the news that Charles
Villiers Stanford, Professor of Music in the University of Cambridge,
was in the congregation at the requiem mass at St Wulstan's Catholic
Church, Little Malvern. The two men had not spoken for sixteen
years — a feud to which Lady Elgar had contributed by describing
Stanford's *Sea Songs* as 'common'. Fortunately Elgar was not aware,
during the service, of Stanford's presence. When he found out he
refused to reciprocate what others believed to be a gesture of
reconciliation.

The death of his wife destroyed much of Elgar's urge to compose.
He remained the grand old man of English music — recording, arrang-
ing and conducting. But the willingness to risk and to dare had
deserted him. Younger composers paid him homage. Arnold Bax
requested 'the pleasure of dedicating a string quartet'[26] and Arthur

Bliss was fulsome in his thanks for the 'rare encouragement' he had received.[27] But they composed in a different spirit for a time to which Elgar had never attempted to adjust. Constant Lambert's description of their attitude was as cruel as it was accurate.

> The aggressive Edwardian prosperity that lends so comfortable a background to Elgar's finales is now as strange to us as the England that produced 'Greensleeves' and 'the Woodies so Wilde' . . . In consequence much of Elgar's music, through no fault of his own, has for the present generation an almost insufferable air of smugness, self-assurance and aristocratic benevolence.[28]

There were continual messages of support from old friends. George Bernard Shaw – chalk to Elgar's cheese, but a friend nevertheless – described the critics of possessing the 'tastes of schoolboys and sporting costermongers'.[29] And there were one or two reassuring signs. At Elgar's seventy-fifth birthday banquet, the BBC – which had been accused of neglecting his work – announced that it had commissioned (with an advance of a thousand pounds) a Third Symphony.

There was a brief revival in Elgar's creative spirit when he found a 'new muse' – Vera Hockman, a young violinist whom he described (with only one accurate noun in four) as 'my mother, my daughter, my lover and my friend'.[30] And, after the merger of Columbia Records and HMV to become EMI, there were constant invitations to make recordings on the new electrical equipment in Abbey Road. But composing had become no more than trawling through old notebooks in search of ideas that could be revived. The one hope lay in the completion of the Third Symphony.

Before the work was finished Elgar was found to be suffering from cancer. The back pain which had troubled him for so long was a tumour pressing on the sciatic nerve. Eric Fenby, Delius' amanuensis, wrote to say that he would gladly perform the same task for Elgar. His offer was firmly declined. Almost the last musical rite was performed thanks to an extraordinary arrangement made by EMI. Elgar – with the aid of a Post Office landline – rehearsed, from his bed, the Triumphal March from *Caractacus* with the London Symphony Orchestra in Abbey Road.

Sir Edward Elgar, OM, died on 23 February 1934 – as he would have wished, in Worcester. A few weeks before the end he had received a letter from T. E. Lawrence, then serving in the ranks of the Royal Air Force. It came from Cloud's Hill, the cottage which Lawrence had renovated in the Dorset woods.

We have just been playing your 2<sup>nd</sup> Symphony, three of us, a sailor, a Tank Corps soldier and myself. So there are all the services present and we agreed that you must be written to and told (if you are well enough to be bothered) that the Symphony gets further under our skin than anything else in the record library . . . Generally we play the Symphony last of all, towards the middle of the night, because nothing comes very well after it.[31]

About a year earlier Lawrence had been taken by Bernard Shaw to meet Elgar. And it is Bernard Shaw whose judgement on the composer is now almost universally accepted. His rebuke to Professor Dent began with the accusation that, by belittling Elgar, Dent was belittling his country. For Elgar, he said, is the only British 'composer who is not dwarfed by the German giants'.[32]

# CHAPTER FIFTEEN

# Power Without Responsibility

I don't know what to believe. I have always admired Mr Baldwin's quiet ways. But if so many papers are against him (Conservative papers too), you have to take notice.

Anne Goodison
aged 85, writing from Newcastle to her daughter
in London, 24 March 1930

On the morning of 14 August 1922 Alfred Charles William Harmsworth, First Viscount Northcliffe – proprietor of *The Times* and *Daily Mail* – died in a wooden hut on the roof of the Duke of Devonshire's house in Carlton House Gardens. One of the symptoms of Northcliffe's madness was claustrophobia and it was hoped that the unusual accommodation high above the Mall would ease his distress. Northcliffe had been mad for more than a year. Two months before he died Wickham Steed, the editor of *The Times*, had visited him in the Plaza Athene Hotel in Paris.

He found him in bed, scantily dressed and obviously excited. For a moment, when the light was turned up, his left eye showed a diagonal squint. His lower lip bore a dark scar as if it had been burned. Seizing Steed's hand he said how keenly he had felt the separation from him and rehearsed, in a gabbling voice, the circumstances of his poisoning by the Germans and the attempted assassination by his secretary in Boulogne.[1]

In the best tradition of journalism, Steed made his excuses and left. When he returned, an hour or so later, Northcliffe was pointing a revolver at his dressing gown, which was hanging on the bedroom door, and announcing that, unless it left at once, he would not hesitate to shoot.

Northcliffe's madness, and subsequent death, came at a time when British newspapers – predominantly Tory – were giving front-page welcomes to the break-up of the wartime coalition. Lloyd George had been generous in the provision of peerages for proprietors. But the press remained resolutely Conservative – until the party was once again split by the age-old battle of protection versus free trade.

Northcliffe was probably the greatest journalist of the age. But his death was accepted by his fellow proprietors with less than over-whelming regret. He had never been willing to subjugate the interests of his own papers to the interests of the industry as a whole – led by men whom he called 'monsters of the Fleet Street deep'. And there is no reason to assume that he would have joined with Beaverbrook in the campaign for 'imperial preference'. He went his own way. Five months before he died he had refused to stand shoulder-to-shoulder with his competitors in their battle with the unions. His telegram from Paris showed little sympathy for organised labour. 'If they tried to dictate how he should run his business, he would fight them.' However, he was 'not likely to join a combination of rich men for grinding down poor men – but regard newspapers as an extension of the commodity market'.[2] To emphasise his point Northcliffe resigned from the News-paper Proprietors' Association. That was bad enough. But he delayed his resignation until after he had prevented the imposition of the wage cut which five of the eight subscribing members had demanded.

Northcliffe's grieving colleagues and competitors found reason for consolation in a second consequence of his death. It seemed certain that his newspaper empire would be split up and that parts of it would be put on sale. So it turned out. Harold Sidney Harmsworth, First Viscount Rothermere, who had inherited his brother's empire, had to sell *The Times* in order to pay the death duties on the Northcliffe estate. He made an offer of £1,350,000 from his private fortune. But John Jacob Astor – a Tory Member of Parliament who had lost a leg fighting with the Life Guards during the First World War – outbid him with an offer of £1,580,000. Wickham Steed, who had done Northcliffe's bidding, was replaced as editor by Geoffrey Dawson who, it was wrongly assumed, would do the same for Astor. It was Dawson's second period in charge of *The Times*. He had been appointed editor (at the age of thirty-seven) in 1911 but had resigned in 1919 when Northcliffe had refused to support the Lloyd George coalition. After four years in Oxford as bursar of All Souls he returned to *The Times* – where he remained until 1941. Throughout his tenure he displayed admirable independence of his proprietor but during the two great crises – Munich and the abdication – was absolutely subservient to the Whitehall establishment.

To emphasise the elevated nature of *The Times*, Astor safeguarded its future by placing a veto on its sale in the hands of trustees – the Governor of the Bank of England, the Lord Chief Justice of England, the Warden of All Souls, the President of the Royal Society and (perhaps more surprisingly) the President of the Institute of Chartered Accountants. Rothermere retained the ownership of the *Daily Mail*, the *Sunday Dispatch* and the *Evening News* and began, at once, to steer a more idiosyncratic course than his brother had navigated. His principal passion was for the renegotiation of the Treaty of Trianon by which Hungary, with a severely reduced border, was separated from Austria. His campaign had no success but was conducted with such vigour that he was offered the Hungarian throne – which he declined with thanks.

A year after Northcliffe died Edward Hulton – the owner of eight newspapers including the *Evening Standard*, the *Daily Sketch* and the *Manchester Evening Chronicle* – decided it was time to sell. In the six years which followed the outbreak of the First World War his profits had averaged £327,000. In 1920 his company made a loss of £216,000. Yet during the first six months of 1923 the circulation figures were still healthy – 1,267,343 for his morning dailies, 868,639 for his evening papers and 4,518,349 for his weekly and Sunday publications.[3]. Hulton had an asset worth selling and the Berry brothers, owners of the *Sunday Times* and *Financial Times*, were ready to buy. The deal would have gone through, but the Berrys' solicitor was ill and negotiations were delayed. While the Berrys waited Rothermere made an offer for their papers and was told that they would not be sold to him at any price.

Hulton was a personal friend of Lord Beaverbrook – a Canadian adventurer who had been raised to the peerage in 1917 after helping Lloyd George to replace Asquith as Prime Minister. At the time of the Hulton sale Beaverbrook was struggling to make a success of the *Sunday Express*, which he had launched on 30 December 1918. It had lost £500,000 in each of the two years of its existence. Fortunately the *Daily Express*, which he had acquired in 1916, was doing better. Circulation, which averaged 550,000 a day in 1920, rose to almost a million in 1922. But the situation was too precarious to last for long. With a success and a potential failure on his hands, Beaverbrook's temperament allowed only one response. He was determined to expand. Unfortunately he lacked the capital to make his aspiration a reality. Beaverbrook made up for that deficiency with one of the most audacious coups in newspaper history.

On 28 September 1923 Beaverbrook learned that Hulton would sell his papers to the Berry brothers on 1 October for £6 million. The deal was to be confirmed with a down-payment of £300,000, with the rest to be paid over a period, the length of which was subject to negotiation. But a second illness intervened. Hulton himself was ordered to rest and his family was determined that the doctor's instructions should not be ignored. There could be no haggling over the details of the sale until his recovery was complete.

Beaverbrook seized the moment. He lived about two miles away from Hulton and, early one evening, he walked from house to house, let himself in by the French windows and found his own way to the sickroom. There he offered Hulton an immediate £1 million with four more payments rapidly to follow. The terms were written out on a sheet of Midland Bank writing paper – which Beaverbrook had providently brought with him. Hulton wrote 'I accept' beneath the offer and signed.[4]

Beaverbrook did not possess five million pounds. Nor did he have

an account with the Midland Bank – a fact that the general manager
confirmed when Hulton's family telephoned to check on
Beaverbrook's resources. But within twenty minutes the manager rang
back to say that the sum would be met. Beaverbrook had hurried
home and telephoned his friend Reginald McKenna, the former
Chancellor of the Exchequer who had become the chairman of the
Midland Bank.[5]

One problem remained. Beaverbrook would owe the Midland
Bank £5 million which he could not repay. However, since his only
real interest in the Hulton empire was the *Evening Standard*, he decided
to sell the rest on as quickly as possible. 'Information was conveyed to
[Sir William Berry] that he could, if he liked, have the rest of the publications but he did not seem to grasp the idea . . . Beaverbrook then
thought of Rothermere . . . [he] called him up and, in his own off-
hand manner outlined the proposition he had to offer. Rothermere,
equally nonchalantly, accepted without ringing off.'[6]

The deal involved Beaverbrook retaining a controlling interest in
the *Evening Standard* as his commission for brokering the sale.
Rothermere kept 49 per cent of the equity – but paid for it with forty
thousand shares in the Daily Mail Trust. In money terms, Beaverbrook
was the clear winner. He had acquired control over one newspaper
and financial interest in another as the reward for visiting a sick
friend – and realising how the visit could be exploited. But
Rothermere pronounced himself satisfied. 'My whole and sole object
was to obtain for [my] shareholders . . . the control of two newspapers
from which they had most to fear.'[7] Beaverbrook's objective was different. 'He wanted political influence . . . But he also wanted fun and
the *Evening Standard* provided an outlet for his excessive radicalism.'[8]

On 3 October 1923 H. A. Gwyne, the editor of the *Morning Post*,
told Stanley Baldwin, 'Beaverbrook is in with Rothermere in the
purchase of the Hulton concerns.'[9] Gwyne feared that the two men
were in league with Lloyd George and were plotting his return to
power. Baldwin was not sure whom Beaverbrook supported, but knew
that he was intriguing to change the leadership of the Tory Party.
The *Express* group of newspapers had begun to develop a distinctive
political position. In 1923 it had argued that 'splendid isolation' was the
right foreign policy for Britain and made a call to the young men of

England. 'If you serve yourself well, you will serve your country well.' The paper went on to suggest that the time had come to harness 'the teeming energies of the imperial race'. The Conservative Party was about to begin one of its regular self-destructive disagreements over the merits of protection – or, as Beaverbrook would have called it, 'imperial preference'.

When a by-election was held in the Abbey Division of Westminster Beaverbrook and Rothermere endorsed an independent candidate who stood on the platform of 'imperial preference and reform'. The *Sunday Times* and the *Daily Telegraph* wrote supportive articles without actually endorsing the rebel. E. R. Thompson, the editor of the *Evening Standard*, refused point-blank to follow the Beaverbrook line and was allowed, in the name of editorial independence, to argue in favour of a Conservative victory. When the election was over – the official Tory candidate won by forty-three votes – Thompson would have been dismissed had he not died of a heart attack 'in the course of being sacked'.[10]

On 18 May 1924, the *People* published an interview with the Conservative leader under the headline, 'Baldwin Turns and Rends His Critics'.

I am attacked by . . . Lord Beaverbrook and Lord Rothermere. For myself I do not care what they say or think. They are both men that I would not have in my house. I do not respect them.

According to the reporter, Baldwin 'yawned with disgust and weariness at discussing, for so long, so unpleasant a subject'.[11] The general public, as always uninterested in the incestuous arguments between press and politicians, accepted Baldwin's attack on his critics calmly. But sections of the Conservative Party were deeply offended by one parenthetical sentence. It referred to Lord Birkenhead – one of the 'sinister and cynical combination' who wanted to revive the coalition which Baldwin had done so much to destroy in 1922. Birkenhead might well return to government, 'if his health does not give way'. Birkenhead was an alcoholic. Drawing attention to his addiction, no matter how obliquely, was hitting below the belt.

Baldwin retreated into the last refuge of recklessly indiscreet politicians. He disowned the reporter and wrote to Lord Beaverbrook, though not to Birkenhead.

> I hope you know me well enough to be certain that I never gave expression to the personal reflections on yourself which are there reported. I am deeply distressed that I should be so misrepresented.[12]

Beaverbrook did not reply.

However, the genie was out of the bottle. The conflict between the Tory Prime Minister and the two paladins of the Tory press was in the open. Other newspapers joined in the battle. The Baldwin-supporting *Morning Post* wrote that there was 'so much truth in what he is alleged to have said that it is almost as good as if he had said it'.[13] The *Daily Herald* noted the similarity between the disowned words and Baldwin's style of speech. 'The Conservative leader talks in that crisp, blunt way.'[14] Freddy Wilson, the reporter who had interviewed Baldwin, and Hannen Swaffer, the *People's* editor, both offered to resign. But, much to his credit, Grant Murdett, the paper's managing director, refused to let them go and, instead, chose to defend and justify the published interview. On 25 May 1924 the *People* described Baldwin as a 'slow thinking, very honest, earnest, likeable man trying to tackle a very difficult subject'. It was not the sort of support that a party leader usually welcomes. But Baldwin was fighting for his life against the combined forces of the two most powerful men in Fleet Street. For the first and only time in the history of British politics two Conservative newspaper tycoons set out to take over the Conservative Party.

Notwithstanding his protestations that he had only bought the Hulton papers in order to keep them from a competitor, in 1925 Northcliffe sold the *Telegraph* and the *Financial Times* to the Berry brothers. The Berrys went from strength to strength. In 1926 they bought provincial dailies in Glasgow, Newcastle, Aberdeen, Cardiff and Sheffield as well as a hundred Northcliffe periodicals. Then, in partnership with Edward Iliffe, they formed Allied Newspapers and bought the Amalgamated Press. Then the almost-automatic peerages followed.

Meanwhile the alliance of Rothermere and Beaverbrook had been solemnised by a share deal which both men had endorsed in strangely sentimental language. On 20 October 1923 Northcliffe had formally asked Beaverbrook, 'Could I purchase an interest in your paper?' and Beaverbrook, as if prepared in advance to respond to the request, had immediately replied, 'Of course, I would like you to purchase an interest in Express Newspapers. Nothing would give me greater pleasure than to work in co-operation with you and with the *Daily Mail*.'[15]

The combined assaults on Baldwin continued almost unabated – only interrupted by the *Daily Mail*'s publication, during the 1924 general election campaign, of the fraudulent 'Zinoviev Letter', which purported to prove that the Labour Party was in cahoots with the Soviet Communist Party. The Tories won and Baldwin returned to Downing Street, but the ferocity of the Northcliffe/Beaverbrook attacks increased rather than diminished. In October 1925 an editorial in the *Spectator* was not sure whether to complain about the press lords' sustained campaign or marvel at Baldwin's insouciant resilience.

> The persecution of Mr Baldwin... has passed beyond reason and decency. Many onlookers are asking 'Can a political party possibly survive when the most popular newspapers, which normally support it, are engaged, day and night, in ridiculing its leader?' . . . [But] the press is less powerful than it seems to be . . . Mr Baldwin passes serenely on his way without paying attention.

The conflict between Beaverbrook and the government was inevitable. But when it came the *Daily Mail*'s animosity was directed less at the Prime Minister, whom Beaverbrook loathed, than at Winston Churchill, by then Chancellor of the Exchequer, who was, by his own definition, one of Beaverbrook's closest friends, though the friendship was to be tested, almost to destruction, during the General Strike. The issue which divided them was not the merits of the dispute itself – though Churchill's attitude was hardened by what he believed to be Beaverbrook's willingness to contain the unions rather than jeopardising the commercial interests at his paper. Before the strike had even begun the *Daily Express* chapel had objected to printing an

advertisement which called for volunteers to man the presses if print-
ers and compositors 'came out in sympathy' with the miners.
Churchill had advised Beaverbrook 'close down. You can afford it.'[16]
The advice had been ignored and the wording of the advertisement
was modified. Churchill expressed his irritation in strong terms. But
the issue which divided them most bitterly was the availability of
newsprint and the effect a shortage would have on Churchill's ability
to run an emergency news-sheet on behalf of the government.

Beaverbrook was a bitter opponent of the TUC's decision to call a
general strike, which his editorials described as the trade unions'
attempts 'to dictate to the nation'.[17] And the *Express*, like other members of the Newspaper Proprietors' Association, endorsed Churchill's
view that, when the strike began, 'something had to be done to prevent alarming news from being spread about'.[18] Churchill wanted to
produce what he called a broadsheet. The meeting with the NPA, at
which the idea was discussed, broke up without a decision being
taken but H. A. Gwyne – the ever-patriotic editor of the *Morning
Post* – regarded his fellow editors' decision as 'shameful'. He volunteered to produce a hundred thousand government newsletters as
soon as the Cabinet thought it necessary, and offered to increase the
emergency print run to four hundred thousand a night within a
week. Volunteers from the *Daily Mail* and *Daily Express* moved into
the *Morning Post*. The *British Gazette* was born.

At the time John Jacob Astor was determined to continue the
production of *The Times*, despite a walk-out by half of his staff.
Encouraged by the conciliatory behaviour of the men on strike –
pickets 'always touched their caps as he passed their lines'[19] – he
recruited volunteer helpers including the Duchess of Westminster and
Lady Diana Cooper. On the first night of the strike forty-eight
thousand copies of a modified *Times* (known as the *Little Sister*) were
printed and sold in London.

Elation at Printing House Square was matched by gloom at the
*Morning Post* temporary office. The *British Gazette* was running out of
newsprint. Its rival was the TUC's *British Worker*. The *Daily Herald* supplied all the newsprint it needed. Churchill requisitioned the *Daily
Herald* supply but – although he temporarily silenced the voice of the
strikers – that did not solve the *British Gazette*'s problem. It was being

given away all over the south of England so it needed more newsprint than the *Daily Herald* possessed. In any case, Churchill wanted a single source of government propaganda – supplied by him.

Churchill informed all Fleet Street that he proposed to requisition all available newsprint. Geoffrey Dawson, the editor of *The Times*, replied with a letter which reflected his bewildered fury. 'The broad effect of this action is to threaten the suppression of *The Times* and, presumably, every other paper which is endeavouring in the face of great difficulties to maintain its daily existence.'[20] Churchill defended himself against Dawson, and the editors who supported him, with allegations that concentrating resources on the *British Gazette* was necessary because of the newspapers' craven capitulation to the trade unions. *The Times*' leader thundered a refutation. 'Mr Churchill . . . stated on Monday that "in a twinkling of an eye the newspaper press went completely out of action" . . . *The Times* has never been out of action'.[21]

Dawson refused to reveal how much newsprint *The Times* possessed, but he told the government that he proposed a daily print run of eighty thousand. Within a week, 405,000 *Little Sisters* were being printed each night. Churchill, infuriated by Dawson's defiant success, requisitioned eighty-nine reels of *Times* newsprint.

At the end of the strike's first week Beaverbrook announced that enough of his employees had returned to work to allow the production of a full-sized edition of the *Daily Express*. Churchill warned him that, if he persisted with that plan, the *Daily Express* building, as well as its newsprint, would be requisitioned. Beaverbrook gambled on the Home Secretary – who was becoming irritated with Churchill's antics – refusing to sign the requisition order for the building. Beaverbrook won. But the Chancellor had the power to requisition newsprint without reference to other ministers. The *Express* therefore made him a grudging offer. Newsprint would be made available, but in such a limited quantity that 'it will not be worth to you the effort you put into its removal'.[22] Leo Amery recorded in his diary that, 'This let Winston loose on a magnificent tirade on the wonders achieved and the selfishness of the press and ended with his determination to suppress the *Express* if, as they intended, they started an evening paper in the next four days'.[23] It was that sort of outburst which prompted

Beaverbrook to judge that, 'On the top of the wave [Churchill] has in him the stuff of which tyrants are made'.[24]

The problem which Churchill created arose from another of the Chancellor's attributes. He retained the enthusiasm of boyhood. Churchill enjoyed being in charge of his own paper and did not intend to have his pleasure spoilt. Towards the end of the strike J. C. C. Davison, the Prime Minister's confidant and deputy commissioner under the Special Powers Act, wrote to Baldwin with an explanation and apology.

> The failure to some extent in the details of the distribution of the *British Gazette* has been due entirely to the fact that the Chancellor occupied the attention of nearly all the staff. He thinks he is Napoleon.[25]

H. A. Gwyne, the editor of the *Morning Post* who had been given nominal authority over the *Gazette*, was even more critical. 'He butts in at the busiest hours and insists on changing commas and full stops until the staff is furious.'[26] He asked the Prime Minister to ban Churchill from his building – an indignity which was only avoided by the collapse of the General Strike.

The *Daily Herald*, which, almost alone, had stood solidly behind the TUC, barely survived the dispute. Just before Christmas 1925 the debenture-holders had announced that they would no longer take responsibility for the paper's debts. In the New Year George Lansbury resigned as editor and a new board of directors – including nominees from the TUC – took control in preparation for what amounted to a rescue operation. At the Labour Party Conference Lansbury – although still general manager – spoke as if the paper was dead or would die without him.

> In the *Daily Herald* there was the life blood of tens of thousands of poor men and women, some of whom sacrificed every-thing . . . for the workers to have a daily paper.[27]

One *Mirror* director arranged for an injection of Russian roubles. It would have put the paper on a firm commercial footing. The readership was consulted and made clear that it was emphatically opposed. The only result of the initiative was vicarious damage to the Labour Party.[28]

To avoid a similar risk of extinction the *Westminster Gazette* merged with the *Daily News* and became the *Daily News Chronicle*. The *Daily Telegraph*, ailing but nothing like as sick as the *Daily Herald*, was bought by William Berry (Lord Camrose by 1929) for a down payment of six hundred thousand pounds and another six hundred thousand in three annual instalments. It cost almost as much to establish new offices and buy new presses, but the result vindicated Berry's view that poor organisation and antiquated equipment, not incompetent journalism, was the cause of the paper's malaise. A new emphasis on news, at the expense of features, combined with a reduction in price from 2d to 1d produced an increase in circulation from one to two million. That figure became the benchmark of success at which every paper aimed.

By 1929 the *Daily Mail* had almost reached the target with a daily sale of 1,845,000 copies. The *Daily Express* at 1,693,000 and the *News Chronicle* with 1,400,000 at least approached the magic figure. But the *Daily Herald* limped along on 300,000. Under the influence of Julius Elias – the managing director of Odhams, a printing company which owned 15 per cent of *Herald* shares – a plan was devised to put the paper on its feet. Readers would be attracted not by the quality of its journalism but by 'special offers'. Other titles – notably and predictably the *Daily Express* – retaliated. The *Daily Herald* (price one penny) offered goods to the value of one pound to everyone who bought the paper for six weeks. The hope was that they would become addicted. Those who did not sowed six shillings and reaped twenty. According to the report on the press published in 1938 by Political and Economic Planning, at the height of the give-away war, 'a whole Welsh family could be clothed, from head to foot, for the price of eight weeks' reading of the *Daily Express*'.[29]

The papers which made special offers risked bankruptcy. Those which did not lost circulation as their readers chose to collect coupons for Box Brownie cameras and cuckoo clocks. The Newspaper Proprietors' Association outlawed, by unanimous resolution, free gifts and offers below cost price. Elias ignored the agreement. In March

1933 the *Daily Herald* offered a sixteen-volume set of the Complete Works of Charles Dickens (value £4.4.0) for 11/- and ninety-six coupons. The proprietors – infuriated by the *Herald's* insubordination – held a special meeting at the Savoy. Beaverbrook demanded an end to the Dickens offer and responded to Elias's refusal with the declaration, 'This is war . . . war to the death. I shall fight you to the bitter end.'[30] He was almost as good as his word. The *Daily Express* offered a rival Dickens edition for 10/-. It sold 124,000 and lost £18,000. During the six months which followed Beaverbrook's threat his papers spent £350,000 on various campaigns. The result was the recruitment of 300,000 new *Daily Express* readers at a cost of 8/3 each. Only 50,000 continued to read the paper after the campaigns were over. But Beaverbrook pronounced himself satisfied. The *Daily Express* circulation rose to 2,329,000. The *Daily Herald* only just topped 200,000.

In 1934, when Lord Rothermere sold his controlling interest in the *Daily Mirror*, its circulation was 720,000. Guy Bartholomew, who had become editorial director in 1934, determined to make progress by a different route. He proposed to attract new readers by the quality of the paper's journalism.

> From the moment he gained control, but particularly throughout 1934, Bart attacked with ferocity the stuffy image the *Mirror* had managed to construct for itself during Rothermere's reign. The prudish schoolmistress that the paper had become was summarily sacked and a jolly jack-the-lad, sensitive but cheeky, supportive but a terrible tease, hired in her place. Had the word streetwise entered the lexicon by then, Bart's new *Mirror* could have been described as streetwise. It was also fun with strip cartoons as a constant ingredient in the editorial mix.[31]

Hugh Cudlipp (editor of the *Sunday Pictorial* when he was twenty-four), William Conor (the columnist Cassandra) and Peter Wilson (sports editor) added zest to the news. Cecil Harmsworth King (Northcliffe's nephew), who became editorial director, described why the *Mirror* became the best-selling paper in Britain. 'Our best hope was to appeal to young working-class men and women . . . the politics had

to be made to match. In the depression of the 1930s, there was no
point preaching right wing politics to young people in the lower
income brackets.'[32] Many of those 'young people' wanted virtually no
politics at all. The *Mirror* catered for their tastes by providing the
razzmatazz of the American tabloids.

It was a brave as well as a shrewd decision. Right-wing policies
were in the ascendant. The Labour Party had formed the government
in 1929. But its success had been short-lived and in 1931 Ramsay
MacDonald had formed the national coalition with Baldwin as his
trusted lieutenant. Beaverbrook's pleasure at Labour's original victory
had not signified a conversion to socialism. He told Lord Birkenhead,
'I rejoice in Baldwin's downfall. I wanted the defeat of the government because I believe it was bad.'[33] However, it seems that Lord
Rothermere continued to support the Tory Party while persisting in
undermining its leader. It is unlikely that Beaverbrook actually
endorsed the demands made in the *Daily Mail* editorial of 14 October
1929. But there is little doubt that he enjoyed reading the demand for
Baldwin to resign. Rothermere's candidate for Tory leader and Prime
Minister was Lord Beaverbrook.

Ward Price – whose job it was to translate Rothermere's opinions
into journalese – moved on from merely demanding that Beaverbrook
become Tory leader to predicting that it would come about. His article in the *Sunday Pictorial* began with a colourful account of why a
new leader was needed. Baldwin had, he wrote, 'made costly but futile
bids for popularity by adding to the country's burdens of pensions and
doles . . . giving votes to millions of flappers who promptly helped to
put the socialists into office and making the unforgivable blunder of
home rule for Ireland'. He then moved on to make clear who the new
leader should, and was likely, to be.

The conviction is fast growing among Conservatives that the
new leader must be found outside the established hierarchy . . .
The name of Lord Beaverbrook becomes steadily more prominent . . . There is no man living in the country today with more
likelihood of succeeding to the Premiership than Lord
Beaverbrook.[34]

The absurdity of the suggestion was emphasised by the argument by which the constitutional nonsense was justified. 'His peerage would only be a temporary handicap, since the reconstruction of the Upper House, with the abolition of hereditary peerages, must soon make it possible for all peers to sit in the House of Commons.'*

On 24 October Beaverbrook himself published a penny pamphlet which looked suspiciously like a manifesto.

> The foodstuffs we need in this country could all be raised either in our own soil or in the British Dominions, Colonies and Protectorates. The coal, machinery and textiles that the increasing populations of our new territories overseas demand, could be supplied by the factories of Britain and the Dominions.

On 2 February 1930 Lord Beaverbrook, pausing only to describe Lord Rothermere as 'the greatest trustee of public opinion we have seen in the history of journalism', launched his United Empire Party. For twelve days news of its foundation and development dominated the *Daily Mail*. Appeals for members and funds appeared as full-page advertisements and were published in other national dailies and in the *Sunday Dispatch*. An article under Beaverbrook's own byline made 'A Plea to Mr Baldwin'.

> Certain individuals have a similar vision of a United Empire and it is their support that we most uncomfortably miss . . . I am in some queer way supposed to be acting in opposition to Mr Baldwin . . . I will stand aside and obliterate myself from the movement if the Conservative leader at the approaching party conference adopts our policy on Empire free trade.

The offer of a truce – as long as the party leader adopted the policy of the dissident minority – has always been one of the political rebel's less subtle stratagems. Beaverbrook recklessly chose to renew his offer in a debate which he initiated in the House of Lords. The *Daily*

---

*The prediction came true – but thirty years later.

*Telegraph* reported that he 'met opposition from all sides'. The *Star* wrote that, 'he finds himself among the obliterati without persuading any old Parliamentary hands to hold the baby', and the *Liverpool Post and Mercury* noted that his noble 'audience was cold'. However the ever-faithful *Daily Express* proudly boasted that 'Lord Beaverbrook was warmly cheered from all sides of the House'.

For a week or two Beaverbrook, despite disliking public speaking, toured the country. At Gloucester he announced that imperial preference was 'necessary to save the country' from an unspecified threat so great that the remedy must be pursued, 'if necessary at the expense of wrecking every political party'. The wrecking which he was prepared to accept would be brought about by the United Empire Party putting up candidates in every seat represented by a free-trade Conservative.

Baldwin's response, delivered to a Conservative rally in the Albert Hall, began typically with a compliment to Beaverbrook which was intended to patronise. 'I pay tribute to his courage – rare in one of his profession – in offering a subject he believes in to criticism in the proper place, the House of Lords.' He went on to welcome at least the initiative of 'bringing before the country once more the idea of a united Empire'. He then made a suggestion. 'An Imperial Conference should meet in an atmosphere of complete freedom and if . . . there should emerge any form of agreement, arrangement or Treaty . . . that does us great benefit and that demands in return a tax on some articles of food from foreign countries, the whole issue could be put before the people.'

The offer amounted to so little that it was a surprise when Beaverbrook described the speech as 'perfectly satisfactory'. But in the *Daily Express* that limited compliment was expanded into gushing praise. 'Mr Baldwin's Great Empire Speech . . . New Conservative Policy . . . Strong Tribute to Lord Beaverbrook . . . Mr Baldwin's Pledge . . . Vision of United Commonwealth.' Alarmed that the exaggerations were intended to manoeuvre the party into endorsing imperial preference, Conservative Central Office issued a leaflet which accused Beaverbrook of misinterpreting – the implication was intentionally – the Albert Hall speech. That put an end to what little hope there was of reconciliation. A rally which the United Empire Party had planned to hold as a celebration of the new unity was cancelled.

The plan to run UEP candidates was put into effect, starting with a by-election in South Paddington.

Vice Admiral Taylor, the UEP candidate, won and at East Islington Brigadier General Critchley split the Tory vote and let the Labour nominee in – a result less satisfactory to the United Empire Party but equally catastrophic for the Tories. On 20 June 1930 Conservative MPs and candidates, meeting at Caxton Hall, prepared for rancorous and destructive disagreement over how far the party should go to meet Beaverbrook's demands. They were united by a speech in which Baldwin dealt less with the merits of free trade than with the iniquities of the press.

> There is nothing more curious in modern evolution than the effects of an enormous fortune, rapidly made, and the control of a newspaper of your own . . . We are told that unless we make peace with these noblemen, candidates are to be run all over the country. The Lloyd George candidates at the last election smelt. These will stink. Here is a letter from Lord Rothermere . . . 'I cannot make it too abundantly clear that under no circumstances will I support Mr Baldwin unless I know exactly what his policy is going to be, unless I have complete guarantees that such a policy will be carried out by his party in office and unless I am acquainted with at least eight of his most prominent colleagues in his next ministry.'

Baldwin added, with mock incredulity, 'His Lordship would want to be consulted on certain offices in the government.' He then added, in a dramatically quiet voice, 'I will fight that attempt at domination to the end.' Affronted by the presumption of Rothermere's demands, candidates and Members rallied to Baldwin's cause. On the following day Lord Rothermere – addressing the world through the pages of the *Daily Mail* – confirmed his animosity was undiminished and his judgement still impaired. 'The hour has come and produced the man – Beaverbrook.'

It was nine months before the assertion could be put to the test of the British people. Then another by-election was called in Westminster.

The Tory candidate, in the St George's Division, was Duff Cooper –
ex-diplomat, socialite and friend of the Prince of Wales. The expenses
of his opponent, Sir Ernest Peller, the United Empire candidate, were
paid personally by Lord Beaverbrook, who spoke in the constituency
sixteen times during the campaign.

The most absurd, as well as the most disreputable, claim of the campaign came from the *Daily Mirror*, then still owned by Lord Rothermere.

> Gandhi is watching St George. The fanatic leader of a fanatic
> Indian sect knows that St George is a test of the people of Great
> Britain on the vital problem of whether India is to be surren-
> dered or governed. Put Peller in and you put Gandhi out.[35]

Beaverbrook's message was less bizarre but more brutal. 'If we win this
fight, the Conservatives will select a new leader, take up our policy
and we shall all live happily ever after.' Nobody doubted that he was
right. Perhaps even Baldwin believed him. That is one explanation for
the violence of his speech at Duff Cooper's eve-of-poll meeting.

> The newspapers attacking me are not newspapers in the ordinary
> sense. They are engines of propaganda for the constantly chang-
> ing policies, desires, personal wishes, personal dislikes of two
> men. What are their methods? Their methods are direct false-
> hoods, misrepresentations, half truths, the alteration of a speaker's
> meaning by publishing sentences apart from the context . . . the
> suppression and editorial criticism of speeches which are not
> reported in the papers.

A *Daily Mail* editorial had accused Baldwin of squandering 'an
immense fortune' left to him by his father. 'The first part of that statement,' the Tory leader said, 'is a lie.' The second (that the imaginary
fortune had been squandered) was 'by implication untrue'. The allegations were, of course, libellous. But he proposed to seek neither an
apology nor damages. 'The first is valueless and the second I would
not touch with a barge pole.' He finished his speech with what was to
become one of the most memorable rebukes in political history –
written for Baldwin by his cousin, Rudyard Kipling. 'What the

proprietorship of these papers is aiming at is power, and power without responsibility – the prerogative of the harlot throughout the ages.'*

Duff Cooper won the St George by-election with a majority of
5,700 – a landslide by the standards of the time. A week later, when he
took his seat in the House, Stanley Baldwin himself was one of his
sponsors. It was not a task which party leaders normally perform.
Baldwin was expressing his gratitude and emphasising an indisputable
fact. Not only had his leadership been saved but,

> the baleful influence of proprietorial journalism was diminished.
> The personal prestige of Beaverbrook and Rothermere, which
> had rarely extended beyond mutual genuflection, plummeted. So
> did their power, though not their pride and arrogance.[36]

Both proprietors were free, for the moment, to return to the business of running newspapers rather than attempting – as it turned out,
with little success – to run the country. But Lord Rothermere had
found another cause to claim his support. In the German elections of
1930, Adolf Hitler's National Socialist Party had increased its seats in
the Bundestag from twelve to 105. The *Daily Mail*'s response to that
achievement was written by George Ward Price. But it appeared in the
paper under the byline of Lord Rothermere.

> These young Germans have discovered, as young men of
> England are discovering, that it is no good trusting the old politi-
> cians. Accordingly they have formed, as I should like to see our
> British youth form, a Parliamentary party of their own.† Under
> Herr Hitler the youth of Germany is effectively organised against
> the corruption of Communism.

---

*It was only one of Baldwin's ferocious attacks on Beaverbrook and Northcliffe.
His reaction to the allegation that he had wanted to capitalise on Indian demands
for independence is discussed in Chapter 4.
†Andrew Carnegie was also impressed by the spirit of the Hitler Youth.
Concerned that the democracies were not matching fascism's offer of 'strength
through joy', he founded a physical training teachers' college in Leeds. It is now
part of Leeds Metropolitan University.

Rothermere, convinced that a new spirit of youthful impatience was sweeping the world, thought it his duty to bring together the men of destiny. Oswald Mosley – Conservative apostate who had defected to Labour and then defected again because of the party's refusal to accept his economic prescription – was the *Daily Mail's* choice for saviour of Britain.

Rothermere was not alone in identifying Mosley as the man on whom the hopes for Britain's future rested. *The Times* thought that he 'might save Britain in a struggle of violence with Communism'.[37] The *Manchester Guardian* accused him of 'deliberately inciting physical opposition and public disorder' like Hitler. But that was not, in Lord Rothermere's scale of values, the outright condemnation that C. P. Scott, the *Manchester Guardian* editor, intended. When Hitler took the oath which made him Chancellor of Germany the *Daily Mail* celebrated 'one of the most historic days in the latter-day history of Germany'.[38] Then Rothermere, having announced his admiration of *The Greater Britain* (Mosley's *Mein Kampf*) without actually reading it, arranged for the *Daily Mail* to support the movement which the book attempted to justify. The *Mail* wrote, 'Hurrah for the Blackshirts . . . The spirit of the age is one of national discipline and organisation.' Britain, the editorial continued, needed 'a Great Party of the Right with the same direction of purpose and energy . . . as Hitler and Mussolini have displayed . . . The socialists who jeer at the principles and the uniforms of the Blackshirts being of foreign origins, forget that the founder and high priest of their own creed was the German Jew Karl Marx.'[39] Three months later it described Mosley as 'the paramount political personality in Britain . . . caught up in such a wave of deep-seated popular enthusiasm as must sweep it to victory'.

Without Rothermere the British Union of Fascists – strutting the streets in military uniforms – might have been dismissed as a collection of unpleasant eccentrics. Even with his backing they never became a threat to British stability or democracy. The Conservative Party provided the bulwark against the supposed Communist threat. But the *Daily Mail* kept Oswald Mosley in the public eye and, for a month or two, gave the BUF a spurious importance. Rothermere arranged for Mosley to meet Mussolini – without whose subventions the movement would have foundered. When Il Duce pronounced himself impressed Rothermere issued a clear instruction. 'If Mussolini believes in Mosley, then let's get strongly behind him with the whole newspaper group.'[40] Rothermere had decided that the BUF was the 'only alternative at the next election to rule by Stafford Cripps'. One of his persistent fantasies was that a fringe group called the Socialist League was going to take over the Labour Party and that the Labour Party was going to take over the country.

The campaign in support of Mosley was more sophisticated than Rothermere's jejune enthusiasm suggested. News of Nazi brutality was gradually reaching Britain. So, in the *Daily Mirror* (still in 1934 a Rothermere paper) an attack was launched on 'concentration camp politicians' who had no 'personal knowledge of countries which are already under Blackshirt government. The idea that a permanent reign of terror exists there has been evolved from their own morbid imaginations, fed by sensational propaganda.'[41]

Neither the *Daily Mail* collectively, nor its proprietor individually, had the slightest excuse for misunderstanding the BUF's policy or underestimating its anti-Semitism. *Mail* reporters went to the rallies and heard what Mosley and his satraps said. Yet the paper did more than support them. It prepared for the Olympic rally of 1934 with the offer of free tickets to readers who sent letters describing 'Why I Like the Blackshirts'.[42] Collin Brooks attended Mosley's 1936 meeting in the Carfax Assembly Rooms in Oxford on the paper's behalf and wrote, 'It was the anti-Jewish references which drew the cheers.'[43] The sub-editors removed the line because of the risk that Jewish advertisers would be offended. The paper also took up the idea of a Jewish Fifth Column. 'Many enemy agents come here as refugees, many of them Jews.'[44] And the *Daily Mail* covered Mosley's assault on London's East End.

On the eve of the BUF's march into Cable Street with three thousand Blackshirts, the party's paper heralded a battle against 'the great Jewish interests which control much of our national life'.[45] The police estimated that ten thousand 'antis have sworn not to let them pass' and stationed a thousand police officers along the route to keep the peace. The protest against the march attracted ten times as many demonstrators as the police had estimated and Mosley's 'Blackshirt Legion' had to be diverted out of the Jewish East End along the

Embankment and into the Temple. The *Daily Mail* was outraged by the denial of free speech and silent on the subject of the march's intention.

Much of the Battle of Cable Street was fought between the police, determined to clear a way for the marchers, and the anti-fascist demonstrators equally determined that they would not pass. Some accounts of the fighting rely on old men who remember with advantages. Jack Spot, later a well-known leader of the London dockers, 'recalled' men armed with cut-throat razors with hollow-ground blades which 'sliced through flesh like butter'. Phil Piratin, a notable Communist, claimed that his group of protesters disarmed the police. One thing is certain. A woman joined the BUF after seeing the way in which the anti-fascists treated the police horses.[46]

The *Daily Mail* fought the campaign for fascism in general and Mosley in particular without the help and support of the *Daily Express*. Its condemnation of *Kristallnacht* was strangely worded but unequivocal.

> There has never been anything quite like it in the history of the world. Jews are still being murdered in concentration camps. They are still beaten in the streets. There is nothing they can do except run around helplessly, in circles, till they die.[47]

There is no way of knowing how long Rothermere would have continued to support Mosley had he not been warned that advertising – always a major preoccupation of the *Daily Mail* – would be lost if he persisted in advocating the Blackshirts' cause. The conversion, when it came – although prompted by commercial considerations rather than a sudden surge of conscience – was absolute and unyielding. Mosley was suitably contemptuous. Northcliffe, he claimed, would have responded to the complaint in simple terms. 'One more word from you and *Daily Mail* placards will carry the words "Jewish Threat to British Press".'[48] Whatever Rothermere's private feelings, standing up to opponents with clout was not his way. Asked by the World Press Agency if his (abandoned) support for the British Union of Fascists had been a crusade or an incident, he replied, 'Definitely an incident.'[49] Unkind commentators made ironic comparisons with the *Daily Mail*'s pre-war campaign for standard bread. That too had been dropped – though the advertisers' complaint was that offering to send every reader a sample of stone-milled flour was making the paper ridiculed for its foolishness rather than reviled for its fascism. The idea of converting the nation to the consumption of standard (as distinct) from white bread had been the brainchild of Oswald Mosley's father.

However, although Rothermere found it expedient to withdraw his support from fascism at home he still championed it abroad. When Mussolini invaded Ethiopia, he was fulsome in his praise for Il Duce's initiative. 'All sound-thinking Britons will wish Italy well in the great enterprise to which she has set her hand.'[50] The *Daily Mail* followed its leader. 'The British people take no interest whatsoever in the slave-owning Abyssinian Empire. And in this war, their sympathy is wholly with the cause of the white race which Italy is so firmly upholding.'[51]

The *Daily Mail* was not alone in its support – indeed admiration – for Mussolini. In October 1931 Winston Churchill wrote in the *Evening Standard*,

> It would be dangerous folly for the British people to underrate the enduring position in world history which Mussolini will hold; or the amazing qualities of courage, comprehension, self control and perseverance which he exemplifies.[52]

Whether or not Churchill's early columns for the Beaverbrook press were guided by judgement and conviction, or the necessity of pandering to the proprietor's prejudices, they were certainly not the future Prime Minister's finest hour.

Churchill made his debut on the pages of the *Evening Standard* on the day that Germany, ignoring the obligations which it accepted at Versailles, reoccupied the Rhineland.

> If the League of Nations survives this ordeal, there is no reason why the horrible, dull, remorseless drift to war in 1937 and 1935 and the preparatory piling up [of] enormous armaments in every country should not be decisively arrested.[53]

Six months later the prophetic opponent of appeasement was no more prescient. *Evening Standard* readers were assured,

> I declare my belief that a major war is not imminent and I still believe that there is a good chance of no war taking place in our time.[54]

And it was not just the Rothermere–Beaverbrook axis that argued passionately for Britain to accept the territorial demands of the dictators. J. L. Garvin in the *Observer* found reasons to justify the *Anschluss*.

> Is it imagined for a moment that Austria is an harmonious unit? It is riven with discord. A powerful section passionately demands closer union with the Reich. Conflict would mean civil war. It is a family issue within the German family. We have nothing to do with it.[55]

*The Times* was equally convinced that Czechoslovakia was expendable.

> It might be worthwhile for the Czechoslovakian government to consider whether they should exclude altogether the project, which finds favour in some quarters, of making Czechoslovakia a more homogenous state by cession of that fringe of the alien population who are contiguous with the nation to which they are united by race.[56]

The execrable literary style should not deflect attention from the even more deplorable principle which *The Times* propounded. It shared Hitler's view of the Greater Germany. Wherever Germans were to be found, there was the Third Reich. At least Beaverbrook did not attempt to justify his cynicism with phoney authority. He simply wrote, or had the *Daily Express* write on his behalf, 'Britain never gave any pledge to protect the frontiers of Czechoslovakia . . . No moral obligation rests on us.'[57] Not content to argue the case for appeasement, the Beaverbrook papers thought it right to exude the irrational optimism which was thought (probably correctly) to be the secret of their success. On 1 September 1935, the *Daily Express* front-page splash made a promise which the British people longed to believe. 'There Will Be No War This Year.' A replica of that front page floated in the sea alongside the lifeboat to which the men from HMS *Torrin* clung after the destroyer was torpedoed in Noel Coward's film, *In Which We Serve*.

The *Times*, in association with the Cliveden set – the friends of the Astors who dined together and argued for appeasement – is generally blamed for making the British press, at least in part, responsible for the government's willingness to compromise with the dictators. Certainly Garvin and, when he became editor, Geoffrey Dawson, together with Robin Barrington Ward, his deputy, were part of the clique and gladly disseminated its views. *The Times* had a baleful influence on the establishment. But the *Daily Mail*, the *Daily Express* and the *Evening Standard* were equally guilty in persuading the people that war could and should be avoided. Those newspapers would not have behaved differently if they had consciously set out to befriend the dictators and promote their interests.

# CHAPTER SIXTEEN

# The Drift to War

The shame is so horrible – the disgust and humiliation. Many of us can't feel anything but horror at Neville Chamberlain & this government. Yes he has done his best according to his lights to save peace at the last minute. Maybe even he will succeed. But look where their disastrous policy has led us. Japan. Abyssinia. Spain. And now this. There is only one hope for the future – to get rid of this government.

Rosamund Lehmann to Jean Talva,
On the eve of Chamberlain's third visit to
Adolf Hitler, 26 September 1938

History is almost unanimous. Neville Chamberlain was the chief culprit among the guilty men who allowed Europe to drift into war. He was the ideal scapegoat – difficult to love and therefore easy to blame. His own brother admitted that, 'Neville's manner freezes people with the result that everybody respects him but he makes no friends.'[1] Part of his problem was the contempt in which he held personal popularity. He reported Stanley Baldwin's critique of his House of Commons style as a matter of fact which caused him neither pain nor pleasure. 'I always give him the impression . . . that I looked on the Labour Party as dirt.'[2]

He was also – as much because of his appearance as his character – an easy object of derision. At the height of the Abyssinian crisis, Mussolini assured his followers that Italy would emerge glorious from its dispute with Britain because 'people who carry an umbrella can never found an empire'.[3] Lloyd George, who had more wit and a better command of English grammar, described him as 'seeing foreign policy through the wrong end of a municipal drainpipe' and Clement Attlee, taking his image from the BBC, said that he was 'permanently tuned in to the Midland region'.[4]

Sir Robert Vansittart – Permanent Under Secretary of State at the Foreign Office when the threat from the European dictators was first recognised – expressed a mandarin's opinion. He was 'an earnest and opinionated provincial [who] was bound to err if he plunged into diplomacy'.[5] Distaste for patrician prejudice should not obscure the truth of what Vansittart wrote. Chamberlain had been an energetic and progressive Minister of Health and a competent, if rigidly orthodox, Chancellor of the Exchequer. His misfortune, and the country's, was that he became Prime Minister at a moment when the nation needed gifts which he did not possess. It was a time for big thinking, but Neville Chamberlain always thought small.

In mitigation of Chamberlain's many failures, it must be said that Baldwin bequeathed him a legacy of drift and prevarication. In Churchill's words, the government was already committed to 'a strange paradox . . . resolved to be irresolute, adamant for drift'.[6] When he moved into Downing Street 'appeasement' was not a term of abuse but an aspiration. Politicians subscribed to the first definition in the Oxford Dictionary. 'To bring to peace, settle (strife etc), 1714.' The fourth definition – 'to pacify by satisfying demands, 1500' – only superseded it after 1939. Chamberlain takes credit for pioneering a change in the language – but little else.

It was not only Chamberlain's dwindling band of supporters who argued that the peace was sold long before he became Prime Minister. Winston Churchill – admittedly more equivocal about appeasement than the history books now suggest – told Harold Nicolson, 'Never has any man inherited a more ghastly situation than Neville Chamberlain.'[7] Not for the first time Churchill was overstating his case. He 'placed the blame wholly on Baldwin'.[8] But responsibility for the Second World War goes back to 1918, when Chamberlain was looking for a Birmingham constituency which would send him, for the first time, to Parliament, and Baldwin was Financial Secretary to the Treasury.

The First World War, unlike the Second, ended with an armistice, not unconditional surrender. Germany, although defeated, felt so far from destroyed that its delegates to the Versailles Peace Conference had sufficient confidence to argue about the terms which they were offered. The terms were sufficiently severe to breed undying resentment, but not so draconian as to prevent an intimidated people from rising up to revenge their humiliation.

Even before the details of peace had been decided, the Allies had agreed that the treaty should establish a League of Nations. The inspiration for the 'reign of international law' came from Woodrow Wilson, President of the United States of America. But the covenant which set out its objectives and powers was drawn up in the British Foreign Office. It provided for escalating sanctions – financial, economic and military – against 'aggressors'. When, in 1922, Turkish aggression in the eastern Mediterranean threatened European peace the League of Nations was not considered as either a suitable forum for the discussion of the crisis or a realistic force by which peace might be enforced.

The Treaty of Sèvres had ended the war between the Allies and Turkey. The Bosporus was declared a permanently neutral international waterway and large parts of the old Ottoman Empire were ceded to France, Italy and Greece. When Kemal Pasha – commander of the victorious Turkish forces at Gallipoli – seized power, he demanded the return of the expropriated lands, the modernisation of the Islamic state and, to prove his commitment to both the state and its reinvigoration, called himself Kemal Ataturk.

France accepted his demands. Greece did not. Kemal Ataturk invaded Greek-occupied Smyrna and, after pausing to massacre a large proportion of the population, passed on to Chanak, where a small British garrison protected what Sèvres had designated a neutral zone. General Harrington, the GOC, was told to stand firm.

Neither France nor Italy offered assistance and Lloyd George's 'Call to the Empire' was only answered by Newfoundland and New

Zealand. With only bluff on which to rely, the Prime Minister instructed General Harrington to issue an ultimatum to the Turks – withdraw or be forced back. Wisely, the GOC disobeyed orders and Ataturk, with equal sagacity, chose not to attack the British troops. A military catastrophe had been avoided. But a political upheaval was to follow. On 6 October 1922 a letter had been published in *The Times* which introduced the British public to a phrase which was going to influence foreign policy for the next seventeen years. 'We cannot act alone as the policemen of the world.' The letter was signed by Andrew Bonar Law, a Canadian Conservative who, it was generally believed, had lost his interest in politics. The Tories had found a leader. The Lloyd George coalition was doomed.

Bonar Law had to be persuaded to attend the Carlton Club meeting – held in the shadow of a by-election defeat in Newport – at which the future of the coalition government was discussed. Stanley Baldwin, until then a competent but undistinguished President of the Board of Trade, made the speech of his life. Lord Birkenhead, the coalition's Lord Chancellor, had called Lloyd George a 'dynamic force'. Baldwin agreed.

> He is a dynamic force and it is from that very fact that the trouble arises. A dynamic force is a very terrible thing. It may crush you and it is not necessarily right. It is owing to that dynamic force and that remarkable personality that the Liberal Party, to which he formerly belonged, has been smashed to pieces. It is my firm conviction that, in time, the same thing will happen to our party.[9]

When Bonar Law spoke – confirming his return to active politics – the business was settled. Lloyd George heard how the meeting had turned out and resigned at once. The dictators had, in their way, claimed their first victim.

Baldwin became Chancellor of the Exchequer and then – within a year Bonar Law was diagnosed as dying of cancer – Prime Minister. In two general elections, 1923 and 1929, he was edged out of office by Ramsay MacDonald. But the second Labour government split, collapsed and gave way to the second coalition in which Baldwin served. The national government, as it was called, took office on 24 August 1931. On 28 September Japan invaded Manchuria. Four days later China appealed to the League of Nations. The League took refuge in generalisations and pledged not to recognise national boundaries which had been redrawn by force. Britain thought it wise to rely on old-fashioned remedies to aggression. As Japanese troops advanced south it reinforced Shanghai.

The supine reaction was always justified by the claim that, having suffered the horrors of 1914–18, a sensible nation, led by rational statesmen, would do everything in its power to avoid a repetition of the slaughter. Baldwin thought it right to warn the civilian population of the dangers it faced. 'I think it is as well for the man in the street to realise that there is no power on earth that can protect him from being bombed. Whatever people may tell him, the bomber will always get through.'[10] Fear, or prudence, as the appeasers called it, encouraged the search for reasons to let the aggressors have their way.

So although it was generally agreed that Japan had behaved illegally, it was argued that it had behaved illegally in a defensible cause. Manchuria was in a state of near-anarchy. Japanese interests and Japanese subjects were under threat. The invasion was certainly reprehensible. But was it so reprehensible that the democracies were justified in taking action which might lead to war? In the ten years which followed, exactly the same questions were to be asked about the aggression of Italy and Germany.

That question was constantly pondered but never answered. Instead the Great Powers waited and hoped. The precedent was set in December 1932 when the League of Nations Commission, inquiring into the causes of the Manchurian War, announced what everybody already knew. The Japanese had justified grievances. But the way in which they had chosen to resolve them was a breach of international law. Japan was 'censured', but Article XVI – identifying an 'aggressor' and initiating sanctions against the offender – was not invoked. Japan, affronted, resigned from the League but China, realising that it could expect no effective international support, accepted the loss of Manchuria. The Truce of Tangku heralded a brief and uneasy peace.

Britain once again felt able to put its faith in treaties. The Kellogg

Pact, named after the American Secretary of State but signed in Paris, had confirmed the nine major world powers' determination to avoid war, but failed to deter the Japanese invasion of Manchuria. But it was a European conflict that was feared in Westminster and Whitehall. However ministers had real faith that the Treaty of Locarno, signed in 1925, would guarantee the peace. A non-aggression pact between France, Germany and Belgium was guaranteed by Britain and Italy. What worries remained concerned France's unremitting hostility to Germany.

Realists – within the civil service and the general staff – argued that Britain should face the possibility of a resurgent Germany attempting to restore its place in Europe by force of arms. They drafted a 'Statement Relating to Defence' which, although it did not contain the usual estimate of weapons and men, made clear that Germany was altering the balance of power. The Cabinet, anxious not to offend Adolf Hitler – Chancellor of Germany since 1933 – moderated the statement's language but agreed to issue it as a White Paper. Moderation did not have the desired effect. Hitler – emboldened by the outcome of the Saar plebiscite, which had resulted in an over-whelming majority in favour of reunification with Germany – announced that Britain's clear intention to rearm left him with no alternative but to strengthen his own armed forces by introducing conscription. Two days later Hermann Goering published details of the new air force he proposed to create. Both initiatives were in direct contravention of the Versailles Peace Treaty.

Ramsay MacDonald – at least still nominal Prime Minister – con-tinued to put his trust in negotiation. At Stresa in Piedmont in April 1935 he signed an agreement with France and Italy which committed each of those nations to uphold and defend the international bound-aries drawn up at the Versailles. The enthusiasm of the Italians, very largely the reflection of a desire to avoid Austria's absorption into Germany, convinced the British delegation that Benito Mussolini – Il Duce since the 'March on Rome' in 1922 – was a potential ally and a man to be trusted. But there was still a profound reluctance to accept that Hitler might be a threat to peace. Stresa 'was not a united front against Germany', and German recalcitrance 'should not stop further negotiations'.

MacDonald was as good as his word. Although the government produced a new White Paper, increasing defence expenditure to £394 million over the next five years, in June 1935 it signed a bilateral Anglo-German Naval Agreement which allowed Hitler's navy to grow to 35 per cent of the Royal Navy's strength and, for the first time since Versailles, the production and deployment of U-boats. Commentators, in London as well as in Paris, wondered if the Stresa Agreement had been more than international window–dressing. Their question was to be answered on the distant borders between Abyssinia and Eritrea.

Five months before the Stresa Agreement had been signed, Italian native levies had opened fire on Haile Selassie's border guards on the disputed frontier. The Emperor had appealed to the League of Nations and, once again, Britain had agonised about the merits of an aggressor's behaviour. His Majesty's Government had formally agreed that Abyssinia was within Italy's 'sphere of influence' and Haile Selassie had been at best dilatory in his dealings with the border commission. What was more, Mussolini had been helpful at Stresa. The British establishment believed that, properly cultivated, he would become a reliable ally against Germany.

In consequence they bent to Il Duce's will. The draft of the final Stresa Communiqué had committed the signatories to oppose 'the repudiation of any treaties which endanger peace'. But the Italian delegation had insisted that the sentence ended 'in Europe'. That was very near to being a declaration of war in the Horn of Africa. Accepting Stresa on Mussolini's terms made Tom Jones – deputy Cabinet secretary and assiduous diarist – conclude that the outcome of the meeting in Piedmont was 'the original blunder' which began the long process of appeasement. Britain, he wrote, 'flunked talking straight with Mussolini because it wanted his support in Europe'.[11] By 'in Europe' he meant 'against Germany'.

In its way, the desire to make one European dictator Britain's ally against another was the most positive strand of the Baldwin government's defence strategy. Its inertia reflected a national mood. The whole country was, or seemed to be, against what the Labour Party denounced as 'the use of force as an instrument of foreign policy'. And the *Daily Herald* – owned by the TUC and faithfully reflecting the policy of 'the movement' – would soon attack the 1935 Defence White Paper as 'a rejection of the entire system of collective security' which did not echo 'the voice of the British people'.[12]

Baldwin's ambivalence towards the dictators sprang from a different view of the British character – which he certainly believed he typified and probably imagined he embodied. Britain was an insular nation, reluctant to become involved in matters which did not concern her. Idealism and self-interest combined to create a majority against rearmament. And potential aggressors knew it. Mussolini told the Italian National Assembly that Britain would never invoke the Stresa Agreement to mobilise the defence of Abyssinia. Nor, in light of the changes in the text which it had negotiated, would it have been entitled to do so.

Although Mussolini announced that he would rather Italy leave the League of Nations than allow international interference in his plans for Abyssinia, he did – realising the advantages of occasional emollience – agree to renewed arbitration in his border dispute. The British Foreign Office devised a plan which it hoped would both satisfy the demands for an honest revision of the frontiers and be sufficiently biased in Italy's favour to win Mussolini's support. They were assisted in their cynical endeavour by the character of the man who became Foreign Secretary immediately Baldwin resumed the premiership, Sir Samuel Hoare.

Before Hoare had time to settle in and make judgements of his own, Sir Robert Vansittart – the Permanent Under Secretary of State – convinced him that Mussolini must be accommodated. The scheme to placate the Duce was devised at a weekend house party which Hoare, Vansittart and Anthony Eden (Minister Without Portfolio for League of Nations' Affairs) all attended. Abyssinia was to cede the Ogaden region to Eritrea and in return would be given the port of Zeila in British Somaliland and a 'corridor' which guaranteed access to the sea. The scheme – which was either to bypass or railroad the League of Nations – was agreed without even notifying Abyssinia of its proposed loss.

Eden – his belief in personal diplomacy not yet dimmed – proposed to put the plan to Mussolini himself. But the Italian government learned of the plan from a spy in the British Embassy in Rome.

Then – as the result of an inadvertent leak by a junior minister – the full details were published in a British Sunday newspaper. The French were outraged at Britain's freelance diplomacy and, when the proposed meeting took place, Mussolini rejected the offer. Italy's alternative involved the acquisition of so much Abyssinian land that, as Eden explained, there was no hope of its endorsement by the League of Nations. Eden reported Il Duce's response to the Cabinet. He said that, 'I must take home with me the clear impression that Italy was going to settle it once and for all.' Mussolini had added that, in the event of failure to accept Italy's proposals, 'the name of Abyssinia will be wiped off the map'.[13] On the day that Eden returned from Rome to London the results of the Peace Ballot were published.

The Peace Ballot had been organised by the National Declaration Committee, an organisation founded and run by Lord Robert Cecil in support of the League of Nations and its Covenant. The ballot asked five questions, ranging from the value of Britain remaining a member of the League to the desirability of prohibiting the production of military aircraft. Neville Chamberlain, Chancellor of the Exchequer and Tory heir presumptive, described the whole initiative as the work of 'League of Nations cranks' who had been 'infuriated by the Defence White Paper'.[14] His chief objection was to question five. It had two parts. Both of them referred to a strangely worded hypothesis.

Do you consider that if a nation insists on attacking another, the other nations should compel it to stop by
a) economic and non-military measures
b) if necessary military measures

Eden, quite rightly, regarded the questions as 'far too complex to admit to simple answers'[15] but 11,559,000 British citizens thought otherwise and voted. Over ten million supported economic sanctions. Only 635,000 were opposed. The majority in favour of military action was smaller – 6,784,368 to 2,351,981.

The government claimed to be unimpressed by what was no more than a statement of minority opinion. But Baldwin thought it necessary to warn the country about the dangers which would follow

treating economic and military sanctions separately. His warning
ended with a revealing comment on the state of Britain's defences.

> If you are going to adopt sanctions you must be prepared for
> war . . . If you are going to enforce a collective guarantee or a
> collective sanction, it means that you have to make the country
> a good deal stronger than she is today.[16]

The indictment against Stanley Baldwin is not that he failed to rearm. It is that he failed to rearm although he knew rearmament was
necessary. His most sympathetic biographer offers an explanation
which is far from a justification. 'The nerve injured in October 1933,
the Fulham nerve, never healed.' The damage was done at a by-
election in which an 'anti-war' candidate converted a Tory majority of
14,521 into a Labour majority of 4,840. In consequence, the Prime
Minister was 'afraid of pacifists'.[17]

It was a terrible indictment made all the more damning by its confirmation by the Prime Minister himself. He made the confession
during a defence debate in the House of Commons on 12 November
1936, when he thought it necessary to reply directly to Winston
Churchill's accusation that the government was 'preparing more
months and years . . . for the locusts to eat'.

> I put before the whole House my own view with an appalling
> frankness. From 1933, I and my friends were very worried about
> what was happening in Europe . . . You will remember at that
> time there was probably a stronger pacifist feeling running
> through the country than at any time since the War . . . You will
> remember the election at Fulham in the autumn of 1933 when
> a seat which the national government held was lost by about
> 7,000 votes on no issue but the pacifists . . .
>   My position as the leader of a great party was not a comfort-
> able one. I ask myself what chance was there – when that feeling
> that was given expression to in Fulham was common throughout
> the country – what chance was there within the next year or two
> of that feeling being so changed that the country would give
> a mandate for rearmament? Suppose that I had gone to the

country saying that Germany was rearming and we must
rearm . . . I cannot think of anything that would have made the
loss of the election from my point of view more certain.

The only error in that remarkable confession – apart from the small
matter of overstating the Tory defeat – was the implication that
Baldwin's reluctance to stand up to the dictators was limited to the
rearmament of Germany. He had failed to resist Italian aggression
because – knowing that economic sanctions could only be imposed
from a position of military strength – he accepted that Britain was too
weak to act. Yet he made no attempt to remedy that weakness.

In 1935 it was by no means clear that Samuel Hoare, the new
Foreign Secretary, shared or accepted the Prime Minister's strictures
about the relationship between military capability and economic sanctions. At the League of Nations he sounded unequivocally committed
to strong action.

> I can say that the government will be second to none in its
> intention to fulfil, within the measure of its capacity, its obliga-
> tion which the covenant lays upon it . . . The attitude of His
> Majesty's Government has always been one of unswerving
> fidelity to the League and all it stands for . . . In conformity with
> its precise and explicit obligations, the League stands and my
> country stands with it for the collective maintenance of the
> covenant in its entirety and particularly for steady and collective
> resistance to all forms of dictatorship.[18]

In his autobiography Hoare defends the 'revivalist appeal' of the
speech with the admission that 'if there was an element of bluff in it, it
was a moment when bluff was not only legitimate but inescapable'.[19]
Not everyone agreed. The official policy of His Majesty's Government
was that another country should make the pace and Britain should
follow suit. Neville Chamberlain set out the exact position. 'We
should not attempt to take on our shoulders the whole burden of
keeping the peace.'[20]

He was not alone in his caution. Winston Churchill – not always as
heroic as history now makes him out to be – was strongly against

Britain becoming 'a sort of bell-wether or fugleman to gather and lead opinion in Europe against Mussolini's Abyssinia designs. We must do out duty, but we must do it in conjunction with other nations. We are not strong enough to be the law-giver of the world.'[21] He was enjoying one of his regular Riviera holidays when Hoare made his 'revivalist appeal'. With the wisdom of hindsight he wrote in his memoirs that the Foreign Secretary had 'united all those forces in Britain which stood for a righteous combination of fearlessness and strength'.[22] But in a letter written to Austen Chamberlain at the time he expressed a different view. 'I do not think that we should have taken the lead in such a vehement way. If we had felt so strongly on the subject, we should have warned Mussolini two months before.'[23]

The Royal Navy was equally alarmed by Hoare's rhetoric. Vansittart had, for some time, argued the necessity to reinforce the Mediterranean Fleet, and the Board of Admiralty – concerned as much by the fear of losing the shortest route to the Far East as by the threat of a European war itself – had warned the government that the Navy needed three months' notice of hostilities. There was no thought that the war at sea might be lost. But the Italians had torpedo bombers. Until the 'open' harbour at Valletta was adequately provided with anti-aircraft cover, Malta was vulnerable. HMS *Hood* and HMS *Renown*, accompanied by a battleship squadron and a flotilla of destroyers, sailed for Gibraltar.

Mussolini reacted to the new disposition of the fleet by sending two infantry divisions through Libya to menace Egypt. When he made clear that they would be withdrawn if he could be convinced that Italy was not under direct threat, Hoare responded that no military action was contemplated and added, gratuitously, that Britain had no intention of closing the Suez Canal to Italian shipping. The assurance emboldened rather than reassured Mussolini. In the small hours of 3 October 1935 Italian troops under the command of General De Bono invaded Abyssinia. At the League of Nations, Italy was formally accorded the status of aggressor. Under the covenant, sanctions automatically followed.

On the day following the Abyssinian invasion the Prime Minister addressed the Tory Party Conference. He spoke strongly in favour of collective security, but dismissed the possibility of Britain fighting the dictators alone. He condemned dictatorship but carefully concentrated his strictures on Germany. Most of his speech concerned unemployment. A general election was, he knew, only weeks away. Elections are won and lost on domestic policy.

There was, however, much discussion within the Tory Party about how defence should figure in the manifesto. Baldwin hoped, but was not sure, that the British people were ready to accept a modest increase in military and naval expenditure. Neville Chamberlain, later to become the high priest of appeasement, wanted 'to take the bold course of actually appealing to the country on the defence programme'.[24] Later he found the £85 million – judged the necessary expenditure by the Defence Requirements Committee – a 'staggering prospect' and insisted that the estimates be reduced to under £26 million. He was, however, strongly – and rightly – of the view that Britain would 'be more likely to deter Germany from mad-dogging if we had an air force which, in case of need, can bomb the Ruhr from Belgium'.[25] But spending on aircraft procurement had, like the rest of the defence budget, to be 'decided in the light of politics and finance'.[26] The government was still not ready to remedy Britain's weaknesses.

The Labour Party – the official opposition – believed that too much was being spent on defence, not too little. Its general election manifesto, published six weeks after Mussolini's invasion of Abyssinia, at least had the virtue of clarity.

> While paying lip service to the League [the government] is planning a vast, expensive armaments programme which will only stimulate programmes elsewhere. Labour will propose to other nations the complete abolition of national air forces.

We do not know what success that initiative would have achieved. On 14 November 1935 the Conservatives won 387 seats, Labour 154.

There was no place for Winston Churchill in the new government, even though he had moderated his criticism in the hope of being recalled. In a letter to his Parliamentary Private Secretary, Baldwin explained why.

I feel we should not give him a post at this stage. Anything he
undertakes he puts his heart into. If there is to be a war – and no
one can say there is not – we must keep him fresh to be our
wartime Prime Minister.[27]

Prophetic though that judgement was, it revealed more than Baldwin's
prescience. The prospect of war was always in his mind, but preparations were rarely on his agenda.

War came a step nearer on 11 November 1935, when the League of
Nations published the list of sanctions which were to be imposed on
Italy. The important commodity was oil. There was hope, but no certainty, that Russia and Romania (between them providing 56 per
cent of Italy's imports) would support the embargo – though Baldwin
had doubts about joining forces with the Soviet Union. President
Roosevelt wanted to prohibit American oil exports but needed
Congress to approve new legislation before the prohibition began.
Fortunately, General De Bono made slow progress and military
experts judged that he would not complete the conquest of Abyssinia
in one campaign before the season and weather changed. Britain, in
conjunction with France, decided that there was an opportunity to
make another conciliatory approach to Italy.

The two powers agreed that, if the Italians halted their advance,
Mussolini should be rewarded with the gift of two towns, Adowa and
Adigrat. Abyssinia would be compensated with cession of two other
towns, Assab and Zeita. Before a decision could be taken – either to
implement sanctions or to pursue the deal – Mussolini moved troops
up to the French frontier. Roman newspapers speculated about the
possibility of Italian air raids on the Riviera.

The French became suddenly uncooperative – not because the
government had lost its nerve but because Pierre Laval, the Foreign
Minister, had been bribed by Mussolini. The Royal Navy was denied
anchorage in Toulon and preparations to impose sanctions were held
up on the pretext that their imposition might provoke Mussolini into
rejecting the offer of new discussions.

It was all becoming too much for Samuel Hoare and, in the middle
of the crisis, his doctor proscribed a recuperative skating holiday in
Switzerland. When he told the Prime Minister of the advice which he

had received he added that he proposed to call in on Laval on his way through Paris. Baldwin was supportive in every particular. 'Have a good leave and get your health back. That is the most important thing. By all means stop in Paris and push Laval as far as you can. But on no account get this country into war.'[28] Hoare left for Paris on 6 December. On the seventh the Foreign Office received sketchy notes of a meeting. On the eighth the Prime Minister received a telegram from his Foreign Secretary requesting that a Cabinet meeting be called for the following day. There was no indication of what the meeting would discuss. However, a communiqué issued in Paris, but not in London, announced that the two ministers had devised a 'formula which might serve as a basis for a friendly settlement of the Italian-Ethiopian dispute'.[29]

The formula was built around what Hoare described as 'an exchange of territories'. Abyssinia would cede the Ogaden and Tigray Province to Italy – sixty thousand square miles in all – and grant Italy the exclusive rights to 'develop' the south and south-west of the country. In return Abyssinia would receive either Assab or Zeita and a 'corridor' to whichever port it chose. However, there could be no railway to the sea. France was not prepared to contemplate competition with its own line to Djibouti. When the Cabinet discussed it, Baldwin urged support without advancing any agreement to justify that view. In Parliament he explained that his 'lips were not unsealed' but assured Members that, if they knew what he knew, they would endorse the Foreign Secretary's proposals. His assurance was greeted with open incredulity.

Public and press were almost universally opposed to the Hoare–Laval Pact and the debate on the subject in the House of Commons was part tragedy and part farce. Hoare was absent. He had fallen while skating and broken his nose. So the Cabinet met again. It talked much of honour – not in relation to the morality of dismembering a small powerless country but in regard to the propriety of repudiating a Foreign Secretary in his absence.

Some Cabinet ministers sagely nodded in agreement with the Prime Minister's continual assertion that Hoare deserved his colleagues' support. But public opinion and parliamentary pressure were irresistible. The Hoare–Laval Pact was dead and Hoare knew it. But

when, on his return to London, he was visited on his sickbed by
Neville Chamberlain, he announced that, when he returned to health,
he would defend the Pact in the Commons as the best prospect on
offer. Hoare, Baldwin reluctantly agreed, would have to go.
Chamberlain made a second visit to the invalid and left with the
Foreign Secretary's resignation in his pocket.

Anthony Eden – a noted foreign affairs expert and a man of legendary charm and good looks – became Foreign Secretary. The
method, or at least the manner, of his appointment was unusual.
Summoned to Downing Street to see Stanley Baldwin, he was asked
by the Prime Minister to speculate about Hoare's successor. His first
suggestion was Austen Chamberlain who, in Baldwin's view, was too
old. His second candidate, Lord Halifax, was ruled out because he was
a peer. After some moments of embarrassed silence Baldwin said, 'It
looks as though it will have to be you.'[30] So Eden travelled to
Sandringham to kiss hands and receive his seals of office from George
V. The King told him, 'I said to your predecessor "You know what
they are saying. No more coals to Newcastle and no more Hoares to
Paris." He didn't even laugh.'[31]

On 7 March 1936 German troops reoccupied the previously
demilitarised Rhineland. But once again Britain could not decide if
the clear breach of the Versailles Treaty was sufficiently serious to provoke an international incident. Historically, the Rhineland was
German territory. Could the presence of a token force of German
troops possibly be called aggression – particularly in the light of a general acceptance that, sooner rather than later, the military prohibition
would be lifted? Anthony Eden warned the Cabinet that 'if Hitler
remains in unmolested military occupation of the Rhineland, war in
two years is a certainty.' But he told France, 'Britain [is] not prepared
to go to war in order that Germany should be compelled to go out of
the Rhineland one week and allowed to come in the next.'[32] The
contradictory statements were less the result of perfidy than of intellectual ambivalence. The British government could never make up its
mind.

The new Foreign Secretary was the beginning of an eventful six
months. No doubt emboldened by Britain's infirmity of purpose,
units of the Spanish army, under the command of General Francisco

Franco, revolted in an overt – and eventually successful – attempt to overthrow the lawfully elected government. Baldwin was less concerned with the possible extinction of democracy than with the cost of saving it. The price to be paid would include fighting on the same side as the Soviet Union – a sacrifice which he was not even prepared to make when an Italian and German aerial bombardment killed 1,645 civilians in Guernica. There is no doubt that he was reluctant to come into conflict – albeit vicariously – with Italy and Germany. But his real objection to intervention was confided to the Foreign Secretary when he told him, 'On no account, French or other, must [you] bring us in the fight on the side of the Russians.' The instruction was repeated before Eden visited Paris to meet Léon Blum (the recently elected 'popular front' Prime Minister). It was, the Prime Minister said, 'important to be careful'[33] about France's inclination to supply arms to the legitimate Spanish government.

Stanley Baldwin resigned the Premiership on 28 May 1937 and was succeeded, without fuss or dispute, by Neville Chamberlain. Eden remained Foreign Secretary. But the style of government changed. The days of Downing Street's studious detachment from Foreign Affairs was over. Back in 1934, when Hoare became Foreign Secretary, there had been much talk of Chamberlain doing the job. But he had chosen to stay at the Treasury because, according to his diary, 'The FO was expensive and I could not afford it. Moreover I should hate the journeys to Geneva and above all I should loathe and detest the social ceremonies.'[34] That did not, however, cause him to question his capacity to succeed in the role. When, three months after Hoare's appointment, a minister was needed to accompany Ramsay MacDonald to Stresa, he had no doubt who was most likely to safeguard Britain's essential interests. 'I believe that the best person to go would be myself, but that of course is impossible.'[35]

Although, when he became Prime Minister, Chamberlain boasted that he 'had only to raise a finger and the whole of Europe was changed',[36] he had no confidence in his ability to bend the Diplomatic Service to his will. Fearful that the Foreign Office – particularly with Vansittart, who despised him, at its head – would pursue an independent policy, he appointed a foreign policy adviser who could be relied upon to follow an independent line. The chosen candidate was Sir Horace Wilson. His strength – from the Prime Minister's point of view – was that he was Chamberlain's man. Foreign policy advisers usually came from, and represented, the views of the Foreign Office. Wilson reflected, indeed shared, Chamberlain's weaknesses – caution, parochialism and suspicion of those around him.

Wilson was a self-educated civil servant who had worked his way up from boy clerk at the Patents Office, through the Ministry of Labour, to become the chief economic adviser to the Prime Minister. That was the position which he occupied – and expected to relinquish – when Baldwin was succeeded by Chamberlain. Much to his surprise, he was offered a new role. By the very nature of his existence he created a gulf between Downing Street and the Foreign Office. He widened it by his character and conduct. Jim Thomas, Anthony Eden's parliamentary private secretary, was both astonished and affronted to be asked to keep the Prime Minister's office informed about Vansittart's behaviour. Chamberlain did not play according to the established rules.

Then, as now, the Security Services theoretically reported to the Foreign Secretary. But Sir Joseph Ball, the head of MI5, established contacts in Italy which were kept secret from everyone except the Prime Minister – including Anthony Eden. Chamberlain's sister-in-law – Dame Ivy, Austen's widow – lived in Rome and was an unapologetic admirer of Mussolini and his regime. Dame Ivy wrote regularly to the Prime Minister with her advice on Anglo-Italian relations and Chamberlain often read her letters to the Cabinet. They invariably urged a rapprochement with Mussolini and were, in consequence, almost always in conflict with the Foreign Secretary's own views.

Eden was a proud, some would say vain, man. But he accepted Chamberlain's behaviour with remarkable patience. Sometimes it seemed that the Prime Minister wanted to humiliate him to the point at which he would choose to resign. Hermann Goering invited Halifax to be his guest at an international sporting exhibition in Berlin, adding that there would probably be an opportunity to meet Hitler. Eden's fears of giving the 'impression of being in pursuit of the German Chancellor'[37] were dismissed out of hand. The meeting with

Hitler was arranged in Berchtesgaden, not Berlin, but the Prime Minister agreed that Halifax should pursue the Führer. The *Evening Standard* published exaggerated reports of the meeting's importance – including the allegation that Hitler had suggested that he be given 'a free hand in Europe' in return for leaving Britain free to dominate Africa. When the Foreign Office complained, the Prime Minister wrote on the memorandum, 'But really that FO. I am only waiting my opportunity to stir it up with a long pole.'[38] The full report of the talks between Hitler and Halifax confirmed that the *Evening Standard* had exaggerated the significance of the meeting – but not by very much. The two men had discussed 'possible alterations in the European order which might be destined to come about with the passage of time. Amongst these questions were Danzig, Austria and Czechoslovakia.'[39] They went on to talk about the need to avoid 'far-reaching disturbances'. The idea of *Lebensraum* had been put on the international agenda.

For more than six months Britain had two foreign policies. One, aimed at holding back Mussolini's drive into Abyssinia, was directed by the Foreign Secretary. The other, committed to a rapprochement at all costs, was dictated by the Prime Minister. The conflict came to a head during the summer of 1937 when the Director of the Conservative Research Department arranged a series of secret meetings between Chamberlain and the Italian Ambassador to London. On 27 July the Prime Minister sent a personal message to the Duce.

> I wish to assure you that the government is activated by the most friendly feelings towards Italy and will be ready at any time to enter upon conversations with a view to clarifying the whole situation and removing all causes of suspicion and misunderstanding.[40]

Chamberlain gladly admitted, 'I did not show the letter to the Foreign Secretary as I had the feeling that he would object to it.'[41]

Chamberlain was moving towards recognition of the Italian claim to Abyssinia and Eden, sensing the Prime Minister's inclination, warned Downing Street that 'Mussolini is a complete gangster. His pledged word means nothing.'[42] Chamberlain was unmoved. 'One

way we can maintain our moral position is to make recognition part
of a general scheme of appeasement in the Mediterranean and the
Red Sea.'[43] The Prime Minister was in head-on conflict with his
Foreign Secretary. Yet he had not the courage to remove him and
Eden – despite his highly developed sense of dignity – seemed willing
to accept every humiliation that Chamberlain heaped upon him.

One of the features of inter-war politics was the frequency with
which ministers abandoned Whitehall for recuperative holidays. Eden
spent the 1938 New Year at Grasse on the Riviera, and he was still
there on 14 January when he received a telephone message urging
him to return to London at once. A crisis had arisen which could not
be discussed on an open line.

At Folkestone he was met by Alexander Cadogan – Permanent
Under Secretary of State since Vansittart had been 'kicked upstairs' to
become Chief Foreign Policy Adviser to the government. He told the
Foreign Secretary that President Roosevelt had suggested that the
United States call an international conference to negotiate 'a new
comprehensive European settlement based on the fundamental principles of international law'. That in itself would not have constituted
a crisis. But, without consulting the Foreign Secretary, the Prime
Minister had responded with a note which the State Department
described as 'a douche of cold water'.[44] Eden's reaction was heroic but
reckless. The British Ambassador in Washington was instructed to
inform the White House that the message had been received while the
Foreign Secretary was abroad. The idea of a conference should not be
abandoned because of Britain's initial hasty response.

Eden was summoned to Chequers to be told of the Prime
Minister's displeasure but Chamberlain agreed not to confirm his
rejection of the President's offer. Then a message from Washington,
reminding him that the United States was 'very strongly against the
recognition of [Italian] Abyssinia', convinced him that Roosevelt's
suggestion would only reduce the prospects of a negotiated settlement
between Britain and Italy. The Prime Minister's chief objection to
Roosevelt's initiative was that, with its strong preference for international law, it would greatly irritate the dictator powers.[45]

A major policy conflict between the Prime Minister and the

Foreign Secretary can end in only one way. The Foreign Affairs Committee of the Cabinet – meeting over several days – considered the Roosevelt initiative and an alternative proposal (much favoured by Dame Ivy Chamberlain) that there should be a bilateral meeting between Italy and Britain. The issues were complicated by concern about the Italian 'volunteers' (who were fighting for the insurgents in Spain) and Mussolini's offer to consider calling them home when his Abyssinia demands had been met. It seemed that Eden's hand had been strengthened when Il Duce strengthened his demands by announcing that recognition of Italy's claim to Abyssinia must precede any meeting.

In normal circumstances Eden's objection to doing business with Mussolini would have been made irresistible by reports of the intelligence service which warned that he had agreed to support Hitler's annexation of Austria and had promised that he would send more 'volunteers' to fight with Franco in Spain. But the situation was not normal. The Italian Ambassador was invited to Downing Street and – at a meeting which Chamberlain had hoped would not include his Foreign Secretary – denied all the allegations. The Foreign Secretary's presence did not inhibit Chamberlain's enthusiasm for détente. The Prime Minister agreed to visit Mussolini in Rome. Once again, Eden registered his objections.

The Prime Minister – as Prime Ministers usually do – got his way. Not even the sinking of British merchantmen by Italian submarines – part of Italy's blockade of what remained of independent Abyssinia – convinced him of the dangers of doing business with Mussolini. Weekend Cabinet meetings – usually regarded as a sign of panic – are normally avoided. But ministers assembled in Downing Street on Saturday 19 and Sunday 20 February. It was clear that Chamberlain would have his way and that a meeting – which Eden thought 'would look like capitulation'[46] – would be held in Rome. At the first meeting the Foreign Secretary offered his resignation. At the second he resigned. Mussolini had won and Britain, apparently willing to accept any humiliation, was diminished in the judgement of both enemy and friend.

Less than a month later – after Eden's resignation and his replacement by Lord Halifax – German troops marched into Austria. The

Prime Minister was host of a luncheon for the retiring German Ambassador when the news reached London and, with infinite faith in his ability to moderate the dictator's territorial demands, he took his guest aside and asked him to send a message to Berlin requesting that the Führer change his mind. He should have realised – from events of the previous three weeks as well as from a reading of Hitler's character – that there was no prospect of holding back the *Anschluss*.

On the day of Eden's resignation Hitler had told the Reichstag that territories on Germany's borders, which were home to ten million ethnic Germans, must be incorporated in the Reich. Schuschnigg, the Austrian Chancellor, had responded by proposing a referendum to determine where the Austrian people's loyalty lay. It was not a test of opinion which the Führer was prepared to allow. Either the referendum was called off or Germany would invade. Schuschnigg was resolute – 'an ill-conceived and ill-prepared act of folly', according to Sir Nevile Henderson, the British Ambassador in Berlin. Henderson had become an admirer of Hitler and the Nazis. In 1937 he attended the Nuremberg Party Day Rally. His description of the event – sent in his official dispatch to the Foreign Office – reveals the extent of his infatuation.

> On Hitler's arrival at the far end, and as he entered the stadium, the 300 huge searchlights surrounding it were turned up into the air, each throwing a broad blue beam some 20,000 feet or more into the sky, where the lights converged to make a square roof which a chance cloud made even more realistic. The effect, both solemn and beautiful, was something like being inside a cathedral of ice . . .
>
> At the word of command 32,000 standard-bearers then advanced from out of sight at the southern end up the main lane and over the further tiers and down the four side lanes. The standards were illuminated by lights on the shafts of a certain proportion of them, and the spectacle of these five rivers of red and gold, one broad and four smaller, rippling slowly forward under the dome of blue lights through the massed formations of brown shirts, and absolutely silently, till, about a hundred yards from where we were sitting, suddenly the tramp of feet was heard, was indescribably beautiful.[47]

This was the man who advised the Foreign Secretary – and ultimately the Prime Minister – on relations with Germany. Sadly it was advice which Chamberlain was happy to accept. Standing up to the dictators was foreign to his nature.

Chamberlain thought that a deal might have been done to save Austria if, during the crisis, it had been 'Halifax at the Foreign Office instead of Anthony'.[48] But he told the House of Commons, 'Nothing could have arrested this action by Germany unless we and others had been prepared to use force to prevent it.'[49] In the meantime Chamberlain, thanks to Halifax, began to placate the dictators one by one. Having described sanctions as the 'midsummer of madness' he gave *de jure* recognition to Mussolini's conquest of Abyssinia. He could not have hoped that by feeding the dictators' appetite for expansion he would, in the end, satiate it. He already knew that, when Hitler asserted that Germany was wherever Germans were to be found, he had more than Austria in mind. The Führer was determined to annex the Sudetenland of Czechoslovakia. And Chamberlain knew it.

It was an intention which Chamberlain was sure could not be frustrated. His brother Austen had warned him two years earlier, 'If Austria goes, Czechoslovakia is indefensible.'[50] It was equally the view of the Foreign Office and the Chiefs of Staff. The Prime Minister set it out in a letter to his sister,

> You have only to look at a map to see that nothing we could do could possibly save Czechoslovakia from being overrun by the Germans if they wanted to do it. The Austrian frontier is practically open, the great Skoda munition works are within easy bombing distance of the German aerodromes, the railways all pass through German territory and Russia is a hundred miles away.[51]

His conclusion was that providing help to Czechoslovakia would be a 'pretext' for going to war with Germany – a strange use of the word which probably revealed his visceral dislike of the rearmament lobby. However, he went on to endorse their views on the state of British preparedness. War was unthinkable unless Britain could 'beat

[Germany] to her knees in a reasonable time'. He ended the letter with the gloomy conclusion, 'of that I see no sign'.

The letter made clear that France (under a treaty obligation to come to the aid of Czechoslovakia in the event of invasion) could not expect Britain to take up arms in the same cause. In the House of Commons the Prime Minister set out the circumstances in which the government would contemplate going to war – in defence of Britain itself or the British Empire, in accordance with the Locarno Pact to defend France and Belgium against unprovoked attack and in compliance with its specific treaty obligations to Egypt, Portugal and Iraq. The League of Nations covenant required member states to protect the victims of aggression. By that, he made clear that Britain had no automatic obligation to fight for Czechoslovakian independence. Hitler must have realised that he had been given a free hand.

Chamberlain was undoubtedly horrified by the thought of war and that was the main inspiration of his determination to appease the dictators. But his response to every act of aggression was influenced by his sympathy for the dictators' cause, if not the dictators themselves. The Rhineland and the Saar were rightfully German and it was difficult to tell Hitler not to reassert his authority over his own country. The near-anarchy in Manchuria and Abyssinia jeopardised Japanese and Italian commercial interests. That did not justify either of the invasions, but it explained what provoked them. Austria and Germany were, as Hitler said, one race and one people. There were equally strong – perhaps even stronger – reasons for changing the boundaries and status of Czechoslovakia which had been arbitrarily decided at Versailles.

Mussolini had made the point in one of his florid speeches. The country should have been called 'Czecho-Germano-Polono-Magyaro-Rutheno-Roumano-Slovakia'. Lloyd George had been opposed to the creation of such a heterogeneous confederation when it was stitched together at Versailles and the promise to amend its original constitution in the interests of the ethnic minorities had not been kept.

Chamberlain, still set on conciliation by concession, asked Walter Runciman – a man notorious for his love of political intrigue and President of the Board of Trade in Stanley Baldwin's government – to search for common ground on which German and Czech interests could be reconciled. It was the Czechs who adjusted their position, as Runciman was determined that they should. He reported to the Foreign Secretary that 'Czechoslovak rule in the Sudeten areas for the last twenty years, though not actually oppressive and certainly not terroristic, has been marked by tactless lack of understanding, petty intolerance and discrimination to a point where the resentment of the German population was inevitably moving in the direction of revolt'.[52]

The British Ambassador in Prague provided an alternative justification for tolerating, while not endorsing, German behaviour. 'Czechoslovakia's present position is not permanently tenable . . . It will be no kindness, in the long run, to try to maintain her in it.'[53] Chamberlain – cynically or naïvely – expressed that view to an American journalist who was a fellow guest at a party given by Lady Astor. He must have realised that, even though the story was published on the far side of the Atlantic Ocean, Adolf Hitler would be told that the British Prime Minister did not regard Czechoslovakia as a viable state. But by then Chamberlain had become positively sympathetic to the Sudeten Germans. They reminded him of the Uitlanders who had been saved from the rapacious Boers by Joseph Chamberlain. Filial piety required him to be on their side.

On the weekend of 19–22 May British intelligence warned the Prime Minister that the Sudeten Germans, supported from Berlin, were about to stage a coup against the Czechoslovakian government. The Germans protested their innocence. In fact, they had been deterred from carrying out their original intention by a risibly inaccurate telegram from the new German Ambassador to London. 'If Germany should resort to military means to reach their objectives, then England would, without any doubt, resort to war at the side of France.'[54]

Chamberlain's prescription for avoiding war was as doomed as it was craven. Instead of resisting the potential aggressors, he put pressure on the likely victim. Doctor Edward Benes, the Czechoslovakian Prime Minister, was presented with Runciman's conciliation plan and urged to make 'maximum concessions' to Hitler and to the Czech minority which he said were under his protection. Benes agreed. But in September the Sudeten German leaders rejected the proposals as offensively inadequate. They wanted to be German with a new definition of the German frontier. When Hitler supported that aspiration at a Nuremberg Rally, riots convulsed the Sudetenland.

It must be said in Chamberlain's defence that even the most militant British patriots 'believed in giving a good deal of autonomy to the Sudeten deutsch'.[55] But, unlike the Prime Minister, they realised that Hitler's 'territorial ambition' would not be extinguished by resolving the grievances of the German-speaking minority. 'The Secretary of State for Foreign Affairs reported that, with the Prime Minister, he had seen Mr Winston Churchill . . . Mr Churchill's proposition was that we should tell Germany that if she set foot in Czechoslavakia we should at once be at war with her.'[56]

Neither the Prime Minister nor the Foreign Secretary agreed. Chamberlain described his alternative approach to the House of Commons.

> I decided that the time had come to put into operation a plan which I had had in mind for a considerable period as a last resort . . . I resolved to go to Germany myself to interview Herr Hitler and find out, from personal conversation, whether there was yet any hope of saving the peace.[57]

Thus began what, fifty years later, was called 'shuttle diplomacy'.

Chamberlain flew to Germany on 15 September and met Hitler in Berchtesgaden. Chamberlain was admirably direct. 'You say that the three million Sudeten Germans must be included in the Reich. Would you be satisfied with that and is there no more you want?' Hitler's response was brutally frank. If the Sudetenland was detached from Czechoslovakia the country would disintegrate and 'what was left would be so small that he would not bother his head about it'.[58] Hitler said that he was prepared to risk war rather than postpone a final solution to the 'Sudeten persecution' and Chamberlain – at least according to his own account as given in a letter to his sister – threatened to bring the meeting to a premature end. 'He then quietened down', allowing Chamberlain to explain that, 'the government accepted the principle of self-determination'.[59] He suggested that he consulted his allies and then returned to Germany ('somewhere near Cologne') to discuss how that could be achieved in Czechoslovakia. His assessment of the likelihood of coming to an agreement with Hitler, made when he had returned home, was to haunt him for the rest of his life.'I got the impression that here was a man who could be relied upon when he had given his word.'[60]

At a meeting in London on 18 September Chamberlain repeated to the French Prime Minister what he had told the Cabinet. 'With the German troops in the position they . . . occupied there was nothing that anyone could do that would prevent . . . invasion unless the right of self determination were granted to the Sudeten Germans and that quickly.'[61] After six hours of argument, Édouard Daladier agreed. On 22 September Chamberlain set off again for Germany.

The meeting – at Bad Godesberg on the Rhine – began with Chamberlain's announcement that France and Britain accepted that Czechoslovakia must lose the Sudetenland and accept new boundary proposals, together with a scheme for the international supervision of population movement. Hitler rejected the Prime Minister's 'solution'. He demanded a settlement within days.The Czechs must immediately withdraw their troops – and all other arms of the Prague government – from the Sudetenland.The final frontier would be eventually decided by plebiscite.There was no question of Germany indemnifying Czechoslovakia for its acquisition of state property or of a new anti aggression pact being signed between the two countries. The meeting adjourned, was reconvened and then abandoned. Chamberlain left Germany 'with heavy heart since he saw the final wreck of all his hopes for peace in Europe'.[62]

It seemed that Britain was left with the alternative of war or total capitulation. And even Chamberlain accepted, albeit with obvious reluctance, that it would be impossible to accept Hitler's demands there and then.The country prepared for the worst. Plans were drawn up to evacuate children from town to country, air-raid shelters were built and tape was stuck on windows to prevent injury from flying glass. In a broadcast to the British people on 27 September Chamberlain demonstrated both his passion for peace and the stunted vision which had prevented him from achieving his aim by standing up to the dictators.

How horrible, fantastic, incredible it is that we should be digging trenches and trying on gas masks because of a quarrel in a far away country between people of whom we know nothing.[63]

On the following day he was repeating the same gloomy message to the House of Commons when the civil servants, in their box behind the Speaker's chair, received a message from the British Embassy in Berlin. They passed a note along the front bench to the Prime Minister, who paused in mid-sentence, stared at the sheet of paper, paused again, and then told the House,

> I have now been informed by Herr Hitler that he invites me to meet him in Munich tomorrow morning. I need not say what my answer will be.

The House of Commons erupted in a frenzy of relief. Most Members stood in their places waving their order papers and cheering, though Winston Churchill struck a balance between hope and doubt by approaching the Prime Minister at the dispatch box and wishing him good luck – a gesture which Chamberlain believed was intended to convey doubt about the outcome of the meeting. Harold Nicolson remained seated and silent. He, at least, had noticed that the future of Czechoslovakia was to be decided by a conference to which Britain, France, Germany and Italy – but not Czechoslovakia – had been invited.

The Munich meeting lasted only a few hours. Hitler obtained everything that he had demanded at Bad Godesberg. German troops would occupy the Sudetenland over a period of ten days rather than immediately – a military necessity rather than a concession. Outstanding issues should be resolved by an international tribunal – composed in a way which guaranteed that Germany would win every dispute. *The Times*, always an advocate of appeasement, saw the agreement differently. 'No conquering hero returning from the battlefields has come home adorned with such laurels.'[64]

Chamberlain's apologists can claim that he represented the will of a nation which was not interested in the merits of the Munich

Agreement but in the pretext which it provided for the avoidance of war. They also argue that, by keeping the peace between October 1938 and September 1939, he bought precious time. There is no doubt that during that eleven months the rearmament programme was accelerated. But the price of the respite was the sacrifice of Czechoslovakia.

The Munich Agreement had changed the country's name by inserting a hyphen between 'Czech' and 'Slovakia'. The disintegration which they presaged came about on 15 March 1939. Slovakia declared its independence. Hungary occupied the Sub-Carpathian Ukraine. Bohemia became a German protectorate – in effect a Nazi dictatorship. Suddenly Neville Chamberlain's words – spoken in triumph to the crowds outside Downing Street on the night of his return from Munich – became a condemnation of his own judgement.

> This is the second time in our history that there has come back from Germany to Downing Street peace with honour. I believe it is peace for our time.[65]

Churchill – during the Munich debate – described the consequences of the settlement more accurately.

> The German dictator, instead of snatching the victuals from the table, has been content to have them served to him course by course . . . All is over. Silent, mournful and broken, Czechoslovakia recedes into darkness.[66]

The House of Commons rumbled its dissent.

At the height of the Czechoslovak crisis, Chamberlain had written a stern personal letter to Hitler.

> It has been alleged that if HMG had made its position more clear in 1914, the great catastrophe would have been avoided . . . HMG is resolved that on this occasion there shall be no such misunderstanding. If the need should arise they [sic] are prepared to employ, without delay, all the forces under their command.[67]

By making the threat, but not carrying it out, Chamberlain con-vinced Hitler that Britain would never go to war to defend the integrity of European frontiers. The worm did turn. But for less heroic reasons than wartime propaganda suggested.

The government was worried about Poland – which was thought, as always, to have ideas above its place in the world. The Poles had seized Tesin from Czechoslovakia after the Munich Agreement broke down and were proving obdurate in their opposition to changing Danzig's 'free city' status. Britain, although feeling some sympathy for the claim that Danzig was essentially a German city, could not afford Poland to be allied with, or occupied by, Germany. Its refusal to come to any sort of agreement with Soviet Russia heartened the ideologues but worried the strategists. It seemed that Poland could only be kept honest by assurances that if its independence were threatened, 'His Majesty's Government and the French government would at once lend all the support in their power.' The proud Poles insisted on a mutual defence treaty signed by the three nations as equal partners.

On 23 August 1939 the Soviet Union and Germany signed a non-aggression pact. In fact, communism and fascism had come together to revive their ancient territorial ambitions. Their real intentions took the form of a secret agreement about the dismembering of Poland and the division of Polish territory between them. At last Westminster and Whitehall were alarmed. On 24 August Parliament met and passed an Emergency Powers Act in one day. On the 25th the mutual defence treaty with Poland was formally signed. Hitler had planned to attack on that day, but postponed the blitzkrieg so that he could go through a charade of negotiation. It is possible that, a couple of months before, Hitler would have accepted a rump Polish state,[68] an idea regarded by Nevile Henderson, the British Ambassador to Berlin, as reasonable. However the pact with the Soviet Union had made that impossible. His territorial ambitions could only be satisfied by conquest.

German troops crossed the Polish border at four forty-five on the morning of 1 September 1939. Seventy-five minutes later German aeroplanes bombed Warsaw. The Poles demanded help under the terms of the non-aggression pact. Britain chose to send a warning rather than an ultimatum and France wanted to postpone hostilities until its forces could be mobilised. For a moment it seemed that Mussolini might fulfil the hopes of earlier appeasers by mediating an agreed settlement. But Hitler refused to prepare for a peace by withdrawing his troops while the discussions were held.

The British Cabinet minutes for 2 September record a unanimous decision to issue an ultimatum which 'should end at midnight'. No ultimatum was issued. In the House of Commons that night Chamberlain still speculated about a peace conference. When Arthur Greenwood (leading for the opposition in Attlee's absence) rose to speak, Leo Amery – for many years a Tory minister – cried, 'Speak for England, Arthur.' It was meant less as an encouragement to Greenwood than as a reproof to Chamberlain. The Prime Minister's speech was received in silence. After the House rose a group of ministers met and decided on an ultimatum of their own. War must be declared next morning.

The ultimatum to Germany was delivered in Berlin at nine o'clock on 3 September. It expired two hours later. The result, as described by Chamberlain – reluctant to the end – was that Britain 'must regard itself in a state of war with Germany'. In the House of Commons he set out the position in more personal terms. 'Everything I have worked for, everything I have hoped for, everything I have believed in during my public life has crashed in ruins.'[69] He might have added that, during the next six years, Britain, France and America would pay the full price of the errors they had made at Versailles.

# NOTES

## Introduction: The Hush Before the Dawn

1. *Times*, 12.11.18
2. Norwich. *Duff Cooper Diaries*
3. Sheffield and Bourne (eds.). *Douglas Haig War Diaries*, p. 487
4. *Ibid.*
5. *The Times*, 12.11.18

## Chapter One: A Child Weeping

1. Sharp. *Versailles Settlement*, p. 37
2. Churchill. *Great Contemporaries*, p. 122
3. Owen. *Tempestuous Journey: Lloyd George, his life and times*, p. 35
4. Lloyd George. *War Memoirs: vol. II*, p. 67
5. Sharp, op. cit., p. 11
6. Rayner. *The Twenty Years Truce*, p. 15
7. Sharp, op. cit., p. 11
8. *Ibid.*, p. 13
9. Owen, op. cit., p. 498
10. *Ibid.*, p. 501
11. *Ibid.*
12. *Ibid.*, p. 497
13. *Ibid.*, p. 500
14. *Ibid.*, p. 507
15. Sharp, op. cit., p. 22
16. *Ibid.*
17. *Ibid.*, p. 19
18. Nicolson (ed.). *Harold Nicolson Diaries*, p. 19
19. Sharp, op. cit., p. 24
20. *Ibid.*, p. 14
21. *Ibid.*, p. 52
22. *Ibid.*
23. *Ibid.*
24. *Ibid.*
25. *Ibid.*
26. Owen, op. cit., p. 510

27. *Ibid.*, p. 511
28. Lloyd George Papers, National Library of Wales
29. *Ibid.*
30. *Collected Writings of John Maynard Keynes*, vol. 11, p. 34
31. Sharp, op. cit., p. 108
32. *Ibid.*, p. 122
33. *Ibid.*, p. 121
34. Lloyd George, op. cit., p. 536
35. Skidelsky. *John Maynard Keynes 1883–1946*, p. 241
36. Lloyd George, op. cit., p. 501
37. *Ibid.*, p. 541
38. Harrod. *Life of John Maynard Keynes*, p. 244
39. Rayner, op. cit., p. 33
40. Nicolson (ed.), op. cit., p. 24
41. Harrod, op. cit., p. 247
42. *Ibid.*

### Chapter Two: Inherit the Wilderness

1. Kee. *The Green Flag*, p. 523
2. *Ibid.*, p. 605
3. *Ibid.*, p. 608
4. *Daily Mail*, 21.10.17
5. Kee, op. cit., p. 610
6. *Ibid.*, p. 611
7. *Irish Independent*, 10.4.18
8. Longford, Earl of and O'Neill. *Éamon de Valéra*, p. 72
9. *Ibid.*, p. 95
10. *Wall Street Journal*, 4.2.20
11. Béaslaí. *Michael Collins and the Making of a New Ireland*, p. 274
12. Kee, op. cit., p. 682
13. *Ibid.*, p. 645
14. *Irish Times*, 22.12.19
15. Coogan. *Michael Collins: a Biography*, p. 123
16. Kee, op. cit., p. 651
17. Owen. *Tempestuous Journey: Lloyd George, his life and times*, p. 56
18. *Irish Times*, 1.5.20
19. Rose. *King George V*
20. Kee, op. cit., p. 690
21. *Ibid.*, p. 693
22. Longford, Earl of. *Peace by Ordeal*
23. *The Times*, 20.10.20
24. Figgis. *Recollections of Irish Wars*, quoted in Kee, p. 248
25. Kee, op. cit., p. 712

26. Nicolson. *King George V*, p. 547
27. Churchill. *The Aftermath*, p. 293
28. Coogan, op. cit., p. 207
29. Owen, op. cit., p. 573
30. Kee, op. cit., p. 714
31. *Ibid.*, p. 719
32. Rose, op. cit., p. 239
33. *Ibid.*, p. 240
34. Owen, op. cit., p. 578
35. Ibid., p. 579
36. Longford and O'Neill, op. cit., p. 148
37. Coogan, op. cit., p. 238
38. *Ibid.*
39. Longford and O'Neill, op. cit., p. 147
40. *Ibid.*, p. 151
41. Coogan, op. cit., p. 220
42. Owen, op. cit., p. 583
43. *Ibid.*, p. 585
44. Longford and O'Neill, op. cit., p. 164
45. Longford. *Peace by Ordeal*, p. 217
46. Longford and O'Neill, op. cit., p. 165
47. *Ibid.*
48. *Ibid.*, p. 166

### Chapter Three: A Wind of Freedom

 1. Nanda. *Mahatma Gandhi*, p. 97
 2. White Paper: Command Number 9109
 3. Nanda, op. cit., p. 78
 4. *Ibid.*, p. 105
 5. *Ibid.*
 6. Marquand. *Ramsay MacDonald*, p. 109
 7. *Ibid.*
 8. *Ibid.*, p. 110
 9. *Ibid.*, p. 112; Nanda, op. cit., p. 113
10. *Ibid.*, p. 129
11. *Ibid.*, p. 130
12. *Ibid.*, p. 129
13. Owen. *Tempestuous Journey*, p. 604
14. Nanda, op. cit., p. 138
15. *Ibid.*
16. Harris. *Attlee*, p. 75
17. Middlemas and Barnes. *Baldwin*, p. 536
18. *Ibid.*, p. 538

19. *Ibid.*, p. 537
20. *Ibid.*, p. 540
21. *Ibid.*
22. *Ibid.*, p. 543
23. Marquand, op. cit., p. 82
24. Nanda, op. cit., p. 155
25. Nehru. *The Discovery of India*, p. 392
26. Nanda, op. cit., p. 312
27. Marquand, op. cit., p. 581
28. Nanda, op. cit., p. 177
29. Marquand, op. cit., p. 582
30. Hoare. *Nine Troubled Years*, p. 54
31. Marquand, op. cit., p. 708
32. *Ibid.*
33. House of Commons debates 5s 1298 3.12.31
34. Jenkins. *Churchill*, p. 456
35. Harris, op. cit., p. 113
36. *Ibid.*, p. 114
37. Middlemas and Barnes, op. cit., p. 714
38. *Ibid.*, p. 713
39. Hoare, op. cit., p. 100
40. Jenkins, op. cit., p. 462
41. *Ibid.*, p. 463
42. Nanda, op. cit., p. 203
43. *Ibid.*, p. 204
44. *Ibid.*, p. 205
45. *Ibid.*, p. 210
46. *Ibid.*, p. 211

## Chapter Four. The King's Matter

1. Nicolson. *King George V*, p. 530
2. Middlemas and Barnes. *Baldwin*, p. 970
3. Airlie, Mabell, Countess of. *Thatched with Gold*, p. 187
4. Ziegler. *Mountbatten*, p. 93
5. Donaldson. *Edward VIII*, p. 158
6. *Ibid.*
7. *Ibid.*, p. 159
8. Windsor, Wallis, Duchess of. *The Heart Has Its Reasons*, p. 192
9. *Ibid.*, p. 194
10. James (ed.). *Chips: the Diaries of Sir Henry Channon*, p. 30
11. Windsor, Wallis, Duchess of, op. cit., p. 202
12. James, op. cit., p. 35. Nicolson (ed.). *Harold Nicholson: Diaries and Letters 1907–1964*, p. 238

13. Hyde. *Baldwin*, p. 419
14. Donaldson, op. cit., p. 156
15. *Ibid.*
16. Middlemas and Barnes, op. cit., p. 979
17. *Ibid.*
18. *Ibid.*
19. Jones. *A Diary with Letters 1931–1950*, p. 163
20. Donaldson, op. cit., p. 208
21. *The Times*, 29.11.55
22. Hyde, op. cit., p. 447
23. Lockhart. *Cosmo Gordon Lang*, p. 598
24. Beaverbrook. *The Abdication of Edward VIII*, p. 117
25. Windsor, Edward, Duke of. *A King's Story*, p. 313
26. Donaldson, op. cit., p. 226
27. Lockhart, op. cit., p. 399
28. Jones, op. cit., p. 277
29. Ziegler, op. cit., p. 95
30. Donaldson, op. cit., p. 236
31. *Ibid.*, p. 240
32. Driberg. *Beaverbrook*, p. 231
33. Middlemas and Barnes, op. cit., p. 468
34. Pope-Hennessy. *Queen Mary*, p. 575
35. Ziegler, op. cit., p. 95
36. Donaldson, op. cit., p. 250
37. *The Times*, 19.11.36
38. *Daily Mail*, 19.11.36
39. *The Times*, 19.11.36
40. *Ibid.*
41. Donaldson, op. cit., p. 258
42. Hyde, op. cit., p. 565
43. Attlee. *As It Happened*, p. 86
44. Harris. *Attlee*, p. 133
45. Hyde, op. cit., p. 451
46. *Ibid.*, p. 451
47. Jenkins. *Churchill*, p. 500
48. *Ibid.*, p. 501
49. Davidson. *Memoirs of a Conservative*, p. 414
50. Nicolson, op. cit., p. 289
51. James. *Bob Boothby: A Portrait*, p. 166
52. Windsor, Edward, Duke of, op. cit., p. 408
53. Nicolson, op. cit., p. 285
54. Donaldson, op. cit., p. 298
55. Ziegler, op. cit., p. 95

56. Donaldson, op. cit., p. 299
57. Driberg, op. cit., p. 238
58. Donaldson, op. cit., p. 300

## Chapter Five: Not a Penny off the Pay

1. Phillips. *The General Strike*, p. 23
2. Bailey. *Black Diamonds*, pp. 268–9
3. Bullock. *Ernest Bevin*, p. 54
4. Phillips, op. cit., p. 11
5. *Ibid.*
6. *Ibid.*, p. 25
7. *Ibid.*, p. 27
8. Minutes of MFGB 5.3.25
9. Jenkins. *Churchill*, p. 399
10. Skidelsky. *John Maynard Keynes – vol. II. The Economist as Saviour*, p. 335
11. Phillips, op. cit., p. 42
12. Middlemas and Barnes, *Baldwin*, p. 380
13. Laybourn. *The General Strike Day by Day*, 1996
14. Phillips, op. cit., p. 47
15. *Ibid.*, p. 48
16. *Ibid.*, p. 51
17. Middlemas and Barnes, op. cit., p. 379
18. Phillips, op. cit., p. 59
19. *Ibid.*, p. 55
20. *Ibid.*
21. Middlemas and Barnes, op. cit., p. 387
22. Marquand, *Ramsay MacDonald*, p. 434
23. Middlemas and Barnes, op. cit., p. 387
24. Young. *Stanley Baldwin*, p. 99
25. Hansard vol. 189 c 233
26. Hansard vol. 187 c 1605
27. TUC Report 1925
28. Bullock, op. cit., p. 78
29. *Socialist Review*, April 1926, p. 4
30. MFGB report on deputation to PM 24.3.26
31. Middlemas and Barnes, op. cit., p. 397
32. Phillips, op. cit., p. 93
33. General Strike Documents, Iron & Steel Trade Confederation (ISTC/45)
34. Citrine. *Men and Work: An Autobiography*, p. 152
35. Phillips, op. cit., p. 92
36. *Ibid.*, p. 55

37. Middlemas and Barnes, op. cit., p. 593, Phillips, op. cit., p. 83
38. Phillips, op. cit., p. 111
39. Middlemas and Barnes, op. cit., p. 406
40. Bridgeman diaries as quoted in Middlemas and Barnes, op. cit., p. 408
41. Royal Archives quoted in Middlemas and Barnes, op. cit., p. 409
42. Hansard quoted in Middlemas and Barnes, op. cit., p. 411
43. Phillips, op. cit., p. 87
44. Jenkins, op. cit., p. 409
45. *Cricklewood and District Industrial Gazette* quoted in Laybourn. *The General Strike Day by Day*
46. Middlemas and Barnes, op. cit., p. 415
47. Marquand, op. cit., p. 433
48. *Ibid.*, p. 437
49. Phillips, op. cit., p. 226
50. *Ibid.*, p. 229
51. *Ibid.*
52. *Ibid.*, p. 230
53. *Ibid.*, p. 232
54. Middlemas and Barnes, op. cit., p. 416
55. *Ibid.*, p. 419
56. *Ibid.*, p. 421
57. *Ibid.*
58. Marquand, op. cit., p. 443
59. Middlemas and Barnes, op. cit., p. 428
60. *Ibid.*, p. 435
61. Jenkins, op. cit., p. 41
62. Laybourn, op. cit., p. 137
63. Perkins. *A Very British Strike*, p. 199
64. Laybourn, op. cit., p. 137

## Chapter Six. A Question of Confidence

1. Rose. *King George V*, p. 325
2. *Ibid.*
3. *Ibid.*
4. Nicolson (ed.). *Harold Nicolson Diaries*, p. 384
5. Marquand. *Ramsay MacDonald*, p. 297
6. *Ibid.*, p. 296
7. Rose, op. cit., p. 341
8. *Ibid.*, p. 333
9. *Ibid.*, p. 327
10. Marquand, op. cit. p. 366
11. *Ibid.*, p. 381

12. *Ibid.*, p. 489
13. *Manchester Guardian*, 10.6.29
14. Shepherd. *John Lansbury*, p. 262
15. Middlemas and Barnes. *Baldwin*, p. 613
16. *Ibid.*
17. *Ibid.*
18. Marquand, op. cit., p. 608
19. Rose, op. cit., p. 370
20. Skidelsky. *John Maynard Keynes III*, p. 393
21. Marquand, op. cit., p. 613
22. *Ibid.*, p. 612
23. *Ibid.*
24. *Ibid.*, p. 615
25. Middlemas and Barnes, op. cit., p. 619
26. MacLeod. *Neville Chamberlain*, p. 149
27. Middlemas and Barnes, op. cit., p. 620
28. *Ibid.*, p. 621
29. *Ibid.*, p. 618
30. *Ibid.*, p. 619
31. Skidelsky, op. cit., p. 394
32. *Ibid.*, p. 365
33. Marquand, op. cit., p. 626
34. *Ibid.*
35. *Ibid.*, p. 628
36. Rose, op. cit., p. 373
37. *Ibid.*
38. Middlemas and Barnes, op. cit., p. 625
39. Marquand, op. cit., p. 605
40. Nicolson (ed.), op. cit., p. 463
41. Marquand, op. cit., p. 634
42. Rose, op. cit., p. 375
43. *Ibid.*
44. Marquand, op. cit., p. 635
45. *Ibid.*, p. 636
46. *Ibid.*
47. Basset. *Nineteen Thirty-One*, p. 166
48. Marquand, op. cit., p. 638
49. Morrison. *An Autobiography*, p. 126
50. Donoughue and Jones. *Herbert Morrison*, p. 164
51. *Ibid.*, p. 165
52. Diary of Ramsay MacDonald 24.8.31
53. Jones. *Diary with Letters 1931–1950*, p. 16
54. Marquand, op. cit., p. 657

55. *Ibid.*, p. 655–6
56. Montgomery-Hyde. *Baldwin*, p. 340
57. Jones, op. cit., p. 20
58. Shepherd, op. cit., p. 278

## Chapter Seven: Tight-Lipped Men in Caps

1. Graves and Hodge. *The Long Weekend*, p. 100
2. Deacon. 'Unemployment and Politics in Britain since 1925' quoted in Showler and Sinfield (eds). *The Workless State.*
3. Dougan. *The History of North East Shipbuilding*, p. 184
4. *Manchester Guardian*, 13.10.36
5. *The Newcastle Journal*, 5.10.36
6. Seaman. *Life in Britain Between the Wars*, p. 181
7. Gazeley. *Poverty in Britain 1900–1965*, p. 102
8. *Ibid.*
9. Seaman, op. cit., p. 32
10. Fraser. *The Evolution of the British Welfare State*, p. 212
11. Hawkins. *The Death of Rural England*, p. 45
12. *Mark Lane Express*, 4.7.21
13. Hawkins, op. cit., p. 50
14. *Ibid.*
15. *Ibid.*, p. 54
16. Fraser, op. cit., p. 207
17. Seaman, op. cit., p. 40
18. *British Social Policy 1914–39*, p. 5 (Fraser p. 195)
19. Fraser, op. cit., p. 200
20. *Ibid.*, p. 197
21. *Ibid.*
22. Fraser, op. cit., p. 201
23. Harris. *Attlee*
24. Shepherd. *George Lansbury – At the Heart of Old Labour*, p. 190
25. *Ibid.*
26. *Ibid.*, p. 192
27. *Ibid.*, p. 191
28. *Ibid.*, p. 196
29. *The Book of the Labour Party vol. III*, p. 16
30. Report of Unemployment Insurance Committee, p. 81 quoted in Fraser, op. cit., p. 203
31. Fraser, op. cit., p. 204
32. Royal Commission on Poor Law 1909 Minutes of Evidence Q2230
33. *Evening Standard* 31.7.28
34. Skidelsky. *John Maynard Keynes 1883–1946*, p. 405

35. *Ibid.*
36. *Collected Writings of John Maynard Keynes* vol. ix, p. 125 (Skidelsky, op. cit., p. 408)
37. Keynes and Henderson. *Can Lloyd George Do It?*, p. 25
38. Hansard Series CLXLX col. 760 12.2.24
39. Marquand, op. cit., p. 534
40. *Ibid.*
41. *Ibid.*, p. 536
42. *Ibid.*, p. 535
43. Orwell. *The Road to Wigan Pier*, p. 108
44. *Ibid.*
45. Taylor. *English History 1914–1945*, p. 112
46. Lawson and Silver. *A Social History of Education in England*, p. 363
47. *Ibid.*, p. 388
48. Rice. *Working-Class Wives*, p. 106
49. Pilgrim Trust. *Men Without Work*, p. 6
50. *Ibid.*, p. 7
51. Gazeley, op. cit., p. 114
52. Beales and Lambert. *Memoirs of the Unemployed*, p. 25
53. Fraser, op. cit., p. 202

## Chapter Eight: My Father's House

1. Iremonger. *William Temple*, p. 538
2. Lloyd. *The Church of England 1900–1965*
3. Fraser. *The Evolution of the British Welfare State*, p. 221
4. Hammerton. *This Turbulent Priest*, p. 73
5. Mowat. *Britain Between the Wars*, p. 510
6. Taylor. *The Church in the Country Parishes*, p. 79
7. Lloyd, op. cit., p. 307
8. *Ibid.*, p. 308
9. *Chronicles of Convocation 1930*, p. 70
10. *Ibid.*
11. *Ibid.*
12. Lloyd, op. cit., p. 316
13. *Ibid.*, p. 318
14. Hammerton, op. cit., p. 73
15. *Ibid.*, p. 52
16. *Ibid.*, p. 45
17. *Ibid.*, p. 81
18. Iremonger, op. cit., p. 382
19. Kent. *William Temple*, p. 136
20. Iremonger, op. cit., p. 520
21. Hammerton, op. cit., p. 83

22. Mowat, op. cit., p. 231
23. Hammerton, op. cit., p. 114
24. *Ibid.*, p. 121
25. Czech–Rechtensee. *Church and Slum*, vol. 1 no. 2, June 1934, p. 96
26. Mowat, op. cit., p. 231

## Chapter Nine: Few Know What They Want

1. Boyle. *Only the Wind Will Listen: Reith of the BBC*, p. 125
2. Briggs. *The BBC: The First Fifty Years*, p. 17
3. Mowat. *Britain Between the Wars*, p. 241
4. Boyle, op. cit., p. 123
5. *Ibid.*, p. 124
6. *Ibid.*, p. 109
7. *Ibid.*, p. 119
8. *Ibid.*, p. 121
9. *Ibid.*
10. Briggs, op. cit., p. 37
11. Boyle, op. cit., p. 146
12. Briggs, op. cit., p. 43
13. Boyle, p. 132
14. *Ibid.*, p. 133
15. Reith. *Broadcast Over Britain*, p. 69
16. Briggs, op. cit., p. 51
17. *Ibid.*
18. Boyle, op. cit., p. 134
19. Briggs, op. cit., p. 52
20. *Ibid.*, p. 53
21. Boyle, op. cit. p. 141
22. Briggs, op. cit. p. 54
23. *Ibid.*, p. 55
24. *Ibid.*, p. 61
25. *Ibid.*, p. 71
26. Reith, op. cit., p. 213
27. Boyle, op. cit., p. 182
28. Briggs, op. cit., p. 85
29. *Ibid.*, p. 98
30. Street (ed.), *Reith Diaries*, p. 96
31. Briggs, op. cit., p. 65
32. *Ibid.*, p. 97
33. Boyle, op. cit., p. 200
34. *Ibid.*
35. Reith. *Into the Wind*, p. 108
36. Boyle, op. cit., p. 201

37. Briggs, op. cit., p. 101
38. *Ibid.*
39. *Ibid.*, p. 105
40. Boyle, op. cit., p. 212
41. *Ibid.*, p. 214
42. Briggs, op. cit., p. 139
43. *Ibid.*, p. 138
44. *Ibid.*, p. 143
45. *Ibid.*
46. *Ibid.*
47. Boyle, op. cit., p. 284
48. *Ibid.*, p. 289
49. Briggs, op. cit., p. 154
50. Boyle, op. cit., p. 298
51. Reith. *Into the Wind*, p. 312
52. Briggs, op. cit., p. 146
53. *Ibid.*, p. 155
54. Briggs, op. cit., p. 161
55. *Ibid.*, p. 164

## Chapter Ten:  As Quick As I Can

1. Penrose. *British Aviation: Widening Horizons 1930–34*, p. 64
2. *Ibid.*, p. 65
3. *Ibid.*, p. 66
4. *Ibid.*
5. *Ibid.*, p. 20
6. *Ibid.*, p. 23
7. *Ibid.*, p. 91
8. *Ibid.*, p. 144
9. *Ibid.*, p. 238
10. *Daily Despatch* 22.1.33
11. Penrose, op. cit., p. 170 (quoting Mollison. *Playboy of the Air*)
12. Gibbs-Smith. *Aviation – An Historical Survey From Its Origins to the End of World War II*, p. 187
13. *Ibid.*, p. 197
14. *Ibid.*, p. 196
15. Segrave. *The Lure of Speed*, p. 54
16. Foreman-Peck, Bowden and McKinley. *The British Motor Industry*, p. 76
17. Bagwell. *The Transport Revolution from 1770*, p. 210
18. *The Times*, 19.9.23
19. Austin, Lord. 'Engineering Gems', *Motor Magazine*, 6.7.55
20. *Autocar*, 28.7.72

21. *Magazine of the Austin Seven*, no. 1973a, p. 4
22. *Autocar*, 28.11.22
23. Foreman-Peck *et al.*, op. cit., p. 70
24. Wyatt. *The Austin Seven*, p. 90
25. Turner. *The Car Makers*, p. 21
26. Richardson. *The British Motor Industry 1896–1939*, p. 64
27. *Ibid.*, p. 116
28. Turner, op. cit., p. 21
29. *Ibid.*
30. *Motor Agent*, 27.9.19
31. Turner, op. cit., p. 23
32. Bagwell, op. cit., p. 312
33. Richardson, op. cit., p. 105
34. Harper (ed.). p.117
35. Occasional Newsletter of Pedestrians Association July 1932, quoted in Richardson, op. cit.

## Chapter Eleven: Taking Part

1. Green (ed.). *Wisden Anthology*, p. 516
2. Birley. *A Social History of English Cricket*, p. 233
3. *Ibid.*
4. Martin-Jenkins (ed.). *Wisden Book of County Cricket*
5. Birley, op. cit., p. 231
6. *Ibid.*
7. *Ibid.*
8. Frith. *Bodyline Autopsy*, p. 70
9. Birley, op. cit., p. 235
10. *Morning Post*, 22.8.1931
11. Birley, op. cit., p. 235
12. Frith, op. cit., p. 171
13. *Ibid.*, p. 181
14. *Ibid.*
15. *Ibid.*, p. 185
16. Whittington. *Time of the Tiger*, p. 175
17. Watman. *History of British Athletics*, p. 26
18. *Ibid.*, p. 27
19. Birley. *Playing the Game. Sport and British Society*, p. 302
20. Matthews. *The Way It Was*, p. 84
21. Public Record Office FO371/22591
22. Matthews, op. cit., p. 84
23. Birley. *Playing the Game*, p. 53
24. *The Times*, 16.6.28

## Chapter Twelve: Private Daydreams

1. Graves and Hodge. *The Long Weekend*, p. 134
2. Johnson (ed.) *Twentieth Century Britain*
3. Miles and Smith. *Cinema, Literature and Society*, p. 201
4. Johnson, op. cit., p. 209
5. Short. *Theatrical Cavalcade*, p. 62
6. Calder-Marshall. *The Changing Scene*, p. 160
7. Richards. *The Age of the Dream Palace*, p. 19
8. *Ibid.*, p. 35
9. *The Cinema and the Public* quoted in Curran and Porter (eds), *British Cinema History*, p. 31
10. Johnson, op. cit., p. 271
11. Orwell. *The Road to Wigan Pier*, p. 80
12. Davis. *Leisure, Gender and Poverty*, p. 75
13. Curran and Porter, op. cit., p. 29
14. *Ibid.*, p. 30
15. Johnson, op. cit., p. 273
16. *Ibid.*
17. Mayor Rawdon Hoa in *This is Our Country*, quoted in Graves and Hodge, op. cit., p. 297
18. Short. *Sixty Years of Theatre*, p. 316
19. *Sunday Times*, 5.5.35
20. *Sunday Times*, 3.5.25
21. Ervine. *The Theatre of My Time*, p. 138
22. Vernon. *The Twentieth Century Theatre*, p. 220
23. Short, op. cit, p. 325
24. Johnson, op. cit., p. 278
25. Pronay and Spring (eds.). *Propaganda, Politics and Film*, p. 81
26. Graves and Hodge, op. cit., p. 135
27. Montgomery. *Comedy Films*, p. 179
28. *Ibid.*
29. Nuttall. *Portrait of Frank Randle*, p. 14
30. Johnson, op. cit., p. 273
31. *Variety*, 3.1.1933
32. Barker and Gale (eds). *British Theatre between the Wars*, p. 141
33. *Bioscope*, 18.3.1920
34. Low. *History of the British Film 1918–1979*, p. 96
35. *Ibid.*, p. 97
36. *Evidence of Departmental Committee on Cinematograph Film* (The Moyne Committee) HMSO London 1936, pp. 109–126
37. *Ibid.*
38. *Ibid.*, p. 20

## Chapter Thirteen: Into the Wasteland

1. Cox and Dyson (eds). *The Twentieth Century Mind 2 1918–45*, p. 310
2. *Ibid.*, p. 311
3. *Ibid.*, p. 180
4. Ackroyd, *T. S. Eliot*, p. 24
5. Eliot. *On Poetry and Poets*, p. 82
6. Ackroyd, op. cit., p. 321
7. The Spencer Memorial Lecture 1951 Poetry and Drama
8. Alan. *Strange Gods*, quoted in Cox and Dyson, op. cit., p. 325
9. Drabble (ed.). *Oxford Companion to English Literature*, p. 782
10. Cox and Dyson (eds), op. cit., p. 313
11. *Ibid.*, p. 379
12. Wilson. *The Shores of Light – A Literary Chronicle of the Twenties and Thirties*, p. 463
13. Blamires. *Twentieth-Century English Literature*, p. 116
14. Judd. *Ford Madox Ford*, p. 4
15. Lawrence. *Lady Chatterley's Lover*, appendix: Introduction to 1901 edition, p. 339
16. *Ibid.*, p. 312
17. Cox and Dyson (eds), op. cit., p. 417
18. Guthrie. *A Life in the Theatre*, p. 85
19. *Ibid.*
20. Gielgud. *Early Stages*, p. 126
21. *Sunday Times*, 3.5.28
22. *Daily Sketch*, 21.5.30
23. *Observer*, 18.5.30
24. *Variety*, 4.6.30
25. Barker and Gale, op. cit., p. 136
26. Agate. *Brief Chronicles*, p. 285
27. Barker and Gale, op. cit., p. 141
28. *Ibid.*, p. 145
29. Olivier. *On Acting*, p. 60
30. *Ibid.*
31. Crick. *George Orwell: A Life*, p. 353
32. Davison (ed.). *Orwell's England: The Road to Wigan Pier*, p. 113
33. *New English Weekly*, 5.4.40
34. Mendelson (ed.). *The English Auden*, p. xviii
35. Davenport-Hines. *Auden*, p. 34
36. *Ibid.*, p. 55
37. *Ibid.*, p. 57
38. *Ibid.*, p. 62
39. *Ibid.*, p. 65
40. *Ibid.*, p. 64

41. *Ibid.*
42. *Ibid.*, p. 68
43. *Ibid.*, p. 64
44. Blamires, op. cit., p. 163
45. Davenport-Hines, op. cit., p. 76
46. *Ibid.*, p. 87
47. *Ibid.*
48. *Ibid.*

## Chapter Fourteen: Shaping the Idea

1. Arnold. *Orpen – Mirror to an Age*, p. 355
2. *Ibid.*, p. 391
3. Spalding. *British Art Since 1900*, p. 91
4. *Ibid.*, p. 62
5. *Ibid.*
6. Foster *et al. Art Since 1900*, p. 268
7. Graves and Hodge. *The Long Weekend*, p. 131
8. *Ibid.*, p. 193
9. Spalding, op. cit., p. 88
10. Foster *et al.*, op. cit., p. 268
11. *Ibid.*, p. 269
12. *Ibid.*
13. 'A View of Sculpture', 1930 lecture quoted in Foster *et al.*, op. cit., p. 270
14. Graves and Hodge, op. cit., p. 194
15. Quoted in Graves and Hodge, op. cit., p. 352
16. Spalding, op. cit., p. 84
17. Spalding. *Duncan Grant*, p. 322
18. Curtis. *Modern Architecture Since 1900*, p. 225
19. Yarwood. *The Architecture of Britain*, p. 238
20. Curtis, op. cit., p. 226
21. *Ibid.*, p. 228
22. Young. *Elgar, OM*, p. 223
23. *Ibid.*
24. Mundy. *Elgar*, p. 165
25. *Ibid.*, p. 172
26. Young, op. cit., p. 214
27. *Ibid.*, p. 215
28. Mundy, op. cit., p. 180
29. *Ibid.*, p. 180
30. *Ibid.*, p. 201
31. *Ibid.*, p. 243
32. *Ibid.*, p. 235

## Chapter Fifteen: Power Without Responsibility

1. *History of Times* vol. IV quoted in Cudlipp. *Publish and Be Damned*, p. 36
2. Griffiths. *Fleet Street: Five Hundred Years of the Press*, p. 207
3. *Ibid.*, p. 211
4. *Ibid.*
5. *Ibid.*
6. Hartwell. *William Camrose*, p. 116
7. Griffiths, op. cit., p. 212
8. Taylor. *Beaverbrook*, p. 215
9. Griffiths, op. cit., p. 211
10. Driberg. *Beaverbrook*, p. 176
11. *Ibid.*, p. 180
12. *Ibid.*, p. 181
13. *Ibid.*
14. *Ibid.*, p. 192
15. Griffiths, op. cit., p. 245
16. Griffiths. *Plant Here the Standard*, p. 228
17. *Evening Standard*, 1.5.26
18. Griffiths. *Fleet Street*, p. 213
19. *Ibid.*, p. 223
20. *Ibid.*, p. 224
21. *The Times*, 12.5.26
22. Griffiths. *Fleet Street*, p. 225
23. *Ibid.*
24. Young. *Churchill and Beaverbrook*, p. 84
25. Griffiths. *Fleet Street*, p. 229
26. *Ibid.*, p. 230
27. Shepherd. *George Lansbury*, p. 222
28. *Ibid.*, p. 187
29. P.E.P. *The British Press*, p. 221
30. Griffiths. *Fleet Street*, p. 244
31. Hagerty. *Read All About It.*
32. Griffiths. *Fleet Street*, p. 243
33. *Ibid.*, p. 248
34. Bourne. *Lords of Fleet Street*, p. 108
35. Cudlipp. *Publish and Be Damned*, p. 41
36. *Ibid.*, p. 43
37. *The Times*, 8.1.33
38. *Daily Mail*, 15.1.34
39. *Daily Mail*, 15.1.34
40. Dorril. *Blackshirt*, p. 271
41. *Ibid.*, p. 272
42. *Ibid.*

43. *Ibid.*, p. 375
44. *Ibid.*, p. 425
45. *Ibid.*, p. 390
46. *Ibid.*, p. 391
47. *Daily Mail*, 30.6.34
48. Dorril, op. cit., p. 309
49. *Ibid.*
50. *Ibid.*
51. *Daily Mail*, 24.7.35
52. Griffiths. *Fleet Street*, p. 258
53. *Evening Standard*, 13.3.36
54. *Evening Standard*, 15.9.37
55. *The Times*, 10.4.37
56. *The Times*, 7.9.38
57. Griffiths. *Fleet Street*, p. 212

## Chapter Sixteen: The Drift to War

1. Thorpe. *Eden.* p. 173
2. Macleod. *Neville Chamberlain*, p. 203
3. Thorpe, op. cit., p. 193
4. *Ibid.*, p. 191
5. *Ibid.*, p. 195
6. House of Commons 12.11.36 Hansard
7. Nicolson (ed.). *Harold Nicolson: Diaries and Letters*, p. 332
8. *Ibid.*
9. Hyde. *Baldwin*, p. 116
10. House of Commons 10.11.1932
11. Jones. *A Diary with Letters 1931–1950*, p. 187
12. Macleod, op. cit., p. 187
13. Middlemas and Barnes. *Baldwin*, p. 834
14. Macleod, op. cit., p. 181
15. Thorpe, op. cit., p. 157
16. Hansard 18.5.35
17. Young. *Stanley Baldwin*, p. 200
18. Hoare. *Nine Troubled Years*, p. 168
19. *Ibid.*
20. Middlemas and Barnes, op. cit., p. 831
21. Churchill. *Arms and the Covenant*, p. 251
22. Churchill. *The Second World War* Book 1, p. 135
23. Jenkins. *Churchill*, p. 485
24. Middlemas and Barnes, op. cit., p. 848
25. Macleod, op. cit., p. 178
26. *Ibid.*

27. Middlemas and Barnes, op. cit., p. 872
28. *Ibid.*, p. 883
29. *Ibid.*, p. 884
30. Thorpe, op. cit., p. 166
31. *Ibid.*
32. *Ibid.*, p. 175
33. Jones, op. cit., p. 231
34. Macleod, op. cit., p. 179
35. *Ibid.*
36. Thorpe, op. cit., p. 190
37. James. *Anthony Eden*, p. 182
38. *Ibid.*, p. 184
39. *Ibid.*
40. Thorpe, op. cit., p. 195
41. Chamberlain diary, 19.2.38
42. Thorpe, op. cit., p. 201
43. *Ibid.*
44. *Ibid.*
45. Thorpe, op. cit., p. 203
46. *Ibid.*
47. Meehan. *The Unnecessary War*, p. 23
48. James, op. cit., p. 208
49. Macleod, op. cit., p. 224
50. *Ibid.*
51. *Ibid.*
52. Documents of British Foreign Policy 3r series vol. 2 p. 675
53. *Ibid.*, p. 55
54. Documents of German Foreign Policy Series D vol. 1 p. 1159
55. Jenkins, op. cit., p. 525
56. *Ibid.*
57. Macleod, op. cit., p. 234
58. *Ibid.*, p. 237
59. *Ibid.*
60. *Ibid.*, p. 239
61. *Ibid.*
62. *Ibid.*, p. 245
63. Feiling. *Life of Neville Chamberlain* Book IV, p. 147
64. *The Times*, 31.9.1937
65. Macleod, op. cit., p. 256
66. Jenkins, op. cit., p. 528
67. Macleod, op. cit., p. 272
68. Kershaw. *Hitler, 1936–45: Nemesis*, p. 238
69. Macleod, op. cit., p. 276

# SELECT BIBLIOGRAPHY

Ackroyd, P. *T. S. Eliot*. London: Hamish Hamilton, 1984.

Agate, J. *Brief Chronicles*. London: Cape, 1943.

Airlie, Mabell, Countess of. *Thatched with Gold: Memoirs*. Leicester: Ulverscroft, 1962.

Arnold, B. *Orpen: Mirror to an Age*. London: Cape, 1981.

Attlee, C. *As It Happened*. London: Heinemann, 1954.

Bagwell, P. S. *The Transport Revolution from 1770*. London: Batsford, 1974.

Bailey, C. *Black Diamonds: The Rise and Fall of an English Dynasty*. London: Viking, 2007.

Barker, F. *The Oliviers: A Biography*. London: Hamish Hamilton 1953.

Barker, C. and Gale, M. B. (eds). *British Theatre Between the Wars*. Cambridge: Cambridge University Press, 2000.

Basset, R. *Nineteen Thirty-One: Political Crisis*. London: Macmillan, 1958.

Beales, H. L. and Lambert, R. S. (eds). *Memoirs of the Unemployed*. Wakefield: E. P. Publications, 1973.

Béaslaí, P. *Michael Collins and the Making of a New Ireland*. London: G. G. Harrap & Co., 1926.

Beaverbrook, Baron. *The Abdication of Edward VIII*. London: Hamish Hamilton, 1966.

Birley, D. *A Social History of English Cricket*. London: Aurum Press, 1999.

— *Playing the Game: Sport and British Society, 1910–1945*. Manchester: Manchester University Press, 1995.

Blamires, H. *Twentieth-Century English Literature*. London: Macmillan, 1982.

Bourne, R. *Lords of Fleet Street: The Harmsworth Dynasty*. London: Unwin Hyman, 1990.

Boyle, A. *Only the Wind Will Listen: Reith of the BBC*. London: Hutchinson, 1972.

Briggs, A. *The BBC: The First Fifty Years*. Oxford: Oxford University Press, 1985.

Brome, V. *J. B. Priestley*. London: Hamish Hamilton, 1988.

Bullock, A. *Ernest Bevin. A Biography* (one-volume edition, ed. Brian Brivati). London: Politico's, 2002.

Calder-Marshall, A. *The Changing Scene*. London: Chapman & Hall, 1937.

Churchill, W. S. *Great Contemporaries*. London: Butterworth, 1937.

— *Arms and the Covenant: Speeches by Winston S. Churchill*. London: G. G. Harrap, 1938.

— *The Aftermath: Being a Sequel to the World Crisis*. London: Macmillan, 1941.

— *The Second World War. Volume 1: The Gathering Storm*. London: Cassell, 1948.

Citrine, W. M. *Men and Work: An Autobiography*. London: Hutchinson, 1964.

Coogan, T. P. *Michael Collins: A Biography*. London: Hutchinson, 1990.

— *Eamon de Valera: The Man Who Was Ireland*. New York: HarperCollins, 1995.

Cox, C. B. and Dyson, A. E. (eds). *The Twentieth Century Mind 2 1918–45*. London: Oxford University Press, 1972.

Crick, B. *George Orwell: A Life*. London: Secker & Warburg, 1980.

Cudlipp, H. *Publish and be Damned! The Astonishing Story of the Daily Mirror*. London: Andrew Dakers, 1953.

Curran, J. and Porter, V. (eds). *British Cinema History*. London: Weidenfeld & Nicolson, 1983.

Curtis, W. J. R. *Modern Architecture since 1900*. Oxford: Phaidon, 1982.

Davenport-Hines, R. *Auden*. London: Heinemann, 1995.

Davidson, J. C. C. *Memoirs of a Conservative: J. C. C. Davidson's Memoirs and Papers, 1910–37*. London: Weidenfeld & Nicolson, 1969.

Davis, A. *Leisure, Gender and Poverty: Working-Class Culture in Salford and Manchester, 1900–39*. Buckingham: Open University Press, 1992.

Davison, P. (ed.). *Orwell's England: The Road to Wigan Pier in the Context of Essays, Reviews, Letters and Poems Selected from the Complete Works of George Orwell*. London: Penguin, 2001.

Donaldson, F. *Edward VIII*. London: Weidenfeld & Nicolson, 1974.

Donoughue, B. and Jones, G. W. *Herbert Morrison: Portrait of a Politician*. London: Weidenfeld & Nicolson, 1973.

Dorril, S. *Blackshirt: Sir Oswald Mosley and British Fascism*. London: Viking, 2006.

Dougan, D. *The History of North East Shipbuilding*. London: George Allen & Unwin, 1968.

Drabble, M. (ed.). *The Oxford Companion to English Literature* (5th edition). Oxford: Oxford University Press, 1998.

Driberg, T. *Beaverbrook: A Study in Power and Frustration*. London: Weidenfeld & Nicolson, 1956.

Eagleton, T. *Exiles and Émigrés*. New York: Schocken Books, 1970.

Eden, A. *The Reckoning: The Eden Memoirs*. London: Cassell, 1965.

Eliot, T. S. *On Poetry and Poets*. London: Faber and Faber, 1957.

Ervine, St J. *The Theatre in My Time*. London: Rich & Cowan, 1933.

Feiling, K. *The Life of Neville Chamberlain*. London: Macmillan, 1946.

Figgis, D. *Recollections of Irish Wars*. London: E. Benn, 1927.

Foreman-Peck, J., Bowden, S. and McKinlay, A. *The British Motor Industry*. Manchester: Manchester University Press, 1995.

Forster, E. M. *Aspects of the Novel*. Harmondsworth: Penguin, 1962.

Foster, H., Krauss, R., Bois, Y-A. and Buchloh, B. *Art Since 1900: Modernism, Antimodernism, Postmodernism*. London: Thames & Hudson, 2004.

Fraser, D. *The Evolution of the British Welfare State: A History of Social Policy since the Industrial Revolution*. London: Macmillan, 1973.

Frith, D. *Bodyline Autopsy: The Full Story of the Most Sensational Test Cricket Series – England v. Australia 1932–3*. London: Aurum Press, 2002.

Gazeley, I. *Poverty in Britain, 1900–1965*. Basingstoke: Palgrave Macmillan, 2003.

Gibbs-Smith, C. H. *Aviation: An Historical Survey from Its Origins to the End of World War II*. London: HMSO, 1970.

Gielgud, J. *Early Stages*. London: Falcon Press, 1953.

Graves, R. and Hodge, A. *The Long Weekend: A Social History of Great Britain 1918–1939*. London: Faber and Faber, 1940.

Green, B. (ed.). *Wisden Anthology 1900–1940*. London: Queen Anne Press, 1980.

Griffiths, D. *Fleet Street: Five Hundred Years of the Press*. London: British Library, 2006.

— *Plant Here The Standard*. Basingstoke: Macmillan, 1996.

Guthrie, T. *A Life in the Theatre*. London: Hamish Hamilton, 1960.

Hagerty, B. *Read All About It: 100 Sensational Years of the Daily Mirror*. Lydney: First Stone Publishing, 2003.

Hammerton, H. J. *This Turbulent Priest: The Story of Charles Jenkinson, Parish Priest and Housing Reformer*. London: Lutterworth Press, 1952.

Harris, K. *Attlee*. London: Weidenfeld & Nicolson, 1982.

Harrod, R. *The Life of John Maynard Keynes*. London: Macmillan, 1951.

Hartwell, M. B. *William Camrose: Giant of Fleet Street*. London: Weidenfeld & Nicolson, 1992.

Hoare, S. *Nine Troubled Years*. London: Collins, 1954.

Howkins, A. *The Death of Rural England: A Social History of the Countryside since 1900*. London: Routledge, 2003.

Hyde, H. M., *Baldwin: The Unexpected Prime Minister*. London: Hart-Davis MacGibbon, 1973.

Iremonger, F. A. *William Temple, Archbishop of Canterbury: His Life and Letters*. Oxford: Oxford University Press, 1948.

James, R. R. *Bob Boothby: A Portrait*. London: Hodder & Stoughton, 1991.

— (ed.). *Chips: The Diaries of Sir Henry Channon*. London: Phoenix Giant, 1996.

Jenkins, R. *Churchill*. London: Macmillan, 2001.

Johnson, P. (ed.). *Twentieth Century Britain: Economic, Social and Cultural Change*. Harlow: Longman, 1994.

Jones, T. *A Diary with Letters 1931–1950*. London: Oxford University Press, 1954.

Judd, A. *Ford Madox Ford*. London: Collins, 1990.

Kee, R. *The Green Flag: A History of Irish Nationalism*. London: Weidenfeld & Nicolson, 1972.

Kent, J. *William Temple: Church, State and Society in Britain 1880–1950*. Cambridge: Cambridge University Press, 1992.

Kershaw, I. *Hitler, 1936–45: Nemesis*. London: Allen Lane, 2000.

Keynes, J. M. *The Economic Consequences of the Peace*. London: Macmillan, 1919.
— *Collected Writings*. London: Macmillan, 1971.
Keynes, J. M. and Henderson, H. *Can Lloyd George Do It? An Examination of the Liberal Pledge*. London: The Nation and Athenaeum, 1929.
Krause, D. (ed.). *The Letters of Sean O'Casey*. London: Cassell, 1975.
Lawrence, D. H. *Lady Chatterley's Lover*. London: Penguin, 1990.
Lawson, J. and Silver, H. *A Social History of Education in England*. London: Methuen, 1973.
Laybourn, K. *The General Strike Day by Day*. Stroud: Alan Sutton, 1996.
Lloyd, R. *The Church of England 1900–1965*. London: SCM Press, 1966.
Lloyd George, D. *War Memoirs of David Lloyd George, vols I and II*. London: Odhams Press, 1938.
— *The Truth About the Peace Treaties*. London: Victor Gollancz, 1938.
Lockhart, J. G. *Cosmo Gordon Lang*. London: Hodder & Stoughton, 1949.
Longford, Earl of. *Peace by Ordeal: An Account from First-Hand Sources of the Negotiation and Signature of the Anglo-Irish Treaty 1921*. London: Sidgwick & Jackson, 1972.
Longford, Earl of and O'Neill, T. P. *Éamon de Valéra*. London: Hutchinson, 1970.
Low, R. *The History of the British Film, 1918–1979*. London: Allen & Unwin, 1971.
Macleod, I. *Neville Chamberlain*. London: Frederick Muller, 1961.
Marquand, D. *Ramsay MacDonald*. London: Jonathan Cape, 1977.
Martin-Jenkins, C. (ed.). *Wisden Book of County Cricket*. London: Queen Anne Press, 1981.
Matthews, S. *The Way It Was: My Autobiography*. London: Headline, 2000.
Meehan, P. *The Unnecessary War: Whitehall and German Resistance to Hitler*. London: Sinclair-Stevenson, 1992.
Mendelson, E. (ed.). *The English Auden: Poems, Essays and Dramatic Writings, 1927–1939*. London: Faber and Faber, 1977.
Middlemas, K. and Barnes, J. *Baldwin: A Biography*. London: Weidenfeld & Nicolson, 1969.
Miles, P. and Smith, M. *Cinema, Literature and Society*. London: Croom Helm, 1987.
Mollison, J. *Playboy of the Air*. London: M. Joseph, 1937.
Montgomery, J. *Comedy Films*. London: Allen & Unwin, 1954.
Morrison, H. *Herbert Morrison: An autobiography*. London: Odhams Press, 1960.
Mowat, C. L. *Britain Between the Wars*. London: Methuen, 1955.
Muggeridge, M. *A Third Testament*. London: Collins, 1976.
Mundy, S. *Elgar*. London: Omnibus Press, 2001.
Nanda, B. R. *Mahatma Gandhi: A Biography*. London: Unwin Books, 1965.
Nehru, J. *The Discovery of India*. London: Penguin, 2004.
Nicolson, H. *King George the Fifth: His Life and Reign*. London: Constable, 1952.

Nicolson, N. (ed.). *Harold Nicolson: Diaries and Letters 1907–1964*: London: Weidenfeld & Nicolson, 2004.

Norwich, J. J. *The Duff Cooper Diaries: 1915–1951*. London: Weidenfeld & Nicolson, 2005.

Nuttall, J. *King Twist: A Portrait of Frank Randle*. London: Routledge and Paul, 1978.

Olivier, L. *On Acting*. London: Weidenfeld & Nicolson, 1986.

Orwell, G. *The Road to Wigan Pier*. London: Penguin, 2001.

Owen, Frank. *Tempestuous Journey: Lloyd George, His Life and Times*. London: Hutchinson, 1954.

Penrose, H. *British Aviation: Widening Horizons 1930–1934*. London: HMSO, 1979.

Penrose, H. *British Aviation: The Ominous Skies 1935–1939*. London: HMSO, 1980.

Perkins, A. *A Very British Strike: 3 May – 12 May, 1926*. London: Macmillan, 2006.

Phillips, G. *The General Strike: The Politics of Industrial Conflict*. London: Weidenfeld & Nicolson, 1976.

Pilgrim Trust. *Men Without Work: A Report made to the Pilgrim Trust*. Cambridge: Cambridge University Press, 1938.

Poel, W. *What is Wrong with the Stage: Some Notes on the English Theatre from the Earliest Times to the Present Day*. London: Allen & Unwin, 1920.

Political and Economic Planning. *Report on the British Press: A Survey of Its Current Operations and Problems with Special Reference to National Newspapers and Their Part in Public Affairs*. London: PEP, 1938.

Pope-Hennessy, J. *Queen Mary: 1867–1953*. London: George Allen & Unwin, 1959.

Pronay, N. and Spring, D. (eds). *Propaganda, Politics and Film, 1918–45* London: Macmillan, 1981.

Rayner, R. M. *The Twenty Years Truce, 1919–39*. London: Longmans, Green & Co., 1943.

Reith, J. C. W. *Broadcast Over Britain*. London: Hodder & Stoughton, 1924.

— *Into the Wind*. London: Hodder & Stoughton, 1949.

Rice, M. G. S. *Working-Class Wives: Their Health and Conditions*. London: Virago, 1981.

Richards, J. *The Age of the Dream Palace: Cinema and Society in Britain 1930–1939*. London: Routledge, 1984.

Richardson, K. *The British Motor Industry 1896–1939*. London: Macmillan, 1977.

Rose, K. *King George V*. London: Weidenfeld & Nicolson, 1983.

Seaman, L. C. B. *Life in Britain Between the Wars*. London: Batsford, 1970.

Segrave, H. *The Lure of Speed*. London: Hutchinson, 1928.

Sharp, A. *The Versailles Settlement: Peacemaking in Paris, 1919*. Basingstoke: Macmillan, 1991.

Sheffield, G. and Bourne, J. (eds). *Douglas Haig: War Diaries and Letters 1914–1918*. London: Weidenfeld & Nicolson, 2005.

Shepherd, J. *George Lansbury: At the heart of Old Labour*. Oxford: Oxford University Press, 2002.

Short, E. *Theatrical Cavalcade*. London: Eyre & Spottiswoode, 1942.

— *Sixty Years of Theatre*. London: Eyre & Spottiswoode, 1951.

Showler, B. and Sinfield, A (eds). *The Workless State: Studies in Unemployment*. Oxford: M. Robertson, 1981.

Skidelsky, R. *John Maynard Keynes 1883–1946: Economist, Philosopher, Statesman*. London: Macmillan, 2003.

— *John Maynard Keynes: A Biography – volume II. The Economist as Saviour 1920–1937*. London: Macmillan, 1992.

Spalding, F. *British Art Since 1900*. London: Thames & Hudson, 1986.

— *Duncan Grant*. London: Pimlico, 1998.

Street, C. (ed.). *The Reith Diaries*. London: Collins, 1975.

Taylor, A. J. P. *Beaverbrook*. London: Hamish Hamilton, 1972.

— *English History 1914–1945*. Oxford: Oxford University Press, 1965.

Thorpe, D. R. *Eden: The Life and Times of Anthony Eden, First Earl of Avon 1897–1977*. London: Chatto & Windus, 2003.

Trewin, J. C. *The Gay Twenties: A Decade of the Theatre*. London: Macdonald, 1958.

— *The Turbulent Thirties: A Further Decade of the Theatre*. London: Macdonald, 1960.

Turner, G. *The Car Makers*. London: Eyre & Spottiswoode, 1963.

Vernon, F. *The Twentieth Century Theatre*. London: G. G. Harrap & Co., 1924.

Warner, P. *Cricket Between Two Wars*. London: Chatto & Windus, 1942.

Watman, M. F. *History of British Athletics*. London: Hale, 1960.

Whittington, R. S. *Time of the Tiger: The Bill O'Reilly Story*. London: Paul, 1970.

Whittle, F. *Jet: The Story of a Pioneer*. London: Muller, 1953.

Williams, R. *Drama from Ibsen to Eliot*. London: Chatto & Windus, 1952.

Wilson, E. *The Shores of Light: A Literary Chronicle of the Twenties and Thirties*. London: W. H. Allen and Co., 1952.

Windsor, Duke of. *A King's Story: The Memoirs of HRH The Duke of Windsor, KG*. London: Cassell, 1951.

Windsor, Duchess of. *The Heart Has Its Reasons: The Memoirs of the Duchess of Windsor*. London: Michael Joseph, 1956.

Wyatt, R. J. *The Austin Seven: A Pictorial Tribute*. Croydon: Motor Racing Publications, 1975.

Yarwood, D. *The Architecture of Britain*. London: Batsford, 1976.

Young, G. M. *Stanley Baldwin*. London: Hart-Davis, 1952.

Young, K. *Churchill and Beaverbrook: A Study in Friendship and Politics*. London: Eyre & Spottiswoode, 1966.

Young, P. M. *Elgar, OM: A Study of a Musician*. London: Collins, 1955.

Ziegler, P. *Mountbatten: The Official Biography*. London: Collins, 1985.

# INDEX

# ACKNOWLEDGEMENTS

Every reasonable effort has been made to contact all copyright holders. If notified, the publisher will be pleased to rectify any errors or omissions at the earliest opportunity.

The following permissions are gratefully acknowledged:

'Bagpipe Music' from *Collected Poems* by Louis MacNeice (Copyright © The Estate of Louis MacNeice 2007) is reproduced by permission of David Higham Associates on behalf of the Estate of Louis MacNeice.

'You that love England' from *Selected Poems* by C. Day-Lewis (Copyright © The Estate of C. Day-Lewis 1992) is reproduced by permission of PFD (www.pfd.co.uk) on behalf of the Estate of C. Day-Lewis.